Soundings in French Caribbean Writing Since 1950

Soundings in French Caribbean Writing Since 1950

The Shock of Space and Time

MARY GALLAGHER

OXFORD
UNIVERSITY PRESS

OXFORD
UNIVERSITY PRESS

Great Clarendon Street, Oxford OX2 6DP

Oxford University Press is a department of the University of Oxford.
It furthers the University's objective of excellence in research, scholarship,
and education by publishing worldwide in

Oxford New York

Auckland Bangkok Buenos Aires Cape Town Chennai
Dar es Salaam Delhi Hong Kong Istanbul Karachi Kolkata
Kuala Lumpur Madrid Melbourne Mexico City Mumbai Nairobi
São Paulo Shanghai Taipei Tokyo Toronto

Oxford is a registered trade mark of Oxford University Press
in the UK and in certain other countries

Published in the United States
by Oxford University Press Inc., New York

British Library Cataloguing in Publication Data

Data available

Library of Congress Cataloging in Publication Data

Data available

ISBN 0–19–815982–X

1 3 5 7 9 10 8 6 4 2

Typeset in Sabon
by Cambrian Typesetters, Frimley, Surrey
Printed in Great Britain
on acid-free paper by
Biddles Ltd., *www.biddles.co.uk*

For

BERTRAND, OISÍN,
EOIN, AND MARIANNE

Acknowledgements

I AM GRATEFUL to several people associated with Oxford University Press: Jason Freeman, who commissioned this book; Sophie Goldsworthy, for her unfailing forbearance; Sarah Hyland and Frances Whistler for able assistance in the home stretch; Janet Moth, whose careful reading and clarity of judgement made all the difference; and the two anonymous but recognizable readers (Bridget Jones, RIP, and Belinda Jack) for their advice on the initial proposal. To the virtual community of writers and scholars who have enabled and enriched the project as it took shape, with a special thought for all those who participated in the conference on Caribbean writing in French held at University College Dublin in 1999, I am indebted. Chief amongst them is Roger Little who pointed the way—via Saint-John Perse—towards French Caribbean space and time. Thanks are also due to my friends at University College Dublin and at NUI Maynooth, but also further afield, for ongoing support and companionship. I am particularly grateful to Michael Brophy, Nick Coates, Maeve McCusker, Maeve O'Brien, Éamon O'Ciosáin, and Douglas Smith for sharing insights and material, and to Dervila Cooke, Patricia Palmer, Susan Portier, and Kitty Shields, whose generosity as readers greatly lightened the final stages. Finally, I extend my thanks to the André Kertész estate and Robert Gurbo especially for permission to reproduce on the jacket a photograph that resonates with so many of my concerns in this book, as well as illustrating J. Hillis Miller's dictum that there is 'always a figure in the landscape'.

M.G.

University College Dublin

Contents

Abbreviations

AE	Patrick Chamoiseau, *Antan d'enfance* (Paris: Gallimard, 1990)
C	Patrick Chamoiseau, *Childhood*, tr. Carol Volk (London: Granta, 1999)
*Él.	Pr.*	Jean Bernabé, Patrick Chamoiseau, and Raphaël Cconfiant, *Éloge de la créolite	In Praise of Creoleness*, bilingual edn., tr. M.B. Taleb-Khyar (Paris: Gallimard, 1993)
ÉOP	Saint-John Perse, *Éloges and Other Poems*, tr. Louise Varèse (New York: Pantheon Books, 1956)
LC	Patrick Chamoiseau and Raphaël Confiant, *Lettres créoles: Tracées antillaises et continentales de la littérature 1635–1975* (Paris: Hatier, 1991)
NT	Paul Ricœur, 'Narrative Time', *Critical Inquiry* (Autumn 1980), 169–90
ŒC	Saint-John Perse, *Œuvres complètes*, Bibliothèque de la Pléiade (Paris: Gallimard, 1972)
Pr.	see *Él.* above
RCN	Joseph Zobel, *La Rue Cases-Nègres* (Paris: Présence africaine, 1950)
T	Derek Walcott, *What the Twilight Says* (London: Faber & Faber, 1998)
VN	Hayden White, 'The Value of Narrativity in the Representation of Reality', *Critical Inquiry* (Autumn 1980), 5–28

Introduction

L'architecture du présent travail se situe dans le temporalité.
Tout problème humain demande à être considéré à partir du
temps.

The resounding prolificacy of French Caribbean writing during the
final half-century of the second millennium prompts many questions. What does this efflorescence mean? For whom is it meaning-
ful? Which urges have driven and sustained it? Is it distinguished
by specific concerns or particular paradigms? Such questions might
suggest a response framed in terms of time and space, since the
passion and the appeal of this literary surge seem to inhere in the
forces—reverberations, strains, and stresses—that stretch and even
splice Caribbean spatial and temporal consciousness.

My subtitle paraphrases Wilson Harris, who has characterized
the Caribbean condition as emerging from the 'shock of place and
time'.[2] There is no doubt that an acute temporal anxiety precipitates
many Caribbean writers into a preoccupation with loss and discontinuity, and a pressing urge to salvage or to imagine a continuity, an
identity, and a legitimacy. However, the fixation on Caribbean
historical aporia usually entails a particularly acute and perhaps
compensatory attention to space. This highly charged relation to
time and space—including the impulse to displace temporality onto

---

[1] Frantz Fanon, *Peau noire, masques blancs* (Paris: Seuil, 1952): 10; tr. Charles
Lam Markmann, *Black Skin, White Masks* (1967; London: Pluto, 1986): 14–15;
'The architecture of this work is rooted in the temporal. Every human problem must
be considered from the standpoint of time.'

[2] In 'History, Fable, and Myth in the Caribbean and Guianas', *Caribbean
Quarterly*, 16 (June 1970), 1–32: 21. Harris sees in the Caribbean mind 'a drama
of consciousness which reads back through the shock of place and time for omens
of capacity that were latent, unrealized, within the clash of cultures and movements
of peoples into the South Americas and West Indies'. However, the revised version
of this essay (1995) in *Selected Essays of Wilson Harris: The Unfinished Genesis of
the Imagination*, ed. Andrew Bundy (London: Routledge, 1999) does not contain
this statement.

spatiality—can be seen at work, for example, in the tremors and spasms that ripple through narrative, sometimes seizing it up altogether; in the constant, almost obsessive emphasis on the enunciative here and now; in the deeply analeptic deferral to continental space; in the effort to register within the more permanent space of writing the ephemeral resonance of the spoken word; and in the extraordinary scriptural density of the alternative or supplementary space of writing or 'textuality'.

The expression 'French Caribbean' employed as a label identifying a particular body of writing suggests the demarcation of a certain fixed cultural, linguistic, and geographical area, and it implies, furthermore, that this putative field produces a distinct, identifiable literature. But as J. Michael Dash has noted, the Caribbean is nothing if not disruptive of such territorial presumptions. In Dash's view,

Including the Caribbean in any survey means ultimately more than simply expanding the literary canon to include new minorities or the heretofore marginalized. It means dismantling those notions of nation, ground, authenticity, and history on which more conventional surveys have been based and exploring concepts of cultural diversity, syncretism, and instability that characterize the island cultures of the Caribbean.[3]

Describing the sea as 'an unstable medium beyond the fixing power of any totalizing discourse',[4] Dash quotes Antonio Benítez-Rojo's suggestion that it is 'the ultimate image of the Caribbean',[5] a postulation apparently echoed in Édouard Glissant's deployment of two gnomic pronouncements from Derek Walcott ('Sea is History') and Edward Kamau Brathwaite ('the unity is submarine') as talismanic epigraphs to his *Poétique de la Relation*.

The Caribbean is held to be unthinkable, then, as a static, demarcated area. Part of the Atlantic continuum, it is first and foremost fluid and, as such, comprises currents, flow, passage, and displacement. For J. Michael Dash, as for Antonio Benítez-Rojo it is '*not a*

---

[3] J. Michael Dash, *The Other America: Caribbean Literature in a New World Context* (Charlottesville: University of Virginia Press, 1998), 5. Dash's title is drawn from Édouard Glissant, *Le Discours antillais* (Paris: Seuil, 1981), 256 n. 12; tr. J. Michael Dash as *Caribbean Discourse: Selected Essays* (Charlottesville: University Virginia Press, 1989), 147 n. 8.

[4] Dash, *The Other America*, 29.

[5] Ibid. 8.

fixed ground, but an open field of signifiers ... a "meta-Archipelago" with neither a boundary nor a centre'.[6] Since movement is four-dimensional, it follows that the Caribbean is not so much a place as a 'taking place'. Its temporality is further underlined by the fact that, for all its flux, the Caribbean sea is still fraught with phantoms. To begin with, it is named for the Caribs, the displaced, not to say decimated aboriginal inhabitants of its islands (the Arawaks being displaced by this naming to a second level of ghostliness). Moreover, its floor was once littered with the now long-dissolved bones of those Caribs who threw themselves into the sea rather than surrender to the European invaders, and also with the skeletons of deported Africans cast overboard the slaving ships. Even the deep, although usually considered to be devoid of (land)marks or traces, can thus be said, in the case of the Caribbean, to have temporal depth.

My principal motive in choosing the term 'soundings' to signal the nature of this study is precisely to advert to the rather unsound cadastral status of what I am calling the 'French Caribbean'. While 'the Caribbean' is certainly a fluid, volatile space/time, it is not just a sea. Indeed the title of Benítez-Rojo's study is *The Repeating Island*, suggesting that, while the Caribbean as a whole is a fluid, open space, it is also, paradoxically, a space of multiple contained, bounded, terrestrial spaces. The reference of the collocation 'French Caribbean' multiplies this paradox. The term 'French' has, after all, both a linguistic (or cultural) and a territorial or geopolitical extension. Here, I am using it—rather uncomfortably—to name the latter, mindful of the relatively discrete, but nonetheless vexed and revealing questions of whether historically French islands such as Haiti, currently (partly) French-speaking islands like St Lucia, French-controlled spaces washed by the Caribbean, such as Guiana, or indeed literary blow-ins to Martinique such as Salvat Etchart or Jeanne Hyvrard, can be kept outside a perimeter that cannot be regarded as stable. The term 'soundings' is also intended to register respect for the integrity or resistance of the writing approached here. In the words of Walter Ong, 'hearing can register interiority without violating it. I can rap a box to find whether it is empty or full or a wall to find whether it is hollow or solid inside. Or I can ring a coin to learn whether it is silver or

---

[6] Ibid. Emphasis mine.

lead.'[7] These scruples should not be confused, however, with the coy precaution of a disclaimer. On the contrary, since 'the field of sound is not spread out before me but is all around me',[8] far from renouncing an encounter with depth, approach by sounding should counteract the temptation to remain safely at the surface. In reality, as Ong reminds us, it is vision, not hearing, and surveys, not soundings, that present surfaces ready to be mapped, 'fixed', explored, colonized, and ultimately, dominated.[9] Finally, the notion of 'soundings' registers the transience of the spoken word, whose impact cannot be rendered in graphic patterns. Indeed, the cognitive dissonance in my title between 'soundings' on the one hand, and 'writing' on the other, adverts to the crucial tension between orality and writing in Caribbean culture.

My principal concern in this study is to show that French Caribbean writing involves a uniquely intense confrontation with the intersection of space and time. This restless and insistent emphasis on the articulation of the two dimensions stands out against the context of the general paradigm shift marking the closing decades of the twentieth century, a sea change that has been described as the 'reassertion of space'.[10] Fredric Jameson writes of contemporary culture as being 'increasingly dominated by space and spatial logic'.[11] Certainly, the discourses of both social theory and literary criticism are overrun by spatial metaphors, and indeed critical studies of French Caribbean literature bear witness to this epistemological trend, which is particularly obvious in the predominance of cartographic rhetoric.[12] Confirming Fredric Jameson's diagnosis of the 'spatial turn'[13] that has led to the 'displacement of time, the spatialization of the temporal',[14] as well as Michel Foucault's much earlier recognition that 'the present era seems to

---

[7] Walter Ong, *Orality and Literacy: The Technologizing of the Word* (London and New York: Methuen, 1982), 71–2.

[8] Ibid. 73.

[9] '(vision presents surfaces) ready to be "explored" ': ibid. 73.

[10] Edward Soja's subtitle is clear in this regard: *Postmodern Geographies: The Reassertion of Space in Critical Social Theory* (London: Verso, 1989).

[11] Fredric Jameson, *Postmodernism, or, the Cultural Logic of Late Capitalism* (London: Verso, 1991), 67.

[12] For example, Patrick Chamoiseau and Raphaël Confiant, *Lettres créoles. Tracées antillaises et continentales de la littérature 1635–1975* (Paris: Hatier, 1991), and Sam Haigh, *Mapping a Tradition: Francophone Women's Writing from Guadeloupe* (London: Maney, 2000).

[13] Jameson, *Postmodernism*, 154.   [14] Ibid. 156.

be more the era of space',[15] the historian Fernand Braudel concludes that 'all the social sciences must make room "for an increasingly geographical conception of mankind" '.[16] Yet, even if we accept Braudel's directive as reasonable and Jameson's diagnosis as accurate, many questions remain, most of them concerning the residual importance accorded to history and to memory, questions of burning interest in cultures that suffered the coercive spatialization known as colonization. Those commentators who reject what they see as the hegemony of postmodern thinking over post-colonial thought (essentially an effort to understand colonialism and its legacy) probably welcome recent developments in critical theory, notably the emergence of a more balanced, less schismatic approach to the relation between space and time. Geographers and historians, being especially concerned by such epistemological mutations, have been particularly quick to comment on this shift.

In a recent study, the geographer Doreen Massey argued persuasively for the need for a four-dimensional approach that would challenge the view that space 'is the realm of stasis'.[17] Massey herself opposes Ernesto Laclau's idea that time is a genuine dynamism diametrically opposed to that time internal to a closed system, a time that some would term *durée* or duration, but that Laclau chooses to call 'space'.[18] In Laclau's view, space is representation and, as such, distortion and closure, since the real is ongoing or temporal. But does spatialization necessarily eliminate temporality? One of the objections raised by Henri Lefèbvre to the unthinking use of spatial metaphors is precisely the frequently underlying failure to relate space to time.[19] Another geographer,

---

[15] 'L'époque actuelle serait peut-être plutôt l'époque de l'espace': Michel Foucault, 'Des espaces autres' in *Dits et écrits, 1954–1988, vol. iv: 1980-88*, ed. Daniel Defont and François Ewald (Paris: Gallimard, 1994), 752.

[16] Fernand Braudel, *On History,* tr. Sarah Matthews (Chicago: University of Chicago Press, 1980), 52; 1st pub. as *Écrits sur l'histoire* (Paris: Flammarion, 1969). Braudel is quoting here P. Vidal de la Blache, *Revue de synthèse historique* (1903), 239.

[17] Doreen Massey, 'Politics and Space/Time', in Michael Keith and Steve Pile (eds.), *Place and the Politics of Identity* (London and New York: Routledge, 1993), 141–61: 142.

[18] Ernesto Laclau, *New Reflections on the Revolution of our Time* (London: Verso, 1990), 41.

[19] 'Si quelqu'un dit "espace", il doit aussitôt dire ce qui l'occupe et comment: le déploiement de l'énergie autour de "points" et dans un temps. . . . L'espace pris

Nigel Thrift, goes so far as to conclude that 'there is little sense to be had from making distinctions between time and space—there is only *time-space*'.[20] Thrift further believes that this view of a hyphenated 'time-space' resonates with Bergson's notion of a 'permanently moving continuity',[21] and with the emergent structure of feeling of our age, which is dominated by movement or flows. Writing of the 'hum of mobility' that characterizes the postmodern age, he asks 'what is place in this new "in-between" world?' and answers his own question as follows: 'compromised: permanently in a state of enunciation, between addresses, always deferred . . . traces of movement, speed, and circulation'.[22] This view of the 'in-betweenness' of contemporary time-space is reminiscent of Marc Augé's 'non-lieux'[23] and consonant with post-colonial thought—'in-betweenness' is one of Homi Bhabha's mantras, after all. Its emphasis on mobility or displacement re-temporalizes space. Thus Thrift's hyphenated time-space suggests not only hybridity, but also fluidity, just as his largely celebratory ontology contrasts with Jameson's disconsolate conclusion that the ascendancy of space has occasioned a 'crisis of historicity'[24] and an attendant 'sense of loss'.[25]

In *The Other America*, J. Michael Dash argues persuasively for the need to approach 'the Caribbean' in the singular, as it were, as 'the other America'. This study has taken, however, a radically different route that fully confirms the validity of Benítez-Rojo's 'repeating island' model. Certainly, in registering some of the major vibrations and gravitations of French Caribbean writing, we can move closer to a sense of the Caribbean in general. However, my study records above all the importance of ever finer degrees of internal variation and relationality within the already restrictive 'area' of French Caribbean writing. Just as the French

---

séparément devient une abstraction vide' ('If someone uses the word "space" he should specify at once what fills that space and how: the deployment of energy around 'points' and within time . . . Space considered independently of these considerations is just an empty abstraction'): Lefèbvre, *La Production de l'espace* (1974; Paris: Anthropos, 2000), 20. All translations mine unless otherwise indicated.

[20] Nigel Thrift, *Spatial Formations* (London: Sage, 1996), 285.
[21] Ibid. 286.   [22] Ibid. 289.
[23] Marc Augé, *Non-Lieux. Introduction à une anthropologie de la surmodernité* (Paris: Seuil, 1992); tr. as *Non-Places: Introduction to an Anthropology of Supermodernity* (London: Verso, 1995).
[24] Jameson, *Postmodernism*, 157.   [25] Ibid. 25.

Caribbean must be seen as part of the wider Caribbean—a fluid, relational field—and as resisting therefore its own separation or restrictive definition, so too a constant tension between differentiation (or separation) and relation (or flow) both structures and limits this study's reach. To begin with, although a body of work in Creole exists, I refer only to French Caribbean writing in French. This restriction increases the strain that must be borne by the expression 'French Caribbean' in my title, reinforcing the tension between its territorial/political and its linguistic/cultural reference. However, in considering the literary dynamic between French and Creole in Chapter 4, I do attempt to discuss some of the implications of that strain for the sounding out of French Caribbean literary space and time. Secondly, prose narrative is given considerably more attention here than either drama or poetry. It is true that the latter two are the least prominent genres in French Caribbean production in the period under consideration here. Furthermore, drama in particular, and poetry to a certain extent, is more likely to be in Creole than in French. And certainly, both genres are more closely associated with voice and performance than with writing—indeed, drama very often does not come into print at all. Nonetheless, the generic and linguistic partiality of this study must be conceded. Thirdly, the 'French Caribbean' with which I am concerned here does not include Guiana. Given its linguistic and cultural isolation or indeed 'insularity' on the South American continent, and its shared historical and cultural status as French colony and then *département d'outre-mer*, it would be misleading to suggest that Guiana is no more 'Caribbean' than Venezuela or Brazil. However, its history as a penal colony, the physical geography that made it unsuitable as a full-scale plantation colony, and its consequent demography, combined with its continental context, are all factors that set Guiana apart from the French Antilles in particular and within the Caribbean cultural economy in general. Haiti, as an independent country, is not, of course, part of the French Caribbean, yet it helps to define the contours of that space. The history of Haiti is unique in the Caribbean: it is unimpeachably different in relation not just to French Caribbean history, but to Caribbean history in general. Haiti has been, indeed, and continues to be for every other Caribbean island, although particularly for the French Caribbean, an over-significant other. Two further factors that distinguish the Haitian literary context are the extremely low levels of literacy in Haiti, and the fact that Haitian writers are largely and for obvious political, cultural, and economic reasons, writers in exile (chiefly in North America, especially Canada and Florida).

Finally, even if the issue of balance between Martinique and Guadeloupe frequently breaks through in the course of this study, it has not proved possible to address fully the important question of Martinique's higher literary profile. Full treatment of this issue, like that of the language question, the genre question, or the relation to Guiana and Haiti, would have required a full-scale comparative study. However, even popularizing histories, such as Ronald Segal's *The Black Diaspora*, counsel against collapsing the difference between Martinique and Guadeloupe. Segal notes, for example, that 'the two islands resemble each other so much in the ascendancy of French culture, their economic dependence on France, and their isolation from their Caribbean context that the differences between them seem all the sharper'.[26] Most of these differences are due to divergences between Guadeloupean and Martinican history, many of which were undoubtedly part of a policy of 'divide and conquer' and served well the cause of colonialism.

The demarcations or restrictions that we have just noted all raise the more general and complex question of the ethics and politics of difference. To what extent is it critically essential not to elide or erase differences and to what extent is differentiation an instrument of intellectual pre-emption and imperialism? Must differentiation precede relation? Is relation conditional on differentiation? These questions must be addressed in the context of the quite extraordinary intersection in French Caribbean writing between literary and poetic endeavour, on the one hand, and, on the other, the conceptualization or theorization of cultural difference that informs and drives a significant proportion of French Caribbean writing. The fallout from the various ideological debates that have raged around different theories of Caribbean cultural difference (negritude, *antillanité* or Caribbeanness, and *créolité* or Creoleness) has included the levelling literary effect of cultural programmes and the blurring of the boundary between propaganda and literary (or indeed criti-

---

[26]   Ronald Segal, *The Black Diaspora* (London: Faber & Faber, 1995).

cal) exploration. This threat to the integrity of writing suggests that the emphasis of literary criticism should be put on relation rather than on difference: on the relation between various theories of Caribbean identity, for example; on the relation between theory and practice; on the relation between criticism and writing, between one part of the Caribbean and another, between the Caribbean and the rest of the world, and so forth.

To take a concrete example, contemporary French Caribbean writing for many readers and critics begins and ends with the work of three or four writers, all of whom are identified with (or against) certain cultural movements, programmes, or manifestos. Furthermore, the positions that these writers are believed to hold have sometimes attracted much more attention than the subtleties of their writing. In this way, specific theories of Caribbean culture create certain exclusions, polarizing writers into partisans and dissenters, and they also encourage critical derelictions (not just the neglect of writing per se, but also the dismissal of writers who do not seem to engage with particular theories or with any). While this study does not aspire in any sense to the status of a survey, as a sonographic study of depth it should surely attempt to register, along with the more visible or dominant trends, the more hidden or perhaps unfairly forgotten writings. More important still, it should consider what distinguishes the fêted from the forgotten, the mediaphilic from the modest. It is crucial to identify the criteria that ensure that certain types of writing capture the imagination of a wide and admiring readership and others do not. In other words, the fact that the most celebrated and widely publicized writing is underwritten by those theories of difference and identity that it is taken to promote or illustrate is something that must itself be interpreted.

Even if I cannot aspire to elucidate them fully here, I have tried not to elide the differences that fissure even that rather artificially constructed 'space apart' that I am calling here the French Caribbean. However, the divergences that must not be ignored are not just the differing orientations of the two islands, but also the disparate approaches to space and to time taken by individual writers from the same island. And even within a given writer's *œuvre*, time, genre, and the vagaries of inspiration and influence can create variations and relations, differences and dynamics.

My approach aims to complement not only the excellent

thematic and chronological surveys that are now available,[27] but also the illuminating monographs that focus either on specific authors,[28] or on various other important questions (self-reflexive writing,[29] for example, or the myth of 'marronnage',[30] the problematic of gender,[31] the Guadeloupean tradition of writing by women,[32] the question of (Creole) identity,[33] etc.), as well as more ambitious, transverse, or oblique approaches, such as those of J. Michael Dash and Antonio Benítez-Rojo. If my own study sidelines the questions of gender, genre, and language, this is not because I underestimate the light shed and the shadows cast by those issues. Rather, the heuristic reach of the concepts guiding my approach is so daunting that it would be difficult to imagine a study that would exhaust their resonances in recent French Caribbean writing. It is easy, however, to imagine how several vectors, such as the highly suggestive ones just mentioned, could productively cross-fertilize the soundings taken here. Hence, while it would be futile to deny that the latter are limited in scope, my hope is that the readings that they yield may prove useful, nonetheless, for the future study of

[27] See especially Jack Corzani's definitive survey, *La Littérature des Antilles-Guyane françaises* (Fort-de-France: Désormeaux, 1978) and Jack Corzani, Léon-François Hoffmann, and Marie-Lyne Piccione, *Littératures francophones*, vol. ii: *Les Amériques* (Paris: Belin, 1998); two works by Régis Antoine: *La Littérature franco-antillaise: Haïti, Guadeloupe et Martinique* (Paris: Karthala, 1992) and *Rayonnants écrivains des Caraïbes* (Paris: Maisonneuve et Larose, 1998); and Sam Haigh (ed.), *An Introduction to Francophone Caribbean Writing: Guadeloupe and Martinique* (Oxford: Berg, 1999).

[28] For example, Celia Britton, *Édouard Glissant and Postcolonial Theory: Strategies of Language and Resistance* (Charlottesville: University Press of Virginia, 1999).

[29] Lydie Moudileno, *L'Écrivain antillais au miroir de sa littérature* (Paris: Karthala, 1997) and Dominique Chancé, *L'Auteur en souffrance. Essai sur la position et la représentation de l'auteur dans le roman antillais contemporain (1981–1992)* (Paris: Presses universitaires de France, 2000).

[30] Richard D. E. Burton, *Le Roman marron. Études sur la littérature martiniquaise contemporaine* (Paris: L'Harmattan, 1997).

[31] Maryse Condé, *La Parole des femmes. Essai sur des romancières des Antilles de langue française* (Paris: L'Harmattan, 1979).

[32] Haigh, *Mapping a Tradition*.

[33] Mireille Rosello, *Littérature et identité créole aux Antilles* (Paris: Karthala, 1992); Maryse Condé and Madeleine Cottenet-Hage (eds.), *Penser la créolité* (Paris: Karthala, 1995); H. Adlai Murdoch, *Creole Identity in the French Caribbean Novel* (Gainesville: University of Florida Press, 2001); Chris Bongie, *Islands and Exiles: The Creole Identities of Post/Colonial Literatures* (Stanford: Stanford University Press, 1998).

questions such as gendered space and time, or the time and space of various literary genres.

Broadly, this study falls into two movements. Although its fundamental thesis denies the value and indeed the possibility of holding the two dimensions apart, it is true that the first stresses time and the second space, with an intermediary chapter emphasizing both equally. The first three chapters probe the imagination of time. The first studies the successive secretion of three models of French Caribbean cultural identity. In addition to examining the teleology claimed for these theories, that is, the tidy, evolutionist narrative of Caribbean identity which is said to pass through the three stages of negritude, Caribbeanness, and Creoleness, I also consider the value attached to time and to space within each of these three visions of cultural identity. The dominant genre in French Caribbean writing from 1950 to the present is narrative, a preference that seems to suggest a preoccupation with linear temporality. However, as we shall see in the second chapter, in most French Caribbean narratives sequential time is interrupted, spatialized, and displaced. In other words, succession tends to be projected onto spatiality, with the result that these narratives register a complex, disrupted relation to history. They combine, rather problematically, a desire to represent sequence or succession—a 'désiré historique' ('longing for history'),[34] to use Édouard Glissant's expression—and a sense of loss, lack, or fracture, caused by the dislocation of historical continuity. For, unlike the immediate and local past, the originary Caribbean past lies elsewhere, and its double remoteness—both spatial and temporal—challenges memory. Continuing to probe the writing of time, the third chapter concentrates on the status of memory in writing, that is, on the connection realized in writing between the past and the present, place and displacement, memory and narrative, and on the dynamic of identity as a process of imagination and remembrance, openness and closure.

The chapter that forms the second, bridging section of the book concentrates on the space and time of writing and intertextuality. Intertextuality could be regarded as a deepening by superimposition or overlay, or as a means of injecting the vibration of diversity into the text. But it could also be envisaged as a form of memori-

---

[34] Glissant, *Le Discours antillais*, 147; *Caribbean Discourse*, 79.

alization—creating or consolidating, that is, a sense of textual tradition. It is also possible, of course, to read the practice as a kind of creolization and thus as the conscious or unconscious actualization of certain cultural theories about Caribbean cultural identity.

The third section turns towards the question of referential space. It opens with a study of the residual memory of the plantation as a seminal space in the French Caribbean imagination. Whereas Aimé Césaire more or less ignored this space and Joseph Zobel highlighted its destructive dimension, Édouard Glissant and his literary heirs are often at pains to emphasize its value as a culturally creative crucible. Issues of memory, nostalgia, and exoticism are raised by this contemporary rehabilitation of a space traditionally viewed as being exclusively coercive and exploitative. The plantation is studied here both as a 'lieu de mémoire' and as a chronotope, more specifically as a (retrospective) projection of temporal and spatial desire. The next chapter in this section follows the rural exodus in contemporary Caribbean writing. We find that the Creole town has taken on in equal measure the aspect of a positive, creative space that takes over from the plantation, keeping alive in its margins the latter's Creole legacy, and the aspect of a fallen domain in comparison with the creative Creole matrix of the plantation. The town as centre, or at least the town's bourgeois centre, is dismissed as being devoid of cultural productivity and centrifugally fixated on importation and imitation: that is, on the consumption of externally sourced models. However, the principal question posed by the Creole town as a whole relates to time: is the 'written' town a site of modernity, change, and dynamism, or of tradition, conservatism, and reproduction?

The fourth and final section of the book studies the reflecting or diffracting mirror held up to the French Caribbean by certain spaces outside it: firstly, the two most decisive source spaces, namely Africa and Metropolitan France. How are these spaces constructed, and how do they configure French Caribbean time? What sorts of displacement are implied by reference to these spaces? Following the consciousness-raising effect of movements such as *négritude*, we might expect Metropolitan France to disappear, or at least to be attenuated as a pole of identification. It would be understandable if writers sought to distance themselves explicitly or implicitly from what came to be widely regarded as a source of alienation. How, then, did writers from the middle of the last century onwards relate to Metropolitan France? To what extent is there circulation between the Caribbean and Europe? What are the directions and motives of that movement and how did the watershed of 1946 inflect the (post)colonial dynamic?

Much has been written about the over-investment of the *négritude* movement in a mythical and ultimately disabling image of Africa. But how does Africa figure in French Caribbean writing in the wake of that movement? Do succeeding generations of French Caribbean writers simply turn away from the African quest, or do they pursue it in a different manner? How does French Caribbean writing relate to African time, and how does it construct African space? In the final chapter, the focus shifts to French Caribbean imagination of other areas of the so-called New World: that is, other Caribbean islands, Francophone, Hispanophone and Anglophone, as well as continental space: South, Central, and North America. To what extent do successive waves of French Caribbean writing relate to contiguous New World space, and what does that relation reveal about French Caribbean time consciousness and about the level of openness to diversity and to interrelation often held to predominate in the Caribbean worldview? Most crucially, is such openness sufficiently prevalent to call into question the limits of this final section, constrained as it is within the triangular framework of an originary relation to Europe and to Africa and a largely analogical relation to the rest of the Americas?

CHAPTER ONE

Theoretical Generations: Writing Identities

[Mycéa] déclarait craindre les théories bien plus que les fièvres dont les épidémies (typhoïde ou paludisme) avaient ravagé naguère encore la plaine du Lamentin.[1]

In 1992, when Derek Walcott was awarded the Nobel Prize for literature, it was the second time that a Caribbean-born poet had been thus distinguished. There was, however, one conspicuous difference between the general perception of the tribute to Derek Walcott and that of the honouring in 1960 of the Guadeloupean-born poet Saint-John Perse. Whereas Walcott's prize secured a prestigious place on the world map of literature both for the tiny island of St Lucia and for the Caribbean basin in general, Saint-John Perse's Nobel was widely perceived, not only in 1960 but for about three decades afterwards, as an honour for 'the' French language and Metropolitan French culture rather than for Guadeloupe, much less the Caribbean.[2] We must be careful, of course, not to misconstrue this shift. Undoubtedly, the general reluctance to link the first Caribbean-born laureate with the 'New World' can be explained as much by the apparent absence of Caribbean texture from the greater part of Saint-John Perse's poetry and by the poet's ambiguous, and perhaps ambivalent, relation with the *pays natal*,[3]

---

[1] Édouard Glissant, *La Case du commandeur* (Paris: Seuil, 1981), 189; '[Mycéa] feared theories more than the typhoid or malarial fever still raging over the Lamentin plain in the recent past'.

[2] Saint-John Perse's Nobel acceptance speech is entitled 'Poésie' ('Poetry'). Derek Walcott, on the other hand, gave his speech the title *The Antilles: Fragments of Epic Memory* (London: Faber & Faber, 1993). The divergence between the two poetics is accurately registered in the contrast between the two titles, one centred in space and time, the other sublimely remote from both.

[3] See also Mary Gallagher, 'Seminal Praise: The Poetry of Saint-John Perse', in

as by the political status of the French Caribbean or the cultural profile of the Caribbean in general during the period in question. Yet the widespread recognition in 1992 of Derek Walcott as belonging to, and as speaking for, the Caribbean does also reflect a general evolution in the cultural status and identity of the geographical area that the Cuban critic Antonio Benítez-Rojo considers to be 'one of the least known regions of the modern world'.[4] More specifically, it illustrates the hearing that twentieth-century Caribbean voices began to claim as such in international literary consciousness.

AN INTERNATIONAL PROFILE

The Caribbean's international cultural currency is founded in large part on the perceived pertinence of this problematically post-colonial, yet unmistakably post-plantation and post-slavery literature to a globalized/globalizing world, increasingly marked by displacement. Furthermore, the gradual acknowledgement of the region's cultural significance is synergistically linked to the vigour of its literary output. The French Caribbean alone—that is, Martinique and Guadeloupe—could boast during the second half of the twentieth century the prolific literary achievement of a long catalogue of widely esteemed writers, including Aimé Césaire, Édouard Glissant, and Simone Schwarz-Bart; Patrick Chamoiseau, Maryse Condé, Daniel Maximin, and Xavier Orville; Myriam Warner-Vieyra, Raphaël Confiant, and Daniel Boukman; Gisèle Pineau, Ernest Pépin, Roland Brival, and Vincent Placoly. As this incomplete inventory implies, the French Caribbean is exceptional in the wider Francophone world in terms of the volume of this late twentieth-century literary surge, whose potency is so disproportionate to the spatial area involved. However, reservations have been expressed in certain quarters about this flood-tide.[5]

Sam Haigh (ed.), *An Introduction to Francophone Caribbean Writing: Guadeloupe and Martinique* (Oxford: Berg, 1999) 17–33.

[4] Antonio Benítez-Rojo, *The Repeating Island: The Caribbean and the Postmodern Perspective*, tr. James Maraniss (Durham: Duke University Press, 1992), 1.

[5] Jack Corzani considers that many French Caribbean novels are repetitive and formulaic, their authors having been tempted into a certain mould by the promise of 'being a hit with a preconditioned European readership' ('un succès facile auprès d'un public européen déjà conditionné'), in Corzani and Piccione, *Littératures francophones*, 158 and 164.

During roughly the same period, the English- and Spanish-speaking Caribbean also led a striking literary assault on the high ground formerly held by Metropolitan literatures. Derek Walcott, Jean Rhys, Wilson Harris, Edward Kamau Brathwaite, V. S. Naipaul, Paule Marshall, Merle Hodge, Michelle Cliff, and Caryl Phillips, along with numerous Jamaican poets, and Hispanophone writers such as Fernando Ortíz, Nicolás Guillén, and Alejo Carpentier, have all played a significant part in shaping the rhythms and mixing the colours of English- and Spanish-language literature. Some of these writers, particularly Derek Walcott, V. S. Naipaul, Alejo Carpentier, Edward Kamau Brathwaite, and Wilson Harris, have invested much energy in speculative cultural theory, although, with the exception of Brathwaite's work on 'nation language', their exertions have been less systematic and less programmatic than Martinican thinking, and have not wielded such widespread influence over other writers. In the case of Derek Walcott, for example, it is remarkable that, although he has been sporadically mentioned by French Caribbean writers (especially since he was awarded the Nobel Prize),[6] his work has had little or no obvious impact on French Caribbean literature, whereas the work of Édouard Glissant and the writing of Patrick Chamoiseau loom large as points of reference for Walcott.[7] Unlike its Anglophone or Hispanophone counterparts, the greater part of contemporary French Caribbean writing has, in fact, evolved in tandem with or in counterpoint to a vigorous body of endogenous cultural ideation. So trenchant is this self-reflexive edge that it must be credited with having carved out for French Caribbean writing a singularly prominent place both in Metropolitan France and in North America.

---

[6] See Maryse Condé in conversation with Françoise Pfaff on the subject of Walcott's Nobel Prize in Pfaff, *Entretiens avec Maryse Condé* (Paris: Karthala, 1993), 163.

[7] It is also possible to read this one-way influence as evidence of French Caribbean insularity, or a patent 'non-engagement with both non-French Caribbean and non-francophone scholarship': Richard and Sally Price, 'Shadowboxing in the Mangrove: The Politics of Identity in Post-Colonial Martinique', in Belinda Edmondson (ed.), *Caribbean Romances: The Politics of Regional Representation*, (Charlottesville: University Press of Virginia, 1999), 123–62: 133.

THEORETICAL FERMENT: MARTINIQUE

Fundamentally, the entire body of theory-driven writing from Martinique and Guadeloupe aims to define and perhaps inflect the cultural specificity of the (French) Caribbean. Jack Corzani is, for his part, suspicious of this trend. He indicts not just the ethnological curiosity and exoticist appetites of the enthusiastic Western readership that would not think of expecting French authors to conduct a similar ontological search for the quintessence of Frenchness, but also those Caribbean authors who play to their (European) gallery.[8] If Corzani were not challenging the more reductive and categorical end of the theoretical spectrum, his censure would be accused of missing the point of the post-colonial dynamic: namely the urge to 'write back' in order to tease out and contest legacies of denial and dispossession. This is, indeed, the dynamic studied by Christopher Miller in his work on the displacement of Europe's historical hegemony as theorizer of Africa by indigenous African self-theorizing.[9] There is a strong tradition of French Metropolitan conceptualization of the French Caribbean: its literary dimension is well documented[10] and its ethnological arm extends from the founding fathers, Du Tertre and Labat, to Michel Leiris and the ongoing work of Francis Affergan.[11] Had French culture been subjected to a proportionally similar barrage of exogenous ethnology, French writers might well have reacted by 'repossessing the gaze'. However, the real question here is whether or not the gaze has, in truth, been 'repossessed': 'the danger faced, predictably enough, is that of control and containment. Authorized marginality means that the production of "difference" can be supervised, hence recuperated, neutralized and depoliticized . . .'.[12]

Whether they are writing inside or outside a specific theoretical movement, most Caribbean authors write about or against the

---

[8] Corzani, *Littératures francophones*, 163.

[9] Christopher Miller, *Theories of Africans: Francophone Literature and Anthropology in Africa* (Chicago: University of Chicago Press, 1990).

[10] See Régis Antoine, *Les Écrivains français et les Antilles. Des premiers Pères blancs aux surréalistes noirs* (Paris: Maisonneuve et Larose, 1978).

[11] See Raphaël Confiant's novel, *Le Nègre et l'amiral* (Paris: Grasset, 1988), 83–105 for a parody of the encounter between the Metropolitan gaze (in the shape of André Breton and Claude Lévi-Strauss) and the realities of Fort-de-France.

[12] Trinh T. Minh-Ha, 'An Acoustic Journey', in John C. Welchman (ed.), *Rethinking Borders* (Minneapolis: University of Minnesota Press, 1996), 1–17: 8–9.

modelling of the collective Caribbean psyche by a shared geography of fragmentation and openness, and by a common colonial history involving genocide, ethnocide, transportation, displacement, slavery, amnesia, assimilation, diversity, contact, economic exploitation, and political marginalization. Layers of relation and creolization (not just between African, Asian, and European cultures, but also amongst Africans, Europeans, or Indians themselves) would alone guarantee a cultural legacy of diversity and variegation and of complexity and complexes with which Caribbean consciousness would somehow have to come to terms. And when the empires exploiting the colonies were several—not just French, British, and Spanish, but also Dutch and Portuguese— the intricacies of the post-colonial scar tissue were guaranteed to be further compounded. Conversely, the already considerable opportunities for creative interrelation were potentially multiplied even further by the linguistic, cultural, and political heterogeneity of the various colonial regimes, although, in practice, such cross-fertilization seems to have been defied if not defeated by geopolitical fragmentation. Culturally and politically, the Caribbean is, then, richly complex or excessively divided, depending on one's perspective. Indeed, despite, or because of this shared inheritance of complexity, division, and diversity, reference to 'the Caribbean' in the singular is often deemed questionable.[13] In this sense, the frequent acknowledgement that the home constituency of Caribbean literature exists only in the virtuality of the future[14] reflects the more

[13] Antonio Benítez-Rojo, in *The Repeating Island*, 37–8, quotes Frank Moya Pons, according to whom 'the Caribbean as a living community, with common interests and aspirations, just does not exist. Practically, it seems more sensible to think of several Caribbeans coexisting alongside one another.' Benítez-Rojo also quotes Sidney W. Mintz, who sees the Caribbean as a 'societal area' without a common culture: 'the cultural panorama of the Caribbean is supremely heterogeneous. How then can one be sure that a Caribbean culture even exists?'

[14] Jean Bernabé, Patrick Chamoiseau, and Raphaël Confiant, *Éloge de la créolité/In Praise of Creoleness*, bilingual edn., tr. M. B. Taleb-Khyar (Paris: Gallimard, 1993; 1st edn. (French only) 1989): 'La littérature antillaise n'existe pas encore. Nous sommes encore dans un état de prélittérature: celui d'une production écrite sans audience chez elle, méconnaissant l'interaction auteurs/lecteurs où s'élabore une littérature' (p. 14) ('Caribbean literature does not yet exist. We are still in a state of preliterature: that of a written production without a home audience, ignorant of the authors/readers interaction which is the primary condition of the development of a literature'; p. 76). Of Édouard Glissant, the authors of the *Éloge* write that he is 'persuaded that he is writing for future generations' (p. 84) ('persuadé d'écrire pour des lecteurs futurs'; p. 23), and indeed Glissant stated in 1986: 'je ne

fundamental question as to whether 'the Caribbean' can truly be said to exist (yet) as a distinct and united post-colonial domain. After all, the educated elites of neighbouring islands often do not speak the same language and, furthermore, the political and economic profiles of the islands vary considerably even within individual archipelagos, and are in some cases—in Haiti, for example—highly unstable and in others supremely anomalous: is the latter not the case, for very different reasons, both of Cuba and of the French Caribbean?

Which factors of Caribbean diversity explain the fact that the self-reflexive tropism took hold so vigorously in the French Caribbean, more especially in Martinique? Although some might point to the Haitian *noiriste* or *indigéniste* movements as demonstrating a comparable ideological commitment, Haitian theories of culture and cultural identity were almost exclusively local. Not only did these theories eschew extrapolation from the Haitian condition itself, but they were also circumscribed in time, failing to endure well beyond the first half of the twentieth century, far less to accelerate, as did their French Caribbean counterparts. Arguably, other restrictions have similarly curbed the theoretical ambition of Anglophone Caribbean writers such as the Guianese novelist Wilson Harris, or Derek Walcott. For example, when the Jamaican poet and critic Edward Kamau Brathwaite theorized creolization at the end of the 1960s, the title of his study was *The Development of Creole Society in Jamaica 1770–1820*; in other words, his approach was more socio-historical than speculative. The restraint and the constraints of such empiricism would be entirely foreign to Édouard Glissant or Patrick Chamoiseau. Moreover, although Edward Brathwaite himself, and also Wilson Harris and Derek Walcott, have authored important speculative essays,[15] they have not attempted to articulate—much less

crois pas qu'il existe encore une littérature antillaise au sens où une littérature suppose un mouvement d'action et de réaction entre un public et des œuvres . . . un projet commun' ('I do not believe that Caribbean literature exists yet, in so far as literature presupposes a dynamic of action and reaction between literary works and their readership'): 'Édouard Glissant, préfacier d'une littérature future', Édouard Glissant in conversation with Priska Degras and Bernard Magnier, *Notre Librairie*, 74 (1986), 14–20: 14. For an analysis of some of these paradoxical statements, see Rosello, *Littérature et identité créole aux Antilles*, 30–4.

[15] Edward Kamau Brathwaite, *History of the Voice: The Development of Nation Language in Anglophone Caribbean Poetry* (London: New Beacon, 1984); Wilson

prescribe—an overarching, tentacular poetics, that is, a pan-Caribbean (or even global) programme of culture that welds an aesthetics and an ethics to an epistemology and an ontology.

In the charged institutional context where Martinican and Guadeloupean authors write in French, publish with French publishers, win French literary prizes, and frequently attract a largely Metropolitan French readership, the programmatic impulse represents perhaps an effort to pre-empt accusations of a sell-out. It could be seen, in other words, as a compensatory and defensive attempt to repatriate and legitimize a literary project by strategically reinforcing it with a discourse of cultural differentiation and resistance. The particularly acute separation anxiety of Martinican as opposed to Guadeloupean intellectuals is no doubt explained by the degree of perceived political and economic emasculation of the *pays natal,* or what J. Michael Dash calls Martinique's 'overwhelming context of adaption and acquiescence' and its 'culture of consent'.[16] It would be altogether plausible if Martinique, as the more assimilated of the two islands, were more anxious to differentiate itself from the *Métropole.*[17] Metropolitan and international receptiveness to Martinican theory, added to the many, often intangible, indications that the implied reader is not (principally) local or Caribbean, suggest indeed a highly intimate dynamic, and one that is perhaps correspondingly fraught on the Martinican side. Certainly, Martinique appears to have provided even more fertile ground than Guadeloupe for dissemination of the ideational, universalizing tropism widely regarded as characterizing Metropolitan French culture, in contrast, again, to the more empirical spirit of 'Anglo-Saxon' thought. This is precisely the point made by Derek Walcott in his open letter to Patrick Chamoiseau, which first appeared in 1996 in the *New York Review of Books.*[18] Walcott observes that the polemical tone of the co-authored pamphlet *Éloge de la créolité* flaunts that faith in new movements

Harris, *The Womb of Space: The Cross-Cultural Imagination* (Westport, Conn.: Greenwood, 1983); Walcott, *What the Twilight Says.*

[16] Dash, *The Other America,* 19.

[17] This is the explanation favoured by J. Michael Dash: 'It is no coincidence that Martinique is a prolific producer of theories of difference. Envisioning opacity at all costs is the only form of resistance open to Martiniquans, and to this extent one is never in doubt as to the political implications of what Glissant is proposing': *The Other America,* 11.

[18] Repr. in *What the Twilight Says,* 213–32.

and theories that marks the history of aesthetic thought in France. He considers the co-authored tract as part of the peculiarly French obsession with 'publishing manifestos', observing that 'nothing is more French than [its] confident rhetoric'. In its 'emphatic isolation' Walcott hears the echo of 'all those pamphlets outlining programs for a new painting, a new poetry, that erupt from metropolitan ferment, and that, reaching out to embrace a public, baffle it by their vehemence'.[19] It should not be forgotten that the *négritude* movement was conceived in Paris, that the seminal moment[20] in Glissant's conceptualization of Caribbean consciousness also took place in France, and that even *Éloge de la créolité* began life as a talk presented in the suburbs north of Paris. Certainly, these 'Metropolitan conceptions' are exceptional given the fact that these writers, with the exception of Glissant,[21] have written almost exclusively in and from Martinique. Yet they reflect the fact that this work was published and promoted primarily in Metropolitan France. The enthusiastic Metropolitan reception of French Caribbean 'theory' does not, however, extend to the two important theoretical works of the Guadeloupean cultural theorist, Creole linguist, and novelist Dany Bébel-Gisler. Whereas this author's works are neither easily available nor widely discussed in Metropolitan France or internationally,[22] Martinican theory

---

[19] Ibid. 223–4.

[20] See my discussion of Glissant's *Soleil de la conscience* (Paris: Seuil, 1956) in Ch. 7.

[21] Although Glissant has also spent substantial portions of his writing life in Metropolitan France and in the United States, his political involvement in the Caribbean from the late 1950s through to the 1960s and his regular if intermittent presence there from 1965 reflects his philosophy of 'errance' and 'relation'. Significantly, his *Le Discours antillais* includes at the end a long list of the occasions (complete with dates and venues) for which the various pieces comprising that work were composed (a much-abridged list is given in the English translation, since the latter comprises a selection only of Glissant's essays). The locations are almost exclusively Caribbean.

[22] Dany Bébel-Gisler, *Le Défi culturel guadeloupéen. Devenir ce que nous sommes* (Paris: Seghers, 1985) and *La Langue créole, force jugulée. Étude des rapports de force entre le créole et le français aux Antilles* (Paris: L'Harmattan, 1976). Sam Haigh, in her study of the specifics of Guadeloupean writing by women (*Mapping a Tradition*), a study that succeeds in its aim of redressing the Martinican imbalance, fittingly does justice both to Bébel-Gisler's thinking on Creole and Creole culture and to her novel, *Léonora. L'histoire enfouie de la Guadeloupe* (Paris: Seghers, 1985), tr. Andrea Leskes as *Leonora: The Buried Story of Guadeloupe* (Charlottesville and London: University Press of Virginia, 1994). See also A. James Arnold, 'The Gendering of Créolité: The Erotics of Colonialism', in Condé and Cottenet-Hage (eds.), *Penser la créolité* (Paris: Karthala, 1995), 21–40.

bedazzles Paris to such an extent that Gallimard brought out a second, bilingual edition of the *créolité* manifesto, featuring the English translation alongside the French text. The discrepancy in the two receptions is no doubt related to the more empirically and sociologically focused nature of Bébel-Gisler's thinking and to the absence of that poetic charge, that literary tension, which immediately identifies the 'writer' in France.[23]

Bespeaking resistance or assimilation (or both simultaneously), the theoretical tropism tends to configure French Caribbean writing as a closed circuit. The various theories act like magnetic poles, not only attracting and influencing other writers, plotting their preoccupations and steering their styles, but also shaping, or indeed curtailing the expectations of readers and critics, who tend, tautologically, to measure writing against the programmes holding strongest currency.

SPACE AND TIME FOR *NÉGRITUDE*

Considerations of space and time are of great importance in the shaping of the theoretical currents directing much French Caribbean literature over the past half-century. To begin with, the various turns taken by the theoretical tide throughout this period—in particular, of course, the Oedipal moments of its teleology—are themselves deeply inscribed in time. Furthermore, the successive movements or currents vary principally in their configuration of the temporal and spatial dimensions of Caribbean identity. However, what I would like to emphasize here is how, over the last two decades of the twentieth century, that body of French Caribbean writing that won itself a respectful Metropolitan and international hearing sedulously promoted a certain narrative of Caribbean identity. This received narrative has Caribbean identity move from *négritude*, where the chief focus is on essence or being, through *antillanité* or 'Caribbeanness', where concern with the contingencies of existence or 'l'étant' predominates, to 'creoleness' (*créolité*/*créolisation*) or relationality. Two features of this histori-

---

[23] 'Dany Bébel-Gisler is not a writer' (n'est pas écrivain'): Chancé, *L'Auteur en souffrance*, 94. This critic suggests that Bébel-Gisler is less committed to 'writing' than to sociological transcription.

cist discourse are particularly striking. Firstly, its marginalization of the work of Frantz Fanon. And secondly, while it makes much of Glissant's writing on *antillanité* (dating from the 1960s and 1970s), it neglects the subsequent work, which in fact goes further and deeper in its exploration of creolization than does the *créolité* movement itself. I am thinking here of Glissant's wide-ranging 'poetics of Relation' or of 'creolization', central to his hallmark visions of the 'tout-monde' or 'chaos-monde'. Moreover, the reductive symmetry of the proposed teleology suggests a certain intellectual insularity or closure, and even a lack of engagement with thinking in the wider Caribbean. The reductiveness of this narrative can also be blamed, however, on its lack of emphasis on the literary, a particularly invidious distortion where *négritude* is concerned. Césaire's polemical pamphlet *Discours sur le colonialisme* is, after all, the only strictly theoretical text of substance in the poet/dramatist's richly literary *œuvre*. A more balanced generic counterpoint of cultural theory and literary practice characterizes the work of the Martinican novelist, poet, playwright, and essayist Édouard Glissant, and that same balance can also be seen in the writing of Patrick Chamoiseau, Raphaël Confiant, and Maryse Condé. However, the *créolité* narrative is founded less on considerations of writing than on the theory of identity that can be inferred from the shorthand of certain political and linguistic choices (the choice of French over Creole, for example).

Even if Caribbean writers, in particular Aimé Césaire and Léon-Gontran Damas, were prominent in the inception and development of *négritude*, the movement did not have a Caribbean patent; it was, after all, Léopold Sédar Senghor who did most to conceptualize the practice, although Roger Toumson is one of many critics who has stressed its lack of any single, strong, or central theoretical underpinning. Indeed, Toumson characterizes *négritude* as a 'pratique sans théorie',[24] that cobbled together an ideological backbone in which anti-rationalism and Marxism predominated. This improvised and uncertain conceptual framework made the notion an easy target for demystification. In 1952 Frantz Fanon attacked *négritude* as an essentialist concept: 'Le nègre n'est pas. Pas plus

---

[24] Roger Toumson, *La Transgression des couleurs. Littérature et langage des Antilles, 18e, 19e et 20e siècles* (Paris: Éditions Caribéennes, 1989). See also Belinda Jack, *Negritude and Literary Criticism: The History and Theory of 'Negro-African' Literature in French* (Westport, Conn.: Greenwood, 1996).

que le Blanc ('The Negro is not. Any more than the white man').[25] Fanon did not take issue, however, with one of the primary projects of the *négritude* movement, a project with which he himself is often associated, namely the critique of self-interested and hegemonic representations of black people, who were routinely stereotyped both in Western and in 'assimilated' Caribbean writing.

Did the French Caribbean writers affiliated to the *négritude* movement neglect the contingencies of space and time as its critics claim they did? In theory, certainly, the 'New World' proponents of *négritude* aspired to counter-cultural assimilation by reconnecting with traditional African values. But did that mean that they necessarily minimized the importance of ('New World') space, displacement, and temporality? Did it automatically mean that they were not particularly interested in the specificity of the Caribbean? Like Fanon's political focus on Africa, the predominantly African wavelengths of Césaire's *imaginaire* are indeed taken to confirm a lack of single-minded concern with 'New World' culture. However, the *writing* of Aimé Césaire or Guy Tirolien, like that of the Guianese poet Léon-Gontran Damas, while it might emphasize the relation to Africa, is often deeply embedded too in the texture of Caribbean space and culture. In so far as Césaire's writing itself is criticized by the *créolistes*, and it must be said that Raphaël Confiant's indictment of Césaire is almost entirely based on the poet's political philosophy and practice,[26] what is condemned is the particular balance between its Afrocentric or Francocentric inflections, on the one hand, and its local Caribbean or American loyalties, on the other.

If *négritude*—in theory at least—does not attend sufficiently to the new creative mix that specifies 'New World' cultural space, can it be accused also of showing scant respect for the strictures of 'New World' time? Certainly, the writing of Caribbean *négritude* eschews the novel, being largely confined to the poetic and dramatic modes. Although this preference for poetry and drama— genres that traditionally highlight voice—may reflect a certain (writerly) suspicion of writing, it might also indicate a reluctance to

---

[25] Frantz Fanon, *Peau noire, masques blancs*, 187; *Black Skin, White Masks*, 231.
[26] In the blurb on the back cover of Confiant's *Aimé Césaire. Une traversée paradoxale du siècle* (Paris: Stock, 1993), Chamoiseau states that his colleague studies 'all of Césaire', the poetic work as well as the politics. This misrepresents Confiant's book, which is in no sense at all a full consideration of Césaire's writing.

expose the idealized and static vision—or illusion—of self-identity suggested by *négritude* thinking to (or within) the linear constraints of narrative. Poetry in particular tends to neutralize the tyranny of syntagmatic relations, with the result that it perhaps lends itself more convincingly to resistance or rupture than to construction, contextualization, or co-ordination. However, while these generalizations may conveniently corroborate the *créoliste* history of Caribbean thinking, only close critical attention to the writing of Aimé Césaire (both the poetry, *Ferrements, Moi, laminaire*, and *Les Armes miraculeuses*, and the plays, *La Tragédie du Roi Christophe, Une saison au Congo*, and *Une tempête*) will confirm or refute them. And since this study does not afford the required critical attention to drama and poetry, I must be particularly careful to sound here a suitably cautionary note. For Édouard Glissant, Césaire's writing can be read as a poetics of incipience, or of becoming, and thus engages frontally with time. Glissant notes in particular that the figure of the Rebel in the play *Et les chiens se taisaient* transcends the historical moment of *négritude* as an anti-racist racism.[27] Moreover, in an analysis that further demonstrates the need to moderate even quite plausible theoretical generalizations by close attention to the density of writing itself, Jean Khalfa and Jérôme Game argue that what is at stake in Césaire's *Cahier d'un retour au pays natal* is, in fact, 'time, or rather modes of experiencing time'. And they continue:

poetry is above all a conflict of temporalities. It always starts with the suspension of the linear or prosaic fragmentation of speech (and therefore consciousness) in time, trying, through rhythm, metre, assonance, rhyme, enjambment, or, later, the space of the page, to keep open the possibility of a discrepancy between the semantic and the syntactic lines, and thus to resist passage, to hold back, to construct the structures of a duration.[28]

This reading presents an alternative view of the poetry of *négritude*, which has often been depicted, even on occasion by Édouard

[27] 'ce qui était moment (le fameux "racisme anti-raciste"), Césaire l'a tué (dépassé) en la personne de son *Rebelle*': Glissant, *L'Intention poétique* (Paris: Seuil, 1969), 147.

[28] Jean Khalfa, with Jérôme Game, 'Pustules, Spirals, Volcanos: Images and Moods in Césaire's *Cahier d'un retour au pays natal*', *Wasafiri*, 31 (Spring 2000), 43–51: 43.

Glissant, as the poetry of the barely articulated 'cri', or scream.[29] It also challenges, however, the notion of poetry as an ahistorical, neo-Adamic naming of the 'New World', in that, according to Khalfa and Game, the *Cahier* confronts the 'fragmented time and space of the present'[30]—which is *'linear, that is without memory'*[31]—with 'the life and depth of a remembered past',[32] that is, 'time perceived as life, as a cycle of creation rather than the linear and repetitive vanishing of the instant'.[33] Such studies look afresh at writing per se. Instead of scanning labels as though they could account for the intensely labile processes of poetic practice, they attend to the flux and contradictions of 'textuality' itself. Perhaps then, if we devoted this level of attention to the writing of *négritude*, we would be led to suggest an alternative, non-Hegelian (and non-Darwinian) reading of the history of French Caribbean thought both before and immediately after 1950. In other words, we might produce a less reductive reading of *négritude* that would be more respectful of generic, textual, and intellectual subtlety than the narrative of transcendence articulated by the *créolité* movement.

ANTILLANITÉ, OR THE TIME OF ANTILLEAN SPACE

Unlike the ideological aura of *négritude*, which, however little it reflects some of the writing that it labels, is supremely remote from reference to space or to time, the vision of *antillanité* is recognized as being radically concerned both with space and with time. If Édouard Glissant anathematizes the 'return' ('retour') practised by the writers of *négritude*, it is because this tropism distracts attention from local space and present time; it fails to ground its vision of identity in the 'New World'. Glissant's alternative perspective is, on the contrary, predominantly local. Etymologically, the name 'Antilles' is derived from the Latin 'ante' and 'illum', meaning 'before the continent'.[34] Although the preposition can function

---

[29] 'Ainsi qualifiera-t-on au mieux l'entreprise de Césaire comme un cri de conscience' ('At best, Césaire's project can be said to be above all a scream of conscience'): Glissant, *L'Intention poétique*, 152.

[30] Khalfa and Game, 'Pustules', 45.   [31] Ibid. 44

[32] Ibid. 45.   [33] Ibid. 47.

[34] See Patrick Chamoiseau, *Écrire en pays dominé* (Paris: Gallimard, 1997), 234–45.

both temporally and spatially (meaning 'in front of' as well as 'prior to'), the temporal reference is the primary one and refers here to the historical fact that the Caribbean islands were reached by the European explorers *before* the latter located the American continent (in the etymology, the monolithic singularity of the pronoun can only refer to the continental land mass anticipated by the 'explorers'). Both the temporal and the historical references implied by the name 'Antilles' are, of course, latent; the name refers to priority and to history only in so far as one recalls the Latin derivation. Moreover, its etymological reference doubly defers to an 'other' space and time. First of all, it defers reference to the islands, naming not the actual islands or archipelagos, but rather their positioning as outposts of continental space; secondly, the vectorization implied in the temporal reference 'ante' means that the name is for ever embedded in a sense of the Western drift of European and African 'discovery' of the Americas, thus deferring to a history seen to emanate from the West, and primarily from Europe. These relational resonances are reinforced in the consistent emphasis within Glissant's 'Caribbean discourse' on the importance of seeing the Caribbean in positional terms. Relationality is, indeed, one of the linchpins of Glissant's thinking, finding its way into the title of his third major essay collection, *Poétique de la Relation*. In this sense, although the etymological subordination of the islands to the pronominal block 'illum' clashes with Glissant's criticism of deferral to other spaces ('l'ailleurs'), at least this reference is prospective rather than retrospective, and it remains within the ambit of the Americas.

CREOLES: FROM SPACE TO DISPLACEMENT?

The first section of *Éloge de la créolité* recounts the gradual twentieth-century movement of the Caribbean psyche towards self-discovery and self-acceptance, a progression leading via Césaire's *négritude* and Glissant's *antillanité* to the ultimate authenticity and self-possession claimed for *créolité*. This evolutionist narrative places the *créolité* movement within a historicist frame. However, the manifesto also invokes time on several other levels: for example, it draws attention to the derivation and history of the term 'créole'. Despite radical fluctuations in meaning, this term has always stressed displacement, even if it has also been overshadowed by what Chris Bongie aptly terms 'resisting memories' of exclusionist racial classification. Referred to by Bongie as a 'shifting signifier',[35] as 'slippery' and 'resolutely unstable', it has always been a locus of considerable semantic confusion. To begin with, its etymology is problematic. In a footnote, the authors of *Éloge de la créolité* state that it 'viendrait de l'espagnol "criollo", lui-même découlant du verbe latin "criare" [sic] qui signifie "élever, éduquer". Le Créole est celui qui est né et a été élevé aux Amériques sans en être originaire, comme les Amérindiens' ('seems to come from the Spanish word "crillo" [sic], itself derived from the Latin verb "criare" which means "to raise, to educate". The Creole is the person who was born and raised in the Americas and who is not a native like American Indians').[36] Here, displacement is highlighted as the chief criterion of creoleness and there is no reference to race. The *créolistes*' use of the conditional tense to signal tentativeness is reinforced by the rather cavalier disclaimer at the end of the same footnote, according to which: 'l'étymologie est, comme chacun sait, un terrain miné et donc peu sûr. Il n'est donc nul besoin de s'y référer pour aborder l'idée de Créolité' ('etymology is, as everybody knows, a dangerous and uncertain field. There is, therefore, no need to refer to it in order to approach the idea of creoleness') (*Él.* 61; *Pr.* 121). However, without embracing the fundamentalism of Heidegger, for whom etymology constitutes the condensed 'wisdom of the tongue', one might consider that the etymological and philological pedigree of the term 'créolité' is, on the contrary, particularly pertinent. After all, usage of the term that the *créolistes* are mobilizing in a narrative of identity based on filiation and displacement has itself followed a complex pattern of variation (or creolization) according to its dissemination and naturalization in different geographical and cultural contexts.

Lexicologists seem to agree that the term 'créole' derives from the Portuguese 'crioulo', meaning a slave born in his master's

---

[35] Chris Bongie, 'Resisting Memories: The Creole Identities of Lafcadio Hearn and Édouard Glissant', *Sub-Stance*, 84 (1997), 153–78. A considerably amplified version of this article features under a similar chapter title in Bongie's *Islands and Exiles*. The fourth chapter of Bongie's book is entitled 'Resisting Memories: Édouard Glissant and the Medusa of History'.
[36] Bernabé et al., *Éloge de la créolité*, 61 n. 12; *In Praise of Creoleness*, 121 n. 10. Further references are given in the text as *Él., Pr.* plus the page number.

house, from the Portuguese verb 'criar' (to breed, but also to bring up), itself derived from the Latin verb 'creare' (meaning to create or beget). The Spanish 'criollo' is said to be based in turn on the Portuguese. The authors of *Éloge de la créolité*, who do not mention the Portuguese usage at all, seem to conflate the Portuguese 'criar' with the Latin 'creare' in their hybrid but ficti-tious 'criare', thus erasing not only the semantic leap between the Latin and the Portuguese, from 'begetting' to 'bringing up', or from generation to acculturation, but also the further shift between the Portuguese and the Spanish meanings. As used in Spanish from the sixteenth to the eighteenth centuries, the term 'criollo' referred not, as in the Portuguese, to the displaced African slave population, but rather to any person of Spanish origin born in the 'New World', as distinct from a Spaniard residing in so-called Spanish America but who had been born in Spain. Clearly, as a term of identification, neither Iberian usage refers exclusively or even principally to racial or hereditary considerations. Rather, they both refer primarily to transportation or migration, that is, discontinuity of *location*: white European born and bred in the 'New World' in the case of the Spanish term and black African born and bred in the 'New World' in the case of the Portuguese. Both in the case of the Portuguese 'crioulos' (African slaves) and in the case of the Spanish 'criollos' (Spanish colonists), this primary distinction, based on differential or adventitious origin, was the premiss of considerable social discrimination in the Americas, particularly in the eighteenth century, in that 'peninsulares' and 'criollos' were regarded as two very distinct, and even opposed, categories. Robert Chaudenson confirms that seventeenth-century French lexicographers, follow-ing the Spanish rather than the Portuguese sense of the word, fixed the meaning of the term 'créole' as being 'Européen né aux Isles',[37] whereas up until the mid-eighteenth century the term designated in France's 'New World' colonies both Europeans and Africans, both whites and blacks, the only significant criterion being birth in the colonies.[38] However, from the middle of the eighteenth century

---

[37] Robert Chaudenson, *Des îles, des hommes, des langues. Langues créoles— cultures créoles* (Paris: L'Harmattan, 1992), 8.

[38] Robert Chaudenson observes (ibid. 9) that dictionary usage (which, until very recently, applied the term 'Creole' to whites only) can be very misleading, and that French lexicography does not take account of regional French and Creole usage, or of usage variations in place and time.

onwards the French Caribbean would follow Metropolitan French usage, reserving for the unqualified noun or adjective 'créole' the exclusionist meaning of white European born in the colonies.

The inclusive contemporary usage whereby the term is taken to refer to all those who share a common Creole (that is, 'New World', or displaced) culture is not a new extension of reference within the French-speaking American colonies; in French Guiana, for example, that inclusiveness had never been surrendered. As the authors of *Éloge de la créolité* point out, black Guianese have always called themselves *Créoles*. Moreover, while the race-specific difference between Spanish and Portuguese usage had been effaced in Guiana from very early on, the term referred there less to the general factor of adventitious 'New World' birth than to perceived cultural assimilation into European ways, that is, to creolization not just as adaptation to a new geographical environment, but as integration into the colonial cultural system. The Guianese *marron* communities would not have been regarded, for example, as Creoles. In neighbouring Suriname (Dutch Guiana), on the other hand, the term 'Creoles' referred exclusively to the descendants of African slaves, that is, it retained the original Portuguese reference.

Without further enumerating all the other meanings of the term 'créole',[39] we can see that its reference fluctuates widely both in space and in time. However, a certain consistency is nonetheless evident regarding the definition of the Creole with respect to place; that is, the (transportation- or migration-based) colonial culture of the 'New World'. The reference to race is variable, however; the emphasis is not, or not always, directly on differentiation by race and, where it is, this stress is superimposed on the primary criterion of deracination or relocation. *Créoliste* discourse ostentatiously cancels the term's historical, geographical, and cultural variability, and also its operation as an instrument of exclusion by race or by culture, declaring that to be 'créole' is to belong to a creolized culture (defined not just as displaced, however, but also—crucially,

---

[39] As Peter Hulme has noted, 'the term "creole" seeps across any attempt at a Manichean dividing line between native and settler, black and white': 'The Locked Heart: The Creole Family Romance of Wide Sargasso Sea', in Francis Barker, Peter Hulme, and Margaret Iversen (eds.) *Colonial Discourse/Postcolonial Theory*, Essex Symposia on Literature Politics Theory (Manchester and New York: Manchester University Press, 1994), 74–5: 75. Bongie, 'Resisting Memories', notes the fluidity of the term's use even within one 19th-century text (Lafcadio Hearn's novel *Youma*).

even primarily—as adjusted, adapted, accommodating, or even crossed or mixed). What is ingenious about the *créolistes'* mobilization of this term is that they thereby harness its aura of indeterminacy and variability in space and time, an aura that could itself be said to be 'creolized'. This very instability may indeed have been intended to protect the *créolité* movement from unwelcome charges of intellectual assimilation into the Cartesian clarity of French thought.

CRÉOLITÉ: CULTURAL RETROSPECTION AND POLITICAL LIMBO

While it cannot be regarded as the inaugural text of the *créolité* movement,[40] the cultural manifesto *Éloge de la créolité* (1989), elucidates certain aspirations already implicit in less doctrinaire form in works such as Chamoiseau's *Chronique des sept misères* (1986). The manifesto's three authors characterize Creole culture as the product of the process of creolization enabled by the plantation system endemic over several centuries in the American South, Central America, Brazil, the Indian Ocean, and the Caribbean. However, they further assert that the entire world is approaching a state of Creoleness in that every people and every culture is increasingly entering into relation with others. In this sense, the pamphlet does not simply theorize Caribbean cultural identity; it also lays claim to certain truths about global cultural identity in the present and future.

Although the spatio-cultural reference of *créolité*, unlike that of *antillanité*, 'theoretically' includes Brazil, Louisiana, and the Indian Ocean, in practice *créoliste* discourse refers almost exclusively to the Caribbean. In *Lettres créoles* Patrick Chamoiseau and Raphaël Confiant date *créolité* from 1635, that is, from the inception of plantation culture.[41] And yet, the notion of Creoleness is injected by

---

[40] After all, many aspects of the ideology and most aspects of the aesthetic are already present in the two novels by Chamoiseau that predate the manifesto: *Chronique des sept misères* (Paris: Gallimard, 1986) and *Solibo Magnifique* (Paris: Gallimard, 1988).

[41] This point is made abundantly clear in the dates given in the subtitle to Chamoiseau and Confiant's *Lettres créoles*, which reads: *Tracées antillaises et continentales de la littérature, 1635–1975*.

its 'authors' with a latent, perhaps compensatory, temporal depth and with infinite spatial complexity or density. It is, after all, rather elliptically identified as 'notre soupe primitive' ('our primitive soup'), 'notre chaos originel' ('our primeval chaos'), and 'notre mangrove de virtualités' ('our mangrove swamp of virtualities') (*Él.* 28; *Pr.* 90). Apart from stressing the tangled or blended texture claimed for creoleness (by analogy with the mangrove swamp and with soup), these metaphors evoke a 'primeval' or 'primitive' time. On the one hand, the *créolistes* acknowledge a definite cultural beginning—a sort of belated big bang, around 1635; on the other, they evoke a primitivity and virtuality designed perhaps to suggest indefinite temporal extension and thus to compensate for this belatedness. The tension between the idea of a new beginning (or 'New World') and notions of primeval latency is reinforced by the tension between definiteness and indeterminacy suggested by the description of *créolité* as a 'spécificité ouverte' (*Él.* 27) or an 'open specificity' (*Pr.* 89).

Despite the striking emphasis on celebration, the pamphleteers have not completely broken with Édouard Glissant's diagnostic discourse of pathology and cure. Their essay is prescriptive in two senses. Firstly, they prescribe the internalization of creolization as a prophylactic measure against the ongoing self-mutilation of cultural assimilation or Frenchification. In an echo of Glissant's emphasis on the value of opaqueness, they insist, however, that this inwardness does not aim at transparency, that is, at the reduction of the Creole to an impoverished self-identity. Secondly, they outline in advance (or pre-scribe) an aesthetic compatible with this overall programme of immunization. The object of this aesthetic and epistemology is to allow Creoles not just to accept their complexity ('Nous accepter complexes'; *Él.* 28), but to discover, know, and explore it: 'Explorer notre créolité doit s'effectuer dans une pensée aussi complexe que la Créolité elle-même … C'est pourquoi il semble que, pour l'instant, *la pleine connaissance de la Créolité sera réservée à l'Art*' (*Él.* 28–9) ('Exploring our creoleness must be done in a thought as complex as Creoleness itself … that is why it seems that, for the moment, *full knowledge of Creoleness will be reserved for Art*'; *Pr.* 90). Only art, it is suggested, can register the impacted yet dynamic complexity of *créolité*.

Although the *créolité* vision is inherently programmatic and future-oriented, the aesthetic outlined in the main body of the pamphlet is strikingly retrospective. The first factor of *créolité* to be singled out is the oral tradition. Orality (in Creole) is identified not just as the chief medium of popular culture, but also as the principal vector of continuity with the past and in particular with the culture of the plantation. Furthermore, it is categorically claimed that, in order to be authentic, the writing of *créolité* must be inseminated by the past via 'la parole créole'. And indeed, even a cursory glance at the literary writing of Chamoiseau and Confiant illustrates this self-conscious transcription into French of spoken Creole constructions and rhythms. The second factor of Creole authenticity to be highlighted, namely 'la mémoire vraie', is even more explicitly retrospective. It is characterized as a careful attentiveness to the voices of the past, even (or especially) when their scream has been swallowed into the gaps of the colonial version of history. The novels of Raphaël Confiant and Patrick Chamoiseau are devoted to remembering this lost and emphatically local past. After orality and counter-history, the third element of the Creole aesthetic is an inclusivist desire to embrace the creoleness of every single aspect of Caribbean reality and history: '*Nous faisons corps avec notre monde*. Nous voulons, en vraie créolité, y nommer chaque chose et dire qu'elle est belle' (*Él.* 39) ('*We are part and parcel of our world*. We want, thanks to Creoleness, to name each thing in it, and to declare it beautiful'; *Pr.* 100–1). It rapidly emerges that this inclusiveness is also temporally inflected, involving a resolute revisionism. The *créolistes* endorse, among other re-evaluations of the past, the rehabilitation of the plantation system and of various other elements of colonial culture, including the '*béké* ethnoclass' (*Pr.* 90). The final elements to be prescribed are openness to the outside world (a corrective to insularity and stagnation) and linguistic plurality: both Creole and French are to be embraced but neither is to be idolized; rather, both languages are to be valued and creatively renewed.

Not only is *créolité* historically founded on the 'New World' 's colonial past, but what passes for Creole cultural authenticity is entirely predicated on that past; indeed, the *créolité* aesthetic is fundamentally an attempt to recover elements of a resistant cultural model held to have been conceived and to have thrived in the colonial past. Although clearly evident in the pamphlet, this past-centredness prevails even more clearly in other texts associated with the movement. *Lettres créoles*, for example, is less a history of Caribbean writing than a lyrical narrative of the development of authentic 'Creole' expression. Just like the literary writing of Chamoiseau and Confiant, this volume presents a further elaboration of their vision of *créolité*, presenting in particular an explicit and developed, nostalgic and revealing panegyric to plantation culture. More specifically, it idealizes the distinctiveness of the smaller-scale version of the plantation that reigned in the Petites Antilles, the relatively compact size of the Antillean plantations being held to explain the peculiar intensity of the cultural interaction that took place in the French Caribbean. The plantation system flourished in the French Caribbean for almost three centuries, and its collapse is lamented by the authors of *Lettres créoles* as a cultural catastrophe that precipitated the decline of Creoleness defined as '*l'agrégat interactionnel ou transactionnel* des éléments culturels caraïbes, européens, africains, asiatiques, et levantins, que le joug de l'Histoire a réunis sur le même sol' (*Él.* 26) ('the *interactional or transactionnal aggregate* of Caribbean, European, African, Asian, and Levantine cultural elements, united on the same soil by the yoke of history'; *Pr.* 87). After the demise of the plantation system, the cultural magic of 'créolisation' or 'métissage' was, according to Chamoiseau and Confiant, gradually replaced by a 'système de consommation globale de la chose extérieure . . . Et nous nous mîmes—mulâtres en tête, à confondre liberté et assimilation, urbanité et civilisation, liberté et francisation' ('system of global consumption of things from outside . . . and we began, starting with the mixed race, to confuse freedom and assimilation, urban culture and civilization, freedom and Frenchification').[42]

Following a final section entitled 'Une dynamique constante', which asserts the open-ended or ongoing process of formation of Creole culture, the *créolité* manifesto ends with a coda entitled 'Créolité et politique'. In what is apparently an afterthought required by some notion of political correctness, the proponents of *créolité* claim that their agenda is in sympathy with the *indépendantiste* movement, which demands sovereignty for the Caribbean *départements d'outre-mer*. However, they explicitly distance themselves from the ideologies that have up until now supported this claim, rejecting, for example, the Marxist tendency to subordinate

---

[42] Chamoiseau and Confiant, *Lettres créoles*, 67.

questions of cultural identity to the 'political struggle'. Instead, they quixotically propose an ideal political evolution based on cultural affinities. More specifically, they envisage a preliminary association of Creolophone islands (here there is no pretence at inclusion of non-Caribbean or non-island space, since only Martinique, Guadeloupe, Haiti, Dominica, and St Lucia are mentioned) as a prelude to wider pan-Caribbean federation with the Anglophone and Hispanophone islands and, ultimately, with Central and South America. The Indian Ocean has thus entirely disappeared from the horizon.

THEORETICAL TELEOLOGY

In a not ungracious moment of their evolutionist narrative, the authors of the *créolité* pamphlet allow that 'c'est la Négritude césairienne qui nous a ouvert le passage vers l'ici d'une Antillanité désormais postulable et elle-même en marche vers un autre degré d'authenticité qui restait à nommer' (*Él.* 18) ('it was Césaire's Negritude that opened to us the path for the actuality of a Caribbeanness which from then on could be postulated, and which itself is leading to another yet unlabelled degree of authenticity'; *Pr.* 80). Here, they depict Césaire's *négritude* as incipiently committed to the geographical and the local ('ici'), a perspective that is held to have flourished in Glissant's fully fledged *antillanité*. Glissant's vision is said to have given way in turn, however, to the *créolité* movement for which an even higher level of authenticity is claimed. *Négritude* is identified in the manifesto, as it had been in Glissant's thinking also, as a necessary stage in the teleology of Caribbean self-recovery and indeed self-discovery. It is nonetheless criticized for having aggravated what the *créolistes* term 'notre instabilité identitaire'; *Él.* 82) ('our identity instability'; *Pr.* 20). This is because it was founded on the illusion of return to the sustaining womb of Africa and also, as Frantz Fanon had recognized, because its universalizing tendencies collapsed the past and present problems specific to the Caribbean within those of black alienation in general. *Négritude* is also viewed by the *créolistes*, however, as self-defeating, in that it challenged colonization and racism in the name of a characteristically Western universalizing or homogenizing concept, thus reinforcing the effects of assimilation or

Frenchification. Hence, although the authors of *Éloge de la créolité* charitably see Césaire as an ante-Creole rather than an anti-Creole, the poet was subsequently the object of a coruscating critique on the part of Raphaël Confiant.[43] This attack was perhaps foreshadowed in the *Éloge*, in that *négritude* is held there to have led its disciples towards an anti-colonial struggle 'hors de toute vérité intérieure, hors de la moindre des esthétiques littéraires' (*Él.* 21) ('outside any interior truth, outside any literary aesthetics'; *Pr.* 82). This comment is damning in so far as the authors of the *Éloge* equate inner depth with authenticity and identify art as the only means of approaching these depths, but it is also deeply ironic given the purely political grounds on which Raphaël Confiant's 1993 assessment of Césaire's contribution is based.

The *créolistes* themselves distinguish their own vision from Édouard Glissant's *antillanité* in terms of heuristic 'added value'. Glissant's *antillanité* is not considered to enable or to map the journey inwards towards authenticity (in the manifesto, the authors refer to the relative difficulty of locating the 'voies de pénétration dans l'Antillanité' (*Él.* 23) ('paths of penetration in [*sic*] Caribbeanness'; *Pr.* 84), and indeed, the only explicit criticism of Glissant concerns the remoteness of his vision. The connection between the two generations is, however, more complex than would first appear. The structure of the manifesto is revealing in that, although Glissant is rarely quoted in the body of the pamphlet, the vast majority of the footnotes spanning the final sixth of the text consist of quotations from his essays. Not only is the manifesto an inflection of *antillanité*, but the model of inter-penetration is continued in much of Chamoiseau's further writing, most notably in the novel *L'Esclave Vieil Homme et le molosse*, which features a number of prominently placed textual implants from Glissant's work. However, although the authors of the manifesto construct themselves as Glissant's successors and as seeking to facilitate the full implementation of his vision, their programme effects a three-pronged shift of emphasis, in addition, that is, to turning 'Glissant's ideas into ideological dogma',[44] and, even more problematically, hypostasizing or foreclosing his thinking.

The factor that most clearly demarcates *créolité* from *antillanité*

---

[43] Confiant, *Aimé Césaire*.
[44] Dash, *The Other America*, 23.

is the whole *arrière pays* of connotation surrounding the two terms themselves. Both movements distance themselves from *négritude* by insisting on the particular rather than the general; but whereas *antillanité* stresses immediate geographical relationality, the proponents of *créolité* focus somewhat less on space than on time, and less on place than on displacement. Moreover, as its authors' choice of *signifiant* suggests, it is through language and culture—that is, through its defence and occasional illustration of Creole and of creolized French—that the *créolité* movement opposes the Caribbean legacy of alienation. Whereas Glissant's vision is held to counter the generality of *négritude*'s reference by anchoring his thinking in the geo-cultural specifics of the Caribbean, *créolité* is claimed, misleadingly I would suggest, as having a deeper cultural reach by virtue of its emphasis on language rather than place.

The second claimed shift between the two visions involves a temporal repositioning. Although Glissant's thinking takes account of the longing directed in the Caribbean towards a painful, splintered, and withheld past, his primary aspiration is vatic. Glissant indeed characterizes it as tending towards a 'vision prophétique du passé' ('prophetic vision of the past').[45] His interest in the past is, in other words, future-oriented and this orientation is not, perhaps, unrelated to the sybilline remoteness for which he is criticized in the *créolité* manifesto: he is said, after all, to be 'pris par son propre travail, éloigné par son rythme, persuadé d'écrire pour des lecteurs futurs' (*Él.* 23) ('taken up by his own work, by his own rhythm'; *Pr.* 84). *Créolité*, on the other hand, is presented less as a divinatory projection than as the endorsement of an accessible present, emerging from a still tangible past; the past is to be rehabilitated, the present celebrated. Thus the *créolité* imovement is a pragmatic programme, rather than the promise or prophecy of what can be imagined of the past or of the future. It is credited, nonetheless, with a residual prophetic status, in that its postmodern model of emergent identity is held to prefigure the future of all culture:

Le terme 'Créole' est donc éminemment moderne, et non passéiste et colonial comme d'aucuns pourraient le croire, et même post-moderne dans le sens où il signale l'émergence d'un nouveau modèle d'identité qu'on pourrait appeler 'multiple' ou 'mosaïque', en train de s'élaborer sous nos yeux partout à travers le monde, notamment dans les mégalopoles occidentales.

---

[45] Glissant, *Le Discours antillais*, 132; *Caribbean Discourse*, 64,

La créolisation a été en quelque sorte la préfiguration, au cours des trois derniers siècles, de ce phénomène irréversible.[46]

We have already seen that Glissant's emphasis on *antillanité* constitutes one moment in the cumulative, poetic movement of his thinking. Furthermore, his work on *antillanité* took shape principally throughout the 1970s by accretion before being collected in *Le Discours antillais* (1981). In many respects, however, Glissant's two later collections of essays, *Poétique de la Relation* (1990) and *Traité du Tout-Monde* (1997), are closer to the vision of the *créolité* movement than is some of the thinking in *Le Discours antillais*. However, although the *Poétique* and the *Traité* were published after the *créolité* manifesto, in many respects they, like the *Discours antillais*, merely draw out the breadth and depth of Glissant's treatment of relationality in *Soleil de la conscience* (1956) and *L'Intention poétique* (1969). Thus, in isolating the moment of *antillanité*, the *créolité* movement does not really register the fundamental dynamic of Glissant's thinking, which is less a teleological unfolding than a process of relation, accumulation, and repetition.

AFTER *CRÉOLITÉ*? DOGMA AND DISSENT

If *créolité* represents the ultimate authenticity, what lies ahead for Caribbean writing? Some light is shed on this question by the rather robust criticism that the *créolité* movement has attracted, much of it based on its perceived contradictions.

The *créolistes* rightly refute, of course, the negative definition of *créolité* in the glossary of *Le Discours antillais*, which decries it as the obsessive intent to establish monoglot Creole linguistic supremacy. In fact, one detects nowhere in the manifesto nor indeed in any other writings by Chamoiseau or Confiant the slightest will to impose or even to promote Creole monolingualism. On the contrary, for all the pious words in praise of Creole, the subtext of *Éloge de la créolité* suggests less lip-service than lucid realism in

[46] 'The term "Creole" is thus eminently modern and not at all old-fashioned or colonial as some might think; it is even postmodern in so far as it bespeaks the emergence of a new model of identity that we could term "multiple" or "mosaic", in the process of being formed under our noses all over the world, but particularly in Western "megalopolises". Over the past three centuries, creolization has, as it were, prefigured this irreversible phenomenon': Confiant, *Aimé Césaire*, 266.

relation to the language (although the dedication is bilingual, the body of the text and the epigraph are monolingual); indeed the same realism is evident in Dany Bébel-Gisler's thinking.[47] None of these writers sees their attempt to remain faithful to the spirit only of Creole (namely, creolization) as betrayal or defeat. And so Michel Giraud's reference to the irony involved in 'dire dans une littérature en français—pour pouvoir trouver un public—que la langue créole est la pierre angulaire des cultures antillaises' ('saying in French—so as to have a readership—that Creole is the cornerstone of Caribbean cultures') is an oversimplification.[48] Certainly, even if Creole is foregrounded much more systematically in the *créolistes*' texts than in the writing of many other Caribbean writers, the frequent use of translation into French, of glossaries, and of periphrastic footnotes means that its status remains complex and even paradoxical. Nonetheless, the defence and illustration of the vernacular—essentially by the ongoing 'creolization' of French—does seem to be held by the *créolistes* as being virtually coterminous with the fundamental creativity of Creole culture and as being a measure of the Creoleness of this or that writing practice. Unfortunately, however, this dogmatic pre-scription would seem more likely to produce formulaic rather than creative results.

In other respects too, *créoliste* dogma seems somewhat contradictory. In proclaiming themselves Creoles, for example, and in confidently writing in the collective first-person plural, the authors of the *créolité* manifesto claim rather presumptuously to speak for Creole cultures everywhere, although their discourse usually refers by implication to one Creole space only, namely the Caribbean.[49] In what is presented as a movement in defence of irreducible diversity, the scant respect shown to the diversity or heterogeneity of Creole 'space' is unexpected. Before claiming rather sweepingly to

---

[47] See also Walcott, *What the Twilight Says*, 224: 'What is the tone of the manifesto if not that of its language, French, being used in the metre of exposition? Why was it not written in Creole if it is that passionate about authenticity?' To add insult to injury, Gallimard, who originally published the *Éloge*, quickly brought out a bilingual edition, but the 'other' language is . . . English!

[48] Michel Giraud, 'La créolité: une rupture en trompe-l'oeil', *Cahiers d'études africaines*, 148 (1997), 795–811. This is just one of the numerous contradictory aspects of *créoliste* thinking identified by Giraud.

[49] See the criticisms of the Caribbean *créolité* movement enunciated from an Indian Ocean perspective by Réunionnais critic Jean-Claude Carpanin Marimoutou, 'Créolie et créolité', *Notre Librairie*, Dix ans de littératures 1980–1990, II. *Caraïbes—Océan Indien*, 104 (Jan.–Mar. 1991), 95–8.

envisage '*notre monde* en pleine conscience du monde'[50] without problematizing either the notion of space (cultural or geographical, Caribbean or Creole?) or, indeed, the deictic reference, the authors of *Éloge de la créolité* could profitably have pondered Homi Bhabha's view that 'the "other" is never outside or beyond us; it emerges forcefully, within cultural discourse, when we *think* we speak most intimately and indigenously "between ourselves" '.[51] It is in this context too that we should consider the stereotyping of women and of gender relations in general in the writing of the *créolité* movement. A. James Arnold in particular takes the *créolistes* to task for their unreconstructed reproduction of the 'age-old' sexual politics of plantation society.[52] What is noteworthy, of course, is that this simplistic, stereotypical, and *passéiste* representation of gender clashes with the *créolistes*' claims to an open, inclusive, creative, and complex model.

In line with most particularisms, especially nationalisms, the writing of the *créolité* movement is accused of being anti-modern and anti-cosmopolitan. Richard and Sally Price consider, for example, that the exoticizing tendencies of literary *créolité* are 'complicitous with the celebration of a museumified Martinique'.[53] Certainly, in Chamoiseau's first three novels and in virtually every line of Raphaël Confiant's work, the writing of particularism shows its dependence on what Timothy Brennan calls the 'populist undercurrents of national thought'.[54] Much *créoliste* writing confirms Bruce King's view that 'nationalism is an urban movement which identifies with the rural areas as a source of authenticity, finding in the "folk" the attitudes, beliefs, customs and language to create a sense of national unity among people who have other loyalties. Nationalism aims at [the] rejection of cosmopolitan upper classes, intellectuals and others likely to be influenced by foreign ideas'.[55] It is all the more difficult not to read the *Éloge* as a fundamentally nationalist tract given that it holds,

---

[50] Emphasis mine.
[51] 'Introduction: Narrating the Nation', in Homi K. Bhabha (ed.), *Nation and Narration* (London: Routledge, 1990), 4.
[52] Arnold, 'The Gendering of *Créolité*'.
[53] Price and Price, 'Shadowboxing in the Mangrove', 138.
[54] Timothy Brennan, 'The National Longing for Form', in Bhabha (ed.), *Nation and Narration*, 44–70: 54. Apart from Michel Giraud, Richard Burton in *Le Roman marron* and Jack Corzani in *Littératures francophones* also make this point.
[55] Bruce King cited in Brennan, 'The National Longing for Form', 53.

fundamentally, a discourse of identity or distinctiveness. Again, what is remarkable here is that the *créolistes* consistently claim that their thinking transcends nationalist boundaries and aspirations, attaining to that higher level of authenticity associated with acceptance of a constant dynamic of complexity, a shifting, open-ended inclusiveness. In other words, they do appear to endorse the 'antinationalist, ambivalent nation-space' that looks towards the 'new transnational culture' of which Homi Bhabha makes so much.[56] What many critics might consider as involuntary self-contradiction is regarded, however, by Michel Giraud as motivated intent.[57] Giraud believes that the absence of political sovereignty in the French Caribbean creates a vacuum, by virtue of which cultural supremacy becomes the prize. In other words, in a society where culture, not politics, confers authority and power, cultural movements necessarily exclude or marginalize. Giraud thus studies in some detail the paradoxical orthodoxy of Creole authenticity on the basis of which the cultural hegemony of *créolité* is imposed and policed.

Certainly, it is in the movement's exclusionary effect that the contradictions inherent in the *créolité* movement appear most clearly. Thus, despite Chamoiseau's manifest conviction that what will prevail of *créolité* is the rendezvous with global diversity and relationality,[58] Richard and Sally Price have noted the rigid insularity of the movement, demonstrated by its failure to relativize itself even within the local Caribbean context:

Setting their ideas within an insular intellectual history of Martinique, the *créolistes* have been able to underscore their difference from earlier generations. But in a more international Caribbean context, the major programmatic claims of the *créolistes*, when first stated, were already widely acknowledged.[59]

---

[56] This critique takes on added historical resonance and irony when one recalls that, according to Timothy Brennan, 'if one discounts the civil wars of England and France, the first nationalists are not Frenchmen, Spaniards, or Englishmen, but the creole middle classes of the New World—people like Simon Bolívar, Toussaint L'Ouverture, and Ben Franklin': ibid. 58–9.

[57] Giraud, 'La créolité', 795–811.

[58] 'ce qui est indépassable, c'est le positionnement de la diversité, l'identité relationnelle': Maeve McCusker, 'De la problématique du territoire à la problématique du lieu: Un entretien avec Patrick Chamoiseau', *The French Review*, 73/4 (Mar. 2000), 724–33.

[59] Price and Price, 'Shadowboxing in the Mangrove', 128–9.

Beyond the Caribbean, the Prices cite, amongst others, Homi Bhabha, Tzvetan Todorov and Anthony Appiah, Sidney Mintz, and Simon Gikandi as intellectuals who have built up a body of work on creolization, hybridity, *mestizaje*, and so on. Where, they wonder, is the *créolistes*' awareness of this intellectual kindred? A similar kind of contradiction, a similar failure to acknowledge diversity and to engage with it in concrete situations, is noted by the same critics in relation to the question of *marron* culture. Richard Price is a noted scholar of 'marron' culture; indeed Eric Hobsbawm sees him as 'the leading authority on marronnage in general' and on the maroons of Suriname in particular.[60] According to the Prices, the *créolistes* underestimate the 'tremendous diversity of African cultures and languages represented in any early Caribbean colony', a diversity that made of the early *marron* communities 'the most thoroughly (and earliest fully) "creolized" of *all* New World communities'. Instead, the *créolistes* are said to depict *marrons* as 'somewhat uncultured isolationists'.[61] This criticism is borne out by the evocation of the maroon in *Lettres créoles* as a figure confined to the realm of disarticulation—scream or silence—and positioned as such outside the economy of creolization, to which he only converts after 1848 when he abandons the hills, bringing with him intact the 'Afrique de ses souvenirs, mythique et irréelle' ('Africa of his memories, mythical and unreal').[62]

The critical debate around *créolité* has involved excesses on both sides. Faced with accusations, for example, of bad faith in their double role as 'social critics railing against French domination *and* beneficiaries of lucrative literary prizes from Paris, both the champions of a fast-disappearing "traditional" Martinique and unchallenged masters of the modern media, expertly harnessing local television, radio, and newspapers to promote their literary careers',[63] the *créolistes* have understandably defended themselves with some animus. However, the tenor of some of this defensiveness (the verbal manhandling reported by Richard Burton, for example)[64] exposes contradictions between *créoliste* relational

---

[60] Eric Hobsbawm, *On History* (London: Weidenfeld & Nicolson, 1997), 193.
[61] Price and Price, 'Shadowboxing in the Mangrove', 130.
[62] Chamoiseau and Confiant, *Lettres créoles*, 34.
[63] Price and Price, 'Shadowboxing in the Mangrove', 139.
[64] At the end of Burton, *Le Roman marron*.

practice, on the one hand, and, on the other, claims to a culture 'qui ne domine pas mais qui entre en relation' and which is governed by a 'désir convivial' (*Él.* 13).[65]

Having registered some of the more programmatic aspects of the *créolité* project, one might be surprised to find that its authors explicitly deny the theoretical status of their thinking. On the very first page of the *créolité* manifesto, they caution: 'ces paroles que nous vous transmettons ne relèvent pas de la théorie, ni de principes savants' (*Él.* 13) ('these words we are communicating to you here do not stem from theory, nor do they stem from any learned principles'; *Pr.* 75). Glissant, for his part, offers in the glossary to *Le Discours antillais* the following definition of *antillanité*: 'Plus qu'une théorie, une vision. La force en est telle qu'on en dit n'importe quoi. J'ai entendu en deux ou trois occasions proposer l'antillanité (sans autre précision) comme solution globale à des problèmes vrais ou fantasmés. Quand un mot devient ainsi passe-partout, on préjuge qu'il a rejoint le réel.'[66] Clearly, both *Le Discours antillais* and *Éloge de la créolité* are concerned with cultural definitions and positionings. Why, then, is the word 'theory' disavowed? For Glissant, there cannot be a theory of *antillanité* because the reality to which it would refer is as yet virtual; it is the projective status of *antillanité* that leads him to prefer the more aspirational term 'vision'.[67] Glissant also disassociates

[65] Patrick Chamoiseau has implicitly recognized the unintentionally annihilative effect of his criticism ('une mise-à-mort totale') and has tried to explain the acidity of some of his writing in *Antilla* by his internalization of a collective wound ('je vis une blessure collective'). See interview with Dominique Chancé (1997) in Chancé, *L'Auteur en souffrance*, 213 and 214.

[66] Glissant, *Le Discours antillais*, 495; *Caribbean Discourse*, 261: 'More than a theory, a vision. The force of it is such that it is applied to everything. I have heard *antillanité* proposed on a few occasions (without further details) as a general solution to real or imagined problems. When a word acquires this kind of general acceptance, one presupposes that it has found its reality.'

[67] As early as the mid-1950s, in *Soleil de la conscience*, Glissant expressed a certain squeamishness about having his work interpreted as theoretical generalization: on the first page of that work, he stresses the personal texture of his views, their strictly positional value: 'Cas très individuel dont nul ne saurait, à des fins diverses, faire un usage d'orientation plus général' (p. 11) '[Mine is] an individual case which nobody will be able to use for whatever ends by seeking to generalize

himself from reductive formulae that might be applied to a range of empirical situations. Indeed, it is tempting to think that the combined aspirational and resistant intent behind Glissant's *antillanité* accounts for what Chamoiseau and Confiant criticize as its arcane remoteness. In other words, the inaccessibility of Glissant's 'vision', or what he himself calls its opacity, is surely directly proportional to his refusal of the transparency of conceptualization. There is thus a certain irony in the *créolistes'* repudiation of the reductive nature of 'Western universalizing concepts', given their critique of Glissant's impenetrability.

Inevitably, of course, the very words *antillanité* and *créolité* suggest an implicit and regressive essentialism.[68] In the *créolité* manifesto, as Chris Bongie puts it:

the authors' praise of an 'identité créole' remains trapped within and committed to a foundationalist politics of identity grounded in claims of authenticity. The opening words of the document—'neither Europeans, nor Africans, nor Asiatics, we proclaim ourselves Creoles' (p. 13)—clearly affirm a New World identity that is logically equivalent to the Old World identities that are being denied [despite] their insistence on the 'torrential ambiguity' of their new 'mosaic identity'.[69]

Bongie seems to believe that, although it is trapped in the same paradox, Édouard Glissant's thinking is not quite defeated by it. In other words, when Glissant affirms that 'ce qui nous porte n'est pas la seule définition de nos identités, mais aussi leur relation à tout le possible',[70] Bongie observes in this assertion 'the prison house of a defined identity and the open field of a chaotic relationality stand[ing] side by side, simultaneously contradicting and supplementing one another'.[71] Whatever the similarities suggested between them, Glissant does distance himself from his heirs by carefully and repeatedly distinguishing between state and process, by espousing creolization and rejecting Creoleness. The 'particularistic logic' that Bongie discerns in that 'inevitable return to what

---

about it'. This caution is also apparent in the disavowal of systematic thinking ('pensée de système') in Glissant, *Traité du Tout-Monde* (Paris: Gallimard, 1997), 18.

[68] See Chris Bongie's 'Resisting Memories' and also his *Islands and Exiles*.

[69] Bongie, 'Resisting Memories', 165.

[70] Glissant (*Poétique de la Relation*, 103) is quoted and commented on in Bongie, 'Resisting Memories', 167.

[71] Ibid.

Glissant's vision of creolization is purportedly bent upon undoing'
is nicely redeemed by the critic, however, who holds it up as a
perfect example of the creolization process itself.

> This apparently paradoxical co-existence of two differing logics is, I
> believe, actually fundamental to the creolizing process, rather than an
> anachronism that must eventually be bypassed in [a] sort of 'epistemic'
> leap ... it is the attenuated prolongation of memories, rather than their
> transcendence, that characterizes this 'process of mutation and adapta-
> tion'.[72]

If some French Caribbean writing is theoretical in all but name,
what, then, is the relation between that writing and the literary
output of the theorists, an output that is typically more extensive
than that of their less speculatively inclined *confrères*? In fact, it
would be difficult to overestimate the extent of the interrelation
between the 'theoretical' writing of Édouard Glissant, Patrick
Chamoiseau, and Raphaël Confiant, and their work in and
between various literary genres. Thus, Ernest Pépin's novel
Tambour-Babel (1996) and at least three novels by Raphaël
Confiant, *Le Nègre et l'amiral* (1988), *Eau de café* (1991), and
L'Allée des soupirs (1994), not to mention Chamoiseau's *Solibo
Magnifique* or his *Chronique des sept misères* could be read, in this
sense, as a defence and illustration of *Éloge de la créolité*. Similarly,
the relation between Édouard Glissant's novel, *La Case du
commandeur* (1981) and the collection of essays, *Le Discours antillais* is one of intense complementarity, if not overlap. Indeed, Celia
Britton has argued in an article on three novels by Glissant that all
three present a 'process whereby the theoretical position developed
in *Le Discours antillais* and *Poétique de la Relation* is gradually
realized in the fiction'.[73] Glissant's more recent work goes even
further, however, in the displacement of traditional generic boundaries: the poem sequence 'Les Grands Chaos',[74] the novel *Tout-
monde* (1993), and the essay *Traité du Tout-Monde* together form
a rhizomatic totality, a kaleidoscopic yet open network of resonances whose interrelation enacts Glissant's vision both of *chaos-*

---

[72] Ibid.
[73] Celia Britton, 'Collective Narrative Voice in Three Novels by Édouard
Glissant', in Haigh (ed.), *An Introduction to Francophone Caribbean Writing*,
135–48: 138.
[74] In Glissant, *Poèmes complets* (Paris: Gallimard, 1994).

monde and creolization. Generic hybridity within a single work can also realize the creolization that is so central both to Glissant's thinking and to the thinking of the *créolité* movement; Chamoiseau's *Écrire en pays dominé* (1997) provides a particularly striking example of such generic indeterminacy.

Where, then, has this interplay of theory and practice, thinking and textuality, brought Caribbean writing at the end of the second millennium? If we accept the *créolité* version of creation or generation, a fundamentally teleological or evolutionist narrative, then French Caribbean writing has followed a mono-linear temporal logic that culminates in a creolization without end. In ignoring synchronic parallels or relations with other 'New World' ideologies, this narrative is locked into a narrow, familial plot of filiation, dialectic, and transcendence. Fortunately, perhaps, several factors at work in *créoliste* writing, in particular the reverberations of intertextual dynamics, along with the impact of the work of Édouard Glissant, combine to subvert that impression of closure.

Glissant's writing has been sedimented from the very outset around certain crucial questions. Despite the constancy of the questions examined, his thinking has changed, of course, describing an erratic spiral dynamic. As such, it exposes the *créolité* narrative of (French) Caribbean consciousness as a reaction to a single fossilized moment of 'thinking in process'. It is thus in the processes and intersections of writing itself that the dynamics and counter-dynamics of French Caribbean theory are most productively worked out. And that fold or crease between theory and practice generates much of the happily inconclusive tension that sustains French Caribbean writing at the start of the twenty-first century.

CHAPTER TWO

Novel Time: Reconstructing the Past?

nous peinons à recomposer nous ne savons quelle histoire débitée en morceaux. Nos histoires sautent dans le temps, nos paysages différents s'enchevêtrent, nos mots se mêlent et se battent, nos têtes sont vides ou trop pleines.[1]

In the Caribbean in general, the past is commonly perceived as problematic and traumatic:[2] it is variously viewed as excessively intrusive or inaccessibly remote. Some authors attempt to distance themselves from its dominion, embracing writing as an opportunity to escape the constraints of temporality, whether these are seen to reinforce the weight of the past bearing down upon the present, or to sever it brutally from a present that is left, bereft, to ponder its own mutilation. However, even in writing that seems more committed to recovering time past rather than to recovering from it (by replacing it, for example, with myth or fiction), the linear flow of time, or time as succession, is frequently neutralized, its specificity denied, or at least translated into spatial terms.

---

[1] Glissant, *La Case du commandeur*, 126; 'we strain to reconstruct we know not what story recounted in fragments. Our stories jump around in time, our various landscapes mingle, our words run into and jostle one another, our heads are empty or else too full'.

[2] In her novel, resonantly entitled *The Chosen Place, the Timeless People* (New York: Harcourt, Brace & World, 1969), the Barbadian author Paule Marshall includes a reference to Joyce's view of history as a nightmare: 'history ... It is a nightmare, as that Irishman said, and we haven't awaked from it yet' (p. 130). Joyce's bon mot ('History is the nightmare from which I am trying to awake') is the epigraph to George Lamming's *The Pleasures of Exile* (1960) and also to Derek Walcott's essay 'The Muse of History' (1974; repr. in Walcott, *What the Twilight Says*, 1998).

THE PAST: MUSE OR MEDUSA?

The tortured logic prevailing over the preamble to Patrick Chamoiseau's first novel to be set entirely in the time of slavery, *L'Esclave Vieil Homme et le molosse* (1997), testifies to the complex, if not conflictive and contradictory, nature of the French Caribbean writer's relation to the past. On the novel's opening page,[3] the narrator observes the paucity of literature on slavery, a poverty explained in terms of the topic's failure to grip 'us'.

Les histoires d'esclavage ne nous passionnent guère. Peu de littérature se tient à ce propos. Pourtant, ici, *terres amères des sucres*, nous nous sentons submergés par ce nœud de mémoires qui nous âcre d'oublis et de présences hurlantes.[4]

If these statements appear ambiguous, or even paradoxical, it is partly because of the ambiguous identity of the enunciating subject. The first 'nous' ('us'), the one that does not find slavery stories interesting, is difficult to locate, although the second one is named, but not unproblematically,[5] as the sugar lands. This second 'us' is said to be deluged by the persistent presences and smoking absences of 'this' knotted past. Is Chamoiseau simply suggesting here that the fascination exerted by the impacted Caribbean past—by the bitter, lingering legacy of trauma—does not lend itself to arresting narratives? The combined effect of the two adverbs 'pourtant' ('however') and 'ici' ('here') surely allows for a rather different reading. For that oppositional or concessive deictic might suggest that the population of the 'sugar lands' is somehow being contrasted with the first 'us'; or at least that it constitutes an exceptional category within it. The first group might then be readers

---

[3] The location of the 'beginning' of this text is problematic. There are several epigraphic texts, one of them part of the 'entre-dire', or interspersed text, quoted at length and at intervals from Glissant's *L'Intention poétique* and his (then) unpublished 'La Folie Celat'.

[4] Patrick Chamoiseau, *L'Esclave Vieil Homme et le molosse* (Paris: Gallimard, 1997), 17; 'Stories about slavery do not really enthuse us. There is very little literature on this subject. Here, however, *bitter sugar lands*, we feel inundated by these knotted memories and tainted by their acrid stench of forgetfulness and screaming presences'.

[5] An unlikely double apposition associates or confuses the deictic 'here', the named space, and the 'we'. The absence of the preposition 'in' and of the article (definite or demonstrative) means that place becomes identified in a particularly literal manner with subjectivity.

(and writers) in general, across the world, who are disinclined to be stirred by stories of slavery. Conversely, the subsequent 'we', identified geographically—the sugar (is)lands—cannot escape this particular past, caught up as they are in this tangle of memories. Indeed, in the very next breath the narrator acknowledges that it is precisely in the old, badly healed wound of slavery that Caribbean literary inspiration is sourced. However, the source is unreliable: 'A chaque fois, quand elle veut se construire, notre parole se tourne *de ce côté-là*, comme dans l'axe d'une source dont le jaillissement encore irrésolu manque à cette soif qui nous habite, irrémédiable' ('Whenever it wants to construct itself, our speech turns in that direction, as though to face a fountain whose still fitful flow is yearned for by that thirst that inhabits us, irremediably').[6] This sentence casts the first two in a different light. The contorted formulation of all three, however, with metaphors of submersion or inundation jarring with images of drought and indecisive flow, emphasizes the unresolved relation between an unavoidable topos—namely, slavery construed as a space ('ce côté-là')—and its verbal articulation ('histoire', 'parole', 'construction', etc.). Just as the narrator contrasted, to begin with, indifference towards stories of slavery with the inescapable, screaming memories inundating the Caribbean mind, so he notes here that the desire to utter ('parole'), on turning for inspiration towards the fountain of slavery, finds there an irresolute stream incapable of nourishing verbalization. Thus the inception of Chamoiseau's first full-length literary foray into the time of slavery bristles with intimations of mismatch: between an enunciative, if not narrative, desire obsessed with slavery and the halting inadequacy of the muse, and between a whole people's fixation on dark memories of slavery and general disinterest in stories on the topic. A fundamental sense of difficulty and dissonance (reminiscent of Édouard Glissant's notion of a 'forced poetics'[7]) thus underlies the opening of Chamoiseau's novel. And it centres on the relation between memory and narrative, or between the past and its verbal or literary articulation.

---

[6] Chamoiseau, *L'Esclave Vieil Homme*, 18. My emphasis.

[7] 'Il y a poétique forcée là où une nécessité d'expression confronte un impossible à exprimer' ('Forced poetics exist where a need for expression confronts an inability to achieve expression'): Glissant, *Le Discours antillais*, 237; *Caribbean Discourse*, 120.

THE POETICS OF AMNESIA

The same unresolved trauma, the same consuming concern with the past, inform both the opening of *L'Esclave Vieil Homme et le molosse* and Derek Walcott's comments on the potency of the Caribbean past, although Walcott's trauma is compounded by the disabling horror of guilt or shame. 'But who in the New World does not have a horror of the past, whether his ancestor was torturer or victim?', he wonders,[8] proceeding to regret that 'in the New World servitude to the muse of history has produced a literature of recrimination and despair, a literature of revenge written by the descendants of slaves or a literature of remorse written by the descendants of masters'(*T* 37). Clearly, Walcott views conventional Caribbean historiography as reductive, a polarizing and paralysing tale of good and evil, a simplifying fable of victim and oppressor. And he concludes that it is, as such, best forsaken for the more subtle palettes of myth and imagination.

If, however, the poet of *Omeros* is reluctant to approach the Caribbean past through history, this is not simply because of the limitations of the Manichaean emotional range imposed by the outrage of slavery; it is also because of history's inhospitality to the poetic impulse. Walcott regards history as the 'medusa of the New World' (*T* 36) because it turns the poetic moment to stone. For him, renunciation of history and of its muse, memory, is the only way to protect the poetic impulse. This is why his tone is approving as he observes that 'in time the slave surrendered to amnesia' (*T* 39). For Walcott, amnesia is not just 'the true history of the New World', but also the corollary of poetic wonder. For he believes that 'it is this awe of the numinous, this elemental privilege of naming the New World which annihilates history in our great poets, an elation common to all of them . . . they reject ethnic ancestry for faith in elemental man'(*T* 40). As Walcott presents it, then, Caribbean poetry is an act of faith that eclipses the historical habit. But although the deflection of memory as a consequence of displacement might serve the extinction of history, the outright elimination

---

[8] Walcott, *What the Twilight Says*, 39. 'For us in the archipelago the tribal memory is salted with the bitter memory of migration' (ibid. 41). Future references in this chapter to Walcott's essays in this collection will be given in parentheses following the abbreviation *T*).

of memory would probably run counter to the temper of Walcott's 'New World' poetics, that is, a matinal freshness predicated on forgetting, memory's flip-side. 'For every poet it is always morning in the world. History a forgotten, insomniac night' (*T* 79). Even if Walcott salutes 'patrician' writers such as Saint-John Perse, whose 'vision of man is elemental, a being inhabited by presences, not a creature chained to his past' (*T* 37), he also considers that the Antillean imagination involves memory, if only residually. For him, there is no such thing as 'imagination as opposed to the collective memory of our entire race' (*T* 83). Indeed, for Walcott, both memory and amnesia, the former freed from all fealty to history, the latter constituting the 'true history of the New World' (*T* 39), are together embedded in 'Antillean geography, in the vegetation itself' (*T* 81) and together guarantee the mutual implication of space and time that is for Walcott the most appropriate muse for the poet or artist. For him, the past can be a 'timeless, yet habitable, moment' (*T* 36) (and this recalls Hölderlin's idea that humans inhabit time/space poetically, or that 'dichterisch wohnt der Mensch') because it is the site of those elemental 'presences' (or ghosts?) that call forth the poetic response. Daniel Maximin shares Walcott's preoccupation with the compatibility of the past and the poetic. 'Comment faire cohabiter poésie et histoire?' ('How can poetry be made compatible with history'?),[9] Antoine asks in *L'Isolé Soleil*, and his perplexity is linked to the numerous reminders throughout the novel of the tension between memory and imagination: 'Tu ouvriras les tiroirs de notre histoire confisquée ... tu rafraîchiras la mémoire des témoignages et des récits; tu mettras la vérité au service de l'imaginaire et non pas le contraire' ('You will open the drawers where our confiscated history lies ... you will renew the witness of testimonies and stories; you will subordinate truth to imagination and not the opposite').[10] The overdetermination of (imagined) forenames, patronyms, and toponyms in Glissant's novels is just one indication of the emphasis that this author too places on imagination, not in contradistinction to memory, but as part of memory.

[9] Daniel Maximin, *L'Isolé Soleil* (Paris: Seuil, 1981),18.
[10] Ibid. 273.

PARTIAL RECALL AND SPLINTERED STORIES

V. S. Naipaul is notorious for having indicted the poverty of the Caribbean past and indeed for having gone so far as to deny the Caribbean any history worthy of the name: 'History is built around achievement and creation; and nothing was created in the West Indies'.[11] How, he wonders, 'can the history of this West Indian futility be written? What tone shall the historian adopt?'[12] Although other writers denounce the extreme negativity and alienation of this view, even their more indulgent visions of the Caribbean past are often laced with some sense of lack. Typically, the pain of the Caribbean relation to the past is imputed not just to the clinging legacy of the slave trade and of slavery itself but also to the difficulty of access to that past: more specifically, the obstruction of the pathways of memory by the disproportionate and anti-mnemonic discontinuity of the Caribbean past. If Walcott commends the creative imagination (or memory) underlying myth, it is not just because of the poetic sterility of history compared with the timelessness of myth which can be inhabited poetically, it is also because of the unreliable recall of memory when summoned as history's muse.[13] As Daniel-Henri Pageaux has observed, historically speaking, myth has always served a compensatory function in historiographical situations perceived as frustrating, or in contexts of suffering and absence.[14] And we have just seen that the start of Chamoiseau's *L'Esclave Vieil Homme et le molosse* stresses the disparity between the past's inspirational status and its lacunary availability: after all, its fascination is construed at least partly in terms of absence or gaps ('manque', 'soif . . . irrémédiable', 'oublis'). Similarly, Orlando Patterson considers that 'to be a West Indian is to live in a state of utter pastlessness',[15] just as

[11] V. S. Naipaul, *The Middle Passage: Impressions of Five Societies, British, French, Dutch in the West Indies and South America* (London: André Deutsch, 1962), 29. See Derek Walcott on Naipaul, 'The Garden Path: V. S. Naipaul', in *What the Twilight Says*.

[12] Naipaul, *The Middle Passage*, 29.

[13] 'These writers reject the idea of history as time for its original concept as myth, the partial recall of the race' (T 37).

[14] See Barbara Webb, *Myth and History in Caribbean Fiction* (Amherst: University of Massachusetts Press, 1992), 6.

[15] Orlando Patterson, 'Recent Studies on Caribbean Slavery and the Atlantic Slave Trade', *Latin American Research Review*, 17 (1982), 251–75: 258.

Édouard Glissant suggests that the 'presence' of Caribbean history is a ghostly one, lodged in 'des ruines dont le témoignage est incertain, dont les monuments furent [si] fragiles, dont les archives sont souvent [si] incomplètes, oblitérées ou ambiguës' ('these ruins with their uncertain evidence, their extremely fragile monuments, their frequently incomplete, obliterated, or ambiguous archives').[16] This epistemological fragility collapses, of course, into complete dysfunction when the envisaged past lies beyond Caribbean space. In that context, what Glissant calls the 'désiré historique' ('longing for history') is left utterly unrequited in so far as the obsessional but doomed search is for 'une trace primordiale' (meaning 'primeval trace', although J. Michael Dash translates it as 'primordial source').[17] Focusing on this 'long-distance' past in his Nobel lecture that is entitled, after all, 'The Antilles: Fragments of Epic Memory', Derek Walcott contemplates the vestiges of certain Asian rituals in Trinidad, and comments on the discomfiture with which such 'fragments' are sometimes regarded in the Caribbean:

Consider the scale of Asia reduced to these fragments ... and one can understand the self-mockery and embarrassment of those who see these rites as parodic, even degenerate. ... Memory that yearns to join the centre, a limb remembering the body from which it has been severed. (*T* 67)

Walcott underlines here the stigmata of loss marking Caribbean re-enactments of Asian epic, adding that 'if the pieces are disparate, ill-fitting, they contain more pain than the original sculpture, those icons and sacred vessels taken for granted in their ancestral places' (*T* 69). Although Walcott understands those who do so, he himself neither derides nor denigrates these efforts to gather 'broken pieces' and 'shards of vocabulary' in order to restore 'shattered histories' (*T* 69). And yet, if his rhetoric is overwhelmingly spatial, referring to 'ancestral places' and 'original continents', centres and margins,

---

[16] Glissant, *Poétique de la Relation* (Paris: Gallimard, 1990), 79; tr. Betsy Wing as *Poetics of Relation* (Ann Arbor: University of Michigan Press, 1997), 65.

[17] Glissant defines this 'longing for history' as the obsession with finding the 'trace primordiale vers quoi s'efforcer par des élucidations qui ont la particularité (comme jadis le Mythe) d'obscurcir en révélant' ('*primordial source* towards which one struggles through revelations that have the peculiarity (like myth in the past) of obscuring as well as disclosing'), *Le Discours antillais*, 147; *Caribbean Discourse*, 79.

entire vessels and scattered fragments, bodies and limbs, this is because his evaluation of remembrance as a response to the mutilation of dismemberment is ambiguous, and perhaps ambivalent. As we have seen, Walcott rejects history for myth. However, the Adamic 'New World' poetics that he favours is based on a certain balance of amnesia and memory, for he recognizes that all creation is recreation, and that memory and imagination are coterminous: 'And this is the exact process of the making of poetry, or what should be called not its "making" but its remaking' (*T* 69–70). If Walcott seems to vacillate between respect for the pain of loss and celebration of the elation of presence, this is because the elation and the privation are in his mind indissociably linked: the elation is indeed conditional on desolation, since Walcott's celebration is fundamentally a commemoration of loss. His espousal of the mysterious 'eucharistic' combination of presence and absence, celebration and loss, allows him, then, to appreciate why some see the staging of Indian epic in Trinidad as a parodic or diminished rite of hopeless yearning. He himself, however, chooses to view it as a celebration of the 'real presence' (*T* 68) of Antillean culture. That is also why he acclaims for their faith in a rather paradoxical 'New World' poetics that is both amnesiac and Adamic, not just the poems of Saint-John Perse's *Éloges* that incontestably consecrate the 'presences' of an Antillean childhood, but also *Anabase*, that epic of often unidentifiable, dislocated cultural fragments, remembered in a 'fresh' poetics that is redolent of myth and of mystery.

A (NON-)HISTORY? CONTINUITY AND DISCONTINUITY

More than any other French Caribbean author, Édouard Glissant has wrestled in his writing not just as an essayist, but also as a novelist, poet, and playwright, with the question of the past in the Caribbean cultural context. Like his St Lucian fellow-poet, the author of *Le Discours antillais* dwells on the seminal fracture of diaspora and transportation, that shock on which 'New World' history is predicated. However, he stresses equally the serial discontinuity permeating the Caribbean past: 'Les Antilles sont le lieu d'une histoire faite de ruptures et dont le commencement est un arrachement brutal, La Traite' ('The French Caribbean is the site of a history characterized by ruptures and that began with a brutal dislocation, the slave trade').[18]

Most working definitions of history highlight the primacy of linear time in historical discourse. For example, Michel Foucault defines history as a discourse about 'le phénomène de la succession et des enchaînements temporels' ('the phenomenon of succession and temporal sequence').[19] The commonsense view of history is that it is a narrative, presenting itself as factual, which addresses the sequential nature of time and its cause-and-effect ramifications. In the Caribbean, however, because of the radical displacement of the vast part of the population with respect to radically diverse origins, the exceptional discontinuity of the past is a decisive impediment to such traditional historiography. For, in addition to the primary, spatio-temporal discontinuity of diaspora, the Caribbean is the site of a plurality of diasporas. One of the principal stresses of Glissant's *Discours antillais* is the dissonance between the explosive plurality of Caribbean origins and histories (lower-case h), on the one hand, and on the other the master narrative of the singular, unified History (upper-case H) fabricated by the West, a History distinguished by its totalizing conception of chronological time. In other words, for the Caribbean population, the sheer multiplicity of 'Old World' cultures from which it has been cut off implies not just a disrupted or severed memory, but also a multiple memory that can only reductively be described as common or collective. Such pervasive discontinuity and disjointed plurality produces the epistemological resistance that is pivotal in Édouard Glissant's value-system: 'Ce discontinu dans le continu et l'impossibilité pour la conscience collective d'en faire le tour caractérisent ce que j'appelle une non-histoire' ('This dislocation of the continuum, and the inability of the collective consciousness to absorb it all, characterize what I call a nonhistory [*sic*]').[20] For Glissant, however, Caribbean 'non-history' is not necessarily an infirmity; on the contrary, it is an ultimately positive value, a sort of '*opassité*', that enables those whom it enshrouds to resist comprehension and reduction to transparency. In his first novel,

---

[18] *Le Discours antillais*, 130; *Caribbean Discourse*, 61.
[19] Michel Foucault, *L'Archéologie du savoir* (Paris: Gallimard, 1969), 216.
[20] *Le Discours antillais*, 131; *Caribbean Discourse*, 62. This 'non-history' recalls Orlando Patterson's notion of 'utter pastlessness': 'Recent Studies', 258.

Patrick Chamoiseau also dramatizes the opaqueness of the past—
the epistemological impossibility of reading the past with the eyes
of the present—when he evokes those things 'que notre esprit de
maintenant ne peut même plus élucider' ('that our contemporary
mind can no longer even clarify').[21]

If I have leant heavily on Derek Walcott's view of the Caribbean
relation to the past, it is precisely because it is foreign in one vital
respect to the thinking and writing of Édouard Glissant. It is no
mere coincidence that, while Édouard Glissant is, like Walcott, a
poet, a dramatist, and an essayist, he is also a novelist and deeply
committed as such to the notion of 'histoire' in all senses of the
word. Walcott's 'other' vocation is painting, however, and it would
indeed seem that space, much more than time, is his preferred
dimension. Although Walcott can understand those who diagnose in
the Caribbean splintered sites of longing for the lost continuity
represented by the continent(s) of the past, he himself clearly relishes
it as the place where the 'sigh of History dissolves' (*T* 68). Édouard
Glissant, on the other hand, although he evaluates discontinuity
positively in many contexts, writes primarily of the desire to reconnect with lived time, and writes out of that very desire himself.
Indeed, in *Le Quatrième Siècle*, Mathieu's desire for history is a
desire for analgesia: 'C'était l'ombre, la fixité, le profond des vérités
révolues qu'il cherchait, pour en recouvrir, comme d'un cataplasme,
l'inquiétude et l'agitation qui boulaient en lui' ('It was the shadow,
the immobility, the depth of bygone truths that he was seeking, as if
they were a poultice to cover the anxious restlessness bubbling up
inside him').[22] Glissant's project is a poetics of relation rather than
elation. His work dwells in and on (doomed) efforts to repair fragmentation, to restore shattered histories, efforts driven by nostalgia
for the twice-distant past, remote in space as well as time. This is
why his writing does not incline towards the numinous. Whereas
Walcott, as we have seen, commends the (amnesiac) act of naming,
the instant of Adamic awe, Glissant has identified the primary challenge facing the Caribbean thinker or writer as being the imagination of lived time. Indeed, Glissant's core aspiration is, according to
himself, the articulation of a poetics of duration:

---

[21] *Chronique des sept misères*, 55.
[22] Édouard Glissant, *Le Quatrième Siècle* (Paris: Seuil, 1964), 257; tr. Betsy Wing
as *The Fourth Century* (Lincoln and London: University of Nebraska Press, 2001),
261.

pour essayer de parcourir les projets que je m'étais fixé (reconquête de la mémoire historique, réapproche d'un temps qui soit notre temps américain et caraïbe), j'ai recherché un temps dévergondé, un temps éperdu. . . . Pour accomplir tout ce travail je me suis donné comme horizon une poétique non plus de l'instant, de la révélation, de la fulguration, mais une poétique de la durée qui permette d'accumuler, d'entasser, de ressasser, de reprendre, de répéter la matière littéraire.[23]

Taking their cue from Glissant, whom they quote on the need to repossess time, the authors of *Éloge de la créolité* also expect of their literary aesthetic that 'elle nous restituera à la durée, à l'espace-temps continu' ('[it will] restore us to duration, to the continuum of time and space').[24]

FROM TIME TO SPACE, OR THE DISLOCATED PAST

It is important to challenge at this point the possible assumption that 'history', even Western history, is a transparent concept or a homogeneous practice. The enthusiastic critical response to the much-quoted distinction made by Édouard Glissant between History and histories should probably be moderated by recognition of the fact that Western historians themselves have held diverging views on what history is or should be. For example, Glissant's desire to bear witness to lost or submerged stories situates his project in line with the kind of grassroots (or social) history, history from below, that Eric Hobsbawm sees as having been launched in post-revolutionary France by the work of Jules Michelet, in particular, and further promoted in the writing of Marc Bloch and Georges Lefèbvre. 'Whatever its origins and initial difficulties', Hobsbawm writes, 'grassroots history has now taken off, trying to

[23] 'in order to work on the projects that I had set myself (the reappropriation of historical memory and of a local American or Caribbean time), I went in search of a dissolute, profligate, boundless time . . . and to this end I set my sights not on a poetics of the revelatory instant or the explosive epiphany, but on a poetics of duration, that would permit accumulation and accretion, and the reworking and repetition of literary material': *Société et littérature antillaises aujourd'hui*, Cahiers de l'Université de Perpignan, 25 (1997), 141–2.

[24] Bernabé et al., *Éloge de la créolité*, 38; *In Praise of Creoleness*, 99. In support of this statement, in note 24 of the original French version of the pamphlet (p. 63), the authors quote Glissant's remark to the effect that in the Caribbean, 'ce temps que nous n'avons jamais eu, il nous faut le reconquérir' ('we must now reclaim this time that we never possessed').

explore an unknown dimension of the past.'[25] Even more significantly, there has also been a tendency, encapsulated in the Annales
school of historiography, to argue in favour of a preferential, or at
least complementary, and compensatory focus on *longue durée*
rather than on the linearity of so-called *histoire événementielle*,
that is, on social rather than on political history. And durational
history, precisely because of its emphasis on lived or experienced
time, tends, as one would expect, to lay much greater emphasis on
space and indeed on the intersection between time and space, than
does a historiography more concerned with sequential time. If colonial and post-colonial history pays particular attention to this intersection it is because colonialism is above all the domination of
space and the spatialization of time.

   While not losing sight of the specific effects of extreme displacement and torsion on the Caribbean sense of time past, it is important to note also the crossings and connections that can be made,
not just between Glissant's historiography and grassroots history
or the history of *longue durée*, but also between the histories of
different spaces. The convergence between developments in
Metropolitan historiographical thinking and the directions taken
by Glissant's work does not take away at all, of course, from the
value of Glissant's poetics of Caribbean time and space. It simply
adds further resonance to the specific parameters of his thinking
and writing. Moreover, Glissant does not shy away from making
connections between different histories: after all, he connects the
history of 'New World' slavery with French feudal history in *Le Sel
noir*, and with contemporary destitution and homelessness in Paris
in *Les Grands Chaos*.[26] True to his preference for relationality over
difference, he distances himself from those who would defend their
difference (including the specificity of their history or historiography) to the death, those who are, as Walcott puts it: 'proud of the
tribal subtleties of their | suffering, its knot of meaning, of blood on

---

[25] Hobsbawm, *On History*, 204. In this book an entire chapter is entitled 'On
History from Below' (pp. 201–16).

[26] On the question of these historiographical parallels, see Bernadette Cailler,
Conquérants de la nuit nue. Édouard Glissant et l'H(h)istoire antillaise (Tübingen:
Gunter Narr, 1988), 15–27. And on the cross-historical references in Glissant's
poetry see ead., 'From "Gabelles" to "Grands Chaos": A Study of the Disode of the
Homeless', in M. Gallagher (ed.), *Ici-Là: Place and Displacement in Caribbean
Writing in French* (Amsterdam and Atlanta: Rodopi, forthcoming).

the street ‖ for an idea, their pain is privilege, a clear | tradition, proud in triumph, prouder in defeat ‖ for which they have made a language they share | in intellectual, odourless sweat.'[27]

There is no doubt that the Caribbean situation lends itself exceptionally well to thinking that refers time to space. A particularly extreme conflation of spatiality and temporality is implicit, indeed, in the use of the expressions *ancien monde* (or *vieux monde*) and *nouveau monde* to refer to certain parts of the planet. After all, these expressions imply that some parts of the world existed prior to others, or that their inhabitants have a longer history than others. As Patrick Chamoiseau puts it in *Chemin d'école*:

> En ce temps-là, le Gaulois aux yeux bleus, à la chevelure blonde comme les blés, était l'ancêtre de tout le monde . . . Nos îles avaient été là, dans un brouillard d'inexistence, traversée par de vagues fantômes caraïbes ou arawaks, eux-mêmes pris dans l'obscurité d'une non-histoire cannibale.[28]

It is impossible to imagine the Caribbean past in non-spatial terms, given that the mass genocide of the indigenous peoples of the Caribbean basin, and the subsequent waves of deportation and migration that deposited there its current population, have ensured that this past lies axiomatically elsewhere. It is a past which is, if not obliterated, then doubly dislocated because of its supplementary geographical inaccessibility.

The superimposition of the historical and the geographical, the temporal and the spatial, is very clearly signalled in many French Caribbean novels. At a primary level, historical time is characteristically projected elsewhere in these texts; that is, onto a distant 'Old World', usually Africa. However, frequently, in a further displacement, in this case a metonymical shift, Africa becomes Guinea, that part of West Africa where most 'New World' slaves embarked on the Middle Passage. Echoing Glissant's thought on the monolithic character of Western 'History' versus the multiplicity and relativity of jostling Caribbean 'histories', Patrick Chamoiseau in his novel *Texaco* identifies the most significant 'histoires' (lower-case and

---

[27] Derek Walcott, *Tiepolo's Hound* (New York: Farrar, Straus & Giroux, 2000), 137.

[28] Patrick Chamoiseau, *Chemin d'école* (Paris: Gallimard, 1994), 159; tr. Linda Coverdale as *School Days* (London: Granta, 1998), 121. 'In those days, the blue-eyed Gaul with hair as yellow as wheat was everyone's ancestor . . . Our islands had been veiled in a fog of non-existence, crossed by phantom Caribs or Arawaks themselves lost in the obscurity of a cannibal non-history.'

plural) as being those which are not just unwritten, but which refer specifically to Africa as the 'Pays d'Avant' ('land of before'), to its gods, its landscapes, and its oral traditions:

Je ne vais pas te refaire l'Histoire, mais le vieux nègre de la Doum révèle, dessous l'Histoire, des histoires dont aucun livre ne parle, et qui pour nous comprendre sont les plus essentielles . . . mémoire des merveilles oubliées: Pays d'Avant, le Grand Pays, la parole du grand pays, les dieux du grand pays . . .[29]

I shall return in the fourth chapter to the tension evoked in the above quotation between the spoken and the written word. However, the immediate issue here is the effect of the geographical displacement of historical time. Surely a heightened sense of alienation must be associated with a past perceived as not just temporally but also spatially remote? Surely such dislocation must disrupt the sense of connection on which history is founded, undermining the vital link between the here and now and the here and then? Does it not, in other words, involve the exclusive association of distant space with the past, and of local space with the absence of history, perhaps even with the absence of time itself?

While such a view of Caribbean historical consciousness is faithful to an extent, it is not the full story. In fact, a great many contemporary writers also look back towards a local, 'New World' past with immense nostalgia. As the geographer Yi-Fu Tuan points out, 'When a people deliberately change their environment and feel they are in control of their destiny, they have little cause for nostalgia. . . . When on the other hand, a people perceive that changes are occurring too rapidly, spinning out of control, nostalgia for an idyllic past waxes strong.'[30] It is not simply the fractures of transportation and enslavement that precipitated Caribbean nostalgia for time past, but also the very rapid changes that came in the wake of *départementalisation* in 1946 and following the near-complete eclipse of the oppressive but familiar plantation structures. 'Les

---

[29] 'I am not going to reinvent a History lesson you've already learned; the old men of the Doum reveal stories beneath History most essential for understanding us, stories no book speaks of . . . Their heads were full of the forgotten wonders: the First Land, the Great Land, its tongue, its gods . . . ': Patrick Chamoiseau, *Texaco* (Paris: Gallimard, 1992), 45; tr. Rose-Myriam Réjouis and Val Vinokurov as *Texaco* (London: Granta, 1997), 35.

[30] Yi-Fu Tuan, *Space and Place: The Perspective of Experience* (Minneapolis: University of Minnesota Press, 1977), 194.

arbres dessouchés, les noms perdus, les voix altérées, les rythmes éteints' ('the uprooted trees, lost names, altered voices, extinct rhythms') evoked in Édouard Glissant's novel *La Case du commandeur* are not necessarily located elsewhere (in Africa, for example).[31] If the distant past is axiomatically spatialized, since it is located elsewhere, the more immediate Caribbean past is also imagined in overwhelmingly spatial terms. The chronotopes of the plantation and the town that will be explored further on eloquently demonstrate this repetition of rupture.

Although the writing of Édouard Glissant and Patrick Chamoiseau is particularly striking in its fixation on place, which for them means, above all, the mutual configuration of space and time, many other writers are attracted by this intersection too. However, in some cases, the two dimensions are kept apart. In Daniel Maximin's first novel, *L'Isolé Soleil*, for example, which is strewn with questions concerning the relation between time and space, those who look to the historical past are contrasted with those who look to space: 'croyez-vous qu'il soit sain d'opter pour l'histoire au détriment de la géographie?' ('Do you think it healthy to opt for history at the expense of geography?').[32] This opposition is, indeed, a leitmotif in Maximin's novel, which refers to the mass suicide of Louis Delgrès and his men in terms of whether Delgrès had chosen to die 'avec la complicité de l'histoire, plutôt que d'espérer le secours de la géographie' ('with the complicity of history, rather than waiting for geography to come to his aid').[33]

NARRATIVE AND TIME

More than any other literary genre, and specifically more than poetry or drama, narrative engages with time. Paul Ricœur argues, for example, that temporality is the 'structure of existence that reaches language in narrativity' and that 'narrativity (is) the language structure that has temporality as its ultimate referent'.[34]

---

[31] Glissant, *La Case du commandeur*, 224.
[32] Maximin, *L'Isolé Soleil*, 225.   [33] Ibid. 86.
[34] Ricœur, 'Narrative Time', *Critical Inquiry* (Autumn 1980), 169–90: 169 (subsequent references to this article are given in the text following the abbreviation NT).

For him, both historical and fictional narratives take for granted that time is a linear 'succession of instants'. More recently, however, Ricœur has become interested in exploring the theory of narrative in relation less to that abstract notion of time than to lived, Bergsonian time.[35] For Ricœur in 1980, narrative links 'sequence and pattern in various ways'. In other words, the 'humblest narrative is always more than a chronological series of events and . . . in turn the configurational dimension cannot overcome the episodic dimension without suppressing the narrative structure itself' (NT 178). In his more recent work, Ricœur might be less inclined to separate temporality from historicality, less insistent on the transformative function of narrative discourse as 'eliciting a configuration from a succession' (NT 178), and less certain that plot imposes almost *a posteriori* 'the "sense of an ending"—to use Frank Kermode's expression—or a modicum of closure on the open-endedness of mere succession' (NT 179). Ricœur's 1980 view is strikingly similar to that of Hayden White, whose seminal article on history as representation saw historical narrative as making the end or the plot appear immanent to the successive events that are recounted. In this perspective, narrative provides a basis for distinguishing between historical and fictional narrative, in that the 'on-going-ness' of historical time precludes the sense of an 'ending'. Having averred that 'the sea is history', Walcott's epic poem *Omeros* ends by making precisely this point: 'When he left the beach the sea was still going on.'[36] What proved initially most controversial in Hayden White's argument was his view that historical narrative attempts to 'give to *real* events the *form* of story'[37] in response to a desire for both closure and moral meaning: the 'desire to have real events display the coherence, integrity, fullness and closure of an image of life that is and can only be imaginary' (VN 27). As White puts it: 'insofar as historical stories can be completed, can be given narrative closure, can be shown to have had a *plot* all along, they give to reality the odor of the *ideal*' (VN 24). More recently, however, phenomenologists such as David Carr and Paul Ricœur himself

---

[35] See Paul Ricœur, *La Mémoire, l'Histoire, l'Oubli* (Paris: Seuil, 2000).

[36] *Omeros* (London: Faber & Faber, 1990), 325.

[37] Hayden White, 'The Value of Narrativity in the Representation of Reality', *Critical Inquiry* (Autumn 1980), 5–28: 8 (subsequent page references are given in the text following the abbreviation VN).

argue that narrative as sequence and plot is inherent in all human being, living and acting rather than being imposed, discovered, or disclosed *a posteriori* by the narratives of history, myth, or literature.

DISRUPTION AND INTERRUPTION: THE WRITING OF DISCONTINUITY

Many French Caribbean novels bear witness to the irrevocable and insatiable desire to make sense of the past. It is also, however, a commonplace of French Caribbean novels that they abound in disrupted or interrupted narratives. Both phenomena are particularly evident in Marie-Sophie's absorption in, and transmission of, Esternome's serpentine story in Patrick Chamoiseau's *Texaco* and in Mathieu Béluse's indeflectable need in Édouard Glissant's novel *Le Quatrième Siècle* to hear the story of the past, as witnessed by his avid patience in the face of Papa Longoué's circuitous recall. When Mathieu tries to elicit the old seer's story, he finds that this narrative is only available in instalments, drawn out over years of patient visits to the hut in the hills. Furthermore, Longoué's *récit* is frequently interrupted when clients arrive in search of cures or potions from the *quimboiseur*. This pattern of interruption and deferral echoes Papa Longoué's perception of himself as the point of fracture in a genealogy or chain of descent that is itself heteroclitic, since many genealogical twists have intermingled the two originally separate and supposedly opposed Béluse and Longoué strains.

Similarly, Joseph Zobel's *chef d'œuvre*, the novel *La Rue Cases-Nègres* (1950), through a number of 'mises en abyme', shows the disruption of chronological time and of the very logic of narrative itself, in particular the defeat of its 'sense of an ending', and thereby its closure and sense of plot. For example, before the plantation *conteur* or storyteller, Monsieur Médouze, can finish telling his story, 'la voix de Maman Tine retentit et vient briser notre duo' ('the voice of M'man Tine rang out and came to break our duet'), with the result that José has to forgo 'la suite de la féérique histoire' ('the rest of the fairy tale [*sic*]'). Worse still, 'il en est ainsi presque chaque soir. Je ne peux jamais entendre un conte jusqu'à la fin' ('that was what transpired almost every night. I could never hear a story right through to the end.').[38] As though to underline the fact that this representation of suspended narration is not fortuitous in the novel, the narrator, this time quoting Médouze, evokes a second interruption of narrative: ' "Chaque fois que mon père essayait de conter sa vie", poursuit-il, "arrivé à 'J'avais un grand frère qui s'appelait Ousmane, une petite sœur qui s'appelait Sokhna, la dernière', il refermait très fort ses yeux se taisant brusquement".'[39] Still further on in the novel, we encounter a third narrative fracture, again in the telling of a traditional *conte* in Creole; but here the agent of untimely disruption is particularly significant: namely, Nemesis in the person of the French-enforcing schoolteacher. In depriving narratives of their endings, these interruptions do not exactly cancel chronological time, but they do prevent the formation of meaning. However, since the broken-off narratives are contained meta-narratives, the ruptures are themselves inscribed in narrative, and of course the written host narrative is not prone to interruption. This structure of continuous, proliferating interruption echos Glissant's description of Caribbean history as 'le discontinu dans le continu'.[40] It is highly significant that all the interrupted stories—those of Longoué and Esternome, Médouze and Vireil—are oral narratives. All three novels thus signify the disruption of oral culture. Furthermore, the agents of this disruption in the case of *La Rue Cases-Nègres* are forces favourable to assimilation: literacy and History.

In a similar use of *mise en abyme*, Édouard Glissant also explores the effects of historical discontinuity through the representation of exploded narrative in *La Case du commandeur*. As pillow-talk, Anatolie, champion lover and *raconteur*, who was told a story by his grandmother Eudoxie, distributes disjointed fragments of this tale amongst his many lovers. These women then relay various fragments to the slavemaster, who in turn repeats them to his wife. The twist in this version of the Chinese whisper is

---

[38] Joseph Zobel, *La Rue Cases-Nègres* (Paris: Présence africaine, 1950): 56, tr. Keith Warner as *Black Shack Alley* (London: Heinemann, 1980), 32.

[39] ' "Every time my father tried to relate his life story", he continued, "once he got to 'I had a big brother called Ousmane, a younger sister called Sonia, the last one', he would shut his eyes very tight and fall silent all of a sudden" ': *La Rue Cases-Nègres*, 57; *Black Shack Alley*, 32.

[40] Glissant, *Le Discours antillais*, 131; *Caribbean Discourse*, 62. The phrase is translated by J. Michael Dash as 'the dislocation of the continuum', whereas I would read it as meaning a continuous discontinuity.

that none of the relaying voices can transmit the entire story. Only Liberté Longoué, the *quimboiseur*'s daughter, is able to reconstruct Eudoxie's broken story (backwards), only to find the beginning swallowed up in a 'trou sans fond' ('bottomless pit').[41] This 'story' clearly relates to the self-reflexive evocation by the novel's collective 'we' narrator of the 'foule des mémoires et des oublis tressés, sous quoi nous peinons à recomposer nous ne savons quelle histoire débitée en morceaux. Nos histoires sautent dans le temps, nos paysages différents s'enchevêtrent, nos mots se mêlent et se battent, nos têtes sont vides ou trop pleines' ('host of interwoven memories and gaps in memory beneath which we strain to reconstruct we know not what story recounted in fragments. Our stories jump around in time, our various landscapes mingle, our words run into and jostle each other, our heads are either empty or overflowing').[42] The notion of the impossibility of complete narrative (re)composition—despite, or perhaps because of the insistence of jostling memories—recalls the opening of Chamoiseau's *L'Esclave Vieil Homme et le molosse*, studied at the start of this chapter. In the case of Eudoxie's story, however, it is less a question of penury or surplus of memory than of two other sources of discontinuity: first of all, severance from the origin or beginning; and secondly, the shattering through narrative relay of sequence and thereby of plot. Where Eudoxie's story differs from the Caribbean past is that, like Zobel's interrupted narratives, it seems to maintain the fiction of a single, original, once complete story, whereas the Caribbean combines and interweaves numerous histories. In Glissant's novel, however, Eudoxie's story is ultimately and unambiguously exposed as splintered from the very outset, and, like all narrative strands in Glissant's work, it is further multiplied and diffracted by relay and interwoven by textual repetitions to such an extent that no sense remains of a prior wholeness, distinctness, or linearity. Yet although Jacques André, like many other critics, identifies narrative disruption as the predominant aesthetic of Glissant's 1975 novel, *Malemort*, a 'récit éclaté dont les différentes séquences sont distribuées de manière irrégulière, au gré d'une linéarité volontairement brisée' ('shattered narrative whose various sequences are irregularly distributed, according to a wilfully broken linearity'),[43]

[41] Glissant, *La Case du commandeur*, 123.　　　　[42] Ibid. 126.

[43] Jacques André, *Caraïbales* (Paris: Éditions caribéennes, 1981), 106–7.

he does not deny the 'narrativity' of Glissant's novels. In other words, however complex or fragmented the narrative mode, it remains identifiably narrative.

POST-NARRATIVE: LOSING THE PLOT OR THE SPATIALIZATION OF TIME

If historical narrative is problematic in the Caribbean context, it is not just because of the open-*endedness* of time; it is also, if not principally, because of the difficulty of locating the beginning.[44] Derek Walcott refers to the amnesiac blow that wiped out the way back in time, and Édouard Glissant frequently evokes the impossibility of following the trail back to the beginning, 'ce commencement qui tout explique *et obscurcit*' ('this beginning that explains *and obscures everything*').[45] For Édouard Glissant, the dislocated quality of the Creole folktale, or its 'discontinuous notion of time',[46] serves to counter the doomed 'désiré historique' ('longing for history') in the Caribbean, that is: 'il est possible que la fonction du conte doit ici ... de nous sauver de la croyance que l'Histoire est la première et fondamentale dimension de l'homme' ('It is possible that the function of the tale is here to combat the sometimes paralysing force of a yearning for history, to save us from the belief that History is the first and most basic dimension of human experience').[47] Indeed, according to Glissant, the folktale also challenges the idea that time itself is the founding dimension of mankind. Without going this far, Glissant's own work favours a non-chronological and thus non-substitutive conception of time, compatible with durative consciousness, as a corrective to the mathematical idea of sequential time, that relentless succession of instants, each one replacing the previous one.

Many French Caribbean narratives are overwhelmed with spatiality, that is, with proliferating points of view and various

---

[44] *Le Quatrième Siècle* ends precisely on the image of a hot season or fever 'qui n'a ni fin ho! ni commencement' ('without beginning or end') (p. 287). At the beginning of the novel, the impossibility of Mathieu knowing the 'but ni le début' ('end or the beginning') sounds the same note (p. 13).

[45] Glissant, *La Case du commandeur*, 224. Emphasis mine.

[46] Glissant, *Le Discours antillais*: 'une conception discontinue du temps' (p. 151); 'a discontinuous conception of time' (*Caribbean Discourse*, 84).

[47] *Le Discours antillais*, 151; *Caribbean Discourse*, 84.

other arabesques that overwrite the linear approach (expected) of narrative. It is not always a case, then, of sequence being interrupted or fragmented; sometimes it is undermined by other structures or configurations, for example, repetition or circularity. Ralph Ludwig has observed that in Caribbean writing 'la causalité fait place à l'association' ('consequence is replaced by contiguity'),[48] and he further notes the frequency of a circular narrative rhythm.[49] Joseph Zobel's *La Rue Cases-Nègres* is a particularly good example of cyclical structure: as Jacques André has noted, the novel's conclusion presents itself as a preface, 'the hero promising himself to tell a story, the one that we have just read'.[50] On several other levels too, this novel represents time in terms of space. Although the narrator recounts the recent past and is separated by time (about twenty years) and by space (the Atlantic) from the childhood that he narrates, the guardian of the (twice) distant African past is Médouze, the *conteur*, José's first mentor. However, when Médouze speaks of Africa (or rather the mythical homeland, Guinea, discussed in Chapter 8), he evokes it in terms of spatial distance alone: 'M. Médouze évoque un autre pays plus lointain, plus profond que la France, et qui est celui de son père: la Guinée' ('Mr Médouze evoked another country even further away, even deeper than France, which was that of his father: Guinea').[51] The notion of time is only present here in the discontinuity implied by the fact that Guinea is neither José's nor Médouze's land; rather it was the homeland of a previous generation, that of Médouze's father. It is as though time can only be conceptualized in terms of space, that is, in terms of geographical distance and that rather strange dimension named 'depth'. The preponderance of space is further underlined as the storyteller begins a tale by evoking an old man who lives alone in a castle 'loin, loin, loin' ('far, far away'). In order to help José to visualize the distance in question, Médouze, in an echoing ternary structure, identifies Guinea as the most truly distant place imaginable: 'Un menteur dirait loin comme d'ici à Grand-Rivière. Mon frère, qui était un peu menteur, aurait dit comme d'ici à Sainte-Lucie. Mais moi, qui ne suis point menteur, je

---

[48] Ralph Ludwig (ed.) *Écrire la 'parole de nuit'. La nouvelle littérature antillaise* (Paris: Gallimard, 1994), 19.

[49] Ibid.　　　　　　　　　　　　　　　　　[50] André, *Caraïbales*, 55.

[51] Zobel, *La Rue Cases-Nègres*, 57; *Black Shack Alley*, 32.

dis que c'était loin comme d'ici en Guinée' ('A liar would say far like from here to Grand-Rivière. My brother, who used to lie a bit, would have said like from here to St Lucia. But I, not being a liar, say that it was far like from here to Guinea').[52] The furthest distance imaginable is thus the distance stretching back past the Middle Passage, as far as the mythical 'pays d'avant' or 'land of the past', what Glissant terms the 'pays rêvé' or dreamed-of land that is simultaneously the past of the real land at hand. Hence Mathieu in *Le Quatrième Siècle* is said to have travelled 'avec le vieux voyant dans ce qui était un pays rêvé en meme temps que le passé frémissant d'un pays réel' ('with the old seer into a place that was both a dream country and, at the same time, the trembling past of a real country').[53] However, while Édouard Glissant's distinction between the real and the imagined, and between time and space, highlights the temporal vibration of the spatial distance, the dimension of time is left entirely implicit, if not cancelled, in the overwhelmingly synchronous impression created by Médouze's references.

In Zobel's novel as a whole, as Jacques André has noted in his illuminating study of the novel, José is rapidly and irreversibly sucked into the order of historical, linear time. The plantation culture from which he becomes ever more distanced, and even estranged, is an oral culture in which time is constructed as repetitive and cyclical: 'Le temps était simplement une alternance de jours et de nuits ponctués par trois jours particuliers dont je connaissais les noms: samedi, dimanche, lundi' ('Time was simply an alternating of days and nights punctuated by three special days whose names I knew: Saturday, Sunday, Monday').[54] This cyclical sense of time appears to be contained and neutralized within José's retrospective 'discours historique' ('historical discourse')[55] of cultural transformation, a discourse that is identified precisely as written narrative by a number of 'mises en abyme' involving the reading or writing of narratives. Yet, although the existence of the written narrative confirms José's alignment with writing, French,

---

[52] *La Rue Cases-Nègres*, 55; *Black Shack Alley*, 31.

[53] Glissant, *Le Quatrième Siècle*, 261; *The Fourth Century*, 266.

[54] Zobel, *La Rue Cases-Nègres*, 59; *Black Shack Alley*, 33. This echoes Glissant's view of the folktale's anti-historical basis being its limitation of all sense of time to the 'balance du jour et de la nuit' (*Le Discours antillais*, 151).

[55] André, *Caraïbales*, 65.

and historical time, and although the novel is chronologically ordered into three numbered sections, the teleological movement of José's evolving social consciousness is undermined, as we shall see in Chapters 5 and 6, by the structural similarities between each of the three spaces—rural, village, and urban—through which he passes and which are his principal sources of enlightenment.

Simone Schwarz-Bart's novel *Pluie et vent sur Télumée Miracle* similarly illustrates the spatiality into which Caribbean historical and temporal consciousness seems to dissolve. This novel comprises two parts: in the first section, the eponymous Télumée recounts the story of four generations of Lougandor women; in the second, she recounts her own 'story'. However, Télumée's life very closely mirrors, magnifies, or reproduces that of her grandmother Toussine, a structural replication that in itself seems to challenge linear or chronological time. Furthermore, the mythical rather than historical status of Télumée's lineage is underlined by the fact that her memory stretches back no further than her great-grandmother who bears the name of the mythical goddess, Minerva. In addition, although the first page of the novel relates to the abolition of slavery and the liberation of Minerve, slavery is subsequently recalled at several points in the text as an ever-present shadow over the Caribbean spirit, thus attenuating the sense of the time that has passed since the abolition. Indeed, Télumée's realization of the anachronistic, ongoing presence and influence of slavery is expressed in spatial terms:

Pour la première fois de ma vie, je sentais que l'esclavage n'était *pas un pays étranger, une région lointaine* d'où venaient certaines personnes *très anciennes*, comme il en existait encore deux ou trois, à Fond-Zombi. Tout cela s'était déroulé *ici même*, dans nos mornes et nos vallons, et peut-être à côté de cette touffe de bambou, peut-être *dans l'air* que je respirais.[56]

Here, place guarantees the continuity between present and past. Most strikingly, the past is present for Télumée in the very air that she breathes in and out, along with the selfsame vegetation that

---

[56] Simone Schwarz-Bart, *Pluie et vent sur Télumée Miracle* (Paris: Seuil, 1972): 62; tr. Barbara Bray, as *The Bridge of Beyond*, intro. Bridget Jones (London: Heinemann, 1982), 39: 'For the first time in my life I realized that *slavery was not some foreign country, some distant region* from which a very old people came, like the two or three who still survived in Fond-Zombi. It had all happened *here*, in our hills and valleys, perhaps near this clump of bamboo, perhaps *in the air* I was breathing.' Emphasis mine.

had witnessed slavery. Finally, at the very end of the text, as Télumée reviews her life and comments on her present situation, she evokes some of the changes she has seen: for example, the electrification of her locality and the advent of running water. Yet, although she avers that there are times when she no longer recognizes her 'pays' ('land'), in the very next paragraph, the last one of the novel, she explicitly concludes that time is cyclical, if not circular, a point eloquently reinforced by the structure of the narrative that ends, as it began, with the narrator standing in her garden contemplating the thread of her life.

Comme je me suis débattue, d'autres se débattront, et, pour bien longtemps encore, les gens connaîtront même lune et même soleil, et ils regarderont les mêmes étoiles, ils y verront comme nous les yeux des défunts. . . . Soleil levé, soleil couché, les journées glissent et le sable que soulève la brise enlisera ma barque, mais je mourrai là, comme je suis, debout, dans mon petit jardin, quelle joie! . . .[57]

In Patrick Chamoiseau's novel *Solibo Magnifique*, a 'narrative' that parades at every turn its non-linear structure, time is 'spatialized' by the hypertrophy of narrative lines or the multiplication of simultaneous narrative positions. The 'narrator' characterizes himself as a 'Marqueur de paroles', whose role is to transcribe the discourse of others. Indeed, the entire text of the novel presents itself as a mosaic of citations, some of the written and some of the spoken word. The spatializing effect of this fragmentation is expressed rhetorically in the following metaphorical evocation of the deceased *conteur*: 'Ceux qui en parlaient le plus volontiers, ou le plus longtemps, n'en détenaient pas une vision globale. Solibo était semblable à un reflet de vitrine, une sculpture à facettes dont aucun angle n'autorisait une perspective d'ensemble' ('Those who spoke more readily or at greater length didn't have a full picture in their heads. Solibo was like a reflection in a window, a sculpture with facets that allowed no angle to reflect the whole').[58] The use of visual, spatial imagery ('vision', 'reflet de vitrine', 'sculpture',

---

[57] Schwarz-Bart, *Pluie et vent sur Télumée Miracle*, 249; 'As I have struggled others will struggle, and for a long time yet people will know the same sun and moon; they will look at the same stars, and, like us, see in them the eyes of the dead. . . . Sun risen, sun set, the days slip past and the sand blown by the wind will engulf my boat. But I shall die here, where I am, standing in my little garden. What happiness!': *Bridge of Beyond*, 172–3.

[58] *Solibo Magnifique*, 220; *Solibo Magnificent*, 154.

'angle', etc.) to define Solibo effects a striking de-temporalization of a life-force 'originally' centred in performance, and thus in time. In stressing the specular, in making of Solibo a figure to be encompassed, the *marqueur de paroles* may well suggest the three-dimensional spatiality of the figure, but this spatialization reinforces, of course, the rigor mortis of the *conteur*'s corpse.

Raphaël Confiant's writing also stresses spatiality by multiplying narrative positions. His aim is to give to his writing the quality of a 'récit étoilé et non linéaire'[59] ('étoilé' means radiating, and the term also describes the 'crazed' pattern of cracked or shattered glass). Thus, Roy Caldwell writes of Confiant's novel *L'Allée des soupirs* that the 'narrative shifts its focus from one figure to another, privileging the perspective or role of none of them. Even the barriers between individual characters fall away.'[60] Caldwell also observes the frequency of anachronic digressions and the lack of 'ordered analeptic systems',[61] concluding that Confiant's text 'does not respect the principle of the dominant temporal key—that time-zero which anchors the narrative chronology. Instead of proceeding through linear analeptic sequences, this tale branches backwards forming rhizomes.'[62]

Maryse Condé's' much-studied *Traversée de la mangrove* is regarded as exemplary in its espousal of narrative discontinuity and its consequent rejection of singularity and linearity. Critics have noted, for example, that this novel does not recount one story but several.[63] However, there is a certain slippage between this notion of a plurality of stories, and the more reductive notion of 'diverses voix narratives qui, chacune, donnent leur interprétation d'une même réalité' ('different narrative voices, each of which gives a different interpretation of the same reality').[64] This second observation recalls Roy Caldwell's view of Confiant's novel, *L'Allée des soupirs* as a narrative that repeatedly 'branches into variants of the same event'[65] or the notion of Solibo as a three-dimensional figure

[59] Raphaël Confiant, 'Quelques pratiques d'écriture créole', in Ludwig (ed.), *Écrire la 'parole de nuit'*, 179.

[60] Roy Chandler Caldwell Jr., 'Créolité and Postcoloniality in Raphaël Confiant's *L'Allée des soupirs*', *The French Review*, 73/2 (2000), 301–11: 303.

[61] Ibid. 305. [62] Ibid. 304.

[63] Pascale de Souza, '*Traversée de la mangrove*: éloge de la créolité, écriture de l'opacité', *The French Review*, 73 (2000), 822-33: 831.

[64] Ibid.

[65] Caldwell, 'Créolité and Postcoloniality', 305.

impossible to apprehend as a whole. For there is surely a difference between various versions or interpretations of what can be identified as the 'same' story or the 'whole story', on the one hand, and a plurality of different stories on the other.[66]

Édouard Glissant's writing, or rather 'overwriting', of narrative, his weaving and relaying of narrative voices, and even Confiant's multiply disrupted narrative, contrast with the clear lines of Condé's novel, which is divided into 'sub-stories' that follow one after the other, each one identified by its narrator's name. In so far as *Traversée de la mangrove* is thus narrated from several individual (and sometimes divergent) points of view, it contrasts with the non-disjunctive, relational tenor of the 'dynamic, internally differentiated collective consciousness'[67] that obtains, according to Celia Britton, in some of Glissant's novels. The relay and overlay of narrative fragments and voices in Glissant's novels foregrounds the text as a space of narrative interweaving. Textual process thus overwrites narrative, radically relativizing all sense of sequence and plot (or sequence as plot). In *Mahagony* (1987), this process reaches paroxysmal proportions in so far as one of the interwoven and relativized narrative voices is identified as that of the author. In what Celia Britton calls a 'process of "unauthorization" ',[68] Mathieu, a character who recurs from novel to novel, challenges and rewrites some of the events or versions of events narrated in previous novels. Rather than suggesting some single version or real story beyond themselves, these narratives thus demand, as Celia Britton has shown, an act of reading that accepts the boundlessness of the narrative 'weave'.

Although Maryse Condé's novel does demote narrative linearity and singularity to an extent, the sheer boundlessness of the rewriting or overwriting of narrative in the work of Édouard Glissant and Daniel Maximin, and to a lesser extent Patrick Chamoiseau and Raphaël Confiant, suggests an even more radical and dynamic challenge to unified narrative identity. In Maximin's novels, as in

---

[66] Delphine Perret observes that in Condé's novel 'chaque personnage dit ici son histoire, et aucun ne dit toute l'histoire' ('each character tells his or her story . . . but no-one tells the whole story'): Perret, 'L'écriture mosaïque de *Traversée de la mangrove*', in Maryse Condé (ed.), *L'Héritage de Caliban* (Pointe-à-Pitre: Éditions Jasor, 1992), 187–200: 200.

[67] Britton, 'Collective Narrative Voice', 147.

[68] Britton, *Édouard Glissant and Postcolonial Theory*, 166.

Glissant's work, open-ended circulation prevails, rather than fragmentation into a limited set of distinct, linear narratives. Maximin
himself notes that in his novel trilogy, 'Le cyclique remplace le
linéaire car il permet de commencer par lire le troisième livre, le
second ou le premier; ainsi c'est aussi éclairant dans un sens que
dans l'autre' ('cyclical structures replace linearity: one can begin by
reading the third, the second, or the first novel; one direction is as
enlightening as the next').[69] Moreover, in his second novel,
Soufrières, the plural form of the title mirrors the narrative multiplication and relativization. Furthermore, both Guadeloupe and St
Lucia have a volcanic mountain called Soufrière, hence this plural in
the title adverts to geographical dispersion and relationality. And
finally, a constant, eruptive syncopation regularly interrupts the
narrative, itself a recital of endless displacement, or constant jour-
neying over the island, especially between Basse-Terre and Grande-
Terre. Against this 'Brownian motion', a criss-crossing circulation in
which the automobile is fetishized, no one trajectory or story (even
if it is one of several) stands any chance of prevailing.

Curiously, the conventional temporal trajectory of narrative is
not so much challenged as inflected in French Caribbean writing by
that sense of place that derives from the constant tension between
narrative and discourse. Far from the narrated events seeming in
some sense to 'tell themselves', and far from them being cut off
from the time of narration, the intrusiveness of the deictic moment,
referring not just to time, but also—and principally even—to space,
is underlined at every turn. The frequency of deictic reference is
matched by the intensity of geographical reference, exemplified by
the sustained use of 'real' toponyms, and by the proliferation of
botanical, zoological, and climatic references. One of the most
striking examples of the predominance of spatial deixis in French
Caribbean writing is the recurrence of the ostensibly paradoxical
Creole expression 'ici-là' that we might translate as 'over here'.[70]
Within narrative, the effect of this distinctive deictic is to draw
attention (back) from the past historic tense to the enunciative
present. In Creole, the definite article 'le' or 'la' is replaced by the

---

[69] Christiane Chaulet-Achour and Daniel Maximin, 'Sous le signe du colibri', in
Alfred Hornung and Ernstpeter Ruhe (eds.), *Postcolonialisme et autobiographie*
(Amsterdam and Atlanta, Ga.: Rodopi, 1998), 210.

[70] See Gallagher (ed.), *Ici-Là*.

demonstrative suffix 'là' (meaning 'there'), which has, of course, a highly deictic spatial value. Appended to the adverb 'ici' (meaning 'here'), the Creole suffix reinforces the demonstrative, deictic charge of the latter. However, in French, the semantic resonance of this hyphenated expression is less pleonasmic than paradoxical or counter-intuitive, since 'ici' and 'là' refer in French to immediate and distant space respectively.

EMPLOTTED SPACE

The flow of time is spatialized but not de-narrativized in Glissant's *Le Quatrième Siècle* (1964) when Mathieu learns to measure centuries, not mathematically by 'l'écart de cent années déroulées l'une après l'autre' ('the gap of a hundred years unfolding one after the other') but by 'l'espace parcouru' ('the space traversed'):

mais aucun d'eux n'avait encore dit . . . 'La mer qu'on traverse, c'est un siècle'. Oui, un siècle. Et la côte où tu débarques, aveuglé, sans âme ni voix, est un siècle. Et la forêt, entretenue dans sa force jusqu'à ce jour de ton marronnage . . . est un siècle.[71]

Not only is space given temporal depth in Glissant's writing, but it is suggested that time is experienced differently in different spaces:

Vers le même temps (si encore on peut savoir qu'un temps est le même: il y a le temps des hauts qui t'enroule à merci, le temps d'en bas qui te traîne dans tous les sillons, sans compter le temps de là-bas qui cogne en éclair dans la tête, et combien d'autres insoupçonnés) . . .[72]

In the above passage, the temporality of the highlands is distinguished from that of the lowlands, from distant space signified deictically (Africa or Metropolitan France, perhaps), and from a host of indeterminate spaces that cannot even be imagined.

---

[71] Glissant, *Le Quatrième Siècle*, 268–9; 'But none of them had yet . . . said: "The sea we cross is a century". Yes, a century. And the coast where you debark, blinded, and with no soul or voice, is a century. And the forest—kept in its prime until the day you became a maroon . . . is a century': *The Fourth Century*, 273–4.

[72] Glissant, *La Case du commandeur*, 148: 'Towards the same time (if, that is, it is possible to decide that a time is the same: there is, after all, the time of the highlands that rolls you forward indefinitely, the time of the lowlands that drags you into all the ruts, not to mention the time of over there that strikes your mind like lightning, and how many other unsuspected times)'.

The alignment of time and space is particularly striking in the quasi-quest novel, *La Case du commandeur*, when Mycéa's search leads her to the 'Mitan du temps' ('centre of time') and to the eponymous 'driver's cabin'. The oxymoron 'centre of time' suggests that time has a beginning and an end and thus negates the idea of time as inexorable flow and double open-endedness. Indeed the specificity of temporality is denied since time now becomes a volume, a notion reinforced by the fact that the 'mitan du temps' section is located in the centre of Glissant's book, or 'volume'. Since the 'middle of time' 'happens' or 'takes place' in the driver's hut, it is identified with plantation time-space. And the latter is thereby identified as a median time equidistant from a beginning and an end, from an original time-space and a 'final' one. Significantly, in this 'median time', Mycéa's delirium dries up. And she appears to be cured—as Celia Britton observes—not by the thought of the ancestors, either original or median, African or Creole, but by the thought of local Caribbean spatial or geographical connections in the present.[73] Perhaps in configuring time for Mycéa, the experience of this median time-space allowed her to distinguish between the distant past, the local past, and the present. Perhaps it allowed her to identify the present, not as an ending, but as the only possible point of temporal reference, and as a point with a future ahead of it.

THE NEUTRALIZATION OF CARIBBEAN TIME

Rien n'est plus étrange que de voir M. Médouze évoquer la Guinée, d'entendre la voix qui monte de ses entrailles quand il parle de l'esclavage et raconte l'horrible histoire que lui avait dite son père, de l'enlèvement de sa famille, de la disparition de ses neuf oncles et tantes, de son grand-père et de sa grand-mère.[74]

At the beginning of the above sentence, the narrator seems about to relay Médouze's evocation of the 'Old World' of Africa: in fact,

---

[73] Britton, *Édouard Glissant*, 129.
[74] *La Rue Cases-Nègres*, 57; 'Nothing stranger than to see Mr Médouze evoke Guinea, to hear the voice rising from his entrails when he spoke of slavery and related the horrible story his father had told him, of the rape of his family, of the disappearance of his nine uncles and aunts, of his grandfather and his grandmother': *Black Shack Alley*, 32.

the relay is double, since Médouze is himself recalling his father's witness. However, before first half of the sentence is completed, the subject of 'Guinée' (Africa) has been replaced by that of slavery. Furthermore, we quickly learn that Médouze is not, as it at first appears, going to evoke the relatively continuous phenomenon of enslavement or 'l'esclavage', but rather the singular ruptures represented firstly by the brutality of the actual sale into slavery, and secondly, by the abolition of slavery. As a result, the phenomenon of slavery is cast as a 'non-histoire', a 'non-history' or a 'non-story', telescoped as it is between two moments of rupture, initial and terminal; moreover, the entire 'duration' of slavery is compressed into a single lifetime, that of Médouze's father, and is associated less with duration, indeed, than with those exceptional and, by definition, disjunctive moments that fracture historical time. However, if the first rupture, the break with Africa, seems to cancel consciousness of a previous place and time (indeed the Middle Passage or transatlantic displacement are not mentioned), the second one, the abolition of slavery, is represented as a fake caesura, and thus as restoring a sense of duration. For, proceeding to recount what his father told him of the abolition, Médouze tells how disappointed the latter was to observe that this development was to change nothing. Instead, Médouze's father discovered that he was neither to be reunited with his family nor with his country, and that he would have to stay on in a *pays maudit* where the power structure had not changed at all. In the absence of the prospect of a return displacement to Africa, nothing can change and time is cancelled.

If Édouard Glissant is right in claiming that the Creole folktale negates temporality, then, given that Patrick Chamoiseau and Raphaël Confiant have spearheaded a movement which argues for the colonizing of written texts by what they term 'oraliture', it would not be surprising to find that these two writers reproduce in their novels the temporal discontinuity and 'non-history' that Glissant has deemed characteristic of 'la parole créole'. In Chamoiseau's *Solibo Magnifique*, the narrator (identified by name as the author) explicitly discounts the significance of dating events: 'Cette récolte du destin que je vais vous conter eut lieu à une date sans importance puisque ici le temps ne signe aucun calendrier' ('The harvest of fate that I shall narrate to you happened on a day whose date is unimportant since time signs no calendar here').[75] Similarly, the measurement of time is frequently dismissed in the writing of *créolité*: of Solibo, the eponymous *conteur*, it is said that he lived 'sans montre et sans calendrier, et surtout sans habitudes' ('without clock and without calendar and, above all, had no habits').[76] In Maryse Condé's novel *La Vie scélérate* the insignificance of calendar time is also noted: 'un beau nègre d'environ trente-deux ans, je dis bien environ, car en ce temps-là, comme chacun sait, on ne se souciait guère d'état civil' ('a handsome black of about thirty-two, I say about, for in those days, as we all know, nobody worried about date of birth').[77]

However, rather than being represented as timeless, the dimension in which the protagonists of many novels exist is represented as the arrested time of plantation life. The oxymoron of frozen time suggests a 'temps mort', or a time in which no (historical) change can take place. Yet in Confiant's claim that 'dans l'oraliture créole règne le temps arrêté de la plantation' ('the arrested time of the Plantation dominates Creole orality'),[78] the neutralization of time is double. Not only is plantation time arrested time, but it is doomed and, at the time of writing, dead. In Chamoiseau's *Solibo Magnifique*, the discourse of the police and of the various witnesses or suspects thus takes as its point of reference a culture which is not just static, but also long disappeared: 'Solibo Magnifique était dans cette vie comme on est à la guerre: en alerte. Fais-toi raconter par les békés anciens ces histoires de nègres-marrons que pièce chien ne pouvait pister … Les vieux chasseurs et les békés d'antan les appelaient *guerriers*!' ('Solibo Magnificent lived life as we live war: always on his guard. Get the old békés to tell you stories about the maroon blackmen that no dog could track down … The old hunters and the békés of bygone days called them *warriors*!').[79] To explain Solibo's disposition, the narrator thus refers us to three defunct systems: the plantation, slavery, and the associated oral culture.

Even more significantly, in the narrator's own asides, as well as in the speech that he transcribes or records, it is claimed that,

---

[75] *Solibo Magnifique*, 25; *Solibo Magnificent*, 8.
[76] *Solibo Magnifique*, 191; *Solibo Magnificent*, 131.
[77] Maryse Condé, *La Vie scélérate* (Paris: Seghers, 1987), 13.
[78] Confiant, 'Quelques questions', 175. On the same page, Confiant uses the term 'atemporalité'.
[79] Chamoiseau, *Solibo Magnifique*, 196; *Solibo Magnificent*, 135–6.

because the only temporal point of reference is this now extinct plantation culture, time has now stopped. In a footnote to clarify one of the police questions 'Quel genre de travail tu fais pour le béké?' ('What kind of work you do for the *béké*?'),[80] it is noted that everything used to belong to the *békés*—the lands, the factories, and all the structures of economic production. Directly or indirectly, everybody was thus working for the *békés*. And the note ends by confirming that the expression lived on, all the more persistently as things had not changed much.[81] Thus no alternative cultural model has replaced the system of slavery that gave this 'New World' its common memory, and therefore its collective solidarity and identity: 'O amis, qui est à l'aise par-ici quand la police est là? . . . Avec elle, arrivent aussi les chasseurs des bois d'aux jours de l'esclavage, les chiens à marronnage, la milice des alentours d'habitation, les commandeurs des champs . . .' ('O friends, who is at ease when the police are around? . . . With cops, the hunting dogs from slavery days return, the maroon-chasing dogs, the militia that watched the plantation, the overseers . . .').[82] All mention of the police reawakens memories of slavery and *marronnage*. And significantly, the resulting sense of discontinuity and anachronism is explicitly associated in *Solibo Magnifique* with the displacement of historical time across the ocean. Sometimes the flow of time is located in France:

Richard Cœurillon et Zaboca parlèrent d'un temps de récoltes et d'usines qui fumaient, en ce temps l'un maniait une machine, l'autre serrait un coutelas, *c'était un temps*, mais aujourd'hui si les champs sont déserts, que les sifflets d'usines ne rythment plus la journée, que tes mains ne savent plus rien amarrer, tresser, clouer, découper, *où passe le temps d'ici*, inspectère? On dit qu'il est en France, que *là il y a du temps*.[83]

---

[80] Chamoiseau, *Solibo Magnifique*, 98; *Solibo Magnificent*, 61–2.

[81] 'Terres, usines, et les structures de production économique (directe ou indirecte) appartenaient aux békés. Quelle que soit sa fonction, l'on travaillait pour les békés. L'expression est restée, d'autant que les choses ont peu évolué' ('Lands, factories, and the structures of economic production (direct or indirect) belonged to the békés. Whatever one's function, one worked for the békés. The expression has stayed on, inasmuch as things have evolved little': *Solibo Magnifique*, 98; *Solibo Magnificent*, 62.

[82] *Solibo Magnifique*, 83; *Solibo Magnificent*, 49.

[83] *Solibo Magnifique*, 146; 'Richard Cœurillon and Zaboca spoke of a time of harvests and smokestack factories, at that time one man handled a machine, the other a scythe, *that was time*, but now if the fields are deserted and the factory whistles no longer give rhythm to the day, now that your hands no longer know how to

And sometimes it is located, rather, in Africa, or at least in those de-colonized spaces characterized in the present by sovereignty and envied their restored ownership of time.

Vous êtes restés combien de temps à écouter ce solo?
  Toutes les dépositions furent les mêmes: *Le temps c'est quoi*, monsieur l'inspectère? ... Solibo avait glissé dans les racines, alors nous on attendait, comme dans ce pays, partout, on attend. Qu'est-ce que hier, qu'est-ce que demain, quand on attend? ... Ti-Cal se réfugia en politique abstruse: *Quel temps?* mais quel temps? Sans Autonomie ou sans Indépendance, il n'y a que tempête ou temps mort ...[84]

The same sense of the French Caribbean being caught in a time-warp, of time standing still, or of being stuck in space, as it were, is powerfully conveyed also in Xavier Orville's novel, *Moi Trésilien-Théodore Augustin* (1996). The first-person narrator of this novel is a revolutionary dictator determined to reform the temporal consciousness of his compatriots: 'Je voulais révolutionner la vie. Tirer mes pieds de la routine. Bousculer montres et calendriers' ('I wanted to revolutionize life. To pull myself out of routine. To upset clocks and calendars'). Instead of regarding his 'subjects' as victims of colonization, he berates their collusion with their own temporal dispossession:

J'ai toujours été révolté par la mollesse de mes compatriotes. ... Ils déclinent l'existence au passé. Oublient que le seul temps réel, c'est le présent ... Ils s'abritent paresseusement derrière l'idée qu'il ne faut rien déranger, que le temps ne leur appartient pas.[85]

Although he recognizes the tragic dimension of their temporal alienation, Trésilien criticizes his compatriots' docility and submissiveness

---

lash a rope, braid, nail, cut anything, *where does time happen*, inspekder? Some say it's in France, that there, *there is time*': *Solibo Magnificent*, 97–8. Emphasis mine.

[84] *Solibo Magnifique*, 145; 'And how long did you sit there listening to his solo? All the statements were the same: *What is time*, Mr Inspector? ... we just waited, like in this country, everywhere, people wait. What's yesterday, and what's tomorrow when you wait?—Ti-Cal took refuge in abstruse politics. *Which Time?* No really, which time? With neither Autonomy nor Independence, there's only tempest or dead time': *Solibo Magnificent*, 97. Emphasis mine.

[85] Xavier Orville, *Moi, Trésilien-Théodore Augustin* (Paris: Stock, 1996), 16; 'I have always found my compatriots' inertia revolting ... For them existence rhymes with the past. They forget that the only real time is the present ... They shelter lazily behind the idea that nothing must be disturbed, that time does not belong to them'.

in the face of imperialism and, himself rather imperially, plots 'des histoires de temps à réformer':

> Ce qui nous arrive est tragique . . . Nous avons habité en tout et pour tout des miettes du temps tombées de la table des autres. Même les événements les plus importants de notre histoire s'affichent aux cadrans étrangers. . . . Nous n'avons fait que nous couler docilement dans le temps des autres.[86]

Echoing Glissant's distinction between history 'made in France' and local history, Trésilien casts this lack of history or 'non-histoire' as a cowardly laziness, castigating his compatriots' refusal of all ownership of their own time, stigmatizing their abdication of all responsibility towards this resource: 'Et qu'avaient-ils fait de leur temps?' ('And what use had they made of their time?'). He does not tire of pointing out energetically 'à quel point il était important pour nous tous que le pays se mît enfin à l'heure de lui-même' ('how very important is was for us all that the country should set its watches to its own time')[87] instead of complacently living in the past, in borrowed time, or the time set elsewhere, by others.

BEING IN TIME, BEING IN HISTORY

Time and space, narrative and post-narrative, history and non-history intersect, then, in a particularly striking manner in the French Caribbean novel. The extensive writing of interruption, disruption, dislocation, displacement, de-temporalization, and spatialization, that I have noted itself takes place in the context of narratives or stories. In other words, the processes of disconnection and fragmentation, and the representation of timelessness, are all contextualized or held, contained and related, within the temporal flow of narrative. However, in order to explore further the narrative relation of time to space, and the particularly important and complex question of narrative and duration, we must now turn to the question of memory.

---

[86] Ibid. 31; 'What is happening to us is a tragedy . . . We have been living essentially off the crumbs of time that have fallen from the tables of others. Even the most important events of our history only registered on foreign clocks . . . All we have done is to slink submissively into the time owned by others'.

[87] Ibid. 111.

CHAPTER THREE

The Place of Memory

Freedom should mean, I think, the action of memory to acquaint us deeply, profoundly, with the perilous voyages of humanity out of its cradles of dream in space and time.[1]

French Caribbean writers appear more preoccupied with memory than with history, and more interested, perhaps, in collective than in personal memory. If we take memory to be, potentially at least, discontinuous and non-emplotted, then the French Caribbean concern with memory resonates with the heightened disjunctive and digressive movement felt to characterize Caribbean time. How, then, is memory written of in the French Caribbean? How does its mobilization resonate with the tendency observed in the previous chapter to translate temporal parameters into spatial paradigms? Is obsession with memory linked to fixation on place? To what extent is memory perceived as being more hospitable than history towards the expression of lived time, or better adapted to the life of consciousness? And is it because of their perception that access to the historical past is highly problematic that Caribbean writers honour the more modest heuristic claims of memory?

HISTORY AND MEMORY: QUESTIONS OF NARRATIVE AND PRESENCE

Because memory is of such importance in Caribbean writing—after all, the authors of the *créolité* manifesto dedicate themselves to exploring what they ambitiously term 'la mémoire vraie'—it is important to take the measure of this phenomenon which has justifiably

[1] Harris, *Selected Essays*, 233.

been pronounced 'amorphous'.[2] Of particular pertinence is the relation of memory to history, a question that has strenuously exercised a number of acute contemporary minds: for example, philosopher Paul Ricœur and historians Jacques Le Goff and Pierre Nora. Paul Ricœur is categorical on this question, taking memory to be the matrix of history, a notion that resonates with the title of Wilson Harris's collection of essays on the Caribbean imagination, *The Womb of Space*.[3] In envisaging the connection between history and memory spatially—the matrix is, after all, the *place* in which something is embedded and formed—Ricœur's thinking diverges slightly, but significantly, from the similarly organic view taken of this connection by Jacques Le Goff. 'Memory is the raw material of history', argues Le Goff, adding that 'whether mental, oral, or written, it is the living source from which historians draw . . . Moreover the discipline of history nourishes memory in turn, and enters into the great dialectical process of memory and forgetting experienced by individuals and societies.'[4] For Le Goff, the relation is less gestational than metabolic, since history consumes and processes memory, although it then feeds back into memory, setting up a circular chain. While both thinkers agree that history depends on memory, for Ricœur it does not supersede memory, whereas for Le Goff history as product does indeed transcend its raw material. Indeed Le Goff is concerned to distance his view of history from those 'recent, naïve trends' that seem almost 'to identify history with memory, and even to give preference in some sense to memory'.[5]

For his part, Pierre Nora, the historian of 'lieux de mémoire' does not collapse the distinction between history and memory; on the contrary, he underlines it, declaring that the two appear to be 'in fundamental opposition'.[6] Far from establishing a generative or

---

[2] Jacques Le Goff, *History and Memory*, tr. Steven Rendall and Elizabeth Claman (New York: Columbia University Press, 1992), 51; *Histoire et mémoire* (Paris: Gallimard, 1986 and 1988).

[3] 'Mon livre est un plaidoyer pour la mémoire comme matrice de l'histoire': Ricœur, *La Mémoire*, 106.

[4] Le Goff, *History and Memory*, p. xi (from preface to 1988 Gallimard edn.).

[5] Ibid., p. xi.

[6] Pierre Nora, 'Between Memory and History: Les Lieux de Mémoire', *Representations*, 26 (Spring 1989), 7–25, repr. in Geneviève Favre and Robert O'Meally (eds.), *History and Memory in African-American Culture* (New York and Oxford: Oxford University Press, 1994), 284–300: 285 (the translator is Marc Roudebush).

metabolic relation between the two, he praises memory as being 'life, borne by living societies founded in its name', and as being 'a perpetually actual phenomenon, a bond tying us to the eternal present'. History, on the other hand, is decried as superficial and inorganic, or the 'reconstruction, always problematic and incomplete, of what no longer is'.[7] In this view, memory is aligned with presence, history with representation and absence. For Nora, it is precisely when memory fails that space takes on the role of retention, or the 'keeping present' of the past. In his work on Caribbean writing, Chris Bongie adapts Nora's opposition, observing that Caribbean memory is a '*lived* as opposed to a *reconstructed* link with the past'.[8] However, in the Caribbean, where collective memory has been so radically and multiply disturbed, not to say damaged or severed, history is unlikely to benefit from a luxuriant matrix. We saw in the last chapter the implications for narrative of this deprivation, namely pervasive interruption, spatialization, and neutralization. Other possible consequences are retrenchment in the discursive present; fixation on memory as loss, blockage, or blank; or retreat into the perceived retentiveness of space (that is, space perceived as holding, but also as withholding, the past).

In their respective works, *Time, Narrative, and History* and *La Mémoire, l'histoire, l'oubli*, David Carr and Paul Ricœur challenge the notion of a schismatic separation between memory and history. As a corrective to overemphasis on memory as present-centred connection with the past, Ricœur emphasizes that every relation to (or of) the past is an acknowledgement that the past is no more. Absolutely fundamental to memory, indeed, is 'l'aporie de la présence de l'absence' ('the aporia of the presence of absence').[9] Phenomenologists do not see memory as denying the flow of time; instead, for them all experience—including experience of memory—is 'organized by a grasp which spans time, is retrospective and prospective, and which thus *seeks to escape from the very temporal perspective of the now which makes it possible*'.[10] David Carr adopts the Husserlian distinction between primary memory or retention and secondary memory or recollection, agreeing that they are 'radically different ways of being conscious of the past'. He

---

[7] Ibid.   [8] Bongie, *Islands and Exiles*, 166.
[9] Ricœur, *La Mémoire*, 11.
[10] David Carr, *Time, Narrative, and History* (Bloomington and Indianapolis: Indiana University Press, 1986), 69. My emphasis.

notes that 'recollections come and go, whereas retention belongs to all experience'.[11] In other words, recollection is aligned in a certain sense with discontinuity: as David Carr points out, 'the past which I retain ... is constitutive of the presence of my object; whereas recollection is like my *imagining* an object somewhere else in space but not within my visual field'.[12] Carr insists, however, that both models of memory imply a temporal arc, that is, a simultaneous sense of the present, past, and future. Recollection is only to a certain extent, then, a temporal circuit-breaker. Certainly, it involves calling to mind something from beyond the horizon of the present and, as such, it might seem to interrupt the temporal charge that passes through the present. David Carr stresses, however, that the process of recollection itself takes place in time and as such implies that temporal flow that simultaneously and continuously empties and fills the present. In Caribbean writing, Édouard Glissant's aspiration to *'une vision prophétique du passé'* (*'a prophetic vision of the past'*)[13] resonates particularly strongly with this phenomenological view of memory. Conversely, however, Derek Walcott's insight in *Tiepolo's Hound* that 'time is not narrative'[14] clashes with it, since, for phenomenologists, narrative is structured precisely by the temporal arc from retention/recollection to protention/projection, and they would argue that time and memory are experienced as narrative.[15] From the phenomenological perspective, in other words, 'life' is 'the same kind of construction of the human imagination as "a narrative" is ... There is no such thing psychologically as "life itself"', or events themselves, or even duration itself.[16] The view that memory and time are configured in the same way as narrative calls into question, of course, Jacques Le Goff's memorable assertion of the epistemological superiority of history over memory: 'The historian must be there to render an account of ... memories and of what is forgotten, to transform them into something that can be conceived, to make them know-

---

[11] Carr, *Time, Narrative, and History*, 22.   [12] Ibid.

[13] *Le Discours antillais*, 132; *Caribbean Discourse*, 64 (emphasis in original).

[14] *Tiepolo's Hound*, 94.

[15] Carr, *Time, Narrative, and History*, 65.

[16] Jerome Bruner, 'Life as Narrative', *Social Research*, 54 (1987), 11–32: 12–13, quoted in Paul John Eakin, *Touching the World: Reference in Autobiography* (Princeton: Princeton University Press, 1992), 198.

able. To privilege memory excessively is to sink into the uncon-
querable flow of time.'[17]

The French Caribbean concern with memory is considerably
elucidated by some of these considerations. To begin with, the radical fractures cutting it off from vast tracts of the past have resulted
in Caribbean collective consciousness being not so much trapped or
carried away in Le Goff's 'inconquerable flow of time', as
marooned outside all sense of temporal flow, even if that isolation
is itself copiously narrativized, especially in writing from 1950
onwards. The extraordinary pre-eminence of narrative in French
Caribbean writing, including the narrativization of landscape and
of duration, makes sense, then, as we shall see, in the context of
phenomenological thought.

TIME AND SPACE: RETAINING THE PAST

We noted in the previous chapter that the distant past of the
Caribbean population is spatialized largely because it lies elsewhere. However, when Édouard Glissant turns his attention to the
immediate past, that is, to local time, he also mobilizes the
language of space. This tendency can be explained in terms of his
concern to render a sense of duration as lived time. As the most
rigorous phenomenologists including Husserl and Merleau-Ponty
have found, and as the historians of *longue durée* confirm, it is
difficult to write of lived time in non-spatial terms. In his work on
the intimate relation between space and duration, Gaston
Bachelard noted that duration cannot be remembered as such; it
can only be intellectualized as mathematical time. Its density or
extension are captured, however—that is, materialized or spatialized—in the sedimented trace.[18]

In French, the word for duration, 'durée', has the same
etymology as 'dur' ('hard' or 'unyielding'). Édouard Glissant
notes the link between endurance and duration ('ils enduraient,
ils duraient dans'—'they endured, they in-dured'),[19] and he
suggests that endurance confers 'l'épaisseur de la durée' or the

---

[17] Le Goff, *History and Memory*, pp. xi–xii.
[18] Gaston Bachelard, *La Poétique de l'espace* (1957; Paris: Presses universitaires
de France, 1970), 28.
[19] Édouard Glissant, *Faulkner Mississippi* (Paris: Stock, 1996), 87.

density of duration.[20] In this context, Glissant's predilection for names—both patronyms and toponyms—incorporating the word 'roche' (rock) confirms his preoccupation with duration, more specifically his conviction that 'New World' poetics is focused on an 'effort de durer' or a 'quête de la durée'.[21] For such names underline what becomes 'dur' in what endures or inhabits duration, that is, its resistance or density, its deflection of flow; indeed, the final chapter of *La Case du commandeur* is entitled 'Roche de l'opacité'. In the toponym 'Malendure' in *Mahagony*, connotations of suffering or difficulty—that is, of duress—overlay the notion of endurance, while the place named 'Trou-à-roches' ('Hole-with-rocks') in the same novel emphasizes the link not just between void ('trou') and presence or matter, but also between memory, duration, endurance, and resistance on the one hand, and amnesia on the other. 'Trou de mémoire' means a 'blank', and *La Case du commandeur* is full of references to these black holes of time.[22] However, it is not just the holes in time, but also the mute rocks of memory that resist narrative. Mycéa is thus represented as pounding the rocks of time in an attempt to release sedimented memories.[23] We might imagine that the more time is inhabited by endurance and thus materialized, as tree or rock, for example, the more impacted or unyielding its sedimentation, and the more the fluidity of the narrative process would be stalled or diverted. Yet this materialization or mineralization is in itself a process, albeit a slow one, of accumulation, growth, or maturation, and is not, as such, incompatible with narrative. Furthermore, narrative can flow around impediments.

This localized confrontation between space and time or time and matter fascinates many Caribbean writers, including Patrick Chamoiseau, who is the author of a poetic meditation on the penitentiary ruins in Guyane, the fragile guardians of that dark (and forgotten) site of the intersecting histories of Metropolitan France

---

[20] Glissant, *Faulkner Mississippi*, 87.

[21] Glissant, *Le Discours antillais*, 244, 254.

[22] Glissant, *La Case du commandeur*, 125: 'Nous devons aujourd'hui regarder ce trou du temps sans vertige'. See also Burton, *Le Roman marron*, 120–1.

[23] As Barbara Webb observes, in *La Case du commandeur*, Mycéa and Chérubin 'are the "stonebreakers" of time who pound the rock of history (the memory blocks) to dust in order to achieve a transformation of consciousness': Webb, *Myth and History*, 128.

and the 'New World'.[24] Chamoiseau also wrote the accompanying text to a book of photographs of ruined plantation and refinery buildings in the Caribbean and to a book of photographs of Caribbean homes or *cases*.[25] For Chamoiseau, in fact, place itself, and in particular, dwelling space, stands guard over the memories that it holds. Thus, on the final page of *Antan d'enfance*, he compares the family home in Fort-de-France to a notary, retaining the deeds of his childhood, and standing as an organic witness to the past, alive with 'ancient sap'.[26]

Conversely, Derek Walcott sees the overwhelming physical intrusiveness of the Caribbean natural environment as thwarting access to the past. More specifically, he considers that 'the sigh of History dissolves'[27] when confronted with the overwhelming presence and profusion of Caribbean landscape and vegetation respectively. In other words, Caribbean ruins, as mute witnesses to the disappearance or absence of the past, are rapidly overgrown and obscured by rampant vegetation. Further demonstrating the problematic nature of Caribbean memory, Walcott makes of the structure of Caribbean space as an archipelago scattered like crumbs on the ocean a spatial enactment of fragmentation and discontinuity, and graphic evidence of severance from an assumed prior wholeness: a 'synonym for pieces broken off from the original continent'.[28] Yet, for him, it is the amputated parts, and not the nervous system from which they have been severed, that preserve the memory of past wholeness. Thus, Caribbean geographical fragmentation is read not just as a correlative of historical fracture, but also as a site of impossible memory: impossible not least because the continent from which the Caribbean islands have been severed is not, of course, the continent that their populations remember.

---

[24] Patrick Chamoiseau, *Guyane. Traces-mémoires du bagne* (Caisse nationale des monuments historiques et des sites, 1994).

[25] Patrick Chamoiseau, *Elmire des sept bonheurs*, photograph by Jean-Luc de Laguarigue (Fort-de-France: Habitation Saint-Étienne, and Paris: Gallimard, 1998); Jean-Luc de Laguarigue and Patrick Chamoiseau, *Cases en Pays-Mêlés* (Habitation Saint-Étienne: Traces, 2000).

[26] Patrick Chamoiseau, *Antan d'enfance* (Paris: Hatier, 1990); tr. Carol Volk as *Childhood* (London: Granta, 1999).

[27] Walcott, *What the Twilight Says*, 68.

[28] Ibid. 69.

INDIVIDUAL AND COLLECTIVE MEMORY,
IDENTITY, AND PLACE

What is striking about French Caribbean writing is that so much of
it testifies to a desire to coordinate personal and collective
memory,[29] and to associate identity and memory. As Jacques Le
Goff suggests, this preoccupation could be regarded as universal in
our times: 'memory is an essential element of what will henceforth
be called individual or collective *identity*, the feverish and anxious
quest for which is today one of the fundamental activities of individuals and societies'.[30] However, because French Caribbean past-
consciousness is affected by the kind of 'neurological devastation'
linked to the 'privation of memory or continuity' that has been
studied in individuals by Oliver Sacks,[31] collective memory and the
associated sense of collective identity and continuity are disturbed.
Again, however, the eclipse of, or at least challenge to, temporal
consciousness throughout the final decades of the twentieth
century was not unique to post-slavery, or even ex-colonial, societies. Indeed, Fredric Jameson analyses the postmodern 'crisis in
historicity' in terms of the 'breakdown of temporality' and the
collapse of syntagmatic organization. He suggests that 'the subject
has lost its capacity actively to extend its pro-tensions and re-
tensions across the temporal manifold and to organize its past and
future into coherent experience'.[32] However widespread and even
universal it might be, a searing awareness of a deficit in collective
memory certainly lies at the heart of the literary endeavour of many
French Caribbean writers. Furthermore, a deep concern with the
co-implication of communal and personal identity distinguishes

[29] Paul Ricœur is explicitly committed to an analysis of the connections one could
make between personal memory, as studied by Husserl, for example, and collective
memory as theorized by Maurice Halbwachs, author of *Les Mémoires collectives*
(1950): 'Ce n'est donc avec la seule hypothèse de la polarité entre mémoire indi-
viduelle et mémoire collective qu'il faut entrer dans le champ de l'histoire, mais avec
celle d'une triple attribution de la mémoire: à soi, aux proches, aux autres' ('We
need to approach history, not with the hypothesis of a polarity between individual
and collective memory, but with the hypothesis of a triple attribution of memory: to
oneself, to one's own, and to the others'): Ricœur, *La Mémoire*, 163.
[30] Le Goff, *History and Memory*, 98.
[31] Oliver Sacks, *The Man who Mistook his Wife for a Hat and Other Clinical
Tales* (New York: Harper, 1987), 29, quoted in Eakin, *Touching the World*, 188.
[32] Jameson, *Postmodernism*, 25-7.

Francophone Caribbean autobiographical writing, and indeed post-colonial life/writing in general, from the model of autobiography put forward by Philippe Lejeune. In envisaging autobiography as the 'retrospective narrative in prose that someone makes of his existence, when he places the main emphasis on his individual life, especially on the history of his personality',[33] Lejeune stresses the particularity of the self. It is clear, however, that the kind of autobiographical writing conducted in the Caribbean emphasizes less the singularity of the individual than the self as it is modelled by the social or collective entity that it also serves to reveal (to itself).[34] Thus, although personal recollection or anamnesis may be distinguished from a sense of collective memory and identity, the two are usually interlinked. The strength of that link is variable however. A relation of identity is suggested, for example, between Pipi and the other *djobeurs* in *Chronique des sept misères*: 'comme une seule mangue dit les essences de l'arbre, ce qu'il fut nous le fûmes . . . parler de nous rend inévitable et juste de vous parler de lui' ('just as a single mango tells of the essences of the tree, what he was, we were . . . to speak of us renders it fitting and inevitable to speak of him').[35] Other, more mediated, relations between the individual and the collective are possible, of course. For example, as the motto of the Canadian province of Quebec is 'je me souviens' ('I remember') and not 'on se souvient' or 'nous nous souvenons' ('we remember'), it gestures towards the cultural potency of the implied individual internalization of collective memory. Indeed, it has been noted that autobiography, 'this act of discovery and confirmation of the self' is frequently the founding act of 'nouvelles littératures naissantes' ('new literatures just coming into being').[36] If this is so, it is because of the potential for reciprocal mirroring between a nascent collective identity on the one hand and the narrative of an individual destiny on the other. Moreover, it is axiomatic that the literature of traumatized and

[33] Philippe Lejeune, *Le Pacte autobiographique* (Paris: Seuil, 1975), 14.

[34] Witness Ernest Pépin's *Coulée d'or* (Paris: Gallimard, 1995), Patrick Chamoiseau's *Antan d'enfance* and *Chemin d'école*, and Raphaël Confiant's *Ravines du devant-jour* (Paris: Gallimard, 1993), as well as Chamoiseau's literary autobiography, *Écrire en pays dominé*, which takes up, in a sense, where *Chemin d'école* left off. Se also Gisèle Pineau's *L'Exil selon Julia* (Paris: Stock, 1996) and Marysc Condé's *Le Cœur à rire et à pleurer* (Paris: Robert Laffont, 1999).

[35] Chamoiseau, *Chronique des sept misères*, 16–17.

[36] Preface to Hornung and Ruhe (eds.), *Postcolonialisme & autobiographie*, 1.

recovering cultures is first and foremost a memorial literature that, typically, abounds in first-person *récits de vie* ('life narratives'). The remembering of an individual life thus seems to go some way towards suturing the torn and alienated collective self-image. Francophone Caribbean writing is no exception to this apparent rule; it is, indeed, particularly rich in first-person fictional, autofictional, or autobiographical narratives of recollection.

The reciprocal relation between the sedimentation of a (collective) literary or cultural tradition on the one hand and the autobiographical act on the other is particularly marked in Patrick Chamoiseau's most recent 'essay' *Écrire en pays dominé*. In a section entitled 'Rêver-pays' ('Dreaming-the-Country'), the author undertakes an introspective voyage in which all that distinguishes the individual subject from collective memory, identity, and place is blurred. The journey is articulated not so much in temporal, as in geographical or at least spatial terms: 'Comprendre cette terre dans laquelle j'étais né devint mon exigence. J'étais en elle et elle était en moi. Aller en elle, c'était aller en moi en une boucle sans rivage' ('My first priority was to understand this land in which I had been born. I was in it and it in me. To enter it was to enter myself in a seamless loop').[37] This acknowledged coextensiveness of place and self reproduces the singularly complete identification between the enunciating subject of the opening sentences of Chamoiseau's novel *L'Esclave Vieil Homme et le molosse* and the place of enunciation, those 'terres amères du sucre' ('bitter sugar lands').[38] Not only does the author of *Écrire en pays dominé* signal that the introspective journey is simultaneously an expedition into place, but he also constructs it as a voyage back in time: 'Je revins au magma de ses émergences. Les livres, la parole, les vieilles mémoires, les traces, les intuitions, les souvenirs bégayés ... tout s'érigeait outil de cette quête du profond' ('I returned to the magma of [the land's] emergence. Books, words, ancient memories, remains, intuitions, stuttered reminiscences ... everything became an implement to use in this seach for depth').[39] In this passage, we note, alongside the reference to memory ('vieilles mémoires', 'souvenirs'), an appeal to orality as well as to writing, along with the notion of a search for

---

[37] Chamoiseau, *Écrire en pays dominé*, 97.
[38] See the beginning of Ch. 2.
[39] Chamoiseau, *Écrire en pays dominé*, 97.

'depth', all ideas that suggest Pierre Nora's idea of memory as an organic, deep, and lived connection. Each of the three sections of the book is named by a term ('anagogie', 'anabase') or neologism ('anabiose') that mobilizes the Greek root 'ana' which has both spatial and temporal connotations, meaning both 'up' or 'up into' and 'back'. In relation to the aspiration to connect both with 'depth' and with the past, we note that 'anabase', meaning expedition 'into the interior', also happens to be the title of one of Saint-John Perse's most famous poems: *Anabase*. In this way, Chamoiseau's quest for depth is self-consciously overlaid with (Caribbean-connoted) textual or literary memory: 'Descendre en moi-même—dans l'âme de ce pays—en vigilance pleine et en bel abandon. J'étais en vouloir. . . . cette expédition vers l'intérieur (pour moi: ce *voyage intérieur*) que Perse avait élue dans le mot *Anabase*' ('Going back down into myself—into the soul of this country—in absolute vigilance and with gay abandon. I was in a state of volition . . . willing this expedition towards the interior (in my case this *interior voyage*) that Perse had opted for in the word *Anabase*'.[40]

As his narrative proceeds, Chamoiseau takes on the voices and the (hi)stories of the various cultural entities that overlaid each other and combined to create Caribbean cultural identity. Hence, on his dream journey back through time that he calls, however, a 'rêver-pays', he takes on the composite 'voice' or memory of the 'Moi-Africains', 'Moi-Indiens', 'Moi-Chinois' in which the singular constant of the self ('moi') is conjugated with a variable, plural, or collective identity. Through this sequence of stories, voices, and identities, each one surfacing in turn, a number of different collective memories appear to dictate or to shape Chamoiseau's cultural consciousness. At the same time, the book articulates memories of reading. These allusions to other texts and to other writers ostentatiously parade their divergence from literary history, presenting themselves rather as discontinuous inscriptions of literary memory. Interspersed, then, with the tale of Chamoiseau's own journey of return through the various strata of the Caribbean past are fragmentary comments on his journey as a reader through various literary works. These passages in italics belong to another level of discourse which is emphatically non-narrative, non-linear, and

[40] Ibid. 98–9.

discontinuous, comprising fragments each labelled by a proper noun: for example, Éluard, Yeats, Saint-John Perse, etc. The discontinuity is mitigated however. Although each snippet is identified by the name of the writer with which it is associated, it is not a quotation. The complex, pithy sentences are rather Chamoiseau's own and the cadences, syntax, and tone are constant. Each writer's work has been processed by Chamoiseau's interpretation and memory, resulting in an 'encapsulation' of the named writer's perspective.

The attempted articulation of a sense of collective identity with an individual destiny drives much French Caribbean writing. In *Le Discours antillais*, Glissant explains his literary practice as a novelist in terms of an effort to write a collective novel, or 'le roman du Nous' which he explains as 'le roman de l'implication du Je au Nous, du Je à l'Autre, du Nous au Nous' ('the novel of the relationship of individual to collectivity, of individual to the Other, of We to Us').[41] This 'we' is not, then, a monolithic undifferentiated subject. In *La Case du commandeur*, the 'nous' characterize themselves as 'moi disjoins qui nous acharnions chacun vers ce nous' ('disjointed me's doggedly trying to reach this we').[42] As Celia Britton shows, the collective consciousness is negotiated as a diversity of individual voices, positions, and visions held together by connections and circuits embedded in the language and structures of the narrative.[43] The collective consciousness that Glissant attempts to construct dialogically is, to use Celia Britton's term, 'stereoscopic' and indeed stereophonic.[44] When Maryse Condé castigates the predominance of an order dictating that 'characters should not be individuals but the collective expression of the West Indian soul',[45] she cannot have in mind, then, Glissant's narrative practice. Indeed, in *Mahagony*, Glissant uses self-reflexivity, irony, and *mise en abyme* to show that one of the principal means of

---

[41] Glissant, *Le Discours antillais*, 153; *Caribbean Discourse*, 87.

[42] Glissant, *La Case du commandeur*, 42. The last word of this novel is 'nous': 'Nous, qui avec tant d'impatience rassemblons ces moi disjoints ... dans cette obscurité difficile de nous' ('We, who are so impatiently gathering these disjointed selves ... into this difficult obscurity of we'), p. 239.

[43] See Britton, 'Collective Narrative Voice'.

[44] Ibid. 146.

[45] Maryse Condé, 'Order, Disorder, Freedom, and the West Indian Writer', *Yale French Studies*, 83/2: *Post/Colonial Conditions: Exiles, Migrations, and Nomadisms*, ed. F. Lionnet and R. Scharfman (1993), 121-35: 128.

ensuring that the 'roman du Nous' is suitably fluid, or prevented from congealing, is through 'rewriting'. Thus, in *Mahagony*, Mathieu censures, tongue in cheek, the reductive effects of his own author's writing in previous novels: he claims that the latter, 'this hagiographer of place', enjoyed merging the characters' identities, descendants, and faces into one blurred and overpowering identity: 's'attardait volontiers à confondre les habitants, leur descendance, leurs visages, dans une même indistincte et trop puissante identité'.[46]

EXPLORING OBLIVION

Narrative is not necessarily threatened by forgetting. Glissant's writing shows that narrative can dwell on the nodes or blockages of oblivion and either dissolve or circumvent them. Furthermore, to know that the past is lost to memory is to remember something, if only absence or privation itself. As Chamoiseau writes in *Chemin d'école*: 'L'oubli | parfois | fait mélancolie douce | C'est mémoire | hors mémoire' ('Forgetting | sometimes | brings sweet sadness | it's memory | beyond memory').[47] Such sanguine acceptance of forgetfulness is entirely foreign, however, to the tense narrative of *La Case du commandeur* (1981), driven as it is by an enduring need to confront the past, by first of all locating, and then pounding, the rocks of time. In this text, Glissant pays remarkable attention to amnesia and, in particular, to the absence of any will or desire to remember. In trying to imagine the extinction of the aboriginal population of the forest, the aboriginally named maroon Aa, transported from so far away ('transbordé de si loin') would have been unable (the narrator presumes) to have imagined how rapidly forgetfulness takes hold and how difficult it can be to move back into or beyond a traumatic past.[48] Mathieu in *Le Quatrième Siècle*, on the other hand, is too young to be able fully to understand the urgency of memory, that link between consciousness and the past:

[46] Glissant, *Mahagony* (Paris: Seuil, 1987), 33. The process of rewriting or intertextuality is discussed at more length in Ch. 4.

[47] Chamoiseau, *Chemin d'école*, 148; *School Days*, 112.

[48] '[Aa] ne pouvait présumer combien vite les têtes deviennent ici oublieuses, comme il y est difficile de rameuter le temps passé, son cortège irréel, sa souffrance qu'on ne veut pas croire': Glissant, *La Case du commandeur*, 165.

'Il s'irritait par moments. Ne sachant pas encore combien il est incommode de vivre sans jamais prononcer en connaissance: "Jadis" ' ('Occasionally he would get irritated. Not yet appreciating how uncomfortable life is when you can never say "long ago" and know what it means').[49] In the later novel, however, Glissant injects the question of memory with a much greater sense of urgency. Although *La Case du commandeur* suggests a gender divide between the future-oriented memory characteristic of men and the more present-centred concerns of women, both genders are united in their common fixation on what was lost to memory.

Mathieu produisait en idées ou en mots ce que Mycéa gardait au plus intouchable d'elle-même et défoulait par bouffées en grands balans de vie exagérée. La remontée dans *cela* qui s'était perdu: comment une population avait été forgée . . . s'était accroupie sur elle-même et avait perduré . . . sécrété un langage; comment elle s'usait pour tant d'outrages subis, à oublier. Marie Celat et Mathieu Béluse, sans se le dire, allaient ensemble au fond de cet oubli.[50]

In writing '*cela* qui s'était perdu' ('that which had been lost'), Glissant suggests two things. Firstly, '*cela*' is part of Mycéa's fully remembered, non-contracted name, Marie *Cela*t: hence the quest for the past is associated with a quest for her-self. This identification of self and past is reinforced by Mycéa's internalization of the return to the past, a return that she then 'acts out'. Secondly, self, past, and place are all linked in so far as '*cela*' can be read as '*ce là*', or 'this there', and thus as highlighting the spatialization of the past—constructed as a place or position in space, inflecting the distance of 'there' with the deictic proximity of 'this' ('this there' rather than 'that there').[51] Moreover, the (lost) past is doubly

---

[49] Glissant, *Le Quatrième Siècle*, 266; *The Fourth Century*, 271.

[50] Glissant, *La Case du commandeur*, 188–9; 'Mathieu verbalized what Mycéa retained in the most impregnable part of herself and expelled in great bursts of exaggerated living. The climb back up into this there that had been lost: how a population had been forged . . . had huddled around itself and endured . . . had secreted a language; and how it was wearing itself out trying to forget after all the outrages it had suffered. Marie Celat and Mathieu Béluse, without admitting it to each other, were together getting to the bottom of this forgetfulness'.

[51] Glissant frequently plays on these residual deictics. The ambiguity of '*cela*' is greatly increased, however, if we remember the Creole use of the demonstrative '*là*' as a suffix functioning as the definite article. This Creole structure would mean that the '*la*' modulates the '*ce*', so that '*cela*' could be read as 'that this' instead of 'this there'.

spatialized in the above passage since it is located in the highlands. By climbing back up there ('remontée'), towards the source or the spring, the searchers will discover or recover how exactly a population was forged; how it 'came to ground', as it were, in a particular place (*ce-là*) and wore itself out forgetting the trauma it had endured. The couple set out together, then, to explore the depths ('fond') not so much of the past, as of the amnesia surrounding it. The 'cela' that Mathieu and Mycéa seek is, precisely, lost. But the lost 'oubli' that the pair want to explore is not just the creation of a people, its endurance, and its creativity, but also its effort to forget. It is, above all, the process of forgetting that they want to remember. In this novel a strong but subtle plea is made, then, for remembrance, if only of the shared loss of memory. And that commonality of oblivion is the horizon to which Mycéa looks out in *La Case du commandeur*, as she calls across to the other islands of the archipelago, trying to awaken some sense of their shared situation and history, an effort that precisely points to the lack of reciprocal historical and spatial consciousness in the region.

WRITING MEMORY

Although all literary genres, including poetry, drama, and prose fiction, can be driven by memory and even by reflection on memory, the most vigorous vector of this preoccupation in contemporary literature is perhaps autobiographical narrative. Certainly, it is memory rather than history that predominates in autobiography, a genre aptly described by Daniel Maximin as being less a quest for the past than 'la proposition de sa présence dans l'aujourd'hui' ('the proposition of its presence in the here and now').[52] Of the better-known contemporary French Caribbean writers, Édouard Glissant and Daniel Maximin are the ones that come to mind as having (so far) resisted this peremptory contemporary summons, where Patrick Chamoiseau, Maryse Condé, and Raphaël Confiant have all succumbed. Moreover, in what is arguably Glissant's most 'auto-graphical' work, dating from 1956, the role of memory is slight.

---

[52] Chaulet-Achour and Maximin, 'Sous le signe du colibri', 212.

It is particularly noteworthy that French Caribbean writers show a marked preference for the *récit d'enfance* rather than for full-blown autobiographies. Unlike the latter, which attempt to construct a substantial, if not quite complete, life story and which are thus usually required to make some sort of teleological sense of a destiny, *récits d'enfance* are both modest and ambitious in their memorial aspiration. Because the childhood recounted rarely extends beyond adolescence, the questions of long-term coherence and temporal closure can be more convincingly dispensed with. However, since the personal past which they recall is relatively remote in time, it considerably stretches the capacity to recollect. In this sense, childhood narrative enacts the preoccupation with 'the beginning' that I identified as pivotal in the previous chapter. Moreover, it would seem plausible to read this preference for remembering the tightly circumscribed time-space of childhood as signalling a nostalgic longing for the sense of self-sufficient completeness often associated with childhood. Caribbean childhood can indeed be seen to function not just like a 'beginning', but also like an island in time, or indeed out of time, mirroring the spatial configuration of the *pays*. Hence the perspective of the writer or narrator of Caribbean *récits d'enfance* is often configured as one of exile or *ex-île*, with the result that the narrative becomes a sort of 'cahier d'un retour au pays natal'. Furthermore, the structure of incipience that is particularly appropriate to childhood narrative is in tune with the plot of cultural emergence present or latent in most accounts of Caribbean cultural identity after 1950.

Autobiographical narratives are not, of course, the only writings that explore memory by combining a concern for a life as lived time ('bio') and a concern with writing ('-graphy'). Prose fiction too can thematize or foreground the processes of memory and forgetting realized within and around narratives. The incipit of Chamoiseau's novel *L'Esclave Vieil Homme et le molosse*, discussed at the beginning of the previous chapter, illustrates this point. Most of the writings of Édouard Glissant and of Patrick Chamoiseau are, indeed, consistently remarkable in their commitment to the exploration of what memory is, how it works, and what it means. Yet despite the fact that Chamoiseau features, often by name, in much of his own writing, and despite some similarities that might lead to Mathieu being considered Glissant's alter ego, both writers' novels are for the most part works of fiction, in contrast to other French

Caribbean narratives that present themselves on one level or another as more or less fictionalized *récits de vie*, for example, Joseph Zobel's *La Rue Case-Nègres* or Simone Schwarz-Bart's *Pluie et vent sur Télumée Miracle*. However, one of the most important tensions in these texts, and also in the writing of Glissant, Chamoiseau, Maximin, and others, concerns not so much the relative emphasis on the imagined and the real, on the individual and the collective, on the autobiographical and the fictional, on the pathological and the recuperative, as the tenor of the attention paid to the intertwined processes of memory and writing.

In so far as it is deeply concerned with the question of identity, we might expect 'self writing' or 'life writing' to highlight the quality of the encounter with memory (and forgetting) and to display an acute awareness of the choices, selections, absences, and exclusions involved in writing as recollection (or Husserl's secondary memory). Paul John Eakin registers his surprise, however, at the paucity of such texts that fulfil this expectation.[53] Yet, were he to consider recent French Caribbean writing in general, that is, not just autobiographical writing, he would find a different story. For cultures that have suffered the shock of loss and displacement, the choice between confronting the Symbolic or taking refuge in the Imaginary is, of course, particularly fraught. In fact, most French Caribbean narratives that are motivated by a 'devoir de mémoire' seem to highlight in one way or another what Lacanians call the 'symbolic order', characterized by moments of lack, split, otherness, flux, disjointedness, or intermittence. However, they often do so in ways that are not immediately obvious, by engaging, for example, with the interstitial space of intertextuality or intergenericity. This is not to deny that some narratives tend, rather, towards the Lacanian 'Imaginary', characterized by the attempt to be and to remain ' "what one is" by gathering to oneself ever more instances of sameness, ressemblance and self-replication'.[54] Simone Schwarz-Bart's novel *Pluie et vent sur Télumée Miracle* comes to mind as an outstanding example of the latter orientation. Although transmission,

[53] 'In fact, however, autobiographies that portray this phenomenological narrativity . . . are comparatively rare . . . On the whole, the characteristically retrospective posture of autobiographical discourse does not seem to lend itself easily to the recreation of past consciousness unfolding moment by moment in the successive presents of the past': Eakin, *Touching the World*, 206.

[54] Malcolm Bowie, *Lacan* (London: Fontana, 1991), 92.

as one of the principal processes of collective memory and identity, is indeed thematized within the narrative of *Pluie et vent sur Télumée Miracle*, the processes of transmission and writing enacted by the novel's narrative itself are not acknowledged, much less foregrounded. Simone Schwarz-Bart has stated in an interview that Télumée is based on a real-life Guadeloupean woman called Stéphanie Priccin (also known as Fanotte), yet this text nowhere problematizes itself as narrative, memory, or transmission. In Zobel's autobiographical novel, the status of the narrative is not directly addressed, either. Indeed the narrative seems to take place 'outside time, apart from the life it is engaged in re-creating'.[55] Yet whereas Schwarz-Bart's novel begins and ends in the same place (with the narrator in her garden looking back over her life), in Zobel's *La Rue Cases-Nègres*, the narrative distance from the diegesis is acknowledged in the novel's dated signature in Fontainebleau. It is significant, indeed, that Euzhan Palcy's film of the novel opens with a sepia-tinted montage of pictures of the colonial Caribbean, as though to underscore the temporal distance of memory, a gap that might not otherwise be adequately registered in the film's diegesis, but that the novel as signed, dated, and located narrative clearly implies.

In general, where memory and identity are problematized, the present tense of discourse predominates over the historical tenses, and the narration tends to be highly self-reflexive. This pattern can be discerned particularly clearly in the writing of Patrick Chamoiseau, Édouard Glissant, and Daniel Maximin, although it can also be seen in the work of Gisèle Pineau and Raphaël Confiant. It is in this sense that these authors highlight, for example, the fitfulness of memory, the bristling jumble of motives that influence narrative processes, or the concern with authentification that often gives way to a wanton delight in the play of imagination and writing. In the next chapter I shall look in more detail at how the highlighting of writing itself relays the exploration of memory.

MEMORY AND DISPLACEMENT

Although many writers, for example Maryse Condé and Gisèle

---

[55] Eakin, *Touching the World*, 207.

Pineau, focus less on place than on displacement, less on location than on dislocation, this does not mean that their work does not examine memory. Rather, the functioning or dysfunction of memory is focalized through the imagination of displacement. In *La Colonie du nouveau monde*, for example, Condé imagines a small and doomed 'New Age', sun-worshipping, utopian colony in Colombia. This colony is, perhaps, a metaphor for all 'New World' communities that bear memories of the lost or abandoned places of the past. 'Tiyi', the Guadeloupean wife of the colony's Caribbean leader-god, is destabilized by memories now grown dim of what she had once been and of what had led her to revolt against her previous condition:

Peu à peu, comme à son habitude, le temps avait fait la toilette du souvenir et elle en était venue à oublier ce qu'elle reprochait aux siens. Son enfance et son adolescence lui revenaient en mémoire comme un paradis perdu. Était-ce bien vrai qu'elle avait été ce qu'elle avait été?[56]

The epistemology of memory, or its uncertain fiduciary value, is also registered as a preoccupation in the epigraph to Gisèle Pineau's autofictional work, *L'Exil selon Julia*: 'Hasards de la mémoire, inventions? Tout est vrai et faux, émotions. Ici, l'essentiel voisine les souvenirs adventices' ('Random memory, or invention? Everything is both true and false, emotion. Here, what is fundamental lies right beside adventitious memories').[57] In this novel, uncertainty regarding memory is indissociably linked to the theme of repeated displacement: the narrator is a second-generation Caribbean immigrant to Metropolitan France and her grandmother, the eponymous Julia, is uprooted from Guadeloupe and transported to France by her family. It is the shock of dislocation that moves Pineau's narrator to question the link between memory, invention, transmission, and usurpation.

Les souvenirs sont déparés ou volés à d'autres mémoires. Seules les photos glacées s'ouvrent sur des flaques de lumière. Le passé vit de l'autre côté des cadres dentelés. Par-delà, une marmaille qui ne grandira jamais continue à

---

[56] Maryse Condé, *La Colonie du nouveau monde* (Paris: Robert Laffont, 1993), 15; 'Little by little, time—as was its wont—had renovated memory and Tiyi had come to forget what she had against her family. Now memory of her childhood and adolescence struck her as a lost paradise. Was it true that she really had been what she had been?'

[57] Pineau, *L'Exil selon Julia*, 7.

courir, à rire et à pleurer. . . . Aujourd'hui encore, j'enjambe le temps avec
facilité pour retomber sitôt dans l'aise de mes cinq ans . . . Se contenter
d'un seul cliché, même si flou, raté, déchiré.
  Reconstruire les heures éboulées.
  Réinventer le soleil du jour.
  Modeler les images qui viennent.
  Défier les temps, les mêler, briser leurs cours . . .[58]

In the above passage, photographs trigger both memory (as reconstruction) and imagination as (re)creation; not only does the imagination embroider memories, but it reinvents or reconfigures them.
For the narrator, glossy photographs are like pools of light, the
liquid image reinforcing the notion of fluidity and flexibility.
Instead of attributing to photographs a retentive role, Pineau
stresses that they inspire the reimagination of the past. Confirming
that the connection between photography and memory is a fertile
one for the writing of memory, the eponymous narrator of Vincent
Placoly's novel *La Vie et la mort de Marcel Gonstran* begins his
'autobiographie' by evoking family photograph albums as a 'pique-
nique du souvenir' ('picnic of memory'), adding, however, that
these 'images saintes' ('holy images') of family history have their
price, in that the memories that they trigger are not always those
that we might choose.[59] Playing on the metaphor of memory as
picnic, he proceeds to recount his memory of an actual family
picnic on the beach that ended with his uncle's corpse being recov-
ered from the sea. For Placoly's Gonstran, then, memory cannot be
denied or disguised, that is, obliterated or rearranged, at will, any
more than his uncle's 'grotesque' and swollen body, which was kept
out of the snapshots of the fateful picnic, but which could not be
erased from his memory of the outing.
  The word 'selon' ('according to') in the title of Pineau's *L'Exil
selon Julia* signifies attribution and transmission, and the novel

---

[58] Pineau, *L'Exil selon Julia*, 51–2; 'Memories are disfigured or stolen from other
minds. Only the glossy photographs open out onto pools of light. The past still lives
on the other side of the jagged frames. Beyond them, children who will never grow
up still run, laugh and cry . . . Even today I step across time with no bother and at
once I fall back into the pleasure of my sixth year . . . just one snapshot is enough,
no matter how blurred, botched, or torn. Enough for reconstructing the avalanched
hours. For reinventing that day's sun. For shaping the images that come. Defying
time, mixing it all up, interrupting its flow . . .'.
[59] Vincent Placoly, *La Vie et la mort de Marcel Gonstran* (Paris: Éditions Denoël,
1971), all quotes from p. 89.

indeed highlights the dialogical dynamic of transmission on which memory (as opposed to imagination) often depends, particularly in cultures affected by displacement and dislocation. I noted in the previous chapter the predominance of meta-narratives, like those of Médouze and Papa Longoué, which are inscribed in a plot of transmission. Like Mathieu in *Le Quatrième Siècle* and José in *La Rue Cases-Nègres*, the narrators of texts as diverse as Patrick Chamoiseau's *Antan d'enfance* and Michel Ponnamah's *Dérive de Josaphat* are in 'belated positions'[60] and so must rely on the memory of others in order to reconstruct their own past. In both texts, the chief informant is the narrator's mother or grandmother, but in Ponnamah's novel, maternal memory is represented as inadequate.[61] Whereas Josaphat's mother can remember the world of the plantation perfectly, her recall of 'le passé indien' is weak. What is original about Ponnamah's representation of memory is that the narrator suggests that his mother's deficient memory is strategic. He singles out for particular criticism the various unsatisfactory versions of her account of how Indians were tricked into coming to the Caribbean as indentured workers. Her failure to name those responsible for this story of betrayal and exploitation, and to identify their Caribbean descendants, is likened to the pacifism of a mother who hides the history of family quarrels and, by implication, to the moral abdication of the folktale that turns Caribbean history into a fairytale that protects the identity of the real-life villains.

In many French Caribbean narratives, secondary displacement represents a supplementary challenge to memory and/or transmission. Hence, for the narrator of *L'Exil selon Julia*, the transmission process is particularly precarious because the temporal erosion of memory is exacerbated by the discontinuity of emigration from the Caribbean to Metropolitan France. Another of Pineau's novels, *L'Espérance-Macadam*, is structured—like Ponnamah's narrative of Indian transportation—not so much around the unwilled erosion or disruption of memory or the fertile tension between imagination and memory, as around the deliberate or strategic

---

[60] 'Quand le négrillon survint, les cuisines étaient mortes' ('By the time the little boy came along, the kitchens were dead'): Chamoiseau, *Antan d'enfance*, 40; *Childhood*, 24.

[61] Michel Ponnamah, *Dérive de Josaphat* (Paris: L'Harmattan, 1991), 98–100.

displacements that can block or disrupt the transmission of memory, filiation, and identity. Similarly, many of Maryse Condé's novels, for example *Desirada* and *La Vie scélérate*, are concerned with the secrets, displacements, and deviations that block access to the truth of the past. In Condé's *Traversée de la mangrove*, too, there is an obsession with retrieving, this time through the multiplication of points of view, the complex and indeed plural truth of an obscured, diverted, or foreclosed past. A luminous example of how displacement inhibits memory is the counter-epiphany that is perhaps the climax of José's narrative of education in Zobel's *La Rue Cases-Nègres*. This revelation that comes in the shape of a black hole in memory, a 'trou de mémoire', occurs towards the end of the narrative, when José's beloved grandmother dies. The boy is far away, being educated in the town, when he learns of his bereavement. His stricken inability to summon up the beloved grandmother's face not only encapsulates his own story of displacement—a story of assimilation and estrangement—but it also condenses the original collective shock of transportation and loss, thus recalling the trauma of an entire population: its wounded memory, broken bonds, and fissured minds.

In the context of Caribbean memory, the leitmotif of the grandmother is particularly significant. Beyond the sociological specificity of post-slavery family structures, in which grandmothers play a particularly crucial nurturing role, the grandmother is—in more general psychoanalytical terms—the 'mère déplacée vers l'origine, la mère de la mère, métonymie maternelle' ('mother displaced towards the origin, the mother of the mother, a maternal metonymy').[62] Thus, in addition to having particular responsibility for transmission and acculturation, M'man Tine in *La Rue Cases-Nègres*, Toussine in *Pluie et vent sur Télumée Miracle*, Eudoxie in *La Case du commandeur*, and Man Julia in *L'Exil selon Julia* are emblematic of a certain continuity of discontinuity (the absence, abdication, or displacement of the mother), yet their ancestral aura compensates, perhaps, for the deficit of 'New World' memory and for the disruption of direct transmission from one generation to the (very) next.

The text that will be explored in the remainder of this chapter is

---

[62] Maximilien Laroche quoting Louis Marin in Laroche, *La Double Scène de la représentation*, GRELCA Essais 8 (Quebec: Université de Laval, 1991), 191.

perhaps the foremost exploration of memory in Caribbean writing between 1950 and 2000. Its fidelity to the vision of *créolité* ensures, however, that its concern with memory is articulated in terms of place rather than displacement, and with regard to intransitive processes of writing rather than the more transitive dynamic of transmission.

COURTING MEMORY: *ANTAN D'ENFANCE*

Antan d'enfance, the first volume of Patrick Chamoiseau's childhood memoirs, is structured into two sections, entitled 'Sentir' ('smelling' or 'sensing') and 'Sortir' ('going out'). As in Jean-Paul Sartre's *Les Mots*, also divided into two sections, 'Lire' ('reading') and 'Écrire' ('writing'),[63] a centripetal movement precedes a centrifugal one, although, whereas 'sortir' clearly refers to space, the centripetal orientation of the verb 'sentir' is only activated by association with the sister-title. This sequence clearly suggests that the first part of the text, set in the home, is concerned with the introspective, private self, whereas the second part represents the first stages of an opening onto public space. The entire second section of *Antan d'enfance* presents, indeed, the child's increased curiosity towards the outside world, or the wider urban community. Yet, in so far as the space represented in this work is restricted to the home and to a limited number of familiar locales in the immediate neighbourhood regarded as an extension of the home, it corresponds to the constraints of the *créolité* programme, which defines itself, as we have seen, as an exploration of the depths of the Creole self, the inscape of Creole identity. It is only in the second volume of Chamoiseau's childhood memoirs, *Chemin d'école*, its title—literally, The Path to School—suggesting a certain mobility and teleology, that the encounter with the machinery of French assimilation is treated. The reservation of the term 'enfance'

---

[63] The sequel to *Antan d'enfance*, entitled *Chemin d'école*, shares this pendulum structure; it is divided into two sections: 'Envie', 'Survie'. And Chamoiseau's first novel, *Chronique des sept misères* (1986), is also divided into two sections, the first again centripetal ('inspiration'), and the second centrifugal ('expiration'). All three texts are in this sense both linearized and vectorized (as internalization, then externalization). The two sections of the novel further suggest orality, and so inscribe the double time rhythm of breathing (and voice production) into the space of the text.

for the first volume is significant, even if this sense of pertinence is undone in the subsequent repackaging of both texts as the two volumes of a single work entitled *Une enfance créole*. Emphasizing the question of cultural identity, this umbrella title effects a certain de-temporalization, in that it obliterates the reference to time central to each of the separate volume titles: 'Antan', derived from the Latin 'anteannum', meaning 'yesteryear', phonetically sounds out 'en temps' or 'in the time of'. The apposition of the preposition 'en' ('in') to nouns, emphasizing containment, dwelling, or interiority as constitutive of their meaning, is a common morphological element of Creole ('en-ville' and 'en-France' thus function as nouns). The rich phonetic echo of this morpheme in the words 'antan' and 'enfance', the latter marking the titles of both the first volume and the two-volume unit, and also indeed in the first subtitle of *Antan d'enfance* ('sentir'), resonates with the importance in this text of retentive space and time. The house, the yard, the attic, under the stairs, etc. are all Bachelardian containing spaces that also indeed hold time, retaining its ceaseless flow. In the second volume, however, the flow is fully released as the child takes the path ('chemin') leading to school, out of childhood and forth from the home.

REMEMBERING AND NARRATIVE, SPACE AND DURATION

The narrator of *Antan d'enfance* enunciates at some length his view of the relation between perception and reality. He believes that childhood is less a state of grace in which the true nature of reality is perceived 'unmediated' than a time of transition, in which a shell is progressively secreted around the self. This carapace will eventually cut us off completely from the immediate, inchoate, even pre-verbal aliveness to reality that characterizes childhood. It is only by not maturing that we could avoid this gradual corruption of the capacity to see things undeformed by the taxonomic grids that gradually adhere to vision. Chamoiseau's narrator distinguishes between what the adult regards as 'réalité' in all its comforting and classified stability, and le 'réel',[64] to which the child has immediate

---

[64] 'On ne quitte pas l'enfance, on se met à croire à la réalité, ce que l'on dit être le réel' ('You never leave childhood, you begin to believe in reality, what is said to be real'): *Antan d'enfance*, 78; *Childhood*, 53 (subsequent page references use the abbreviations *AE* and *C*).

perceptual access, and which is uncomfortable, jagged, complex, shifting, and unpredictable. Thus growing up, as Chamoiseau constructs it, means replacing latency by cognition; maturing is a defensive process, a matter of constructing 'entre cette perception et soi le bouclier d'une enveloppe mentale. Le poète—c'est pourquoi—ne grandit jamais, ou si peu' ('a mental shield between this perception and the self. That's why poets never grow up, or so little') (*AE* 79; *C* 53). Time thus brings loss and abdication rather than acquisition, in that, paradoxically, as the child proceeds in his or her inventory of the world, reducing to familiarity the strangeness of things, this very process neutralizes the capacity to perceive mystery, and so the world is denuded not just of its magical aura but also of its chaotic truth. Only the poet escapes, more or less, this encasement.

Childhood is, then, a time of passage. And Chamoiseau's text is an attempt to re-enter this passage (of time) on which the narrator has superimposed a particular plot: loss as sclerosis. The 'envelope' to which the text is to bear witness is thus sealed as the child gradually takes it inventory of the world: it was an 'enveloppe' (translated as 'enclosure') 'construite à mesure qu'effeuillant le rêve et le mystère, tu inventoriais le monde' ('constructed while plucking off petals of mystery and dream, you were taking inventory of the world') (*AE* 11; *C* 3). This process cuts childhood off fairly definitively. Worse, there is, then, no memory. 'Il n'y a pas de mémoire, mais une ossature de l'esprit, sédimentée comme un corail, sans boussole ni compas' ('just a skeleton of the spirit, sedimented like coral, with neither chart nor compass') (*AE* 158; *C* 113). It is impossible, then, to break through this coral of cognition; it is rigid, impacted, and fixed, and no way can be found through it back to 'le réel'. The only way to bear witness to childhood vision is perhaps to recognize its foreclosure and its irrecuperable loss. There is an apparent tension, however, between this admission of impossibility and the impression that the entire weight of anamnesis will be brought to bear on an attempt to pace out childhood, 'l'arpenter dans ses états magiques, retrouver son arcane d'argile et de nuages' ('survey it in its magical states, recover its mystery of clay and clouds') (*AE* 11; *C* 3). How is anamnesis to render a sense of the strangeness and magic of childhood? In aiming at a moving target (namely a process of transformation or sedimentation), the narrator chooses a mobile mode of recovery: active traversal. In attempting to track the 'en-temps' ('in-timeness') or the in-passage quality of childhood, he will sabotage his narrative by resorting more and more often to snatches of poetry. These fragments are discrete islands of text that hold (narrative) time still. Their puncturing of the prose and disruption of the chronological flow of the narrative give, perhaps, a sense both of the unmastered relentlessness of time and also of the ruptures of that flow, breaks or suspensions said to be germane to the child's vision of the world. The narrator has pointed out explicitly, after all, that the child's gaze is similar in quality to that of the poet. Rather, then, than approaching childhood by recollection (alone), the narrator will mobilize poetry, because the poet's vision is analogous to that of the child. Hence, while apparently attempting to recover the past and to establish its sequence, this text suggests at another level that the gaze of the child survives only in the discontinuities, detours, inventions, and ellipses germane to poetic insight.

Not only is the entire project of *Antan d'enfance* framed by lyrical passages of reflection on the problematic nature of memory, but this self-reflexive strategy is underlined by recurrent references throughout the text to the operation of memory. And yet, despite his attempt to structure his approach in more creative ways than the conventionally chronological, Chamoiseau nonetheless refers to these conventions: 'où débute l'enfance?' ('where does childhood begin?') he asks towards the beginning of his text. And symmetrically, towards the end, 'Où s'achève l'enfance?' ('Where does childhood end?') (*AE* 157; *C* 112). However, his concern here is precisely to question the closure that would inscribe time in spans marked out by a clear beginning and a clear end. In the same spirit of scepticism, he also acknowledges his lack of mastery over memory: 'Quelle est cette dilution? Et pourquoi erres-tu dans cette poussière dont tu ne maîtrises pas l'envol?' ('What is this dilution? And why do you wander in this dust whose scattering you cannot contain?') (*AE* 157; *C* 112). Even more fundamentally, he raises the question of agency: 'Mémoire, qui pour toi se souvient? Qui a fixé tes lois et procédures? Qui tient l'inventaire de tes cavernes voleuses?' ('Memory, who remembers for you? Who fixed your laws and procedures? Who keeps inventory in your thieving caves?') (*AE* 157; *C* 112). Despite the chronological concern of the apostrophes directed at memory and despite the frequent invocation of his mother, 'la haute confidente', the chief guarantor of the accuracy of certain memories,[65] the narrator's apparent interest in authentication and linearity is explicitly undermined on several occasions. As an example of this ambivalent attitude towards the relation between memory and imagination, or memory and truth, we could cite an incidence of memory policing the border between fact and fiction and catching out memory as imaginative reconstruction: 'La seule crainte de Man Ninotte en course derrière le sien (cochon) était qu'on le lui vole mais, à l'écrire, j'ai soudain souvenance que rien à l'époque ne se volait' ('Ma Ninotte's only fear as she ran after her own [pig] was that it would be stolen, but as I write this, I suddenly remember that nothing at the time was stolen') (*AE* 51; *C* 32). Similarly, in the question 'Mémoire, tu t'emballes?' ('Memory, are you taking off?') (*AE* 156; *C* 111), memory is represented as getting carried away with itself. As the pig runs away, so the writer's imagination runs off too, but it is apprehended and carried back to the facts by the vigilance of memory's own border patrols. The narrator is ultimately complicit, however, with the organic link between memory and imagination. After all, he addresses memory thus: 'Mémoire, je vois ton jeu: tu prends racine et te structures dans l'imagination, et cette dernière ne fleurit qu'avec toi' ('Memory, I see your game: you take root and form in the imagination, and the latter blossoms only through you') (*AE* 58; *C* 37). The virus of memory thus invades the imagination, but the host thrives on this occupation, and the play of this symbiotic pair manipulates not just chronology, but also spatial relations. In addition to confusing different chronological stretches, it also mixes up sensations and places, creating, for example, relations that never existed between certain places and certain feelings: 'Enfance, c'est richesse dont jamais tu n'accordes géographie très claire. Tu y bouscules les époques et les âges, les rires et l'illusion d'avoir ri, les lieux et les sensations qui n'y sont jamais nés' ('Childhood is a treasure whose geography you never clearly reveal. In it you mix up eras and ages, laughter and the illusion of having laughed, places and sensations that weren't even born there') (*AE* 11-12; *C* 3).

In the face of vacillating recall, rather than lamenting memory's

---

[65] The narrator's mother, usually referred to as 'la haute confidente' ('the Prime Confidante') (*AE* 13; *C* 4), is frequently invoked as a guarantor of the narrator's memories.

unreliability, the narrator vaunts his freedom to choose the version of events that he prefers:

O mémoire sélective. Tu ne te souviens plus de sa disparition. Dans quels combles as-tu rangé sa mort? L'as-tu vu flottant ventre en l'air dans le bassin de la cour, ou gardes-tu trace de son corps recroquevillé sur une marche d'escalier? . . . Il s'est peut-être campé entre deux rêves, et il reste là, momifié dans une insomnie devenue éternelle. Mémoire, c'est là ma décision. (AE 49)[66]

In this way, *Antan d'enfance* demystifies memory and promotes writing. Not only does the writer suggest that memory is impossible, and the past irrecoverable, but he also shows how false memory can convince us that we have lost something that we never, in fact, possessed or experienced at all.

Et quand s'écoule d'un au-delà des yeux, sans annonce ni appel, un lot de souvenirs, quand s'élève en bouffée la mensongère estime d'un temps heureux, que l'on réinvestit cette période sorcière transformative où chaque brin du monde donnait lecture des possibles du monde . . . et que l'on s'y sent, non pas étranger, mais en humeur d'exilé. (AE 12)[67]

In this passage, the narrator begins by evoking the involuntary or uninvited nature of memory and the aleatory rag-bag of memories that it turns up. Then the emphasis shifts to the question of illusion or delusion linked to mendacious regard ('estime') for a 'happy time'. The focus on memory slips then, and it is the remembered time, the time of childhood, and *its* transformative wizardry that is emphasized. Yet, the effect of memory in this instance is that we feel, not as we should, like foreigners in unfamiliar territory, but rather as exiles, cast out from a once familiar place or time. If the nostalgic haze can delude us into yearning to recover a regard ('estime') that we never felt, another source of illusion is the

---

[66] 'O selective memory. You no longer remember his disappearance. In which attic did you store his death? Did you see him floating belly-up in the courtyard tub, or do you retain a vision of his hunched body on one of the steps . . . Perhaps he set up camp between two dreams and remains there, mummified in an eternal insomnia. Memory, that is my decision' (C 31).

[67] 'And when from somewhere beyond the visible a batch of memories flows, unannounced and uncalled, when the illusory reckoning of a happy time rises in a burst of wind, when one re-examines this bewitching period in which every scrap of world gave a reading of the world's possibilities . . . and when one feels there more exiled than foreign, is it I who remember, memory, or you who remember for me?' (C 3–4).

erosion of the distinction between experience and transmission. Thus, the narrator wonders whether he himself remembers certain things, whether memory is acting in some sense independently of him, or whether he has been told about his childhood so often that he has come to remember the emotions that he is supposed to have felt then: 'Celle-ci lui fut par la suite tellement évoquée que l'homme d'aujourd'hui en conserve une douleur rémanente' ('Subsequently the episode has been mentioned so often that the man of today bears a residual pain') (*AE* 60; *C* 39).

Antan d'enfance ends on a note that remains faithful both to the absence and presence at the heart of memory.[68] It combines the inflection of desire, that untold longing that bespeaks lack, and the inflection of fulfilment, reflected in the completeness, the phatic fullness, of the circular letter 'O'. The text does not so much come to an end—there is no full stop—as rebound or reverberate on the word 'dire'. It peters out on the desire 'to say' or 'to tell', reaching out in communion to a confraternity of listeners, thus refusing narrative closure in favour of discursive openness: 'Mes frères O, je voudrais vous dire' ('My brothers, oh, how I want you to know').

[68] *AE* 165; *C* 117. This final appeal echoes an earlier acclamation—one of the two epigraphs to the text, 'partageurs ô | Vous savez cette enfance! | (il n'en reste rien | mais nous en gardons tout)' ('O sharers, | you know how childhood is! | (there's nothing left of it | but we keep it all)'); *C*, p. ix)—which also reconciles loss and plenty, absence and presence, emphasizing too, like the last line of the book, the phatic dimension of an enunciative relation constructed as a relation of community or belonging, and the lack of anything more to say. The poetry and the poignancy of this 'ending' are heightened by the reverberation of these closing words in the sister or sequel text, *Chemin d'école*, which opens with these selfsame words: 'Mes frères O, je voudrais vous dire' (p. 17).

CHAPTER FOUR

The Time-Space of Writing: Voicing Continuities and Texturing Traditions

tout s'oublie, tout se recrée[1]

ORALITY AND WRITING IN THE FRENCH CARIBBEAN

The dynamic between the spoken and the written word is a particularly productive one in French Caribbean culture. Given the crucial, if corralled, place of oral culture in the colonial era, and given the historical use of literacy, particularly perhaps in French, as an instrument of colonial domination by assimilation, the standing of writing in the ex-colonial or neo-colonial Caribbean is bound to be complex. While recognizing the special place of oral production in French Caribbean history and culture, Édouard Glissant is careful to distinguish between the status of the oral tradition in what he terms 'cultures ataviques' or 'atavistic cultures', on the one hand, and in 'cultures composées' or 'composite cultures', on the other.[2] This distinction allows him to avoid setting up a binary opposition between Caribbean orality and writing. Such facile polarization, apart from being a distortion of the two cultural modes, would negate the hybrid spirit of the Creole language, which is the principal vector, after all, of French Caribbean orality. In a deft turn of phrase, Glissant sidesteps dialectic, describing the dynamic between writing and orality in

---

[1] 'everything is forgotten, everything is recreated': Glissant, *Mahagony*, 95.
[2] Édouard Glissant, 'Le Chaos-Monde: L'oral et l'écrit', in Ludwig (ed.), *Écrire la 'parole de nuit'*, 118.

terms of writing 'recomposing' oral production.[3] The notion of recomposition suggests both the creation of a new composite, and also the recreation, recovery, or renewal of what was *already composite*. In this sense, Glissant sees Creole oral culture as being different in kind to African oral culture, and he denies that the former is directly descended from the latter, the *conteur* from the *griot*, the *parole* from the *palabres*.[4]

Since it champions Creole, the *créolité* movement is predictably attentive to the value of oral culture, which is coterminous to a large extent with the poetics of the vernacular. In their reverence for the *conteur*, or *maître de la parole*, the authors of *Lettres créoles* set the storyteller's verbal mastery against the power of the colonial master. More specifically, they replace the myth of the heroic maroon or fugitive slave with the myth of the 'Master of the Word', whose ascendancy is attributed to his/her role as keeper of the tongue and guardian of Creole community. In other versions of Creole culture, however, the role of *conteur* merges with that of the *quimboiseur*, sorcerer or medicine man/woman. Significantly, and unlike Édouard Glissant or Simone Schwarz-Bart, for example, the writers of the *créolité* movement do not emphasize this convergence of verbal and extra-verbal vocations, although they do stress the subversive power of the *conteur* during slavery. For them, 'la Parole' (the spoken Word) is *the* instrument or locus of power and no further magic is necessary. In the literary landscape after 1950, the *conteur* is still, then, a crucial figure: Médouze, Papa Longoué, Toussine, Solibo, Esternome, and Julia are all memorable in the role.

The style of spoken utterance, and of associated cultural production—for example, the *conte* or Creole folktale—is deeply embedded in much French Caribbean writing. Simone Schwarz-Bart's *Ti Jean l'Horizon* (1979), Xavier Orville's *L'Homme aux sept noms et des poussières* (1981), and Ernest Pépin's *L'Homme au bâton*

---

[3] Ibid. 113.
[4] Chamoiseau and Confiant observe a similar distinction in *Lettres créoles*, noting of the *conteur* that: 'même s'il cherche à mobiliser en lui uniquement l'Afrique mère, il est créole—c'est-à-dire déjà multiple, déjà mosaïque, déjà imprévisible, et sa langue est la langue créole, elle-même déjà ... mosaïque et ouverte' (pp. 37–8) ('even if he seeks to mobilize Mother Africa alone, he is Creole—in other words, already multiple, already mosaic, already unpredictable and his language is Creole, itself already an open mosaic').

(1992) are just three novels which show that short fiction—
Myriam Warner-Vieyra's collection of stories, *Femmes échouées*
(1988), or Roger Parsemain's work, for example[5]—is not the only
literary genre to recycle the folktale or to be imprinted with oral
modes of expression. The fact that the title of a dialogical volume
comprising short prose fiction and critical essays by several major
Caribbean authors and critics is *Écrire la 'parole de nuit'* (Writing
the 'Nighttime Talk') and that the subtitle reads *La Nouvelle
Littérature antillaise* (New Caribbean Literature), further confirms
that the connection between the written and the spoken word (in
that title reduced rather unfortunately to a transitive relation) is
still one of the principal dynamics fuelling contemporary
Caribbean writing. Other titles in the primary or secondary literature invoke orality too: for example, Maryse Condé's *La Parole des
femmes* (1979; Women's Talk), Myriam Warner-Vieyra's *Le
Quimboiseur l'avait dit* (1980; As the Sorcerer Said), or Colette
Maximin's *La Parole aux masques* (1991; The Spoken Word and its
Masks). But given that cultural authenticity and authority are
consistently related to the dynamic of orality by Glissant,
Chamoiseau, Pineau, and others, one might expect even more titu-
lar reference to orality. That this expectation is not met reflects, of
course, the bald fact that the principal *lieu de mémoire* of oral
culture in the French Caribbean after 1950 is, precisely, the written
word. Just as the vernacular needed to be written down in order to
survive, so too the tensions and crossings between oral tradition
and scriptural modernity keep alive the memory of oral culture.
Indeed, it is often when French Caribbean texts are at their most
writerly, when they emphasize their own 'textuality' most insistently, that they are most successful in 'memorializing' the spoken
word.

Ralph Ludwig introduces *Écrire la 'parole de nuit'* by underlining what he calls the division ('clivage')[6] between two cultures, oral
and written, going on to suggest the predominance of a 'concern
with [the] synthesis'[7] that would link them. While it is undoubtedly
helpful to point to the apartness of the time and space of Creole
oral culture, the notion of a dialectic based on an orality/writing

[5] Roger Parsemain, *L'Absence du destin* (Paris: L'Harmattan, 1992) and *Il chantait des boléros* (Pointe-à-Pitre: Ibis Rouge, 1999).
[6] Ludwig (ed.), *Écrire la 'parole de nuit'*, 15.
[7] Ibid. 18.

dichotomy and on an eventual or desired synthesis is misleading. By over-emphasizing the supposed dichotomy, this approach reduces a complex relation rather dramatically in comparison with the anti-teleological circumspection of Édouard Glissant's chiaroscura. Glissant is careful to recognize that, in the Caribbean, oral culture always existed *alongside* writing. Even if most of those who spoke Creole were not literate, they were living in a world where the French matrix of many Creole words existed in written form, and was indeed written down, if only in plantation registers. Moreover, Glissant's use of the term 'recomposition' ('recomposer') to refer to the readjustment of a pre-existing relation between orality and writing echoes the French expression 'composer avec', meaning to compromise. His notion therefore suggests the renegotiation of a prior compromise. In the Caribbean, it is not just a question of two 'different' languages, Creole and French, occupying the same time (diglossia)[8] and much more rarely and restrictively the same socio-cultural space too (bilingualism), as did Irish and English in colonized Ireland, for example. For Creole is itself a composite, a compromise that incorporates at least one highly literate language. Furthermore, the notion of a dichotomy between writing and orality is just as flawed as the notion of a division between Creole and French. Writing cannot, in fact, be conceptualized independently of orality, any more than Creole can be thought of independently from French. Hence, any 're-composed' relation between the two languages or between the two modes of language, oral and written, will of necessity be incestuous.

SOUNDING WRITING, OR FROM ETYMOLOGY TO *ÉCRITURE*

For Walter Ong, the word is 'articulated sound', and writing commits the word to space.[9] He notes, furthermore, that writing is

---

[8] We must imagine Zobel's Médouze as a 1930s *conteur* officiating even as Césaire is penning his *Cahier* and as MacKay is writing *Banjo*, the novel that will make such an impression on the newly literate José. Much earlier still, the plantation chronicles and registers and the accounts of Le Père Labat and Le Père du Tertre were being written in French even as the Creole language was being 'composed' and mobilized both in the heights and on the plains.

[9] See Ong, *Orality and Literacy*, 7.

a 'particularly pre-emptive and imperialist activity', making it extraordinarily difficult for literate cultures to conceptualize 'pure' orality, or what he calls 'primary' oral cultures.[10] Although Ong does not cite it as such, etymology is perhaps one of the more significant vectors of the colonizing reach of writing. Certainly, our understanding of words can be greatly influenced by our perception of their temporal depth, a dimension usually revealed in the orthography, or the written form of the word. Our earlier etymological consideration of the terms 'Creole' or 'Antilles' shows that etymology, as one of the chief vectors of the history of meaning, is indeed tracked through literation.

One of the most vigorous late-twentieth-century movements in literary criticism centred on the semantic reverberations of the signifier triggered by writing. These provisional, textually specific, semantic relations generated by phonetic patterns are defined and promoted as 'écriture' or 'writing' by late-twentieth-century French critics and writers such as Jacques Derrida, Julia Kristeva, and Hélène Cixous. As the semantic productivity of *écriture* shows, and as Derrida's *De la grammatologie* seeks to explain in detail,[11] sound thus can and does reclaim, and indeed overgrow, the space of writing: for example, in the phonetic echoing suggested in the previous chapter between *en*-ville, *en-temps*, *antan*, and *enfance*. This fundamentally poetic reactivation or recomposition of phonemes is enabled by their spatialization in writing. Their simultaneous availability on the page allows an exponential increase in the possible phonetic combinations and this idea is at the heart of the formalist and structuralist theory behind the notion of the 'travail du texte' that we might translate as 'textual process'. However, the vocabulary of colonization, or at least occupation (Walter Ong's 'imperialist pre-emption', for example) would probably not come to mind in this connection as it seems to do almost unbidden in the context of writing *qua* literation. For example, in his comments on the spatiality of writing, Antoine Compagnon notes that writing 'n'échappe jamais tout à fait à un modèle spatial' ('never completely avoids a spatial model')[12] even when '*l'occupation* de cet espace, *l'habitation* de la lettre prend, historiquement,

---

[10] Ong, *Orality and Literacy*, 12.

[11] Jacques Derrida, *De la grammatologie* (Paris: Minuit, 1967).

[12] Antoine Compagnon, *La Seconde Main, ou le travail de la citation* (Paris: Seuil, 1979), 399.

des formes diverses' ('the way it *occupies* that space, its mode of *dwelling in the letter* takes, historically, different forms').[13] In what Derrida and others call 'écriture', however, poetic meaning does not inhabit or occupy the letter; rather, it flashes through sounds that momentarily, and as a function of the written context, are recombined in order to recreate or recompose meaning. Thus, here, the appropriate analogy is clearly not the spatial one of dwelling or occupation, but rather the temporal notion of pulses or currents passing through a switch.

WRITING AS 'NEOTOPIA'

In his searching but limpid study *Orality and Literacy*, Walter Ong elegantly teases out the relation between the culture of the voice and the culture of the written word, acknowledging the importance of the temporal dimension of this relation. As Ong notes, 'the basic orality of language is permanent', since 'written texts all have to be related somehow, directly or indirectly, to the world of sound, the natural *habitat* of language, to yield their meanings'.[14] Furthermore, because literacy has only existed for at most one-sixth of the history of mankind, oral language is significantly older than writing. In the development of most languages, the oral 'phase' precedes the written one, but this is not, of course, entirely true of Creole. For this reason, oral (or 'Creole') culture in the Caribbean is *both* an 'Old' and a 'New' world. Creole may be a 'new' language, but orality is the oldest mode of language. The emphasis placed by Walter Ong on the difficulty for literate cultures of imagining 'pristine' oral cultures is not really pertinent, then, to the French Caribbean linguistic dynamic. Nor is his view that the term 'oral literature' is preposterous. Creole came into being, after all, by deforming and reforming, decomposing and recomposing French, as well as other languages. From the very outset, it incorporated both morphological and lexical elements of French, 're-oralizing' them.

In the passage from orality to the 'New World' of literacy, writing becomes the secondary or adventitious context of the spoken

---

[13] Ibid. My emphasis.
[14] Ong, *Orality and Literacy*, 8. My emphasis.

word. While, in some respects, the 'New World' of Caribbean writing is more rewriting or transliteration than writing, it is represented, nonetheless, as a space-time riven with the loss, silencing, and occultation that are a function of the displacement from voice to page. Even when it is not represented as being analogous to the Middle Passage, the acquisition of literacy is always figured as a rite of passage that resonates self-reflexively throughout the work. In Zobel's *La Rue Cases-Nègres*, the entire plot turns on José's literacy; not only does he himself learn to read and write, but he subsequently initiates his friends Carmen and Jojo, and his essay on Médouze (that the schoolmaster believes to be plagiarized) foreshadows his concern to tell (or write) his own story. Simone Schwarz-Bart's *Pluie et vent sur Télumée Miracle* represents school as an oasis of ease for Télumée, and her brief brush with literacy as the short-lived lightening of a life of hardship. Similarly, in Glissant's novel *La Case du commandeur*, Pythagore, who is taught to read by his daughter Mycéa, finds that writing does not unlock all doors to the past. In Glissant's *Mahagony*, Hégésippe is another belated initiate, whose writing is regarded by his illiterate wife Eudoxie as otiose, a poor substitute for the progeny that they have been unable to produce. However, subliminally, the narrative represents Hégésippe's secret writing as hidden treasure, and as life-affirming, since it is 'planted' in the earth and thus recalls both the eponymous tree and Gani's placenta, buried beside the latter.

CREOLIZING/ORALIZING WRITING: ORALITY AS HETEROTOPIA AND *ALLOCHRONIE*

The Creole language, as mobilized or embedded in French Caribbean writing, is no doubt intended principally to inscribe orality in the text. If this strategy is effective, it is partly because of the phonetic spelling of Creole. This orthography, although it has been criticized as 'coarsely phonetic' and 'visually crass' by Derek Walcott, and as being intent on denying 'its almost completely French roots',[15] is much closer to the sounds of spoken language than French spelling. In Creole, the sound o is written 'o' and not

---

[15] Walcott, 'A Letter to Chamoiseau', in *What the Twilight Says*, 228.

'eau'. Similarly, the hard 'c' is written 'k' instead of 'c', and 'fw' is written instead of 'fr' to communicate one of the most marked characteristics of the Caribbean pronunciation of French, namely the non-pronunciation of the 'r' phoneme. However, when Creole expressions are translated into French either immediately or in a footnote or glossary, the effect is to suggest that the Creole text is serving, in some sense, as a hollow or empty marker of orality. Rather than communicating a 'signified', the Creole signifier signals to many readers nothing other than Creole itself or perhaps orality as an 'other' space or heterotopia, an undissolved block of language that refuses to yield its meaning to non-Creolophone readers, who are thereby made dependent on in-text translations, footnotes, glossaries, etc.

Patrick Chamoiseau's in-text reference to himself as a 'marqueur de paroles' (usually translated as 'wordscratcher') makes of him a scribe who transposes the spoken word. But, apart from introducing Creole words into the French text, French Caribbean writers have many other means at their disposal for 'oralizing' their work. Walter Ong notes several stylistic characteristics of orality, but one of the more obvious is the saturation of the text with 'dialogue' or direct speech, usually reinforced with the indices of deixis, in other words, the coordinates of the act of enunciation: references to the speaker, the addressee(s), the place, and the time of enunciation (although deixis is not, of course, peculiar to the spoken utterance, it is a consistently stressed feature of oral culture). Highlighting the more strictly phenomenological and existential resonances of the writing/orality dynamic, Édouard Glissant identifies orality for his part with the 'ressassement' ('redundancy', 'repetition'), 'étalement' ('spread'), and 'étendue' ('extension') that 'make space' in writing for time experienced as duration, whereas he credits writing with sharpness and compression.[16] Glissant's portrayal of Creole poetics, with its emphasis on baroque accumulation and enumeration, or what Colette Maximin terms the 'geometry of repetition', is entirely consistent with Walter Ong's 'psychodynamics of orality', and especially with the latter's additive, redundant, or 'copious' modes of thought and expression. Moreover, in his work on memory and history, Paul Ricœur suggests that the metrical or rhythmic characteristics of what he calls stability—a notion that he

[16] See Glissant, 'Le Chaos-Monde', 113.

links both to Pierre Bourdieu's 'habitus'[17] and to the phenomenological notion of duration—are precisely accumulation and reitera-
tion.[18] Thus Ricœur makes the same link as Glissant does between
the 'techniques' of orality and the measure of duration, or lived
time. While recognizing also that orality is inscribed in Glissant's
work in the use of 'long unpunctuated sentences, frequent repetition and parenthetical digressions, [and] rhetorical questions',
Barbara Webb notes that these structures are always combined
with a strong scriptural effect as 'the "we" narrator's commentaries
and speculative reflections and the general use of the self-referential language of writing emphasize the literary nature of the text'.[19]

Creole, orality, and indeed the whole culture secreted around the
vernacular could be considered as 'heterotopic' in Michel
Foucault's sense of the term, and, indeed, as 'allochronic' too,[20]
when integrated into the space of writing. In other words, in draw-
ing upon the matrix of oral culture, Caribbean writing sets off
vibrations of an 'other' temporal order of repetition, extension,
accumulation, dilation, and duration. As Walter Ong observes,
'before writing was deeply interiorized by print, people did not feel
themselves situated every moment of their lives in abstract
computed time of any sort'.[21] Ong goes on to observe that the
calendar was not relevant to people's lives in medieval or even
Renaissance Western Europe, and he notes that in modern Nigeria
and Ghana, that is, in places where 'an oral economy of thought'
is predominant, 'matters from the past without any sort of present
relevance commonly drop[ped] into oblivion'.[22] I have already
noted that French Caribbean narrative often articulates a sense of
pastlessness and even timelessness. However, it would be at best
tautological, and at worst misleading, to explain this relation to

---

[17] For a brief discussion of Bourdieu's notion in relation to notions of dwelling
and duration, see the section entitled ' "Plantation" or "Habitation": What's in a
Name?' in Ch. 5.

[18] 'des aspects métriques de la durée . . . accumulation, réitération, permanence':
Ricœur, *La Mémoire*, 289.

[19] Webb, *Myth and History*, 126.

[20] See Johannes Fabian, *Time and the Other* (New York: Columbia University
Press, 1983). Fabian uses this term to characterize the discourse of anthropology as
being subject to the conflicting demands of 'coeval research and allochronic
discourse' (p. 60). For Fabian 'allochronic' and 'coeval' are antonyms, and 'coeval'
would appear to be a synonym of 'synchronous'.

[21] Ong, *Orality and Literacy*, 98.

[22] Ibid. 98.

time in terms of the predominance of oral culture in the Caribbean. Surely these two phenomena, that is, the pre-eminence of oral culture and this 'different' time-consciousness, can both be seen as consequences of the colonial blow that severed the present from the past and that imprisoned a displaced and culturally diverse population within a static system of exploitation. In that context, within the same geographical and institutional space, the culture of the plantation entails not only a sense of 'abstract computed time', the time of production, but also the absence of that temporal consciousness in the slaves' or ex-slaves' folk culture, just as it accommodates both oral and written culture, functioning coevally—but as two separate time-frames.

How can writing be seen as a process of cultural recomposition that opens up the space and time of written narrative to an 'other' temporal and spatial vibration? How does it function as the host 'economy of thought' into which oral sensibilities percolate? We have seen that the *créolité* movement promotes the 'insemination' of the written word with the spoken word, and of French with Creole. This strategy in itself can certainly produce a differential effect that reflects the heterotopic structure of colonial space. As we have already seen, a specifically Creole sense of place, an 'other' orientation in deictic space, is inscribed in the pervasive use in French Caribbean writing of the paradoxical deictic 'ici-là'.[23] Moreover, forty years before the *créolité* programme was launched, in Joseph Zobel's use of the Creole title *Diab-là* for his 1947 novel, the (French) adverb 'là', meaning 'there', features prominently, appended to an attenuated form of the word 'diable', meaning 'devil'. In Creole, this adverb used as a suffix re-places as the definite article. Creole morphology thus serves in this instance (as in many others) to communicate a strong deictic inflection, typically underlining the spatial or positional dimension of the enunciative context. However, not only does the presence-absence of Creole in the French text inject values of voice and vernacular, along with heightened reference to the moment and context of enunciation, but it can also bear intimations of the demotic or even carnivalesque dimensions of oral culture. This effect of 'otherness' is

---

[23] See my introduction to Gallagher (ed.), *Ici-là*. In *Chronique des sept misères*, for example, we read 'qu'en créole d'ici-là on appelle raziés (p. 22) ('called *raziés* in Creole from over here').

further magnified by two considerations. Firstly, the fact that Creole oral culture was, from the beginning, not just a 'popular' culture, but a culture of the colonized and the oppressed, and it was often therefore, but not necessarily, a culture of resistance. And secondly, the fact that Creole orality resounds with 'otherworldly' (or supernatural) intimations that blend magic and realism. As examples of the magic paradigms mobilized in Glissant's narratives, Barbara Webb points to the mysterious appearance of the foundling Cinna Chimène in the forest, the fatal kick of the mule named Mackandal, the flying bed, and the miraculous mirror of the great hurricane. And Webb concludes that these 'plantation stories' are 'verbal feats that defy the destructive force of history and oblivion aimed at putting an end to voices of resistance'.[24]

In his second novel, *Solibo Magnifique*, Patrick Chamoiseau applies the full force of his literary talent to emphasizing a further level of 'otherness' associated with oral culture, a dimension that derives from the impossibility of transferring to the written word the full impact of the spoken word, which is located in time: its evanescence, its stresses, its rhythm; the timbre, intonation, and tonicity of the speaker's voice; the eloquence of the body, the kinetic energy of the gestures; the spirit of performance; the ripples of the dynamic between speaker and audience. In this novel, even if the dialogical and corporal life of the word dries up on the page, and even if all that remains of that life are traces, letters, the desiccated shells of meaning, the reader is made aware on every page of his or her deprivation and is made to 'feel the distance':

Solibo Magnifique me disait: '. . . Oiseau de Cham, tu écris. Bon. Moi, Solibo, je parle. Tu vois la distance. . . . Moi, je dis: On n'écrit jamais la parole, mais des mots, tu aurais dû parler. . . . Tu me donnes la main par-dessus la distance. C'est bien, mais tu touches la distance . . .'.[25]

---

[24] Webb, *Myth and History*, 126.
[25] Chamoiseau, *Solibo Magnifique*, 53; 'Solibo Magnificent used to tell me: "Oiseau de Cham, you write. Very nice. I, Solibo, I speak. You see the distance? . . . Me, I say, One writes but words, not the word, you should have spoken. . . . You give me your hand over the distance. It's all very nice, but you just touch the distance" ': *Solibo Magnificent*, 27–8.

VOICING WRITING

In general terms, the literary genres that can be considered to be—
or to have remained—closest to oral culture are drama and,
perhaps, but to a culturally variable extent, poetry. However, in the
French Caribbean context, drama is often not written down at all
(although the availability of a written text, whatever the drawbacks, at least guarantees a play's longevity), and furthermore the
language of theatre is often Creole rather than French.[26] As for
poetry, in the French Caribbean, as in France, it is an overwhelmingly written genre. In this tradition, prose narrative is much more
clearly marked by oral culture than is poetry, even the poetry of
Aimé Césaire or Édouard Glissant.

French Caribbean written narrative frequently asserts its oral
foundation by subverting the conventional distinction between
récit and discourse, highlighting the indices of direct speech. It is
often, in other words, dramatized in the manner of the *conteur*'s
performance, or even multiply dramatized as in theatrical performance, its phatic function stressed, its dynamic of emission and
reception, writing and reading, speaking and hearing, underlined,
often by rituals of question and response. Maryse Condé's polyphonic novel *La Traversée de la mangrove* provides an example of
such dramatization, as does Patrick Chamoiseau's *Chronique des
sept misères*, *Solibo Magnifique*, and *Chemin d'école*. Thus,
Chronique des sept misères begins as an address: the first words
apostrophize the 'Messieurs et dames de la compagnie' ('Ladies and
Gentlemen of this gathering'). And the incipit proceeds: 'l'histoire
des anonymes n'ayant qu'une douceur, celle de la parole, nous y
goûterons à peine' ('the story of the nameless being sweet in one
respect only, in its telling aloud, we will scarcely taste it here').[27]
Furthermore, the 'we' narrator is dramatized as speaking rather
than writing: 'parler de nous rend juste et inévitable de parler de
lui' ('to speak of ourselves we must inevitably and in all fairness
speak of him').[28] Édouard Glissant's preface to the novel further

---

[26] See Bridget Jones and Sita E. Dickson Littlewood, *Paradoxes of French
Caribbean Theatre: An Annotated Checklist of Dramatic Works, Guadeloupe,
Guyane, Martinique, from* 1900 (London: Roehampton Institute, n.d.).

[27] Chamoiseau, *Chronique des sept misères*, 15.

[28] Ibid. 17.

stresses the pressure of voice in the text: he states that the novel is straining 'à l'écoute d'une voix venue de loin dont l'écho plane sur les lieux de notre mémoire et oriente nos futurs' ('to hear a voice come from afar whose echo hovers over the places of our memory and drives our future').[29] However, because of the relatively enduring nature of the written word, which contrasts with the transitory passage of the embodied spoken word, writing favours continuity and historical consciousness: 'Je pars, mais toi tu restes' ('I'm going and you're staying'),[30] admits the storyteller or *maître de la parole* to the *marqueur de paroles* in *Solibo Magnifique*. As Raphaël Confiant has written: 'la logique de l'écriture est celle du temps, du déroulé, qui permet l'entrée dans l'Histoire avec un grand H' ('the logic of writing is a logic of temporality, of unfolding, that allows for participation in History with a capital H').[31] And indeed, Chamoiseau's text, with its constant emphasis on the gulf between writing, an ersatz for speech, and the embodied, fleeting *parole* itself, gives a sense of the historicity and also the ephemerality of the spoken word, of its belonging to a specific, unrepeatable moment in time. It is important, of course, not to confuse the general enunciative structure of language with the specifics of orality. For example, while emphasizing writing, the relational dynamic of Françoise Éga's *Lettres à une noire* (1978), written as an epistolary diary, addressed to a 'sœur brésilienne', stresses the relational 'je–tu' dynamic of enunciation. The epistolary dimension renders it relentlessly phatic, underlining a constant straining towards the immediacy of spoken communication and against the mediation of writing, while the journal form makes for a highly deictic, and somewhat de-narrativized text. Although this foregrounding of the moment and context of enunciation is taking place within writing, it is highly suggestive of displaced voice, realizing meta-discursively the very problematic of exile that is the subject of Éga's novel of Metropolitan immigration.

In the French tradition, poetry readings (where the poet reads her or his work aloud) are extremely rare, whereas in Britain as well as Ireland, for example, poets traditionally give public readings (whether they write in English, Irish, or Scots Gaelic). In

---

[29] Chamoiseau, *Chronique des sept misères*, 6. (Glissant's preface is entitled 'Un marqueur de paroles'.)

[30] *Solibo Magnifique*, 53; *Solibo Magnificent*, 28.

[31] Raphaël Confiant, 'Quelques questions', 179.

primary oral culture, memorization and recitation were the traditional modes of performance, but in our times of secondary orality, a complex overlay of written and oral culture ensures that reading is the accepted contemporary mode of contemporary public performance of poetry. Regardless, however, of whether the poem is recited or read, poets' voices in this tradition typically become 'imprinted' on their work in a manner unimaginable in the French-language context. A reader who has heard a poet read aloud will memorize that voice—its accent, timbre, cadences, and tone—and will superimpose that enunciation, that music, upon all that they themselves will henceforth read of that poet's work. This is as true of Derek Walcott as it is of Seamus Heaney, Ted Hughes, or Philip Larkin. It would be rare for a major Irish or British poet's voice to be unfamiliar to her or his readers, and even more rare for a writer—poet or novelist indeed—to participate in a literary event without being called upon to *read*, instead of, or as well as, to speak. The importance attached to this public dimension of the traditionally private act of writing and reading, in addition to the 'popularity' of this traditional reassociation of voice and text, orality and writing, perhaps explains why some English-language poets, such as Derek Walcott, like to foreground textual space. It is as though it were the visual, the spatial, or the textual dimension of poetic writing that needed to be highlighted or reinforced in the English-language tradition, or as though writing rather than orality were the ghost at the banquet. In *Tiepolo's Hound*, for example, Walcott frequently draws attention to textual space. Underlining the continuity between the visual space of writing and of landscape, for example, he draws an analogy between the latter and textual marks, evoking 'the blue, gusting harbour, where like *commas/*in a shop ledger gulls *tick* the *lined* waves'.[32] The dynamic is dramatically different in the French-language tradition. In Édouard Glissant's poetry, for example, and indeed in his novels also, the meta-poetic or meta-discursive references are much more likely to highlight orality. As though, with poetry in French being deprived of that tradition of public reading and organic re-embodiment, French Caribbean writing must somehow, in some other way, draw attention to voice. And, of course, the Creole language, the techniques of the folktale, the figure of the *conteur*, and,

---

[32] Walcott, *Tiepolo's Hound*, 3. Emphasis mine.

crucially, the dramatization of enunciation are mobilized precisely to this end.

As Derrida writes in *L'Écriture et la différence*, much ink has been spilled over the question of whether 'graver sauve ou perd la parole' ('inscription ruins or redeems utterance').[33] And this is, as we have seen, the question that motivates Chamoiseau's novel, *Solibo Magnifique*. The eponymous *conteur* is an anachronism whose death launches the police investigation that is the basis of the novel. Solibo is identified as a Force, a Strength, and the 'magnificent' aura emanating from his voice belies his unremarkable daytime appearance. Once darkness falls, he is transformed. His gradual disappearance from public life is blamed on the demise of folk culture, and on the weakening of the grip of Creole. Chamoiseau, the author, proposes himself as a sort of poor substitute for the *conteur* who has perished, having, significantly, choked on his own tongue one night during Carnival. What is termed the 'parole' takes up the whole central part of the book. Instead of being presented as a purely written text, the body of the novel is configured as a polyphonic wake oration or inquest, a theatrical relay with a cast of colourful characters who pass on the baton of speech from one to the other. Early on, the author spells out that what he is offering is a 'parole', and to highlight its spoken status he sandwiches it between two texts that are labelled 'écrits': the police report of the scene of Solibo's death and the written transcription of one of Solibo's performances. The first, written in legalese, bears no trace of oral fluidity. The second is ostentatiously missing the intonation, the breath, the rhythm, the tone, the gestures, the audience participation, and the drumbeat of Solibo's performances. Although the main part of the book is presented, then, as *parole* or spoken word, and the writer, Chamoiseau, as the 'marker of the spoken word', what we read is a written-down 'spoken word' that explicitly proclaims its own shortcomings. Moreover, the scribe's asthmatic condition and his defective tape-recorder are further emblems of deficiency.

What is perhaps most intriguing in this context is the hypertrophy of Chamoiseau's text, or the overdevelopment of the marks of textuality, the 'overkill' on writing. In one sense, this scriptural hypertrophy is produced by the very strategies used to render oral-

---

[33] Jacques Derrida, *L'Écriture et la différence* (Paris: Seuil, 1967), 19.

ity. For example, the epigraphs that set out the 'rules of the game', so to speak, or the propaedeutics of reading, mimic the riddles and responses that mark the opening of the *séance* around the *conteur*, as the audience rehearses the tenor of its participatory role. Similarly, just as Solibo's discourse is said to be a patchwork of different registers and languages and to highlight the 'dire' (act of saying) at the expense of the 'dit' (what is said), so too, Chamoiseau's text is a patchwork of citations and allusions to other texts, as well as being a choral or polyphonic work that flamboyantly resists the reduction of a 'saying' to a simple, summarizable 'said'. In this way, the reader can perhaps conclude that not only does writing preserve the trace of a threatened culture, lending it whatever future it can hope for, but it can also in its own way—that is, through Bakhtinian 'heteroglossia', or the reflection of a multiplicity of dramatic moments and voices—oppose the clarification of that opaqueness which constitutes the last defence of utterance against assimilation or reduction. In one of the many latent allusions to Bakhtin's work on dialogism, the chapter numbered 'one' begins 'Une soirée de Carnaval' ('During a Carnival evening'), the reference to Carnival echoing the connotations of popular, subversive, shifting discourse mobilized in Bakhtin's use of the term.

POLYPHONY, INTERTEXTUALITY, AND DIALOGUE

When Maurice Blanchot writes in *L'Entretien infini* (The Infinite Conversation) that all works are generated from pre-existing works, his paradigm is not only temporal, but also spoken, since 'entretien' means conversation (from 'entre' meaning 'between' and 'tien', 'hold'), and since he refers the idea of reproduction to the spoken or the sung word:

personne ne songe que pourraient être créés de toutes pièces les œuvres et les chants. Toujours ils sont donnés à l'avance, dans le présent immobile de la mémoire. Qui s'intéresserait à une *parole* nouvelle, non transmise? Ce qu'il importe, ce n'est pas de *dire*, c'est de *redire* . . .[34]

---

[34] Maurice Blanchot, *L'Entretien infini* (Paris: Gallimard, 1969), 459; 'none would dream of thinking that songs and works could be created from nothing. They are always there already, in the immobile present of memory. Who would be interested in a new utterance, as opposed to a mediated one? What is important is not to say something, it is to say it again . . .'. Emphasis mine.

Similarly, for Daniel Maximin, writing provides a means of continuing the 'conversation of books', or of maintaining the 'possibility
of dialogue': 'Pour moi, écrire, c'est continuer la *conversation* des
livres. . . . Écrire, c'est une façon, tout seul à une heure du matin,
de postuler toujours la *possibilité* des *dialogues*' ('For me, writing
is a way of prolonging the conversation of books . . . of maintaining the possibility of such dialogue, even when one is alone at one
o'clock in the morning').[35] It is significant that both Blanchot and
Maximin, along with the critic Mikhail Bakhtin, should want to
link the 'textuality' or 'intertextuality' of writing with the notions
of dialogue and conversation. At issue here is not so much the
distinction between the spoken and the written word, as the
distinction that can, and indeed must, be made between the kind of
relation that we might call 'intersubjective' and the kind of relation
that we might term pluri-subjective or 'polyphonic', in other
words, between a relation of otherness and a relation of plurality
or diversity. Although some critics have noted a connection
between the thinking of Martin Buber and Bakhtin, the latter is not
concerned exclusively with dialogue in the sense of the reciprocal
approach of two subjects engaged in discourse, which is the basis
of the I–Thou relation studied by Martin Buber as an 'ontology of
the between'.[36] Rather, he wants to highlight the relations that link
individual expression to the socially constituted fabric of language
composed by the voices of others, voices that have first been internalized, then re-externalized. Clearly, Bakhtin's effort to link the
I–Thou relation to the relation of reverberation or resonance is
extremely valuable, but, equally clearly, these are two different
types of relation which should not be confused. The second is the
type of relation that many critics would term intertextual, but that
can only metaphorically be described as 'dialogical'. In other
words, this circulatory relation is usually mobilized within a
primary relation that is often truly dialogical. While the intertextual relation may not be completely 'mastered' or 'contained'
within this primary relation—or indeed may not be heard or read
at all—it is, nonetheless, 'held' as a potential resonance within a

---

[35] Daniel Maximin, 'Entretien', *France-Antilles*, 315, 7–13 Oct. 1995, 2. Quoted
in Chaulet-Achour and Maximin, 'Sous le signe du colibri', 213–14.
[36] Michael Theunissen, *The Other: Studies in the Social Ontology of Husserl,
Heidegger, Sartre, and Buber*, tr. Christopher Macann (Cambridge, Mass.: MIT,
1984), 271–2.

given discursive time-space and within a primary discursive relation (for example, between the author of a letter and its addressee). The reading relation is, for the most part, a circulatory rather than a dialogical relation. The relation between the face-to-face, the I–Thou enunciative relation, on the one hand, and the circulation and superimpositions effected by intertextuality, on the other, is a complex question, far beyond the reach of this study, and one in which a lot is at stake, notably, the relation between otherness and difference, ethics and ontology.[37]

It is less to ethics than to ontology that we are referred by J. Michael Dash's observation that 'the only useful approach to Caribbean literature is an intertextual one', an observation that he bases on Glissant's vision of the Caribbean as a 'multiple series of relationships'.[38] This vision suggests the fundamentally poetic nature of the Caribbean and, indeed, of Caribbean writing, both of which are intensely overdetermined, just like poetry. Certainly, contemporary literary theory holds that intertextuality is one of the principal vectors of literary meaning and significance, although it is usually argued that its mobilization is heightened to an unprecedented degree in the postmodern age. It could be argued, however, that the intertextuality of French Caribbean writing is a function not just of universal time, not just of the postmodern age, but also, if not primarily, of Caribbean space and displacement. Is this not why the Caribbean presents a particularly hypertrophied version of a general trend? Indeed, it would be impossible to give here a full account of the prevalence of intertextuality in French Caribbean writing and probably futile to attempt to explain all of its numerous and far-reaching resonances. Instead, I shall try to see how some of the principal effects of this literary phenomenon feed into the (de)construction of French Caribbean apprehensions of time and space and are in turn reinforced or directed by those apprehensions.

Before evoking particular examples of the intertextual impulse

---

[37] For two very different approaches to this problematic, see Gregory Clark, *Dialogue, Dialectic, and Conversation: A Social Perspective on the Function of Writing* (Carbondale: Southern Illinois University Press, 1990) and Mary Gallagher, 'La Poétique de la diversité dans les essais d'Édouard Glissant', in Yves-Alain Favre (ed.), *Horizons d'Édouard Glissant* (Biarritz: J&D Éditions, 1992), 27–35, a comparative study of the ethics of Emmanuel Levinas and the poetic ontology of Édouard Glissant.

[38] Dash, *The Other America*, 20.

at work, we should consider briefly the relation between the Caribbean imagination of space and time, on the one hand, and the processes and implications of intertextuality, on the other. In the abstract, and often in practice too, intertextuality is semantically labile. It can mean filiation or affiliation; foundation or affinity; resistance or assimilation; hybridization or ironization. It can create a sense of tradition and continuity or a sense of density and network; it can suggest renewal or creative exhaustion; and it can revise, reject, or reinforce 'old meanings'. It is always, however, based on displaced textual elements, located on a paradigmatic axis, from which they are selected and integrated into a 'New World', that is, a different textual structure into which they inject a sense of paradigmatic possibility. These elements thus function as a poetics (in the Russian formalist sense). The intertextual displacement is, at the very least, an enrichment, creating a poetic surplus, a density or an opaqueness of meaning in the host text, whether it is read spatially, as rhizomatic proliferation, or temporally, as a factor of flow between different time-frames. In all its manifestations, intertextual mobility highlights and subverts not only spatial, but also temporal boundaries: 'the semantic fabric of the text, like the fabric of the universe, can be theorized as a space-time continuum, alive with memory of probabilities, memory of alternatives, and memory of change'.[39] Intertextuality can build up, then, both a sense of tradition and a transverse or synchronic sense of simultaneity. While it may raise temporal questions of originality and of priority, stressing the re- in re-creation, it can also create a sense of simultaneous interconnection.

For Umberto Eco, the 'postmodern reply to the modern consists of recognizing that the past, since it cannot really be destroyed, because its destruction leads to silence, must be revisited: but with irony, not innocently'.[40] This view of postmodernism is not, however, the full story. Linda Hutcheon would consider, for example, that postmodern irony is attenuated by an element of nostalgia. According to her, 'postmodernist intertextuality neither repudiates nor simply ironises the past; nor does it simply repro-

---

[39] Wae Chee Dimock, 'A Theory of Resonance: Literature and Temporal Extension', *PMLA*, 112/5 (Oct. 1997), 1046–59: 1060.

[40] Umberto Eco, 'Postmodernism, Irony, the Enjoyable', in Peter Brooker (ed.), *Modernism/Postmodernism* (London: Longman, 1999), 225–8.

duce the past as nostalgia'.⁴¹ These combined motives of desire and challenge certainly seem to correspond to the effect produced by much Caribbean intertextuality, which cannot be corralled, then, within the exclusively spatial dimension of Edward Soja's definition of postmodernity as 'a geography of simultaneous relations and meanings tied together by spatial rather than temporal logic'.⁴² The tension between the temporal and the spatial stresses of intertextuality is well illustrated by Chris Bongie's interpretation of Daniel Maximin's writing. For Bongie, Maximin approaches the 'words of others' as having to be, not expelled, but, rather, 'cautiously inhabited'.⁴³ Yet he also acknowledges the temporal inflection of Maximin's intertextuality, which produces 'a mutual transformation of the past by the present and of the present by the past'. Here, however, the critic, echoing Maximin's intertextual practice which he regards as 'exemplary of the creolization process',⁴⁴ immediately re-spatializes the temporal reference again, arguing that the intertextuality of Maximin's novels 'create[s] the unstable *ground* for a future that does not so much lie beyond as within the interstices of ... ambivalently, and ineluctably, *conjoined worlds*'.⁴⁵ Bongie thus constantly interweaves or overlays the two dimensions and effects—spatial and temporal—of the intertextual process, but tends to favour the former.

In the Caribbean context, the general poetic effect of intertextuality is often linked to a philosophical or political effect that has implications for the conceptualization of space and time. In Glissant's work, for example, intertextuality actualizes the author's preponderantly spatial vision of relation as rhizomatic, extensive, and opaque, even if it is also faithful to his concern with duration as accumulation. In the case of Daniel Maximin, the effect of intertextual repetition is somewhat similar. It is easy to agree with Clarisse Zimra that Maximin's novel *L'Isolé Soleil* is a 'novel of and about (re)writing'. Moreover, since one of the most insistent

⁴¹ Linda Hutcheon, 'Telling Stories: Fiction and History', in Peter Brooker (ed.), *Modernism/Postmodernism* (London and New York: Longman, 1992), 229–42: 229.

⁴² Soja's *Postmodern Geographies*, as referred to in Lisa Lowe, 'Literary Nomadics in Francophone Allegories of Postcolonialism: Pham Vanky and Tahar Ben Jelloun', *Yale French Studies*, Post/Colonial Conditions, 1 (1993), 43–61: 47.

⁴³ Bongie, *Islands and Exiles*, 356.

⁴⁴ Ibid. 355.   ⁴⁵ Ibid. 358-9. Emphasis mine.

motifs of this text is the questioning relation to the putative heroes of Caribbean history, Maximin's 're-writing' has both political and psychoanalytical oppositional resonance. However, like Chris Bongie, Clarisse Zimra ultimately locates the significance of Maximin's intertextuality in the spatial realm: his writing is described as a 'post-modern crazy quilt', as 'montage', and as a 'dizzying narrative space'.[46] Moreover, this leaning towards space is thematized in the novel, since, as we saw earlier, Maximin seems to place his hopes for the Caribbean future in geography rather than history.

INTERTEXTUALITY AT WORK: CONSOLIDATION OF A TRADITION?

The importance accorded by some French Caribbean writers to the sense of belonging to a cultural tradition in the making is predictable. Indeed, given the significance of rupture and discontinuity in Caribbean history and identity, the Caribbean subject might be expected to crave the sense of continuity and tradition that intertextuality would seem capable of fulfilling. The intertextual impulse is not always at work, however, where one might expect to find it. In the case of Guadeloupean writing by women, for example, there is little intertextual echoing at work within this gendered field itself. In other words, while Maryse Condé's writing resonates extensively with work of Césaire, Saint-John Perse, Emily Brontë, Victor Hugo, et al., there are few echoes in her writing of texts by French Caribbean women writers. Similarly, the work of Lucie Julia and Gisèle Pineau does not really refer intertextually to that of Simone Schwarz-Bart, Maryse Condé, Michèle Lacrosil, or Jacqueline Manicom. It is worth wondering why these writers, unlike their male counterparts, are not more drawn to intertextuality as a cohesive, structuring reinforcement of a tradition of 'women's writing'.

Patrick Chamoiseau's writing, along with that of Daniel Maximin, provides perhaps the most striking example of inter-

---

[46] Clarisse Zimra, 'Daughters of Mayotte, Sons of Frantz: The Unrequited Self in Caribbean Literature', in Haigh (ed.), *An Introduction to Francophone Caribbean Writing*, 177–94: 191.

textual proliferation in French Caribbean writing. While it is true that the works of other writers, especially Édouard Glissant, Aimé Césaire, and Maryse Condé, but also Raphaël Confiant, Daniel Radford, and Gisèle Pineau, are also studded with intertextual allusions, the density of these references does not reach the paroxysmal proportions that it consistently demonstrates in the work of Chamoiseau and Maximin. The modes of allusion are very different in each case, however. Whereas Patrick Chamoiseau usually identifies the other voices in his work, Maximin's references are often more discreet, and are more rarely labelled by proper names. Just as the rhythms and cadences of Édouard Glissant's poetry are marked to an extraordinary extent by the poetics of Saint-John Perse, so too Chamoiseau's language is infinitely but implicitly enriched by Glissant's thinking. However, in his novel of 1997 in particular, Chamoiseau opts to declare the debt and even makes room in his own writing for several long offset passages of Glissant's work in a mosaic that stresses the separateness of the incorporating and incorporated texts. In this novel, the displaced segments of Glissant's writing are set apart in italic print and are explicitly entitled an 'entre-dire', or 'between-speak'. In his intergeneric essay *Écrire en pays dominé*, published in the same year as the mosaic novel, the most clearly highlighted references to other writers barely qualify as intertextual, in that they are not textual references as such, but refer instead, as we saw in the previous chapter, to proper names and to the literary styles and intellectual preoccupations that these names have come to signal. The broadness of Chamoiseau's 'intertextual' reach in this work indicates a desire to escape the imaginative and referential closure against which Glissant too has so sedulously set his face from the very beginning of his intellectual effort. Yet, even if we leave aside the assimilative processing to which these references are subjected (they are not quotations, but rather pithy one-liner interpretations of a given writer's perspective), Chamoiseau's thesaurizing intent is implicit in the collective title given to these references—'sentimenthèque'—on the model of 'bibliothèque', the Greek root 'thekè' denoting 'depot', 'store', 'holding place'. In other words, the classificatory and curatorial connotations of Chamoiseau's 'sentimenthèques' could produce a hypostasizing effect at odds with the (no doubt) desired emphasis on the open dynamic of relationality.

Of all French Caribbean writers, including Aimé Césaire and

Maryse Condé, Daniel Maximin's intertext boasts perhaps the most extensive extra-Caribbean dimension. His *L'Ile et une nuit* recalls the *Arabian Nights*, for example, and Hélène Cixous is a constant textual presence in his work. Moreover, Cixous's largely anagrammatic work on the signifier and on proper names in particular is one of the key influences on Maximin's writing (for example, 'Son Adrien-Soleil, avec son nid d'aide caché dans son prénom'—'Her Solar-Adrien with his *nid d'aide* or nest of succour hidden in his forename'—although this author is also invoked intertextually, as in the allusion to the title of one of her works, *La Jeune Née*: 'Tu es aussi une jeune née').[47] Maximin also refers extensively to Caribbean texts, however. The following allusion to the poetry of Léon-Gontran Damas, author of collections entitled *Pigments*, *Névralgies*, and *Black-Label*, is characteristic: 'une Marque noire pour déguster ses névralgies et pigmenter ses insomnies . . .' ('a black label for savouring your neuralgia and spicing up your insomnia').[48] Similarly, an allusion to the Haitian writer Jean Métellus, author of *Au pipirite chantant*, emerges in the interstices of Maximin's text: 'Malgré l'enfant à naître bientôt, Gerty se lève toujours au pipirite chantant'.[49] Virtually every page of *L'Isolé Soleil* shimmers in this intertextual haze.

Usually the more latent the intertextual relation, the more potent its poetic effect. In other words, when the repeated text is not labelled the reader has a greater sense of active co-creation. And while the insights yielded by individual incidences of echo may be slim (what can we deduce, for example, from the ludic correspondence between the eponyms Solibo—a Creole word for a fall or tumble—and Tituba—echoing the French word 'tituber' to stumble or fall?),[50] we cannot deny the intensity of the effect of connection, density, and poeticity produced by the sheer insistence and volume of intertextual correspondences across French Caribbean writing. Collectively, they create a sense of the infinite capillary flow of text, imagination, and meaning, through an organically interconnected system. However ostentatious or seemingly gratuitous the echoing, the reader retains the residual sense both of the internal continuity and consolidation of a Francophone

---

[47] *L'Isolé Soleil*, 145.   [48] Ibid. 54.   [49] Ibid. 143.
[50] Chamoiseau, *Solibo Magnifique*; Maryse Condé, *Moi, Tituba sorcière . . . Noire de Salem* (Paris: Mercure de France, 1986).

Caribbean literary corpus in the making, and, to a variable extent, of the interrelation between that corpus and Metropolitan (or other) writing.

THE DENSITY OF PLACE: THE 'COMÉDIE ANTILLAISE'?

One highly significant factor of textual continuity throughout the corpus of Caribbean writing is, without doubt, the common spatial and temporal reference to the islands. Because the islands are so small, the same toponyms recur with almost mesmerizing frequency across the work of various periods and authors. As well as producing an effect of consolidation and stability, this continuity also, however, creates a sense of saturation, closure, and limitation. Sense of place is privileged at the expense of the openness and indeterminacy of fiction, and a certain impression of 'déjà lu', of constriction, and monotony can be imputed to the extraordinary level of repetition of locales and place-names from one work to another. Space is, unquestionably, elevated thereby to an unprecedented level of meaningfulness, functioning as well as a register of duration. Moreover, the sense of the world beyond the horizon of the islands—or the archipelagos—takes on, against the sense of saturation and constriction, an undeniable urgency. The tension between intertextuality that refers out to non-Caribbean works and strictly Caribbean intertextuality, not to mention the intertextuality internal to a given *œuvre*, is also, largely, a tension between inside and outside, restriction and extension, insularity and connection, separation and relation.

French Caribbean intertextual reference is at its most striking—and perhaps at its most productive too—as a source of cohesion, texturing, and echoing within the *œuvres* of individual writers. Édouard Glissant's work provides the most striking Caribbean example of a textual universe that is peopled by the same characters, moved by the same concerns, constantly recycling or recomposing the same cast, the same segments of text, the same keywords, the same concepts, in addition to repeating its reference to the same locations, the same historical moments and relations, building up thereby an overwhelming sense of the relational density of time and place. Each text relates intertextually to the rest of Glissant's work, recycling the same concerns, adapting them to a different textual context, thus expanding and relativizing (or indeed creolizing) their former significance. What makes this continuity even more striking is the fact that it is highly self-reflexive and also intergeneric. In other words, it comments on itself untiringly, and it constantly crosses the generic boundaries between essays and novels, novels and poetry, in an ever more complex dynamic of circulation. Other writers repeat this paradigm, but on a more nineteenth-century scale, confining their reworking to one genre: for example, the novels of Confiant's diptych or of Maximin's trilogy, which feature the same nucleus of characters, the same locations, and related preoccupations. Apart from reinforcing a sense of the autonomy of the individual *œuvre* (in a further manifestation of Benítez-Rojo's 'repeating island'), this intense rewriting or texturing lends the *œuvre* in question a surfeit of internal relationality and continuity. Unlike the serial fresco of Balzac's 'Human Comedy' or the sagas of Dumas or Scott, there is little sense, however, of individual works inscribing themselves as sequels in a sequence. Rather, the density of intertextual correspondence creates a powerful sense of simultaneity and a correspondingly limited sense of linearity as development or change. In Confiant's work, the plantation overseer Firmin Léandor, the *béké* planter de Cassagnac, and the 'driveur' or townie corner-boy Rigobert reappear from one novel to the next, as do the various named quarters of Fort-de-France or the rural sites where they act and circulate. More importantly still, all three characters recur in Confiant's childhood memoirs, a recurrence that knits together reality and fiction.

On yet another level of superimposition, not only do all three of Daniel Maximin's novels feature with just some variations the same cast of characters and the same Guadeloupean locales, but these intertextual constants sometimes gesture towards other Caribbean *œuvres*. For example, Siméa, one of the principal voices in Maximin's work, recalls Édouard Glissant's narratives in that her name is a phonetic anagram of Glissant's Mycéa.

RECLAIMING THE LITERARY PAST

The text considered in some detail at the end of the previous chapter provides a compelling insight into the temporal dimension of intertextuality. Like the memoirs of Raphaël Confiant's childhood,

Ravines du devant-jour (1993), Chamoiseau's work recalls not just the author's childhood, but also, intertextually, the poetry of Saint-John Perse, the poetic alter ego of Alexis Leger, born in Guadeloupe in 1887 and thus belonging to the generation of the two *créolistes'* grandparents. As we saw, *Antan d'enfance* is a text of remembrance that explores the limits and the texture of memory. However, it simultaneously, but implicitly,[51] and much less imposingly than Confiant's memoirs, deploys intertextuality as 'supplementary' textual and inter-generic memory, that is, as a specifically poetic mode of re-vision.

I have elsewhere studied in some detail the seminal value of Saint-John Perse's writing for the Caribbean imagination, a question that would be difficult to explore exhaustively.[52] Already in 1980, Roger Toumson saw Caribbean writing as 'rewriting' and one of the principal objects of this rewriting was, in his view, the work of Saint-John Perse.[53] The intensive reactivation of Saint-John Perse's poetry in the work of Aimé Césaire, Patrick Chamoiseau, Raphaël Confiant, Maryse Condé, Édouard Glissant, Daniel Maximin, Daniel Radford, Guy Tirolien, and Joseph Zobel, amongst others, suggests a wide spectrum of different relations: irony, homage, awe, demystification, and so forth. Whereas much of this rewriting of Saint-John Perse takes on a revisionist meaning and is strictly positional in intent and effect, the status of other echos is much less easy to define. For example, when we read in Édouard Glissant's *Sartorius* the phrase 'seule longue respiration sans césure', a quotation from Saint-John Perse's *Exil*, there is a sense that the novelist is simply convoking an entire field of poetic and literary echo in order to 'densify' his own writing.[54] As this example shows, the effects of intertextual relation are, like the effects of creolization, multiple, complex, and unpredictable, and do not lend themselves to generalization. While the evocation in *La Rue Cases-Nègres* of 'l'économe qui passe sur son mulet' ('the overseer passing by astride his

---

[51] One precise intertextual reference would be the echoing of the line from 'Pour fêter une enfance': 'je me souviens du sel, je me souviens du sel', Saint-John Perse, *Œuvres complétes*, Bibliothèque de la Pléiade (Paris: Gallimard, 1972), 24) in 'Je me souviens de l'icaque | oh je me souviens de l'icaque': *Antan d'enfance*, 161.

[52] See Gallagher, 'Seminal Praise'.

[53] Roger Toumson, 'Les écrivains afro-antillais et la réécriture', *Europe*, 612 (Apr. 1980), 115–227.

[54] Édouard Glissant, *Sartorius* (Paris: Gallimard, 1999), 13.

mule')[55] or of the 'cases couvertes en tôle ondulée' ('huts of corrugated iron') (*RCN* 19) may evoke the world of Saint-John Perse's 'Écrit sur la porte', they do not operate intertextually. However, 'tout cela est beau nous les enfants nous en jouissons royalement' (*RCN* 20), because of its celebratory connotations and because of the link suggested between childhood and an aesthetic well-being connoted as royal privilege, comes much closer to implying an ironic textual rapprochement between the world of the small and almost destitute black plantation boy and the privileged plantocracy figured in 'Pour fêter une enfance'. This collection is indeed connoted as royal in the epigraph 'King Light's Settlements' (*ŒC* 21)[56] and in the allusion to the child's dazzling 'blanc royaume' ('the white kingdom') (*ŒC* 23; *ÉOP* 22). Similarly, the twice-repeated description of José's absent mother Délia as lost to her son, working in the distant town 'derrière les chaises des békés qu'elle sert' ('behind the chairs of the békés she served') (*RCN* 42 and 74) is an unmistakable echo of the poem that serenely signals the reassuring, valorizing presence of those mute, servile shapes frozen into hieratic poses of attendance in the colonial dining-room: 'pour longtemps encore j'ai mémoire | des faces insonores, couleur de papaye et d'ennui, qui s'arrêtaient derrière nos chaises comme des astres morts' ('I shall still long remember | mute faces, the colour of papayas, and of boredom, | that paused like burnt-out stars behind our chairs' (*ŒC* 27 , *ÉOP* 29).

Whether reverential or irreverent, the extent of the stylistic and referential relation to Saint-John Perse in Chamoiseau's writing confirms the revisionist stance of the *créolité* movement. Much of that movement's claim to originality is based on its new emphasis on celebration at the expense of lament. Indeed, this sense of 'recovery' is evident in the very title of the movement's 'manifesto', *Éloge de la créolité*, which inevitably calls to mind that of Saint-John Perse's first poetic masterpiece and which was, indeed, inspired by the latter.[57] Moreover, the manifesto's reference to

---

[55] Zobel, *La Rue Cases-Nègres*, 38. Remaining page references are given in the text following the abbreviation *RCN*.

[56] The quotations from Saint-John Perse refer to his *Œuvres complètes*, abbreviated to *ŒC*. The translations are from Saint-John Perse, *Éloges and Other Poems*, tr. Louise Varèse (New York: Pantheon Books, 1956), abbreviated to *ÉOP*.

[57] Chamoiseau makes this point explicitly in McCusker, 'De la problématique du territoire'.

Saint-John Perse as epitomizing the 'ethnoclasse béké' underlines the poet's pivotal importance in the movement's programme of reconciliation with the totality of Caribbean culture, including the colonial dimension.[58]

Like Confiant's and Chamoiseau's memoirs of childhood, although written some eighty years previously, Saint-John Perse's *Éloges*, a collection that includes the two poem sequences, 'Pour fêter une enfance' and 'Éloges', was inspired by a Caribbean childhood. 'Pour fêter une enfance' celebrates the plantation, 'Éloges' the town. Of the two sequences, the second is the more resistant, owing largely to the poet's oblique yet insistent foregrounding of the process of remembrance, a concern that generates, as we saw, considerable complexity in *Antan d'enfance* also. Not only do 'Éloges' and *Antan d'enfance* evoke many of the same daily sights and experiences of an urban Caribbean childhood, but both texts share, in addition, a predominantly celebratory tone. They also have in common an appeal to poeticity and the explicit imprint of the spoken word in their regular recourse to apostrophe and direct speech, meta-discourse and reported speech. However, the most notable similarity between these two texts is the fact that they are both marked by reflection on their respective programmes of re-presentation. Both self-consciously invoke memory directly.

In contrast to the extensive citation of Saint-John Perse in Confiant's *Ravines du devant-jour*, Chamoiseau's actual intertext is very discreet. For example, at the end of the last chapter I noted in *Antan d'enfance* a passage about false memory, more specifically, the false memory of an 'estime d'un temps heureux' ('esteem for a happy era'). This recalls Saint-John Perse's laudatory expression of assent and reverence 'je parle dans l'estime' ('I speak in esteem')— in 'Pour fêter une enfance' (*ŒC* 25). However, whether or not Chamoiseau's text recalls 'Éloges' depends on the extent of the reader's (literary) experience and memory. The English translator of *Antan d'enfance*, for example, did not make the connection (and so translated 'estime' by 'reckoning').[59] In her study of Édouard Glissant's 'camouflaged language', Celia Britton notes that the meaning of Glissant's novels depends on the reader's memory, which is stretched to capacity by the density of textual links

---

[58] Bernabé et al., *Éloge de la créolité*, 29; *In Praise of Creoleness*, 90.
[59] See Ch. 3, n. 67.

between different parts of a single work or between different parts of Glissant's *œuvre*.[60] This observation on the role of memory could, as we see, usefully be applied to the entire Caribbean inter-text.

For Chamoiseau, writing about his childhood is a means of conserving and sharing a collective past, even if he is led to high-light in addition a discontinuous, pre-eminently poetic reality. In 'Éloges', the speaker's song offers an opportunity to re-view and to communicate past perceptions and experiences that are, however, less communal than personal. Intertextual allusion to Saint-John Perse underlines, then, the differing orientation of the creative act in the two instances, and the common centrality of memory and nostalgia. Moreover, despite the serial movement of its numbered poems, 'Éloges' shows a marked tendency towards abstraction, impersonality, and discontinuity, while Chamoiseau's narrative follows a broadly linear movement. And yet, we have seen that discontinuity and opacity are explicit values in Chamoiseau's text too, even if the writer modestly intimates all that separates his writing from poetry.

REMEMBERING IN 'ÉLOGES', OR THE DOUBLE PASSAGE

The structural pivot of 'Éloges' is a conventional trope, a common-place of the French poetic tradition: namely, a comparison likening the launching of the processes of memory and/or imagination to a departure on a sea voyage. Here, however, the spatial image (the sea journey) has literal relevance in this poetic project, since the poet is imagining the Caribbean from 'overseas' (in Metropolitan France). The images all bear the mark of this double distance: refer-ential and spatial remoteness, on the one hand, displacement of imagination and memory on the other. Since the images presented in the first three poems are hallucinatory, the reader is, so to speak, at sea right from the beginning of the sequence. However, the third poem presents a transition to relative clarity as the speaker enunci-ates a mission of return or recall:

---

[60] Britton, *Édouard Glissant*, 155.

Sois un homme aux yeux calmes qui rit,
... et du bord immobile du cil il fait retour
   aux choses qu'il a vues, empruntant les
   chemins de la mer frauduleuse ...
il nous a fait plus d'une promesse d'îles,
comme celui qui dit à un plus jeune: 'Tu verras!'   (ŒC 35)

(Be a man with calm eyes who laughs
... and from the immobile rim of the lashes
   he turns back to the things he has seen,
   borrowing the paths of the fraudulent sea ...
more than one promise has he made us of islands
as one who says to someone younger: 'You will see!')   (*ÉOP* 37)

The return will be an internal or imagined one, then, a return of the mind's eye ('du bord immobile du cil'), represented as flying ('perfection du vol') or sailing back across a sea said to be fraudulent, presumably because the return is merely imagined. This promise cataleptically clarifies the organization of the rest of the poem sequence. Thus, following several poems evoking a boat journey, the tenth text evokes disembarcation, with the remainder of the sequence evoking things said or seen on dry land, in the town. In the revelatory passage of poem III, the only clue that the displacement will be temporal is the expression 'back to the things he has seen'. Similarly, in Chamoiseau's text, the narrator's remarks on memory as a return to childhood vision and experience both frame and determine, as we saw, the structure and significance of the entire text. Furthermore, Chamoiseau, like Saint-John Perse, acknowledges the unreliable fiduciary value of his memories. But whereas Saint-John Perse does so rhetorically through the image of the 'fraudulent sea', Chamoiseau's flirtation with narrative leads him to ask much more searching questions about agency. Of course, for the Martinican writer, the displacement effected by memory is temporal only, whereas Saint-John Perse's lyrical return involves a much more radical deception, in that an imaginary displacement—from Metropolitan France where the poet's family settled when he was 12—is grafted on to the imagined return through time, thus compounding the illusion of writing, that heaving sea of words. The promise of this process is that it will restore a vision of 'islands'. The island that was the scene of the poet's childhood will be revisited, as will the island in time that is childhood, and both will be made visible to those for whom the poet sings.

Both texts defer to the traditional progression of childhood from home-centredness to self-assertion in a realm beyond the limits of the house.[61] However, the final poems of '*Éloges*' express the speaker's peremptory intention to withdraw from the programme of recollection and communication and his determination to retreat into communion with his own body or with nature. In this sense, the trajectory of *Antan d'enfance* inverts that of '*Éloges*'; at the outset of *Antan d'enfance*, the child is absorbed in solitary games at home with fire, insects, rats, and the elements and only gradually turns towards the wider human community and its doings which then become the new centre of his preoccupations. Although *Antan d'enfance* is concerned with the dynamic between domestic and extra-domestic space, there is little sense in that text of the sea as a space of passage, and no sense of openness to arrivals from outside or to departures. This is consistent with the emphasis of the *créolité* movement on interiority: unlike the writing of *antillanité*, the *créoliste* imagination does not privilege the sea as a space of displacement, even if Raphaël Confiant's novel *Eau de café* (1991) is exceptional in its relatively maritime orientation, and even if that author claims that as a child he signed 'un pacte d'amour indéfectible avec cette mer que des générations d'hommes ont décrétée maudite' ('an indefeasible love pact with this sea that generations of men and women had declared cursed').[62] Conversely, towards the end of 'Pour fêter une enfance', having reviewed at length what goes on in the house and the organization of the *habitation* more generally, the poet/child concentrates on comings and goings across the sea.[63] And, in '*Éloges*', the 'sea' as the space-time of return (as memory) is present throughout the entire sequence.

---

[61] 'Et la Maison! la Maison? . . . on en sort!' ('And the House! the House? . . . we go out of it!') (*ŒC* 48; *ÉOP*, 53); 'L'enfant veut qu'on le peigne sur le pas de la porte' ('The child wants his hair combed on the doorstep) '(*ŒC* 51; *ÉOP*, 57) and, further on: 'A présent, laissez-moi, je vais seul. | Je sortirai, car j'ai affaire' ('And now let me be, I go alone. | I shall go out, for I have things to do') (*ŒC* 52; *ÉOP*, 57).

[62] Confiant, *Ravines du devant-jour*, 140.

[63] 'Alors | une mer plus crédule et hantée d'invisibles départs' ('In those days | a more credulous sea and haunted by invisible departures') (*ŒC* 28; *ÉOP*, 31); 'La barque de mon père, studieuse, amenait de grandes figures blanches' ('Reverently, my father's boat brought tall white forms') (*ŒC* 29, *ÉOP*, 31).

MEMORY AND COMMUNITY

'Éloges' does not simply evoke the mechanism of memory in terms of an introspective, specular, and subjective mission of memory. Rather the avowed function of the speaker's return to things he has seen is to share them with another. In this way, memory is presented not just as exalted lyricism; it also enables an intersubjective activity of revelation or initiation. In poem III, where the poetic mission is announced, the speaker or grown man addresses a person younger than he, promising that the latter 'will see' for himself what he, the speaker, had seen presumably in his youth. And further on, in poem XI for example, we read: 'Pour voir, se mettre à l'ombre. Sinon, rien' ('To see, go into the shade. Otherwise, nothing') (ŒC 43; ÉOP 47); then further on, in poem XIV: 'ô mes amis où êtes-vous que je ne connais pas? Ne verrez-vous cela aussi?' ('O my friends where are you, whom I do not know . . . Can't you see this too . . .?') (ŒC 46; ÉOP 51). Although Chamoiseau remembers his childhood as being full of solitary moments that he now deems unlikely, his text is saturated with marks of solidarity with the community or fraternity for whom he is remembering the childhood that they have in common. Thus, the universalizing connotations of the rather abstract and remote figures of the *songeur*, the *conteur*, and the *enfant* of 'Éloges' contrast on several levels with the child of Chamoiseau's memoirs, usually identified as the 'négrillon' or small (black) boy. This term is not simply an affectionate diminutive; it is also a social and racial marker identifying the narrator's ethnic allegiance, the connotations of 'grillon' (cricket) adding an actively expressive, oral dimension to the child's identity. Furthermore, in his wilful withdrawal from communication—'À présent laissez-moi, je vais seul | . . . et vous me laissez également, | assis, dans l'amitié de mes genoux' ('And now let me be, I go alone . . . and also you'll let me be, | sitting, in the friendship of my knees') (ŒC 52; ÉOP 57)—and in his (apparently) involuntary eviction from favour: 'Et moi, plein de santé, je vois cela, je vais | près du malade et lui conte cela: | et voici qu'il me haït' ('And I, full of health, I see this, I approach | the sick man and tell him about it: | and then how he hates me') (ŒC 39; ÉOP 43)—the child/speaker of 'Éloges' is much less socially integrated than the *négrillon* of *Antan d'enfance*. Whereas 'Éloges' ends with the peremptory dismissal of all human company, *Antan d'enfance* tapers off reluctantly into silence.

Much of the striking intertextuality between *Antan d'enfance*, on the one hand, and 'Éloges', on the other, centres on the congruent patterns of orality which mark each text. These patterns involve extensive use of direct address and pre-eminent self-referential discourse: for example, 'Je parle d'un Noël sinon amer, du moins très sombre' ('I'm talking about, if not a bitter Christmas, at least a sombre one') (*AE* 58; *C* 37). In their use of direct address, both texts address memory in the first place and, secondly, a certain audience or readership. In 'Éloges', however, memory is indirectly addressed as the 'maître du navire', whereas in *Antan d'enfance*, it is called upon directly and intimately: 'Mémoire ho, cette quête est pour toi' ('Memory ho, this quest is for you') (*AE* 11; *C* 3). Moreover, whereas Saint-John Perse's poetry seems to master memory, Chamoiseau's narrator tries to reassure and to cajole it, promising to submit to its flow.[64] In contrast to 'Éloges', where those who are to share the poet's memories are referred to as 'O mes amis . . . que je ne connais pas', in *Antan d'enfance* they are 'O mes frères'. Thus, Saint-John Perse's readers are not identified in time or in space, whereas the identity of the projected readers of *Antan d'enfance* is quite clear, since they are assumed to share the same past as the narrator. A dedication at the beginning of the text is addressed to these readers who will identify with the narrator's childhood: 'Partageurs ô/vous savez cette enfance!' ('O sharers | you know how childhood is!') (*AE* 7; *C*, p. ix) (unfortunately, the translation does not register the specificity of the shared childhood as indicated by the demonstrative). *Antan d'enfance* thus presents itself as being written for and addressed primarily to a specific community of readers for whom the remembered world will be familiar. This sense of recognition and solidarity resonates with the attempt on Chamoiseau's part to reconstruct, to recollect, or to remember the experience of a specific and shared (Caribbean) way of life.

---

[64] See *AE* 12: 'Mémoire, passons un pacte le temps d'un crayonné, baisse palissades et apaise les farouches, suggère le secret des traces invoquées au bord de tes raziés. Moi, je n'emporte ni sac de rapt ni coutelas de conquête, rien qu'une ivresse et que joie bien docile au gré (coulée du temps) de ta coulée' ('Memory, let's make a pact long enough for a sketch, lower your palisades and pacify the savages, reveal the secret of the traces that lie at the edge of your brushy borders. I bring neither sack for kidnapping nor knife for conquest, nothing but intoxication and a mighty docile joy at the rhythm (flow of time) of your flow'; *C* 4).

In raising issues such as differences of genre (poetry, autobiography, narrative, etc.), social and racial affiliation and integration, spatial orientation, relation between speaker and audience, between writer and readership, between the narrator's (or singer's) voice and those other voices 'quoted' or otherwise reported, the relation between the two texts principally illuminates the vastly different milieux, times, ideologies, poetics, and readerships of the two writers. And yet, unlike 'Pour fêter une enfance', 'Éloges' does not directly confirm the prevalence of the considerable social and historical differences between the childhood experiences evoked by each text. The world of the Caribbean town, as presented in 'Éloges', is a significantly less hierarchical milieu than the Caribbean plantation evoked in 'Pour fêter une enfance'. Consequently, the passages that economically outline in *Antan d'enfance* what Chamoiseau terms the 'ruine intérieure' of racism resonate less in relation to 'Éloges' than in relation to the casual privilege of the plantation childhood celebrated in 'Pour fêter une enfance'. Thus, while the two authors converge to a certain extent in the picture that they present of the Caribbean, in their evocation of its cultural and racial diversity, for example, or of the somewhat decadent texture of the urban environment, the contiguity of life and death, etc., this evocation is located, in Chamoiseau's case, in relation to an implicit collective affiliation and an implicit cultural agenda. 'Éloges', on the other hand, although it is also an exploration of the process of memory as imagination and dream, has as its agent the figure of a serenely universalized, idealized *enfant/songeur*. Between the writing of the self-styled 'Français des Iles', a Frenchman and Poet first and foremost, and that of the *Créole* who identifies himself as the 'négrillon'-turned 'Marqueur de paroles', this disparity is predictable. However, a closer reading of the convergences between the two works (in tone, genre, and self-reflexivity) provides much more than confirmation of a crudely determinist thesis. Apart from encouraging the reader to dwell on the texture of memory instead of reading through it, Chamoiseau's discreet raising of the ghost of 'Éloges' encourages us to review the complex relation in the French Caribbean context between self and community, past and present, memory and poetry, imagination and reality, personal expression and collective engagement, colonialism and neo- or post-colonialism.

All writing may be rewriting, all French Caribbean writing

recomposition, but it would be a mistake to dissolve the specificity of individual instances within some general theory of what intertextuality is or does. In the first place, there are as many examples of intertextuality as there are texts. Even within the *créolité* movement, even within that movement's foray into the genre of memoirs of childhood, and therein, even in relation to intertextual reference to the same poet and the same work, Raphaël Confiant's *Ravines du devant-jour* creates an entirely different intertextual relation to Saint-John Perse than the one realized in *Antan d'enfance*. Intertextuality can perhaps be best regarded in this context as a poetic language of relation, each time unique, but always engaging the reader in a *process* of relation, not just between texts, *œuvres*, genres, and writers, but also between places and times.

CHAPTER FIVE

The Plantation Revisited: Revising Time

> Maintenez-vous en état de veille . . . la plantation, immuable
> dans le tremblement, vient jusqu'à vous.[1]

In the French Caribbean imagination of local time and space, few 'chronotopes' are of greater significance than those of the plantation and the town. It is in relation to these two nodal topoi that most other micro- or macro-spaces on the islands are defined, usually as tributary or oppositional. They configure not only Caribbean space, but also Caribbean time. Although it would be tempting to discuss here questions such as the relation of natural or uncultivated space (sea, forest, river) to planted space, or the rich semiology of toponyms, this chapter attempts to keep both space and time in focus together. This aim is facilitated by the fact that, given the collapse of the plantation system in the mid-twentieth century, 'plantation writing' is fundamentally retrospective. Unlike the urban chronotope, it is, axiomatically, a 'lieu de mémoire'.[2]

DEFINING A TOPOS

In the Caribbean, as in the American 'Deep South', the Brazilian north-east, and the islands of the Indian Ocean, the plantation—growing sugar, cotton, coffee, or tobacco—was the pivotal element

---

[1] 'Keep yourselves in a state of watchfulness . . . the plantation, immutable in the quaking, will come right up to you'; Glissant, *Mahagony*, 249.
[2] Keith Alan Sprouse, '*Lieu de mémoire, lieu de créolité*: The Plantation as Site of Memory', *Cincinnati Romance Review*, 18 (1999), 153–61. The title of this article, more than its content (a critique of *créoliste* positions on gender and *marronnage*), is suggestive of the resonance of the plantation *imaginaire* in contemporary writing.

in the imperial equation. Throughout these three zones, as Édouard Glissant puts it, 'la même organisation rythme la production économique et fonde un style de vie' ('the same organization would create a rhythm of economic production and form the basis of a style of life').[3] Given that the plantation system was the cradle of Creole society and culture and that it flourished for about three centuries, the writing of these regions might be expected to recall, if not reproduce, its rhythms. Whether or not late-twentieth-century French Caribbean writing repeats the plantation paradigm on a structural level, it is certain that, on a much more banal, strictly referential level, it has revisited the scene of the plantation compulsively. Indeed, in one of its more productive contemporary veins, it subjects that system to a radical reassessment, itself symptomatic of a far-reaching revisionism in contemporary French Caribbean thought.

Édouard Glissant defines the plantation as an 'une organisation socialement pyramidale, confinée dans un lieu clos, fonctionnant apparemment en autarcie mais réellement en dépendance, et dont le mode technique de production est non évolutif parce qu'il est basé sur une structure esclavagiste' ('an organization formed in a social pyramid, confined within an enclosure, functioning apparently as an autarky but actually dependent, and with a technical mode of production that cannot evolve because it is based on a slave structure').[4] This definition dwells on the spatial and temporal dimensions of the institution, which is represented as an enclosed and constricted space, and as a non-evolving or indeed static organization, largely because of its dependence on slavery. Glissant also underlines the constraints imposed by the colony's fixation on the distant European centre. This 'extraversion' causes a great deficit of autonomy and, combined with dependence on slavery, it limits change and creativity.

Joseph Zobel's *La Rue Cases-Nègres*, set in 1930s Martinique, is perhaps the most widely read and most comprehensive literary representation of the structure of plantation space and time in the French Caribbean.[5] The socio-spatial configuration of Zobel's

---

[3] Glissant, *Poétique de la Relation*, 77; *Poetics of Relation*, 63.

[4] *Poétique de la Relation*, 78; *Poetics of Relation*, 64.

[5] Although less well known than *La Rue Cases-Nègres*, Zobel's novel *Diab'là* (Paris: Présence africaine, 1946) is even more fundamentally a rural novel than the better-known work, which concentrates principally on the rural–urban shift.

plantation as a hermetically sealed time capsule, located in Petit-Morne, is sketched out by the narrator at the very start of the novel. The hierarchical regimen of plantation society is mirrored in the pyramidal organization of physical space: the *blanc créole* of this particular plantation is an absentee who leaves no mark on the visible landscape; beneath him is the *géreur*, the manager or agent, who alone lives in a proper house, and subordinate to the *géreur* is the *économe* (or overseer), followed by the *commandeur* (driver), then the *nègres* (blacks), and finally, at the base of the pyramid, the *petite bande* or child gang. The row of cabins housing the plantation workers is the protagonist/narrator's place of origin and the seminal location of the story; it is so significant that the entire novel bears its name. In fact, the expression is less a name than a generic term, since every plantation had its own 'black shack alley'.

The rigid social structure of the plantation is comfortingly Euclidean and resonates as such with its Newtonian calibration of time. This explains its deep-rooted attraction for De Cassagnac, the *béké* of Raphaël Confiant's novel, *Eau de café*:

> la canne est toute une civilisation, vous comprenez. Elle règle la vie de quatre heures du matin à six heures du soir. Chacun est à son poste: le commandeur qui distribue les tâches et en surveille l'accomplissement, les coupeurs . . . les amarreuses . . . les petites bandes de négrillons . . .[6]

This inflexible temporal order is reflected in the strict management of space (memorably celebrated by Saint-John Perse in 'Pour fêter une enfance')[7] and exacerbated by the pervasive sense of closure. In Raphaël Confiant's *Commandeur du sucre,* what Glissant has termed the plantation's 'autarky' is expressed in spatial terms: 'L'habitation est un enclos. Le monde extérieur n'existe pas pour ceux qui y vivent' ('The plantation is an enclosure. For those who

---

[6] Raphaël Confiant, *Eau de café* (Paris: Grasset & Fasquelle, 1991), 39. 'a whole civilization is based on the sugarcane, you see. The cane regulates life from four in the morning to six in the evening. Everyone is at their post then: from the driver who assigns the work and oversees the labour, the cutters . . . the binders . . . the child gangs.'

[7] 'A droite | on rentrait le café, à gauche le manioc'; 'Et par ici étaient les chevaux bien marqués, les mulets au poil ras, et par là-bas les bœufs; | ici les fouets, et là le cri de l'oiseau Annaô—et là encore la blessure des cannes au moulin' ('To the right | the coffee was brought in, to the left the manioc'; 'And over here were the horses duly marked, smooth-coated mules, and over there the oxen; | here the whips, and there the cry of the bird Annaô—and still there the wound of the sugarcanes at the mill'; *ŒC* 25; *EOP* 25).

live inside it, the outside world does not exist').[8] The same association of constriction and confinement is highlighted in *La Rue Cases-Nègres* by the fact that the alley where the labourers live is located right beside the canefields. There is thus no room for a hiatus between labour and life, between exploitation and existence. Moreover, the double echo—alliteration and assonance—linking the terms 'cases' and 'cannes' underlines this confining contiguity (a similar effect operates in English too: 'cane | cotton' and 'cabins'). A further index of closure, this time capitalist closure, is the plantation shop, run by the wife of the *géreur* (agent). The claustrophobic effect of this closed circuit of exchange, this absence of internal boundaries between life and work and between shelter and exploitation, is reinforced by the fact that the workers metonymically refer to this shop as 'la maison'.[9] In Zobel's novel, the factory or sugar-processing plant (often linked to a rum distillery) is also a significant locus, a fundamental part of the plantation's production system. The refinery reproduces the structures of the plantation, its organization of labour mirroring the racial hierarchy that obtains in the canefields. Thus, the factory foreman, Justin Roc, a *métis*, is a former plantation *géreur*. The closed circuit of agricultural production and industrialized processing is also exposed in Raphaël Confiant's diptych, *Commandeur du sucre* and *Régisseur du rhum*,[10] both set, like *La Rue Cases-Nègres*, in 1930s Martinique, the first in the canefields, the second in the distillery, and both figuring the same cast of characters.

Placing the plantation at the centre of his reflection on the 'repeating island' paradigm, Antonio Benítez-Rojo characterizes it as a machine in the Deleuzian sense:

This family of machines almost always makes cane sugar, coffee, cocoa, cotton, indigo, tea, bananas, pineapples, fibers, and other goods whose cultivation is impossible or too expensive in the temperate zones; furthermore, it usually produces the Plantation, capitalized to indicate not just the presence of plantations but also the type of society that results from their use and abuse.[11]

Benítez-Rojo's reading of the Caribbean is based on what he terms

[8] Raphaël Confiant, *Commandeur du sucre* (Paris: Écriture, 1994), 51.
[9] *La Rue Cases-Nègres*, 105; *Black Shack Alley*, 61.
[10] Raphaël Confiant, *Régisseur du rhum* (Paris: Écriture, 1999).
[11] Benítez-Rojo, *Repeating Island*, 9.

the 'brand-new paradigm' of Chaos Theory, according to which 'within the (dis)order that swarms around what we already know of as Nature, it is possible to observe dynamic states or regularities that repeat themselves globally'.[12] In the Caribbean context, the Cuban critic sees not so much shapes as tropisms or movements repeating themselves. For example, as the title of his study suggests, he notes the dissemination across the Caribbean of a dynamic of disconnection or separation. In this way, the islands' spatial discreteness is repeated in the strict and closed organization of plantation and factory labour, and in the further repetition of discrete or isolated units in the plantation's residential arrangements. Indeed, in Glissant's *Le Quatrième Siècle*, it is the entire (post-plantation) island of Martinique that is represented as a 'closed space', set apart from the 'world', the latter being configured as a kind of outer space that occasionally hits the island like a meteor. Its population is bedazzled 'par tout ce qui, légitimement ou non, se proclamait l'émanation et la représentation de l'ailleurs. Comme si c'était un morceau miraculeux du monde qui venait chaque fois traverser en météore l'espace clos de l'ici' ('by anything that, legitimately or not, proclaimed that it emanated from and represented that somewhere else—coming every time like a miraculous bit of the world, like a meteor passing through the enclosed space here').[13] One could expand on Benítez-Rojo's insight by observing the importance for the Caribbean imagination of temporal disconnection too, as in the intense interest manifested in discrete 'islands of time', for example journeys or childhood.

'PLANTATION' OR 'HABITATION': WHAT'S IN A NAME?

Although historians still refer to the late sixteenth- and early seventeenth-century colonization of Ireland as the Leinster, Munster, and Ulster 'plantations', the term functions in the Irish context as an overwhelmingly figurative allusion to the English conquest, clearing, and settlement of Ireland. Sheltering behind its benignly organic primary meaning (cultivation of the land), the term 'plantation' euphemizes in the Irish context what was primarily, and in

[12] Ibid. 2.
[13] Glissant, *Le Quatrième Siècle*, 255; *The Fourth Century*, 259.

most cases, purely a policy of agrarian dispossession and usurpation.[14] In the Caribbean, the term enacts a similar elision, less dramatically than in the Hibernian situation, only in so far as the superimposition of literal and figurative meanings is much more motivated in the so-called 'New World': there, the colonial settlement was, in fact, based on the plantation of labour-intensive crops and on a punishing system of production sustained by slavery and indenture. And yet, regardless of this literal reference, the principal and permanent object of plantation in the 'New World' context also was the displaced population. Hence, in the Caribbean, the term 'plantation' designated the entire colonial system of production and resettlement based on transportation and slavery. Furthermore, whereas in Ireland the indigenous population was colonized, and its space occupied, in the French Caribbean islands, virtually the entire indigenous population was either eliminated or expelled. In this sense, voluntarily or involuntarily, outsiders came to occupy the islands completely. Most colonial contexts produced a certain level of the 'extraversion' indicated in Glissant's definition of the plantation. But in the Caribbean, this tension between colonial space, on the one hand, and the umbilical pull tugging the settlers' attention back towards some original space or other characterized almost every single element of the population. Local observers like Moreau de Saint-Méry in the eighteenth century,[15] European travellers like Anthony Trollope in the following century,[16] and contemporary historians[17] alike draw attention to

---

[14] See Nicholas Canny, 'Early Modern Ireland *c.*1500-1700', in R. Foster (ed.), *The Oxford Illustrated History of Ireland* (Oxford: Oxford University Press, 1989), 104–60: 131–9.

[15] In Saint-Domingue, in the first part of the 18th century, 'talk of definitive or provisional return to France is all the rage . . . everyone considers themselves as just passing through in a land where they often find their last rest': Moreau de Saint-Méry, *Description topographique, physique, civile, politique et historique de la partie française de l'isle Saint-Domingue* (1779; Paris: Société française d'outre mer, 1984), i, 34.

[16] Trollope's comments are quoted in Ch. 7.

[17] The historian Pierre Pluchon distinguishes between the planters of Saint-Domingue (present-day Haiti) and those of the smaller Windward Islands: the former are expatriates who see their tenure as strictly provisional, whereas the latter are more likely to be settled and adapted, or 'Creoles'; 'les Iles du Vent ont une société plus enracinée que celle de Saint-Domingue': Pierre Pluchon, *Histoire des Antilles et de la Guyane* (Toulouse: Privat, 1982): 171. Similarly, Gabriel Debien notes that the planter in Saint-Domingue, although he might call himself a 'habitant', is not a builder, his aim being rather to make a quick fortune: 'le colon de

the unstable, provisional nature of the parenthetical attachment often formed with the Caribbean colonies by the first generations of European settlers. All these writers recognize, however, that the planter population of the French Leeward Islands put down roots much more rapidly than those of other islands.[18]

Significantly, in the French Caribbean context, the term 'plantation' is usually jettisoned altogether, or else—in the collocation 'Plantation-Habitation'—it is yoked to the term that frequently replaces it. The word 'habitation' would seem to be derived, as Régis Antoine suggests, from the expressions 'habitué' and 'habitant' used to qualify the planter over the 'first centuries of French settlement of the Antilles'.[19] It is in this historical sense that Édouard Glissant resurrects it: 'Il y eut une servante de cuisine pour hasarder de demander à *l'habitant* s'il comptait vendre le nouveau né, une fois enfant' ('There was one kitchen slave who ventured to ask the *planter* if he was intending to sell the newborn infant once it had become a child').[20] Régis Antoine notes that certain Creole idioms and toponyms retain this historical usage: 'crabes zhabitants' for example.[21] In Haiti, however, the term 'habitant' has survived up to the present to denote peasants working the land.[22] The temporal implications of these cognate expressions, especially

---

Saint-Domingue, quand il se dit "habitant" n'est pas un bâtisseur. Son but est de faire fortune au plus tôt . . .': 'Les Grand'cases des plantations à Saint-Domingue aux XVIIe et XVIIIe siècles', *Notes d'histoire coloniale*, 138 (1970), 1.

[18] The Creole residences described by Le Père Labat have an air of permanence, boasting 'beautiful avenues, tall trees, oak or elm, planted in rows and carefully tended', Le R. P. Jean-Baptiste Labat, *Nouveau voyage aux isles d'Amérique*, iii (1742), 16 (repr. Fort-de-France: Éditions des Horizons Caraïbes, 1972).

[19] Antoine, *La Littérature franco-antillaise*, 35.

[20] Glissant, *La Case du commandeur*, 159. Emphasis mine.

[21] Antoine, *La Littérature franco-antillaise*, 35.

[22] Jacques Roumain, *Gouverneurs de la rosée* (Paris: Éditeurs français réunis, 1944); tr. Langston Hughes and Mercer Cook as *Masters of the Dew* (Reynal & Hitchcock, 1947; repr. with introd. by J. Michael Dash (London and Kingston: Heinemann Educational, 1978): 'il n'y a d'autre Providence que son travail d'habitant sérieux, d'autre miracle que le fruit de ses mains' (p. 47). In the English translation, the word 'habitant' is not translated ('And there's no providence but hard work, no miracles but the fruit of your hands', p. 54), although from the context it clearly refers to those who toil on the land. Émile Ollivier uses it in the same sense: 'Personnellement, il n'avait rien contre ces gens de la ville qui voulaient s'enrichir de plus en plus, mais les habitants ne devraient pas faire les frais de leur prospérité' ('On a personal level he had nothing against the townsfolk who just wanted to get richer and richer, but the country dwellers should not have to pay for their prosperity'): *Passages* (1991; Paris: Le Serpent à Plumes, 1994).

their connection with the notion of 'habitude', are highly significant. André Leroi-Gourhan recognizes that the term 'demeure', or
'dwelling', a more poetic synonym of 'habitation' in French,
suggests a somewhat sentimental notion of vague duration and
sedentary space.[23] Pierre Bourdieu, for his part, uses the term
'habitus' to refer to the positions in social space associated with the
system of 'durable dispositions' ('dispositions durables') or persistent world-views characteristic of different 'classes'. Bourdieu thus
harnesses both the temporal connotations of duration or durability
implicit in the term 'habit' and the spatial notion of (dis)positions
in order to suggest social grooves, ruts, or furrows, thus echoing
the 'rhizomatic' philological and semantic network linking notions
of habit, settlement, persistence, custom, culture, and cultivation
latent in the hybrid expression 'Plantation-Habitation'.

Use of the word 'habitation' as a synonym for 'plantation' is
very widespread in the French Caribbean and not only within
those contemporary discourses that seek to dissociate the entire
plantation system from the negative associations to which it has
long and legitimately been tethered. Thus Patrick Chamoiseau and
Raphaël Confiant point out in their survey of Caribbean literature, entitled *Lettres créoles*: 'aux Antilles, le système des plantations devrait s'appeler "système d'habitation" ' ('in the Caribbean
islands the plantation system should be called the "habitation"
system').[24] They justify their prescription of this terminological
distinction, widely observed in the French-colonized Antilles from
the seventeenth century onwards, by referring to the disparity in
area between the vast latifundaria of continental America and the
more restricted colonial demesnes of the French Caribbean. For
the reduced scale of the latter is held to explain the special intensity of French Caribbean creolization or cultural mixing. In other
words, since the Big House of the *béké* was a real and visible
centrepoint in the Caribbean plantation, slaves or labourers came
into closer contact with its values or, to quote Chamoiseau and
Confiant: 'tout cela amplifia les interactions de la créolisation'
('this all amplified the opportunities for creolization').[25]

---

[23] 'connotation sentimentale de durée vague et d'espace sédentaire', André Leroi-
Gourhan, 'Demeure: "Espace construit dans lequel on vit" ', *Corps écrit, La
Demeure*, 9 (1984), 9–13: 9.
[24] Chamoiseau and Confiant, *Lettres créoles*, 35.
[25] Ibid. 36

Limitation of scale is also held to explain the relatively porous nature of the *habitation*'s periphery. Towns, ports, and, thereby, the Metropolitan connection would all have impinged on the life of the French Caribbean plantation rather more intensely than would have been possible in the vast continental plantations or even in the estates of larger Caribbean islands such as Cuba or present-day Haiti.

Clearly, however, the *créolité* movement also promotes the term 'habitation' because of its connotations. Firstly, it suggests the quasi-ontological category of dwelling (witness Heidegger's capitalization on the rich phenomenological and ontological associations of Hölderlin's 'dichterisch wohnt der Mensch' or 'man dwells poetically'), rather than a provisional economic arrangement; secondly, it replaces the harsh realities of toil and exploitation in the canefields with the altogether more clement and congenial connotations of residence. Whereas the term 'plantation' implies a functional, economic paradigm, a proto-industrial unit of production, the word 'habitation' suggests instead a human habitat, an ecology, much more in tune with the *créoliste* rewriting of the time and space of the plantation. Thus, whereas the chapter devoted by Beverley Ormerod to the French Caribbean plantation novel is entitled 'The Plantation as Hell',[26] the inferno is not the comparison that comes to mind on reading many of the more recent French Caribbean plantation novels.

As though to underline the fact that the term 'habitation' is not neutral, the Haitian critic Maximilien Laroche writes of the plantation and the 'habitation' as two distinct and even dichotomous socio-spatial models, which he sees as emblematic of two successive approaches to Haitian literary creation, still caught up, according to him, in an evolutionary plot centred on the plantation:

L'esprit de la littérature haïtienne est celui d'une rupture d'avec l'ère des plantations. Dans la réalité le passage des plantations aux habitations n'est pas encore achevé. . . . Dans l'utopie des écrivains haïtiens, la plantation est le lieu carcéral, concentrationnaire et ségrégationnaire où le planteur esclavagiste . . . isolait l'esclave noir pour le forcer à travailler. L'habitation dont rêve cet ancien esclave devenu homme libre et écrivain, est un espace

---

[26] Beverley Ormerod, *An Introduction to the French Caribbean Novel* (London: Heinemann, 1985).

ouvert choisi par lui et bâti à sa convenance, où il veut avoir le loisir de faire, selon la définition de la liberté, 'tout ce qui ne nuit pas à autrui'.[27]

Laroche believes, then, that Haitian writers are still only dreaming of the imaginative or literary freedom that one might associate with the term 'habitation', since, in order to lay claim to this desired freedom, they must first of all break free from the prisonhouse of racialization ('se déprendre de cette logique de la racialization dans laquelle il se voit enfermé contre son gré'), synonymous for Laroche with the plantation system:

Car c'est cela la plantation: se trouver obligé, malgré soi, de faire de la négritude. On ne vous jette peut-être plus directement dans l'esclavage mais on vous oblige davantage encore que par le passé à être commandeur des vôtres. On ne vous interdit plus en principe de quitter la plantation mais vous n'avez nulle part où aller ni le choix d'*habiter la maison* qui vous plaît.[28]

Laroche's view of the plantation as a symbol of literary limitation and aesthetic/intellectual coercion, and his promotion of the 'habitation' as a figure of imaginative freedom, could be applied to much contemporary French Caribbean writing. Yet, ironically in the French Caribbean context, the obsessive return to the literal space and time of what is termed there the 'habitation' indicates an inability or an unwillingness to choose freely an open literary agenda. But then, in so far as dwelling or habitat is an obsessive Caribbean (or post-slavery) paradigm, and in so far as the French Caribbean plantation has colonized and even, perhaps, corrupted this paradigm by transforming the generic term 'habitation' mean-

---

[27] Maximilien Laroche, *Sémiologie des apparences*, GRELCA Essais 11 (Quebec: Université de Laval, 1984), 109–10; 'The spirit of Haitian literature is informed by a break with the plantation era. In reality, however, the transition from plantation to "habitation" is not yet complete . . . In the utopia of Haitian writing, the plantation is a site of incarceration, a concentration camp, a space of segregation where the slave-owning planter . . . used to isolate the black slave and force him to work. The "habitation" dreamt of by this former slave become free man and writer, is an open space, chosen by him and constructed to his taste, where he wants to have the leisure to do, according to the definition of freedom, anything that does not interfere with somebody else's liberty.'

[28] Ibid. 110; 'Because that is what the plantation means: it is about being forced to enforce negritude. Although you are not technically enslaved, even more than in the past, you are turned into a driver. Nobody says that you cannot leave the plantation, but you have nowhere else to go and you cannot choose *where you want to live*.' Emphasis mine.

ing 'dwelling', into a synonym for itself, it is inevitably going to be difficult for writers to break out of that conceptual prisonhouse.

It must surely be significant that all Caribbean writing, in French at least,[29] should be so very preoccupied with representing inhabited space in general. Along with education, this is the single most predominant theme of *La Rue Cases-Nègres*, and it is also at the forefront of writing by Simone Schwarz-Bart, Gisèle Pineau, and Patrick Chamoiseau.[30] Michel Gresset, a specialist in William Faulkner's work, has observed that American culture in general is particularly concerned with the notion of the dwelling-place or the home. However, he believes that this is particularly true of Southern culture, in which space is perceived as 'the materialization of time' ('une culture qui perçoit l'espace comme du temps matérialisé']).[31] The notion that the relation to time can be translated into a relation to space is not unrelated to the phenomenology of Gaston Bachelard. For Bachelard, memory cannot really register Bergsonian duration: in other words, we cannot relive *as such* past duration, we can only recall it as abstract linear time, deprived of all density. In a particularly illuminating statement, Bachelard suggests that fossils are materialized duration, duration made concrete by long periods of dwelling.[32] We have already noted Édouard Glissant's concern with duration. He has made a connection, for example, between the fact that in Faulkner's poetics Southern blacks are not involved in linear plots or storylines of foundation and filiation, on the one hand, and on the other their

[29] This preoccupation makes itself felt in Caribbean writing in English too. See Maeve McCusker, 'No Place like Home? Constructing an Identity in Patrick Chamoiseau's *Texaco*', in Gallagher (ed.), *Ici-Là*.

[30] For example, in Schwarz-Bart's *Pluie et vent sur Télumée Miracle*, Toussine's house is the envy of the entire locality, Télumée represents herself as a tortoise, carrying her house around the island with her, and her grandmother represents the community as a set of homes linked by a spider's web of relations; in Gisèle Pineau's *La Grande Drive des esprits* (Paris: Le Serpent à plumes, 1993), Léonce builds his own house, and in Chamoiseau's *Texaco* Esternome is a carpenter and house-builder, while the eponymous 'Driver's Cabin' is at the heart of Glissant's fourth novel, *La Case du commandeur*.

[31] Michel Gresset, '*Going* la maison', *Corps écrit*, 9, *La Demeure* (1984), 119–26: 122.

[32] 'La mémoire … n'enregistre pas la durée concrète, la durée au sens bergsonien. On ne peut revivre les durées abolies. On ne peut que les penser, les penser sur la ligne d'un temps abstrait privé de toute épaisseur. C'est par l'espace, c'est dans l'espace que nous trouvons les beaux fossiles de durée concrétisés par de longs séjours': Bachelard, *La Poétique de l'espace*, 28.

ability to endure or to inhabit duration (like cats attaining to eternity by sheer immobility and somnolence).[33] In Daniel Maximin's *L'Isolé Soleil*, the plantation is called 'l'Habitation (des) Flamboyants', the flame trees for which it is named preserving the reference to the plant-ation, but the apposed phrase 'la maison de ton grand-père', underlines the notion of dwelling. A sense of duration is introduced by the further description of the house as a 'vivant rêve d'histoire', a living dream of history.[34] Similarly, in Saint-John Perse's 'Pour fêter une enfance', the house, foregrounded by capitalization, is associated both with trees and with duration: 'Et la Maison durait sous les arbres à plumes' ('and the House endured under the plumed trees').[35] In Patrick Chamoiseau's celebration of childhood, the house also ensures a sense of continuity, although it is, in addition, a locus of community; it becomes, after all, the objective correlative of collective memory, (with)holding the steadily retracting archive of the past, standing guard over an ever more distant era: 'O mes frères, vous savez cette maison que je ne pourrais décrire, sa noblesse diffuse, sa mémoire de poussière ... la maison a fermé une à une ses fenêtres ... se refermant à mesure sur sa garde d'une époque—notaire fragile de nos antans d'enfance' ('O my brothers, you know this house I could never describe, its noble aura, its dusty memory ... the house has closed its windows one by one ... gradually closing around its guardianship of an era—the fragile archive of our childhood yore').[36] However, one of the most striking poetic images of duration as materialization through dwelling is, perhaps, Chamoiseau's eponymous 'old man slave'. This figure (significantly defined not just as a slave, but also as a man) is said to 'last', to 'dwell' in his corner over years and years, his features 'sculpted' by the glow of his pipe,[37] his skin aged like the

[33] Glissant notes that, in Faulkner's poetics, 'les Noirs sont capables de se couler dans la durée (comme on a dit que les chats, à force d'immobile et de somnolence, ont fini par vaincre l'éternité'), and he attributes this to the fact that 'ils ne maîtrisent pas l'histoire': *Faulkner Mississippi*, 87.

[34] 'L'habitation des Flamboyants, la maison de ton grand-père, est un vivant rêve d'histoire': Maximin, *L'Isolé Soleil*, 21.

[35] Saint-John Perse, *Œuvres complètes*, 30; *Éloges and Other Poems*, 33.

[36] *Antan d'enfance*, 164; *Childhood*, 117.

[37] 'il demeure dans son coin, des années durant, suçant une pipe de tabac-macouba dont l'incendie sévère lui sculpte la figure'; 'il dure, il piète dans la friche qui ne procure'; 'rugueux comme l'écorce d'un arbre qui a passé mille ans': Chamoiseau, *L'Esclave Vieil Homme*, 22 and 17.

'bark' of a tree more than a thousand years old, his whole being ultimately evoked as 'un minéral de patiences immobiles' ('a mineral formed by still patience').[38]

A SPACE OF EXILE AND EXPLOITATION

Antonio Benítez-Rojo notes that the plantation machine was astonishingly productive in socio-economic terms: it produced, after all,

no fewer than ten million African slaves and thousands of coolies (from India, China and Malaysia) . . . turned out mercantile capitalism, industrial capitalism . . . African underdevelopment . . . Caribbean population . . . imperialism, wars, colonial blocs, rebellions, repressions, sugar islands, runaway slave settlements, air and naval bases, revolutions of all sorts, and even a 'free associated state' next to an unfree socialist state.[39]

All this to remind the reader that the Caribbean is 'not just a multiethnic sea or a group of islands divided by different languages' but an 'important historico-economic sea'.[40] The plantation's prodigious productivity was predicated, however, on intensive oppression. In many of the major texts of the French Caribbean tradition, it appears as an abrasive, corrosive environment. The physical mutilation of Zobel's M'man Tine and of Simone Schwarz-Bart's eponymous Télumée in the canefields is emblematic in purely physical terms of the brutalization rampant under slavery. Maximilien Laroche uses the term 'concentration camp' to qualify the plantation, and certainly, it is represented as a carceral space and a site of hard labour, even when the workers are not technically enslaved:

Un contremaître me désigna ma tâche et je me trouvai d'un seul coup plongée au cœur de la malédiction. Les sabres coupaient au ras du sol et les tiges s'affaissaient, les piquants voltigeaient, s'insinuaient partout, dans mes reins, mon dos, mon nez, mes jambes, pareils à des éclats de verre . . . J'avais entouré mes mains de bandages serrés très fort, mais ces diables de piquants s'enfonçaient dans le linge, mes doigts comprimés ne m'obéissaient plus et bientôt je rejetai toutes ces bandes, entrai carrément dans le feu des cannes.[41]

---

[38] Ibid. 17.   [39] Benítez-Rojo, *Repeating Island*, 9.
[40] Ibid.
[41] Schwarz-Bart, *Pluie et vent sur Télumée Miracle*, 199; 'A foreman told me what my job was, and I found myself plunged at a blow into the heart of maledic-

Canefield labour is idealized at the start of *La Rue Cases-Nègres*; it is represented through the eyes of a child as an innocent paradise, an entertaining spectacle, and a forbidden playground, only to be denounced once the child matures sufficiently to perceive it as a living hell. The narrator's eventual disillusionment is rendered all the more bitter by his previous failure to perceive the adult workers' infantilization by plantation managers and their collusion in this process as they too treat the plantation as a holiday camp following payday.[42] As the child's insight grows, the world of the black 'adult' workers is exposed as irredeemably stunted by their childlike dependency, and the novel's plot thus prefigures Édouard Glissant's indictment in *Le Discours antillais* and elsewhere of the temperamental irresponsibility and economic parasitism fostered by the plantation system.[43] In *Le Quatrième Siècle*, a novel that attempts to recover and reappropriate the story of the French Caribbean from 1788 to 1944, Édouard Glissant lampoons the fatuous tropical pastoral that would whitewash the harshness of plantation labour:

Dans un pays où chanter est comme devenir libre, les chantres étaient inévitables . . . et ils naquirent de leur propre béatitude. 'Qu'il était beau et bon, en rangs coordonnés, au rythme du tam-tam, et dans la joyeuse confiance du travail de couper la canne: pendant qu'au loin les alizés caressaient la douceur des fleurs, des fruits, des feuilles et des branches!' . . . Le chantre se balançait, feignant la volupté. Ayant oublié, non seulement le morne et sa raide exigence mais encore l'épuisement, les fourmis rouges, la saignée, le désert des cannes étendues sous le soleil. Et c'est que le chantre dansait sur un chemin qui n'était pas tracé pour ses pieds; il rejetait loin de lui jusqu'au souvenir de la boue primordiale.[44]

---

tion. The machetes skimmed low, the stems fell, and the prickles flew everywhere, like splinters of glass, into my back, my nose, my legs . . . I had put tight bandages on my hands, but the infernal prickles stuck into the cloth, my constricted fingers wouldn't obey me, and soon I tore off the bandages and entered outright into the fire of the canes': *Bridge of Beyond*, 136. For a more dystopian view of plantation labour in *La Rue Cases-Nègres*, see pp. 89 and 210–11.

[42] See, for example, *La Rue Cases-Nègres*, 81.

[43] Glissant argues that dependence on enslaved human resources explains the technological irresponsibility of the planter class, just as slavery accounts for the tendency on the part of the ex-slaves to participate in an economy of subsistence ('généralisation des petits métiers, djobs, économie parcellaire'): *Poétique de la relation*, 79.

[44] *Le Quatrième Siècle*, 222; 'In a country where singing is like becoming free, bards were bound to come. They were born of their own bliss . . . "How lovely and

Le Quatrième Siècle is not the only one of Édouard Glissant's novels to dwell at length on the institution of the plantation. Numerous novels of the 1980s and 1990s—including Glissant's own *La Case du commandeur* (1981) and *Tout-monde* (1993)—are shot through with flashbacks to the plantation scene. In addition, Patrick Chamoiseau's *Texaco* (1992), Vincent Placoly's *Frères Volcans* (1983), and Roland Brival's *Montagne d'ébène* (1984), all emphasize resistance to slavery, while Chamoiseau's more recent novel, *L'Esclave Vieil Homme et le molosse* (1997) concentrates poetically on slave subjectivity and the dynamic between master and slave. 'Emancipation' in 1848 did not directly cause the demise of the plantation system nor did it dispel its traumatic associations. Hence the plantation's representation in novels set in the twentieth century as a realm that continued, long after the abolition of slavery, to be exploited for the sole profit of the *béké* and his administrators; a realm where the workers, descendants of the enslaved and/or the indentured, are all, from the very old to the very young, caught in the poverty trap of which the plantation becomes the symbol. Right up to the middle of the twentieth century, deprivation stalks the 'rues case-nègres' of Caribbean writing; hunger is a leitmotif not just of Césaire's *Cahier*, but also of Joseph Zobel's work, both in *La Rue Cases-Nègres* and also in the earlier novel, *Diab'là*, where the narrator, opening the narrative, admits that he is starving: 'et moi, je meurs de faim'.[45]

Most narratives emphasize less the material hardship of the post-slavery plantation than the spiritual rot at its core. In *Pluie et vent sur Télumée Miracle*, Élie and Amboise both avoid plantation work at all costs, being too conscious of its spiritually toxic effect.[46] Several novels underline the sexual abuse endemic in the

---

how fine it was to cut cane in orderly lines to the tom-tom's beat, joyful and confident in one's work while in the distance the sea breeze caressed the sweetness of the flowers, the fruits, the leaves and the branches!" . . . The bard rocked back and forth pretending sensual delight in this bright spot. He had forgotten not just the hills and their steep demands, but also the exhaustion, the red ants, the bleeding, the desert of cane stretched out beneath the sun, because the bard was dancing along a road not made for his feet. He drove even the memory of the primordial mud far from him': *The Fourth Century*, 224–5.

[45] Zobel, *Diab'là*, 12.

[46] 'Quant à Élie, le seul mot de canne le faisait entrer dans des transes, des fureurs incompréhensibles. . . . [Il] criait, jurait tous ses grands dieux que la canne ne le happerait pas, jamais, jamais il n'achèterait de coutelas pour aller dans la terre des blancs. Il préférait plutôt se trancher les mains avec . . .' ('As for Élie, the very word

plantation hierarchy, from predatory *commandeurs* to rapacious *békés*. Underlining the diffuse sense of dispossession that survived well beyond the nineteenth century, Michèle Lacrosil in her novel, *Demain Jab-Herma* (1967), has the Martinican Cragget articulate his tortured sense of dispossession, and his fixation on the white Metropolitan Philippe, who is and has everything that Cragget desires. In a context dominated by the power struggle between the Metropolitan White, the Creole White or Grand-Blanc, and the eponymous black *quimboiseur*, Cragget, the *métis*, craves a place of his own. It is highly significant that, in the following passage, the object of his yearning is a shelter, a dwelling-space, a home, a site, or even just a place of his own, on 'his' island:

> L'Autre est partout chez lui; Cragget est partout un étranger . . . Où trouver dans ce pays, les terres ayant été distribuées aux Autres il y a deux ou trois siècles, un lopin, un abri, et un concept permettant de se ressaisir et d'être soi? . . . Dans les pires moments des crises, il devient ce fou qui, pour *posséder une maison* décente et un coin de la terre où sa mère esclave est née, fouille depuis des années à la recherche d'un or légendaire.[47]

The dynamic between the plantocracy and the *Métropole* was a complex one, particularly following the abolition of slavery. Although the former entertained vague aspirations to secession in response to perceived Metropolitan interference in 'home affairs', the failure of these vague aspirations to independence and the copper-fastening of the Metropolitan connection in 1946 did not disturb the racial balance of socio-economic power. Indeed the *békés* and *grands blancs* managed to keep in place the structures of plantation apartheid well beyond the near total collapse of the plantation system. Thus, in Ernest Pépin's *Tambour-Babel*, the contemporary plantation, despite its predominantly vestigial aura,

---

cane drove him wild, filled him with incomprehensible fury . . . [he] railed and swore by all the gods the cane would never get him, he was never going to buy a knife to go work on the land of the white men. He'd rather use it to cut his own hands off'): Schwarz-Bart, *Pluie et vent sur Télumée Miracle*, 84; *Bridge of Beyond*, 54.

[47] Michèle Lacrosil, *Demain Jab-Herma* (Paris: Gallimard, 1967), 42. My emphasis. 'The Other is all over his island; and he Cragget is everywhere a stranger . . . The land having been distributed amongst the Others two or three centuries ago, where can we find a patch, a shelter, or a concept that will allow us to regroup and be ourselves . . . At the darkest moments of his attacks, he becomes this madman who has being digging for years for legendary treasure, in order to possess a decent home and a corner of this earth where his slave mother was born.'

is still a by-word for socio-economic stratification along racial lines and remains, as such, an ongoing reminder of slavery and of all that remains to be reformed in the material and social conditions of post-abolition Caribbean society.

THE DIALECTIC OF ALIENATION AND RESISTANCE

Post-1940s writing cannot be accused of representing the plantation as an unopposed institution, immune to historical forces. On the contrary, much emphasis is placed on the possibility and practice of resistance and subversion. Central to Édouard Glissant's version of the past is the distinction between the *marron* or runaway and the plantation slave. In the historical fresco painted on one level at least by the narrative of *Le Quatrième Siècle*, this distinction and its legacy are projected as generating much of the ambivalence at the heart of contemporary Caribbean identity. Caribbean history, as Glissant creatively 'recovers' it, was determined, then, not only by the primary relation of slavery, a relation of domination/subordination itself bristling with ambivalence,[48] but also by the imagined dynamic or tension (impossible to recover properly across the temporal distance) between those who submitted and those who resisted, or at least between those who adopted different strategies of resistance.

Outside the pale of the Caribbean plantation, beyond the limits of those regulated and policed plains, are the *mornes* or hills. And to the *mornes* belong, traditionally, the fugitives. Even in the mid-twentieth century, the highlands still symbolized resistance or opposition. When José's friend Jojo eventually rebels against his victimization at the hands of a racist mixed-race stepmother, José imagines him fled to the hills, the traditional refuge of the *marron*, and indeed Jojo's classmates spread the rumour that he had 'marronné'. This figurative use of the term suggests a parallel between plantation slavery, on the one hand, and the ravages of the racism internalized by so-called 'assimilated' blacks, on the other hand. Although many Caribbean writers make much of the resistance of the *marrons*, magnifying the

---

[48] See Glissant's *Discours antillais*; even in the glossary entry under 'abolition', Glissant notes the father fixation of the Caribbean mentality. The seminal father figure in this context is the colonist, but Schoelcher becomes a surrogate.

overt revolt of those who escaped the lowlands of the plantations to found more or less free and fierce outlaw or scavenger communities in the highlands, others concentrate much more on the covert resistance practised on the plantations by those slaves who expressed their opposition by poisonings, arson, and abortions or, indeed, more indirectly, by the elaboration of a counter-culture, a hidden, disguised culture transmitted orally through the *conteur*, descendant of the African *griot*.

Over two centuries, however, *marronnage* provided the principal focus of opposition to the plantation.[49] In so far as it was a reaction against the plantation, it was, of necessity, determined by that system and dependent on it. Yet the very existence of the *marrons* (or the *négateurs* ('negators') as Glissant has termed them) does define an alternative space, however partial or porous the plantation boundary. Indeed, many writers prefer to stress the interstitial space of *petit marronnage* involving a certain degree of symbiosis or negotiation between plantation and *marrons*. But whatever the balance between 'grand' and 'petit marronnage', the fact that the plantation system inspired its own negation inevitably mitigated its perceived closure and attenuated its perceived supremacy. One of the most significant aspects of Édouard Glissant's emphasis on the figure of the *marron* is, as we have seen, the refusal to polarize creolization and *marronnage*. Whereas the *marron* of Chamoiseau and Confiant's *Lettres créoles* preserves intact the beauty of mythical Africa in the hills over more than a century until it is safe to come down to the lowlands to participate in the Creole challenge, Glissant's 'marron originel' does not hold back from that adventure.

LABOUR POLITICS AND REVOLT

In post-slavery times, the persistent pattern of subjection at the heart of the plantation system continued to be challenged by the sedition, labour revolts, and confrontations depicted in several novels of the 1960s and 1970s: in *La Rue Cases-Nègres*, Jojo's exposure of the corrupt *économe* foreshadows the more extensive

---

[49] For a full discussion of *marronnage*, see Cailler, *Conquérants de la nuit nue*; Burton, *Le Roman marron*; Suzanne Crosta, *Le Marronnage créateur. Dynamique textuelle chez Édouard Glissant* (Laval: GRELCA, 1991).

treatment of labour relations in, for example, Jacqueline Manicom's *Mon examen de blanc*,[50] Vincent Placoly's *La Vie et la mort de Marcel Gonstran*,[51] Simone Schwarz-Bart's *Pluie et vent sur Télumée Miracle*,[52] and Bertène Juminer's *Au seuil d'un nouveau cri*.[53] While Juminer's novel vaunts the revolutionary efficacy of subversives undermining the plantation from within, in most representations—Placoly's novel, or Schwarz-Bart's, for example—the balance of power is less favourable. In the former, striking workers are met by the firepower of the army, and many of them are felled. These rumblings of revolt echo through time, of course, notably recalling the violent but usually abortive or ill-fated slave uprisings. In contrast to mostly unrecorded and thus forgotten resistance, the dramatic group suicide which ended the (rather ambiguous) uprising of Delgrès and his men left an indelible mark on the French Caribbean consciousness. These historical echos also subtend Dany Bébel-Gisler's *Léonora*, a novel that evokes the rise of unionized labour. However, Lucie Julia's novels,[54] which depict the fraught labour relations, industrial instability, and rampant emigration of the 1970s (as well as the scaled-down production, lock-outs, closures, and redundancies that are central to the plot of Léonard Sainville's *Au fond du bourg*),[55] break with the plantation paradigm, opening up instead the disarray, confusion, and distress of an erstwhile labour force that finds itself utterly expendable to Metropolitan capital.

ALTERNATIVE SPACES: DISPLACEMENT AS RESISTANCE

Following the abolition of slavery, the principal alternatives to plantation space were less the highland retreats of the *marron* communities or the cultural traditions sustained by the memory of the mythical homeland of Africa, than urbanization, education, and emigration (to France). The urban environment appears to

[50] Jacqueline Manicom, *Mon examen de blanc* (Paris: Presses de la cité, 1972).
[51] See *La Vie et la mort de Marcel Gonstran*, 113–14.
[52] See *Pluie et vent sur Télumée Miracle*, 221–2.
[53] Bertène Juminer, *Au seuil d'un nouveau cri* (Paris: Présence africaine, 1963).
[54] Lucie Julia, *Les Gens de Bonne-Espérance* (Paris: Temps actuels, 1982) and *Mélody des faubourgs* (Paris: L'Harmattan, 1989).
[55] Léonard Sainville, *Au fond du bourg* (Paris: Messidor, n.d.).

promise deliverance from servile labour to rural, Creole-speaking agricultural workers, yet, as we shall see in the following chapter, it continues the pattern of alienation and segregation. While urbanity, formal education, assimilation, and the myth of France may well offer alternatives to the dead end of plantation labour, they prove unlikely to offer, in themselves, an escape from dispossession. On the contrary, these 'alternatives' can turn out to be inscribed in an ineluctable chain of estrangement. José of *La Rue Cases-Nègres*, who spends much of his young life fretting about freeing his grandmother from plantation servitude, himself escapes that fate by moving from plantation to village to town, from Creole to French, from illiteracy to initiation into 'high culture', and he is eventually drawn into exile in Paris, an exile explored in the sequel to *La Rue Case-Nègres*, entitled *Quand la neige aura fondu*.[56] José's schooling is a place of transformation and, on one level at least, a space of liberation via literacy. As Colette Maximin observes, he wants to put as much distance as possible between himself and the cruel world that had worn out Médouze. In relation to the myth of Africa and the myth of France, the plantation is exposed as the irredeemably deleterious, mutilating environment from which the child must rescue his grandmother.[57] Similarly, although on a less messianic level, at 12 years of age, Albert in Maryse Condé's novel *La Vie scélérate*, stares at his father's corpse, promising himself that he will not live and die like Mano, but rather 'Quitter la plantation. S'établir ailleurs' ('Get away from the plantation. Settle elsewhere').[58] These echos of the slogan 'Canne c'est maudition' ('the curse of the sugarcane')[59] beg the question: is it really possible to

---

[56] Joseph Zobel, *Quand la neige aura fondu* (Paris: Éditions caribéennes, 1979).

[57] 'José s'éloignera d'autant plus de l'ancien monde que le sort du vieux Médouze lui en offre des raisons: c'est la plantation qui a détruit le Nègre. Une seule porte de salut: l'école républicaine. L'assimilation se nourrit donc de l'aversion qu'engendre la souffrance. Les mythes, solidaires, de l'Afrique et de la France servent à négativer l'univers créole' ('José distances himself from the old world all the more radically since the fate of Médouze makes that choice the logical one: after all, it is the plantation that destroyed the black man. There is only one salvation, namely formal schooling. Assimilation is thus fortified by the aversion caused by suffering. Moreover, the two mutually reinforcing myths of Africa and France both serve to detract from the Creole world'): Colette Maximin, *Littératures caribéennes comparées* (Pointe-à-Pitre and Paris: Jasor and Karthala, 1996), 41–2.

[58] Condé, *La Vie scélérate*, 16.

[59] This is the refrain of Léandor's mother in Raphaël Confiant, *Commandeur du sucre*, 81.

escape the plantation? And if so, does the alternative necessarily lie outside rural space and/or beyond the Caribbean?

For those who remained on in the countryside, the *case* and its garden could sometimes constitute in themselves a space apart, a space that, although it might be located within the limits of the plantation, had nonetheless the potential to be oppositional, when it was, for example, appropriated by the worker and disassociated from his labour. As an example of this claiming of the 'jardin créole', we could point to Monsieur Saint-Louis's mysterious secret garden in the *Rue Cases-Nègres*. But Télumée's plot in *Pluie et vent sur Télumée Miracle* and Julia's plot for growing healing herbs in *L'Exil selon Julia* are two further examples of a reclaiming of rural space. In contrast to those who are drawn by an apparently more desirable 'elsewhere', the eponymous Télumée never aspires to find redemption beyond the patch of ground outside her home, wherever that home might be. Indeed, her Voltairean garden presents an alternative not just to the plantation, but also to the Frenchification and implied self-alienation of the town. Télumée's garden, like the plots cultivated on the hills or *mornes* by the descendants of the *marrons*, is an empowering and organic anti-plantation founded on love and solidarity, just as her little cabin or 'case' is an authentic *habitation* built on self-acknowledgement and self-possession. It is this redeemed relation with place and space that enables not just Télumée, but all the heroic figures of this novel to (re)possess themselves. The narrative closes upon Télumée's refusal to leave her patch, and upon her determination to enjoy her autonomy during the years that are left to her, an autonomy synonymous with a complete absence of exploitation.

J'ai transporté ma case à l'orient et je l'ai transportée à l'occident, les vents d'est, du nord, les tempêtes m'ont assaillie et les averses m'ont délavée, mais je reste une femme sur mes deux pieds, et je sais que le nègre n'est pas une statue de sel que dissolvent les pluies. . . . Soleil levé, soleil couché, les journées glissent et le sable que soulève la brise enlisera ma barque, mais je mourrai là, comme je suis, debout, dans mon petit jardin, quelle joie!. . .[60]

---

[60] *Pluie et vent sur Télumée Miracle*, 248–9; 'I have moved my cabin to the east and to the west; east winds and north winds have buffeted and soaked me; but I am still a woman standing on my own two legs, and I know a Negro is not a statue to be dissolved by the rain. . . . Sun risen, sun set, the days slip past and the sand blown by the wind will engulf my boat. But I shall die here, where I am, standing in my little garden. What happiness!' *Bridge of Beyond*, 172–3.

CULTURAL RESISTANCE: IN PRAISE OF PLANTATION
CULTURE

We have seen that Édouard Glissant represents the equivocal relation between resistance and compromise as explaining many of the
gaps and complexities of the opaque Caribbean past. Although
Glissant's novels show the ambivalence of both positions, and
although he seems concerned above all with the in-between, or the
relational space in which the one encounters the other, it was,
essentially, the initiative of *marronnage* that facilitated, according
to the author of *Le Discours antillais*, the development of an interstitial space and with it, the perspective necessary for a collective
prise de conscience. The critic Jacques André notes that the plantation is inevitably regarded by some writers as a space of social and
linguistic compromise ('espace social et linguistique qui recoupe
celui des compromissions').[61] And indeed, one school of thought
would go so far as to reject everything that emerged from the plantation system. This would include the Creole language, which
would be dismissed on the grounds that it suggested an 'entente
illusoire' or an illusion of understanding. Glissant's *Le Quatrième
Siècle*, however, stages the momentous consummation of the relation between the first Longoué, the original *marron* who escapes
from enslavement as soon as he disembarks in the Caribbean, and
Louise, the apparently compliant plantation slave, mistress to the
white planter, whom he abducts. The consummation of their relation is triggered by Longoué's effort to communicate with his own
captive, the woman whom he has liberated from plantation
bondage, by uttering in Creole the words meaning sea, earth, and
lightning. The subsequent bond between the two depends on
communication in Creole: 'Il accepta donc qu'elle lui apporta
quelque chose: la parole nouvelle' ('He therefore accepted her
giving him something: the new language').[62] If Glissant thus
creolizes the space of the highlands and, by extension, the space of
marronnage, traditionally viewed as the ultimate resistance to the
plantation, it is because his view of the relation between compliance and resistance is open to ambiguity and ambivalence.

Patrick Chamoiseau and Raphaël Confiant celebrate both in

[61] André, *Caraïbales*, 17.
[62] Glissant, *Le Quatrième Siècle*, 95; *The Fourth Century*, 91.

their fiction and in their theoretical writings the resistance mounted against the plantation from within the system itself. Not simply, however, the poisonings, the arson, or the abortions to which the plantation slaves resorted as a sort of underground sedition nor the slave revolts, nor indeed the labour struggles that followed the era of slave labour. The resistance that they honour is principally cultural in nature and is outlined in their manifesto, *Éloge de la créolité* (1989), as well as in their literary work. In the chapter devoted to the 'La Plantation, l'Habitation' in *Lettres créoles*, the two authors concentrate on the contrast between the *marron* and the *conteur*. Whereas the *marron* is held to sustain the unarticulated primal scream of the displaced and enslaved population, the *conteur* is said to have articulated this scream; in fact, the *conteur* was an artist, 'l'artiste du cri' ('the artist of the scream').[63] Although both figures are said to represent resistance, the authors of *Lettres créoles* favour verbalization over revolt, the folktale over the primal scream, narrative over poetry, *créolité* over *négritude*, and Creole cultural continuity over political rupture. Putting it at its simplest, the *conteur*'s art, even if it amounted to adaptation, and even if it did involve compromise, survived 'to tell the tale'; whereas the *marron* did not leave any verbal trace as such. Certainly the champions of *créolité* do not fall into the trap of denying that the plantation was essentially an 'outil de conquête et de défrichement' ('a tool of conquest and colonization'), a 'machine à exploiter et à enrichir' ('a mechanism of exploitation and enrichment') (*LC* 35). Yet they insist that when they celebrate plantation culture as the cradle of *créolité*, they are celebrating resistance rather than assent. It is here that we could locate the radical shift represented by their interpretation of the plantation system. Their benediction of the cultural richness that emerged from the plantation context is based on the belief that such accommodation left room for resistance.

Chamoiseau and Confiant argue that the plantation system secreted Creole culture and that the *habitation* was, in this sense, a fruitful, sustaining womb, an 'amniotic space' ('espace créole quasiment amniotique') (*LC* 38). Presented as pragmatic in the first instance, the secretion of Creole culture was a matter of survival,

---

[63] Chamoiseau and Confiant, *Lettres créoles*, 39. Subsequent page references are given in the text (*LC*).

involving the essential acquisition of a 'savoir faire d'habitation pour l'habitation' ('insiders' plantation know-how') (*LC* 40). In other words, for the slaves and plantation workers, their popular culture amounted to no more than a sort of 'users' guide'. Yet Chamoiseau and Confiant insist that this acculturation was a form of clandestine resistance, in so far as survival and creativity in adverse circumstances are in themselves resistance. Michel De Certeau's complex notion of the tactic, and Glissant's notion of opaqueness as resistance, are implicitly being drawn upon here as models of opposition. Creole culture came into being, according to this interpretation, not just within but against slavery, and it was based on ruse and dissimulation; Creole *oraliture* is said to attack the 'valeurs du système' ('values of the system') and to 'installe[r] le lieu de marronnage dedans l'habitation' ('relocate *marronnage* within the plantation') (*LC* 58).

It might seem quixotic, to say the least, to insist that Creole popular culture was from the start a culture of resistance. Even if survival can be seen as a form of opposition, it necessitated in the first instance (and possibly beyond) a culture of compliance. In that sense, the so-called resistance of the *conteur* was recuperated and institutionalized. As Chamoiseau and Confiant openly admit, his art was 'dans la norme de l'habitation' ('normalized in the plantation') (*LC* 59), sanctioned by the *béké*, who, according to the two critics, failed to understand this secret subversion of plantation order. They go on to suggest, however, that the *conteur* was also the guardian of the group's cohesion, counteracting the slaves' original cultural diversity. Giving voice to the group and to its collective, fragmented memory, the *conteur*, even while offering distraction, might have enunciated, in his entertaining wake orations, a struggle against death that could have been heard as a struggle against the symbolic death of the slaves. But to leap from that plausible hypothesis to the deduction that 'ainsi, une grande part des esclaves n'a pas été esclave' ('in this way, a substantial proportion of the slave population were not really slaves') (*LC* 61) is a radical redefinition of the power of culture and an underestimation, perhaps, of the disempowerment of enslavement. Clearly, this positive re-evaluation of the plantation system is an essential part of the project of *créolité*. Equally clearly, its conflation of issues of power and identity and of politics and culture is consonant with that sidelining of political issues noted in the first chapter of this study.

If the plantation system failed, it was not because of a proliferation of *marrons* or because of sporadic or organized resistance on the part of the labour-force; nor was it because of some mass exodus to the towns or the following the abolition of slavery. And it was certainly not because of the conception and development of Creole culture. It was rather because of the rise of European-grown sugar beet as a competitive crop. Yet the plantation was doomed in any case, because, and this brings us back to Glissant's definition, it was a system stunted from the outset by its dependence on the *Métropole* and on slavery. This is the reason why, in the words of Glissant, 'partout le système des Plantations s'est brutalement ou progressivement effondré, sans engendrer ses propres dépassements' ('the Plantation system collapsed everywhere brutally or progressively, without generating its own ways of superseding itself').[64]

VISTAS OF LOSS: LOOKING BACK TO THE PLANTATION

Most of the writing of Patrick Chamoiseau and Raphaël Confiant is foundational, looking back to the origins of Creole culture and seeking to represent, to explain, or illustrate its mode of functioning. This retrospection is determined by a concern to locate and validate the advent of a new culture, a new people. Certain novels by both writers are substantially concerned with the dynamics of the plantation system; others, and indeed the majority of Confiant's work falls into this second category, are more concerned with the Creole town, although even then, the urban dynamic is consistently referred back to the seminal, ghostly space-time of the plantation. Chamoiseau's novels *Chronique des sept misères* and *Texaco* are both founded on a plantation narrative—'les dix-huit paroles rêvées d'Afoukal' ('Afoukal's eighteen dream statements') in *Chronique* and Esternome's story as relayed by Marie-Sophie in the case of *Texaco*—while the sense of time that predominates in *Solibo Magnifique* is based, as we saw in Chapter 2, on plantation time.

Although Édouard Glissant's writing demonstrates intense interest in the plantation—indeed, his gravitation towards the two talis-

---

[64] Glissant, *Poétique de la Relation*, 77; *Poetics of Relation*, 63.

manic figures of Saint-John Perse and William Faulkner is explained in terms of their shared status as writers of the plantation—he refrains from idealizing that space-time. In *La Case du commandeur* Marie Celat (Mycéa) and Mathieu Béluse represent two different approaches to the demise of the plantation system. Marie Celat allows herself to drift, passively registering the island's absorption into the colourless morass of modernity and the bland alienation of global consumerism: 'elle subissait le pays, sa lente absorption dans la vie neutre et blême' ('she suffered the land passively, its slow absorption into a pale and neutral life'). She is convinced that she must leave behind plantation time ('ce temps des Plantations'), and prepare to live with the new 'platitude irréparable' ('irredeemable flatness'), the alliteration of 'platitude' and 'plantation' resounding here in the reader's ears. The spatial metaphor is paradoxical in that the memory of plantation time is preserved, not in the lowlands, where this time has fallen into oblivion, but in the island's relief, up in the highlands. Mathieu Béluse, on the other hand, holds on to the 'rêve d'avant, fuligineux et incertain' ('obscure and uncertain dream of before').[65] He even persuades Mycéa to visit the old *quimboiseur/conteur*, Papa Longoué, one last time. The latter is said to be 'abandonné du temps, incompris de ce qui gagnait là comme une gangrène en surface: les agents de la fonction publique, les voitures à crédit, la Lézarde tel un filet de boue au long de la piste d'atterissage' ('abandoned by time, misunderstood by what was taking over here like a surface gangrene: bureaucracies, cars sold on credit, the Lézarde river like a trickle of mud running along the landing runway').[66] However, although Longoué is said to be outside time, excluded and misunderstood by those who are 'in time', that time is itself silted up, its sluggish or arrested flow is evoked in terms of gangrene and mud. After their visit to Papa Longoué, represented as a visit to the past, the pair come back down to the lowlands, returning to what the narrator terms the present ('revinrent donc au temps présent'). For Mathieu, however, the present is the site of loss. He asks Marie Celat if she has ever counted all the words that are now extinct, all the gestures made defunct by the collapse of the plantation system. The litany of loss includes all the plantation work with bananas and yams, and all the skills and specialist

---

[65] Glissant, *La Case du commandeur*, 190–1.   [66] Ibid. 191.

vocabulary linked to the closed-down refinery. Included in the enumeration also are the *commandeurs* and the *géreurs*, and oral culture, especially the folktales.

Non, pas un ne se souvient par ici du temps longtemps . . . Non, la distillerie est fermée depuis on ne sait pas quand . . . En ce temps-là les commandeurs et les géreurs avaient disparu du paysage. On en voyait encore quelques-uns, zombifiés. Les chiffres officiels décomptaient une usine et demie dans le pays: une qui marchait pour la récolte pleine, l'autre pour une moitié de la saison. Plus personne ne croyait aux contes . . . c'est-à-dire à l'opportunité d'en réciter, pas plus qu'à l'importance sans poids de ce qu'ils disent.[67]

In addition to the sense of loss of a whole way of life, there is, here, a sense of fracture: it is not just that a culture, a hierarchy, a way of life, a set of values and meanings, and a language have disappeared but that a whole tradition, a whole line of descent or continuity has been broken. Monsieur Chanteur is one of those who regrets the changes. He laments in particular the abandon of the canefields: 'mais c'est parce qu'il regrettait le temps où les commandeurs à cheval (le plus souvent à mulet) régentaient le pays alentour . . . lui qui descendait de tant d'économes, de commandeurs; qui avait été un des meilleurs cuiseurs à la distillerie' ('but that is because he missed the time when the drivers on horseback (mostly riding mules) governed the land for miles around . . . as the descendant of so many overseers and drivers . . . he who had been one of the best boilers in the distillery').[68]

Losing her senses, Marie Celat begins to haunt the countryside like a lost soul, but her compulsion is characterized as banal, since she is said to be one of many in modern Martinique to have become fixated with their rural roots, trying to reconnect with the countryside regarded as the space of authenticity, a space to be cultivated,

---

[67] Ibid. 201; 'No, not one person around here remembers the time that lasted a long time . . . No, the distillery has been closed for no one knows how long . . . By this time, the drivers and the agents had disappeared from the landscape. You might still see one or two wandering around like zombies. The official figures showed one and a half refineries on the island: one that operated for the whole harvest, the other for half a season. Nobody believed in folktales any more . . . that is, in the wisdom of telling them, or in the importance of what they were about' (ibid. 201). The same sense of loss is registered in the evocation of 'les gestes que plus personne ne faisait, les mots morts, disparus avec les gestes' ('the actions no longer accomplished by anybody, the dead words, gone with the actions they had denoted').

[68] Ibid. 202.

that is, reclaimed through planting crops or gardening.[69] The (collective) narrator concludes from all this evidence that something is missing.

il manquait donc quelque chose. Nous avions beau être actifs, efficaces, modernes, équipés, il manquait quelque chose. Nous avions beau manipuler des gadgets, il manquait quelque chose. . . . nous levions les yeux sur ce qui de l'alentour nous échappait tellement. Nous ne savions à la fin comment faire marcher notre usine, ni par quoi remplacer sa vacance terrible. On nous divertissait d'activités de remplacement, qui nous saturaient d'une jouissance au bout du compte insupportable.[70]

This Pascalian pronouncement is confirmed by the growing delirium of Marie Céelat, as she finds the countryside that she roams more and more encroached upon by modernity, tarred roads and cement-built houses. Her distress is contrasted with the lazy, uncritical, unresistant pragmatism of the 'rusés d'en bas' ('wily plains people').[71] The latter, taking refuge in the urgency of artificial busyness, avoid confrontation with the terrifying cultural hollowness (or 'vacance') at the centre of their lives. For those who barely register their own cultural bankruptcy and political paralysis, Mycéa is a crank ('une enquiquineuse'). They delude themselves that 'le pays n'allait pas si mal' ('the country isn't doing so badly'), implicitly contrasting it with Haiti, with Africa, or with countries afflicted by dictatorships and other ills, such as endemic famine, massacres, death squads, fascist dictators, and so forth.[72]

What, then, is *La Case du commandeur* saying about the plantation? Clearly, the novel does not endorse nostalgia for that system, given the implicitly ironic portrayal of Monsieur

[69] 'Depuis peu, il est vrai, tout un chacun revenait aux sources. Les fonctionnaires, qui continuaient d'investir en clandestins dans les taxis et les autobus, commencaient d'acheter des morceaux de terrain et de faire planter des ignames' ('recently, it is true, everybody was returning to their roots. The civil servants, still investing on the black market in taxis and buses, were beginning to buy plots and have yams planted on them') (Glissant, *La Case du commandeur*, 211).

[70] 'so something was missing. No matter how active, efficient, modern and well-equipped we were, something was missing. No matter how well we manipulated our gadgets, something was missing . . . we looked up at what was escaping us so completely. At the end of the day we could not make our factory work, nor did we know how to replace its dreadful absence. We were being distracted with displacement activities that were saturating us with a pleasure that we found unbearable in the final analysis') (ibid. 212).

[71] Ibid. 214.   [72] Ibid. 214–15.

Chanteur's pining after slave-drivers on horseback. Nor does it idealize a system that had betrayal, coercion, and brutalization at its core. Yet the novel acknowledges that the system's collapse has left in its wake a yawning abyss. The replacement of production by consumption, the withdrawal of a reassuring routine, of valorizing know-how, and of a social relief dependent on clear distinctions and hierarchies has led to an unrelieved sense of emptiness in which the population is both 'at a loss' and 'at a loose end'. However, these withdrawal symptoms are in themselves an eloquent indictment of a system that was not so much unable to, as unconcerned with engendering a system to replace it.[73] In Glissant's view, then, the plantation *produced* above all this very void. In contrast to the *créolistes*' claims that it was an eminently productive time and space, Glissant's assessment, even in his propositional or theoretical work, is more muted and nuanced. What he does acknowledge is that the plantation is perceived, retrospectively, as a source of structure, order, certainty, and routine, as a locus of endurance and duration, as habit as well as habitat. He is both able to imagine the demise of the plantation as eviction from duration, and intent on criticizing colonial nostalgia. Even in 1981, his discourse on the plantation was complex. He was already noting darkly the paradoxical extraversion of this solipsistic space, but, commenting that a year would not suffice to describe this world, he limited himself to outlining the oral and written literature that it occasioned. The entire thrust of Glissant's thinking on the plantation is thus shot through with a deep ambivalence. He regards it, along with the slave ship, as the 'difficult and opaque' source or matrix of the Caribbean people: 'Mais c'est bien à cette deuxième matrice de la Plantation, après celle du bateau négrier, qu'il faut rapporter la trace de nos sources, difficiles et opaques' ('This second Plantation matrix, after that of the slave ship, is where we must return to track out difficult and opaque sources').[74] However, one of its chief secretions was the deep-seated and long-lived neurosis of unproductivity: 'aujourd'hui notre collectivité ne produit certes plus rien en tant que telle . . . notre conscience d'un tel manque nous constitue pour une part' ('these days, collectively, we produce nothing as such . . . and our awareness of this lack partly makes us what we are').[75]

---

[73] See Glissant, *Poétique de la Relation*, 77.   [74] Ibid. 87.

[75] Glissant, *Le Discours antillais*, 183 (not included in *Caribbean Discourse*).

In *Faulkner Mississippi*, Glissant notes that a literary caesura divides Caribbean writing between the plantation and the town:

nous ne sommes pas loin d'une sorte de césure littéraire, entre une écriture de la source, de la matrice, du temps lent et de l'espace ouvert dans un lieu clos (la Plantation), et une écriture de la multiplicité, de la vitesse foudroyante, de l'entassement et du détachement (la Ville). Le verdural, et le concassé.[76]

In thus characterizing the plantation/town dichotomy, he defines the plantation as an open space enclosed within boundaries, and as a space of gestation and slow time, whereas the town is a space of crowding, severance, or at least disengagement, and speed. Although the two chronotopes are clearly being contrasted, their difference cannot be reduced to a simple binary or dialectical structure. The relation between 'verdural' and 'concassé' further confirms this rejection of symmetrical opposition or polarization. Glissant's neologism 'verdural' is derived from 'verdure' meaning vegetation or greenery. Not only does it connote the rhythms of organic life and growth, the slow process of gestation, but its central syllable suggests the word 'durée' or duration, as well as endurance, thus suggesting long-term organic sedimentation and lived time foreign to the urban economy of speed, fragmentation, and detachment. Through his choice of the caesura metaphor, which suggests both break and suspension, both rupture and continuity, Glissant inscribes the relation between plantation and town into a kinetic, rhythmical pattern. In the poetics of French, the caesura traditionally divides the alexandrine into two hemistiches, balancing the line between two periods, neither of which replaces or displaces the other. This poetic logic explains the plantation's literary endurance as locus of duration and gestation, its poetic persistence or 'rémanence'.

[76] Glissant, *Faulkner Mississippi*, 334; 'We are not far from a sort of literary caesura between writing of sources, gestation, slow time and open space in a closed place (the plantation), and writing of multiplicity, lightning speed, accumulation and detachment in (the Town). The verdurant and the pulverized.'

CHAPTER SIX

Urban Time: The Reproduction of Space?

A writer's heaven.[1]

A 'FERMENT WITHOUT A HISTORY'?

In *Tristes tropiques* Lévi-Strauss recalls the mischievous description of America as bypassing civilization in its race from savagery to decadence and from newness to decrepitude, although he himself reserves this description for the cities of the New World.[2] Refining this view, the Canadian writer Pierre Nepveu contrasts the cities of the American north with the paradigmatic city of the southern hemisphere, 'ville du sud, sublime et tragique magma, espace de décomposition qui fournit un merveilleux creuset aux métaphores organiques et aux hyperboles flamboyants' (a 'magma no less tragic than sublime, a space of decomposition that provides a wonderful crucible of organic metaphors and flamboyant hyperbole'), and instances Émile Ollivier's Port-au-Prince as just such a frenzied site of premature blight.[3] Although similar in many

---

[1] Walcott, *What the Twilight Says*, 71; the context of this phrase is quoted on p. 176.

[2] 'Un esprit malicieux a défini l'Amérique comme un pays qui a passé de la barbarie à la décadence sans connaître la civilisation. On pourrait, avec plus de justesse, appliquer la formule aux villes du Nouveau Monde: elles vont de la fraîcheur à la décrépitude sans s'arrêter à l'ancienneté. . . . Certaines cités d'Europe s'endorment doucement dans la mort; celles du Nouveau Monde vivent fiévreusement dans une maladie chronique: perpétuellement jeunes, elles ne sont pourtant jamais saines': Claude Lévi-Strauss, *Tristes tropiques* (1955; Paris: Plon, 1993), 105.

[3] Pierre Nepveu, *Intérieurs du nouveau monde. Essai sur les littératures du Québec et des Amériques* (Quebec: Boréal: 1998), 333; 'lieu d'enlisement et de décadence' ('morass of decadence') and 'foyer de délire' ('site of delirium'): ibid. 333.

respects to these exogenous assessments of 'sub-tropical' cities or indeed tropical 'sub-cities', Derek Walcott's portrayal of the Trinidadian capital Port-of-Spain excises all traces of tropical melancholy, celebrating as utopian this 'downtown babel of shop signs and streets, mongrelized, polyglot, a ferment without a history, like heaven. Because that is what such a city is, in the New World, a writer's heaven. A culture, we all know, is made by its cities.'[4]

Common to Lévi-Strauss's and Walcott's visions is less the impression of feverish ferment verging on chronic pathology than the conviction that these cities share an anomalous relation to time: for Lévi-Strauss they bypass maturity and for Walcott they are devoid of history. While their baroque febrility might confirm the acceleration towards doom discerned by Lévi-Strauss, Derek Walcott's view that they lie outside history is more problematic. Indeed, their common history is evoked by Édouard Glissant in his essay *Faulkner Mississippi*, which highlights not just the 'similar and fascinating nature' of nineteenth-century Creole cities such as New Orleans, La Havana, Port-au-Prince, or Saint-Pierre, but their similarly bleak twentieth-century fates. Glissant's description evokes the manifestly dated atmosphere of much Francophone and Hispanophone writing[5] set in the nineteenth-century Caribbean.

Un même goût du baroque et de l'Opéra les distingue, en liaison avec une vie dissipée, saisonnière, une activité à la fois d'aristocratie neuve et de racaille ancienne, une folie de Carnaval et de fêtes religieuses, un négoce intense et aucune activité industrielle, un port (fluvial ou maritime) grouillant et des remparts ou des allées retirées pour les duels, des masses d'esclaves à merci et des gens de couleur libres exerçant toutes sortes de métiers, . . . une justice paradante et souvent expéditive, des ébauches très sérieuses de vie artistique (peintres et musiciens, chroniqueurs et romanciers, sans compter les pamphlétaires) . . . un frémissement et un énervement sans fin.[6]

---

⁴ Walcott, *What the Twilight Says*, 71.

⁵ Glissant explains that the Anglophone Caribbean baroque was less mixed and less exuberant. See *Faulkner Mississippi*, 336.

⁶ Ibid. 334–5; 'They are all marked by the same taste for Opera and for the Baroque, for dissipated seasonal activity, beloved of the new aristocracy and the old trash, and by their passion for Carnival and religious festivities. They all boast a vibrant business culture but no industrial activity, they have thriving river or sea ports, ramparts and alleys perfect for duels, masses of slaves, and many freed coloureds practising all sorts of occupations . . . an ostentatious and often expedi-

These sparkling nineteenth-century cities are doomed, as Glissant explains: New Orleans wilts following the demise of the plantation system; Port-au-Prince is the victim of chronic underdevelopment; and Saint-Pierre of outright annihilation, buried in 1902 beneath the volcanic ash of the Montagne pelée. Is there, then, a life and a history after decadence? The urban focus of the late-twentieth-century surge in Caribbean writing would suggest that there is. Moreover, if Derek Walcott and V. S. Naipaul rank among the most memorable writers of Caribbean urban space, within the French Caribbean tradition long-lingering lines were traced in the dust much earlier by two poets: in 1911 by Saint-John Perse (or Leger Saint-Leger as he signed himself in those days) in *Éloges*, and in 1939 by Aimé Césaire in the *Cahier d'un retour au pays natal*. Without exploring here the heavy intertextual debt owed to these two poems by contemporary writing, it is fitting to recall them, if only to stress that the French Caribbean tradition of writing the 'ville créole' has a certain temporal depth.

IN PRAISE OF THE CREOLE TOWN?

In the first poem sequence of the collection *Éloges*, entitled 'Images à Crusoé', the poet sees detritus at the heart of every town: 'toute ville ceint l'ordure',[7] and he views the (generic) Town as an open sore, describing it as a suppurating abscess that flows through the river to the sea (*ŒC* 13). The Caribbean town is not being singled out here; on the contrary, most critics interpret the city of 'Images à Crusoé' as being Bordeaux. However, the association of urban space with waste matter and with pathology is even more pronounced in the poetry evoking the tropical splendour of the native island. From the outset of the eighteen-poem sequence itself entitled 'Éloges', one of the principal topoi is the intrusive presence of death within life; indeed the morbidity of the town is due in large part to a surfeit of life. The hillside cemetery presides over the entire town; it is visible at the end of the main street, where it overlooks the noisy market and the lively quays. The town's sticky torpor ensures that the

---

tious judicial system, worthy attempts at an artistic culture (painters, musicians, chroniclers and novelists, not to mention pamphleteers) . . . an endlessly palpitating state of enervation.'

7 Saint-John Perse, *Œuvres complètes* (*ŒC*), 13; *Éloges and Other Poems* (*ÉOP*), 157: 'for every city encompasses filth'.

backdrop to the vivid street-market activity is decomposition: the streets are teeming with detritus (for example, the fish's head and the empty coconut shell likened to a death's head) and peopled by local dignitaries carrying corpses sealed into zinc coffins[8] and by blacks bearing flayed (animal) carcasses.[9] Death is also implicit in the sun-quickened explosiveness of the town's sultry temper,[10] and the apocalyptic rumbling of ever-threatening natural calamities (earthquakes, volcanic eruptions, and cyclones) undercuts the urban bustle. Thus the remains contained in the coffins are the victims of a recent 'cataclysm' and the dappled sky seems to be predicting an imminent earthquake.[11]

Although muted, the marine backdrop is frequently adumbrated: for example, the main thoroughfare is 'barrée d'eau verte' ('barred with green water'), but it is as though the sea were somehow a constraint, putting a stop to the town's gallop. The poet nowhere evokes the thundering energy of majestic ocean breakers, but rather the standing water of an urban basin: for example, the sordid trickle in the street gutter (in which the poet sees, however, 'la splendeur des eaux pourpres lamées de graisses et d'urines, | où trame le savon comme de la toile d'araignée'(*Œ*C 45) ('the splendour of purple [*sic*] waters mottled with grease and urine, | where soap weaves a spider's web'; *ÉOP* 47); the water of the enclosed harbour;[12] the courtyard wells and ponds; and indeed the town's water-tower. The sea is present, of course, both as the tepid water ('eau tiède') and cool currents ('courants frais'), where people go paddling. But the predominant impression is nonetheless one of containment, if not stagnation, and it resonates with the restricted space of the island and with the sense of the Caribbean sea as a basin rather than a stretch of open ocean.

---

[8] 'Les morts de cataclysme, comme des bêtes épluchées, | dans ces boîtes de zinc portées par les Notables' ('The victims of disaster, like plucked animals, | in those zinc boxes borne by the Notables') (*Œ*C 44; *ÉOP* 47).

[9] 'des nègres porteurs de bêtes écorchées' ('Negroes, porters of skinned animals') (*Œ*C 46; *ÉOP* 51).

[10] 'La Ville est jaune de rancune. Le Soleil précipite dans les darses une querelle de tonnerres' ('The city is yellow with rancour. The Sun in the roadsteads precipitates a quarrel of thunders') (*Œ*C 43; *ÉOP* 47).

[11] 'le ciel pommelé annonce pour ce soir un autre tremblement de terre' ('the dappled sky for this evening predicts another earthquake') (*Œ*C 44; *ÉOP* 49).

[12] 'havres crépitants' ('harbours crackling') (*Œ*C 46, *ÉOP* 51); 'au fond des cours gluantes . . . bassins clos' ('at the back of viscid courtyards . . . enclosed baths') (*Œ*C 46; *ÉOP* 51).

It could be said that the space of 'Éloges' recalls less a 'true city'[13] than one of those market towns that Derek Walcott memorably defends against those who would belittle them: 'cities create a culture, and all we have are these magnified market towns'.[14] Apart from the difference in scale and grandeur between city and town, the emphasis on the 'market' highlights small-scale commerce and economic practicalities. The opposite semantic shift operates in the euphemistic replacement of the term plantation by *habitation*, where reference to the economic context is erased. Glissant himself points out that, historically,

ces villes étaient des prolongements de la Plantation et ne se concevaient pas sans elle: le coton, le tabac, les rhums et le sucre, les épices, l'indigo (l'or et l'hévéa au Brésil), le plus souvent brocantés contre les produits fins de l'Europe ou les produits manufacturés du nord des Etats-Unis.[15]

Traditionally, both visitors and inhabitants are attracted to the buzz and colour of the Caribbean market: in the early twentieth century, the diplomat and writer Paul Morand, evoking his first impressions of Pointe-à-Pitre in *Hiver Caraïbe*, registers the charm of the Caribbean market: 'Ce qu'il y a de charmant, à Pointe-à-Pitre, c'est la grand-place du marché. Je me trouve soudain au milieu de trois à quatre cents négresses' ('What is really enchanting in Pointe-à-Pitre is the market square, where I found myself all of a sudden in the midst of between three and four hundred black women').[16] Many *créoliste* representations of the Caribbean capital are set 'au mitan de Fort-de-France, dont le marché aux légumes était le cœur' ('in the plumb centre of Fort-de-France, in the vegetable market that was the city's beating heart').[17]

Before considering the dystopian images from the opening pages of Césaire's poem, it is worth returning briefly to Derek Walcott's musings on Port-of-Spain and more specifically to his definition of the 'ideal Caribbean city' as one which would be 'so racially various that the cultures of the world—the Asiatic, the Mediterranean,

---

[13] Walcott, *What the Twilight Says*, 24. [14] Ibid. 73.
[15] Glissant, *Faulkner Mississippi*, 335; 'these towns were an extension of the Plantation and would have been unimaginable in any context other than that of [the trade in] cotton, tobacco, rum, sugar, spices, indigo (gold and rubber in Brazil), usually bartered for European luxuries or for manufactured goods from the American North'.
[16] Paul Morand, *Hiver caraïbe* (1928; Paris: Flammarion, 1991), 36.
[17] R. Confiant, *Le Nègre et l'amiral* (Paris: Grasset, 1988), 15.

the European, the African—would be represented in it, its human variety more exciting than Joyce's Dublin'.[18] Walcott's idealization of the Trinidadian capital as a 'writer's heaven' contradicts the dismissal of Caribbean cities and culture by outsiders or alienated insiders. Moreover, despite being evoked in the conditional tense, his ideal Caribbean city corresponds in its ethnic variety to the urban Caribbean celebrated by many contemporary French Caribbean writers. Especially striking, however, is his suggestion that Port-of-Spain's ethnic variety might compare favourably with Joyce's Dublin. Certainly, when Joyce was writing *Ulysses*, and even when Walcott penned this comparison, there were very few non-white faces to be seen on the streets of Dublin: indeed, racially, Ireland and its capital were virtually entirely homogeneous and utterly parochial. However, critics have noted that, in *Ulysses*, Dublin is 'placed in direct proximity to the rest of the world-at-large' and is furthermore redeemed from 'allochronic' representation, that is from the 'poetics of anachronism' synonymous with the 'paralysis and stagnation'[19] that had predominated in the Dublin of Joyce's earlier work, *Dubliners*. Given that in 'Éloges', no less than in the *Cahier*, the Creole town is represented as stagnant and as turning its back on the connective space of the ocean, to what extent, one might wonder, does French Caribbean writing in general represent the Creole town as being linked to the 'world at large' and as being synchronous with the latter's temporal dynamic?

CÉSAIRE'S MEAN STREETS

The focus of Aimé Césaire's *Cahier d'un retour au pays natal* is on the Caribbean town as subject (or subjected) space, rather than as mere backdrop, spectacle, or townscape. His text vomits out the passivity, ineffectuality, and submissive lowliness of the Caribbean town: 'elle rampe sur les mains sans jamais aucune envie de vriller le ciel d'une stature de protestation' ('it crawls on its hands with

---

[18] Walcott, 'The Antilles', in *What the Twilight Says*, 74.
[19] Joep Leersen, *Remembrance and Imagination: Patterns in the Historical and Literary Representation of Ireland in the Nineteenth Century* (Cork: Cork University Press, 1996), 229–33.

never any impulse to pierce the sky with a posture of protest').[20]
Despite their squalor, the timid, makeshift shacks are somewhat
more indulgently delineated than the town as a whole: 'Le dos des
maisons ont peur du ciel truffé de feu, leurs pieds des noyades du
sol, elles ont opté de se poser superficielles entre les surprises et les
perfidies' ('The backs of houses are scared of the fire-truffled sky,
their feet of sinking into the ground, they have chosen to perch
gingerly between surprises and perfidies').[21] The saving grace of
flora and fauna is deemed absent from the arid and abject urban
desert that is itself said to be stunted—'rognée, réduite, en rupture
de faune et de flore' ('clipped, diminished, alienated from its own
flora and fauna').[22] Furthermore, the town's population, sometimes distinguished from the town per se, is an undifferentiated,
strident crowd lacking in awareness: 'cette foule criarde si étonn-
namment passée à côté de son cri comme cette ville à côté de son
mouvement, de son sens' ('this squabbling crowd so strangely
swayed from its own cry as the town is swayed from its own movement and meaning').[23]

Césaire's portrayal of urban space is not, however, without a
certain sense of movement: the poet notes, for example, that the
town encroaches each day a little bit further into the countryside:

Et pourtant elle avance la ville. Même qu'elle paît tous les jours plus outre
sa marée de corridors carrelés, de persiennes pudibondes, de cours gluantes,
de peintures qui dégoulinent. Et de petits scandales étouffés, de petites
hontes tues, de petites haines immenses pétrissent en bosses et creux les rues
étroites où le ruisseau grimace longitudinalement parmi l'étron . . .[24]

However, this urban growth is presented as pathological, as pustu-
lent or cancerous. Moreover, while the 'cours gluantes' or 'viscid
courtyards' have found their way from *Éloges* (ŒC 46; *ÉOP* 51)
into the *Cahier*, the dripping paintwork and grimacing gutter
reflect Césaire's projection from the spatial order onto the moral:

[20] Aimé Césaire, *Cahier d'un retour au pays natal/Notebook of a Return to the
Native Land*, tr. Mireille Rosello and Annie Pritchard (London: Bloodaxe, 1995),
82–3.
[21] Ibid.   [22] Ibid.72–3.   [23] Ibid. 74–5.
[24] Ibid. 84–5; 'And yet, this town does move along. Look at it, every day, it grazes
further on the tide of its tiled corridors, prudish shutters, slimy yards, dripping
paintwork. And petty hushed scandals, petty silenced shames and petty immense
hatreds knead bumps and holes in the narrow streets where the gutter grimaces
longitudinally among turds . . .'.

from narrowness onto pettiness, from cramped streets onto stunted lives. The *Cahier*'s town seems devoid of high culture, yet there is no sense here, as there is in Walcott's vision of the Antilles, that some deprivations nourish artistic inwardness and provide a release from 'high mediocrity'.[25] Apart from dwelling too on urban morbidity, Césaire's town recalls the spirit of Saint-John Perse's Caribbean in one other crucial respect as well, namely in its under-lining of the democracy of natural disasters. In *Éloges,* grandeur of scale and permanence of privileged tenure (the 'Maison' or Big House) are as much under threat from the destructive natural envi-ronment as the improvised dwellings with their corrugated iron roofs. Indeed, in the *Cahier* Césaire's downtrodden street is called the 'rue paille' ('straw street'), its name chiming with the inflam-mable and easily blown away lives to which it affords such scant protection. Behind both works lurk not only the fires that devas-tated Pointe-à-Pitre at the end of the nineteenth century, but also, and principally, the biblical proportions of the destruction in 1902 of Saint-Pierre, that urban jewel in the French Caribbean crown and a monument to the fragility of the operatic glitter of the colo-nial Caribbean. In extinguishing the lights of Saint-Pierre, the volcano laid down a store of nostalgia in the French Caribbean imagination. This nostalgia for what Glissant calls 'vivacité créole' or 'Creole intensity' suffuses Chamoiseau's *Texaco*.[26]

THE RURAL–URBAN SHIFT

There is little sense of mobility or change in the *Cahier* and even less in *Éloges*. Both texts lack the narrative-driven sense of succes-sion that makes of the problematic of time such a pivotal one in French Caribbean prose (fictional, historical, or autobiographical). Indeed, one of the criticisms of *Éloges* made from within the French Caribbean itself concerns precisely the fixed or frozen qual-ity of the poem's imagery. Narrative is, however, generically more in tune with the dynamic missing from the poems of *Éloges*. In Caribbean writing, the distinction between rural and urban space is often constructed as a transition from repetitive, seasonal, or cyclical time on the one hand, and from one culture (illiterate and

---

[25] Walcott 'The Antilles', 73.   [26] Glissant, *Faulkner Mississippi*, 336.

Creole) to another (literate and French). Not only is the relation between country and town temporalized, but it is frequently constructed as successive and hierarchical, construed either positively as upward mobility or negatively as the irreversible passage from an 'authentic' and distinct Caribbean culture to the inauthentic ersatz of urbanized, globally homogeneous culture: 'tout bougera, ou plutôt s'écroulera, quand le mouvement inarrêtable aura dépeuplé le lieu clos pour amasser dans les marges des villes sa population' ('it all began to shift, or rather collapse, when the unstoppable evolution had emptied the enclosure of people to reassemble them in the margins of cities').[27] Or, as one of Raphaël Confiant's characters puts it: 'Quand on vient vivre ici . . . on coupe les ponts avec son passé. Moi-même, je ne suis jamais retournée dans ma commune d'origine, le Gros-Morne et ça depuis 1938 que je suis descendue en ville' ('when you come to live here . . . you cut your ties with your past. For example, I have never been back in my townland, Gros-Morne, not since 1938, when I first came down to the town').[28] 'Ici' or 'here' refers to the quarter of Fort-de-France called Morne-Pichevin, a rehabilitated shanty town. Clearly, in this extract, urban space as a locus of permanent deracination and resettlement could be read as a paradigm of the vast part of the Caribbean, or indeed as a metaphor for the entire 'New World' as a space of dislocation and relocation. However, whereas the Caribbean was in no sense the chosen destination of its black population, the town is indeed the elective home of the population that migrates there en masse after the abolition of slavery, and that associates urban space with liberation, if not with freedom. However, the transition model does not quite indicate the complexity of the post-colonial rural–urban dynamic, a complexity that lurks behind Raymond Williams's notion that 'one of the last models of "city and country" is the system we now know as imperialism'.[29] Williams notes that, from the middle of the nineteenth century, 'distant lands became the rural areas of industrial Britain'.[30] He is not blind, of course, to the fact that the colonies

---

[27] *Poétique de la Relation*, 86; *Poetics of Relation*, 72.
[28] Raphaël Confiant, *Le Meurtre du Samedi-Gloria* (Paris: Mercure de France, 1997), 20.
[29] Raymond Williams, *The City and the Country* (1973; London: Hogarth Press, 1985), 279.
[30] Ibid. 284.

had their own rural–urban dynamic and that consequently, from this perspective at least, colonial urban space enjoys the paradoxical status of 'peripheral centre' or 'rural city'.

LA RUE CASES-NÈGRES: A NOVEL OF MOBILITY?

It has been held that the urban novel was inaugurated by the writers of the *créolité* movement.[31] In fact, however, Joseph Zobel's most famous novel is as much an urban as a rural novel, as well as sharing many of the attributes of the *Bildungsroman* (novel of education or acculturation), a genre distinguished by its attention to linearity. From the very outset, the representation of space serves to track José's transformation from the plantation child of the novel's opening to the disillusioned and politically aware Fort-de-France *lycéen* of the conclusion. José's mobility is determined by the dream of formal education entertained on his behalf by his grandmother and mother, a dream that will take him ever further away from the dead-end plantation alley, not just towards an increasingly urban space, but also towards an ever more complex, ambivalent, and literate life. The expectation held of this trajectory is that it will effect social and economic ascent. And yet, socially and economically, José seems to move in an exclusively horizontal plane, from Petit-Morne, to Petit-Bourg, to Petit-Fond. After all, the prefix 'petit' characterizes each one of these locations as lowly or inferior, its fateful recurrence denying hopes of social advancement and working against any notion of deep metamorphosis. However, notwithstanding this index of stasis, the narrator's range of experience and awareness is indeed exponentially extended by his lateral mobility in space. As a fledgling *lycéen*, José learns as much from his exploration of the town of Fort-de-France, from his outings to the cinema or to the bars, and vicariously from the urban experience of his friends Jojo and Carmen, as he does from his studies. His formal education is supplemented by this informal, nomadic initiation into the meaning of space, both inhabited space

---

[31] 'il faudra attendre Patrick Chamoiseau pour qu'un écrivain antillais s'attache à vraiment comprendre la ville' ('Patrick Chamoiseau was the first Caribbean writer who made a real effort to understand the town in some depth'): Burton, *Le Roman marron*, 81.

and public space (a distinction that is not dissimilar in the colonial context to Henri Lefèbvre's differentiation between appropriated and dominated space).[32] José's new insight into the configuration of space, and its appropriation and domination, proves just as instructive as his schooling. From his relegation to the hall or yard at Madame Léonce's house for example, he learns to locate and to decode social and racial structures and discovers that village and urban space is modelled on the same immutable racial lines that structured the plantation. The analogy between the two universes is further reinforced, indeed, by the 'French leave' taken by the small child and even by the *lycéen*, who, in a gesture of disaffection or resistance that recalls *marronnage*, wanders off alone during school hours into the hills or parks, those alveolae of the urban landscape.[33]

The prime mover behind José's escape from the closure of the plantation is his progressive yet assimilated grandmother, M'man Tine. Her assimilation is evidenced by her dream of hearing her grandson speak French rather than Creole and by her disdain for the attempts made by Médouze to keep alive within the plantation an alternative frame of reference: a Creole-based culture looking back towards Africa. But, if she participates as little as possible in the accommodations of folk culture,[34] she also rejects, but in her own way, the oppressive closure and the exploitation of the plantation; she refuses, for example, to compound her own oppression by spending her wages in the plantation shop and she also refuses to allow her daughter or grandson to labour in the plantation's *petites bandes*. Her will and her vision bring about the physical and emotional distance that separates Délia, her daughter, from José, and they also lead to José's agonized sense of distance from his grandmother's death. The effects of formal education are thus complex, entailing both loss and gain. The very divisions of the text underline the fact that José's schooling is founded on a fundamental exclusion: not just of the plantation, but also of the whole

---

[32] See Henri Lefèbvre, *La Production de l'espace* (1974; Paris: Anthropos, 2000), 191–5.

[33] The reference to hedge school or 'école buissonnière' underlines the element of return (to rural space) latent in this regular punctuation of José's formal schooling: Zobel, *La Rue Cases-Nègres*, 250.

[34] José recalls that his grandmother 'voisinait très peu' ('socialized very little in the neighbourhood'): ibid. 139.

mentality represented by Médouze, including oral culture and the folk memory of Africa, of transportation, and of slavery. Médouze's death precedes the onset of José's schooling at the start of the second part of the novel. This latter process will carve a chasm of critical distance separating José from both the social space of the plantation and the mental space of traditional culture, the two predominant realms of the first part of the novel. Allied to the replacement of rural life with urban life, formal education eventually supplants the innocent, childish, Creole-speaking self by the enlightened, literate, French-speaking self and also replaces the old familiar grandmother with the unfamiliar biological mother.

Formal education also opens up the alternative dimension of literacy for José. As he learns to live through books, he develops the capacity to abstract himself from the misery of his immediate surroundings. It is on his own initiative, however, and partly because of the denatured literary response required by an inappropriate and desiccated pedagogy, that he extends his reading *outside* the syllabus, thus resisting the programme's closure to his African heritage and to the Creole history of cultural diversity and interpenetration. In a sense, then, in reading Claude McKay and René Maran, and in writing the story of his childhood, he uses his literacy to reconnect in a different way with the space from which he has emerged. In teaching Jojo and Carmen to read, and in telling his own story, José is presented as paying a debt, as atoning for a betrayal. Although estrangement is explored exhaustively in the novel, the final pages (already commented upon in Chapter 3) express this chasm most graphically. When José's grandmother dies he is not present and, worse, he is unable, after he learns of her death, to summon up the image of her face. He can visualize her hands and coffin and imagine her burial, but he can no longer picture her face. He is stricken less by the fact that she died before he was able to rescue her from destitution than by the fact that he has become the unwilling instrument of her depersonalization in death. The distance that occasions this perceived betrayal is both magnified and made manifest in the novel's signature (in Fontainebleau), which confirms that the narrator had become so estranged from the plantation—and from the Caribbean—that the only possible outcome was emigration.

The cultural ambivalence marking Zobel's novel recurs in many texts of the colonial tradition of education writing, including

Camara Laye's *L'Enfant noir* (1953) and Cheikh Hamidou Kane's *L'Aventure ambiguë* (1961), as well as two further Caribbean texts: Guy Tirolien's poem 'Prière d'un petit enfant nègre' and the second volume of Patrick Chamoiseau's *récit d'enfance, Chemin d'école* (1994). The 'Prière' invokes some 'messieurs de la ville' who have been held up as the model to be emulated by the 'petit enfant nègre'.[35] Assimilated to the point of self-betrayal, however, these educated urban gentlemen are dismal and disconnected, having lost touch with the earth, the body, natural rhythms, and even the cosmos. All the emphasis of Tirolien's text is on what has been lost by urbanization and education (shorthand for assimilation), rather than on what has been gained. Although forty years separate them, Chamoiseau's account of his Fort-de-France schooling is very similar to José's narrative. Both strike a highly ambivalent note, since they temper their narrative of assimilation and alienation with the grateful hindsight of the wordsmith. However, Chamoiseau's untiring foregrounding of the collective, oral, and dialogical dimensions of his memories and of his writing, and his constant emphasis on the value of Creole and on the ravages of linguistic indoctrination are the principal points of divergence between the two works.

RURAL–URBAN DICHOTOMY?

The nineteenth-century history of Caribbean rural–urban polarization along racial lines can be explained in terms of the urban supremacy of a mixed-race population that saw itself as several cuts above the black labouring classes and as having left the mud of the canefields far behind. The Haitian tradition also foregrounds the overlap between the rural–urban dichotomy, on the one hand, and divisions of class and race, on the other. Jacques Roumain, for example, stresses the tension between the city-dwellers and those whom the latter term 'nègres pied-à-terre' or 'nègres va-nu-pieds' (the barefoot). In the French Caribbean context, the survival well into the twentieth century of this sense of urban superiority is confirmed in much contemporary fiction. In Édouard Glissant's novel *La Case du commandeur*, in a scene of striking social polarization, the town's European-identified officials show their

---

[35] Guy Tirolien, *Balles d'or* (Paris: Présence africaine, 1961).

contempt for Pythagore, a rural blow-in who has the temerity to wish to consult public records on the Dahomean king (Béhanzin) exiled to Martinique by the French. Pythagore retreats, leaving behind him 'ce vague émoi des gens de la ville dérangés de leur sieste ou de leur sorbet, qui s'inquiétaient de ce qu'un Nègre des champs, un coupeur de cannes, eût la pretention de faire des recherches . . .' ('that vague fluster of urbanites disturbed in the middle of a siesta or a sorbet, annoyed that a field worker, a mere canecutter, should presume to carry out research . . .').[36] The urban environment is associated in this novel with fiercely defensive, small-minded, cultural prejudice, and in Simone Schwarz-Bart's *Pluie et vent sur Télumée Miracle* with a stilted estrangement parading as refinement. Télumée's sister Régina is described as having become 'une dame élégante de la ville' ('an elegant city lady'). Her mother's pride and joy, she is literate and eats apples imported from France. However, Schwarz-Bart's sketch of Régina's apparent social elevation must be read in relation to the aesthetic of the novel as a whole, where the recurrent motif of physical beauty is inseparably linked to spiritual nobility, serving indeed as a sign of exceptional inner resources of compassion and endurance. Moreover, in each portrait of physical grace, pride of place is given to praise of (black) skin. Blackness is deconstructed, however, into a multiplicity of colours identified as such—wine-red and rose-wood, for example—rather than as racial markers ('câpresse', 'chabine', etc.). In Régina's portrait, however, reference not only to skin colour, but also to beauty, is conspicuously absent. Instead, her apparel—clothes and gloves—elide all possible impression of her own distinct appearance and thus of her inner self. It is as though the acquired social markers of her urbanity overwhelm, disguise, even efface nature, making it impossible to see the individual or her beauty. Moreover, Régina's estrangement from her origins is figured as a fissure in memory, revealed as she extends in some embarrassment a gloved hand to her half-sister whom she barely recognizes: 'Vous êtes bien Télumée, n'est-ce pas?' ('Why, you must be Telumée').[37] Towards the end of the novel, Télumée recalls her own brief experience of urban life, and how, removed from sources

---

[36] Glissant, *La Case du commandeur*, 41.
[37] Schwarz-Bart, *Pluie et vent sur Télumée Miracle*, 65–6; *The Bridge of Beyond*, 41.

of natural sustenance, she had been afraid that she would starve. However, given the importance of plants in Télumée's powers of physical and spiritual healing, this fear implies that the urban environment is a spiritual desert. As in Césaire's *Cahier*, the town's remoteness from nature is negatively connoted and serves to underline the separateness and difference of the two spaces, rural and urban.

I have already noted Glissant's reference to the search for rural roots in *La Case du commandeur*,[38] and Roland Brival's *Biguine Blues* also evokes this fashion for the 'retour aux racines'.[39] The latent exoticism of this focus on the vanishing point, as it were, of what is wistfully regarded as a coherent, cultural quiddity, recurs in *créoliste* representations of urban space where cultural authenticity seems to be axiomatically linked to the countryside. This is indeed the assumption behind Bertène Juminer's comment that 'De nos jours ... le bain culturel créole est en voie de tarissement ... L'exode rural bat son plein' ('Today ... immersion in Creole culture is no longer possible ... the rural exodus is in full swing').[40]

We must distinguish between two types of (sub)urban 'creolization': in the first, rural time/space is present in the urban setting, but the distinction between the two is not lost. In the second, urban space/time can be seen to reproduce the structures of rural space/time and the two are not distinct, but rather the former reproduces the latter. Thomas Spear defines the space of Creole 'récits d'enfance' as the 'En-ville créole imprégnée des histoires de la campagne antillaise' ('town centre impregnated with stories of the Caribbean countryside'). For Spear, 'cette autobiographie antillaise et urbaine est donc mixte, créolisée avec son pendant campagnard' ('Caribbean urban autobiography is thus mixed, creolized by its country dimension').[41]

En ces temps, Fort-de-France abritait la campagne, il y avait dans les rues, des mulets des chevaux des bœufs de Porto-Rico en route vers l'abattoir,

---

[38] See above, Ch. 5, n. 69.
[39] Brival, *Biguine Blues* (Paris: Phébus, 1999), 17.
[40] Bertène Juminer, 'La parole de nuit', in Ludwig (ed.), *Écrire la 'parole de nuit'*, 131–49: 148.
[41] Thomas C. Spear, 'L'enfance créole: la nouvelle autobiographie antillaise', in S. Crosta, *Récits de vie de l'Afrique et des Antilles*, GRELCA Essais (Quebec: Presses universitaires de Laval, 1998), 143.

des canards volant sans tête, des poules egaillées, des cabris en rupture d'un sacrifice indien, des oiseaux pas farouches, et des chiens errants dessous leurs cicatrices.[42]

Nostalgia for a time when town and countryside were more permeable to each other is certainly evident in Chamoiseau's *Antan d'enfance*, although the two spaces are kept further apart in the childhood narratives of Maryse Condé and Raphaël Confiant;[43] in the latter the one is highlighted after the other, and in the former they alternate, as the narrator's family lives in the town, where appearances have to be kept up, but holidays and relaxes 'upcountry'.

Autobiography is not, of course the only genre to highlight this hybridity, for the representation of creolized urban/rural space is widespread in Caribbean writing in general. It is registered too in Caryl Phillips's portrayal of streets 'in which hens played in drying and dried mud, and goats either wandered free or were tethered on chains . . . This area, which resembled the country in its poverty, had always impressed Bertram as the unassembled, peopled, animaled heart of Baytown.'[44] But, whereas this critical observation is devoid of nostalgia, the positive connotation of creolization—even the creolization of life and death that I have noted both in Saint-John Perse's poetry and, in Chapter 4, in the portrayal of Solibo—ensures that the presence of the country in the town is desired and celebrated in the writing of *créolité*. Thus the urban migrants of Chamoiseau's first novel gravitate to the only part of the town to offer them the 'présence rassurante de leurs campagnes natales: les places de marché' ('the reassuring presence in the markets of their native countryside').[45]

---

[42] Chamoiseau, *Antan d'enfance*, 51; 'At that time, Fort-de-France was home to the country; in the streets were mules, horses, Puerto Rican oxen headed for the slaughterhouse, ducks flying headless, scattered chickens, goats that had broken away from an Indian sacrifice, tame birds, and dogs meandering with a bodyful of scars': *Childhood*, 32.

[43] Maryse Condé, *Le Cœur à rire et à pleurer*; Confiant, *Ravines du devant-jour*.

[44] Caryl Phillips, *A State of Independence* (London: Faber & Faber, 1986), 57–8.

[45] Chamoiseau, *Chronique des sept misères*, 16.

DIFFERENCE AND REPETITION: PLANTATION
SEGREGATION REPRODUCED

In the second part of *La Rue Cases-Nègres*, José's impression of the village's familiarity confirms the spread of the iniquitous parameters of plantation structures far beyond the plantation perimeter. Many factors underline that morphological continuity between plantation and urban space, from the similarities between the room occupied in the village of Petit-Bourg by grandmother and grandson and M'man Tine's *case* on the plantation, to the fact that José's mother, Délia, and his friends Jojo and Carmen remain locked into the status of domestic servants in the town (they may no longer work the land, although Jojo is a gardener, but they do still labour for whites). Indeed, the social organization of Fort-de-France closely mirrors that of the plantation in Petit-Morne. Both worlds are strictly tiered, with little or no mobility between the various strata. Three distinct types of urban space are singled out for particularly close attention: firstly, the popular quarters of Sainte-Thérèse and the Morne Pichevin; secondly, the chic white district called Route Didier—its name suggestive of connection and mobility; and finally, Petit-Fond, or the satellite quarter housing the servants who work on the Route Didier, the term 'Fond' (bottom, depth, end) suggesting the same sort of subaltern positioning as that connoted by the seemingly inescapable epithet 'Petit'.

As a result of his exposure to these 'new' spaces, José at first sees the 'Rue Cases-Nègres' with even more critical eyes, comparing his memories of the inside of his grandmother's shack there with the opulent interior of the Route Didier villa where his mother works. However, his initial admiration of the affluent white quarter gives way to an understanding of its shameful foundation in slavery and exploitation. In the novel's most sustained analysis of urban space, José contrasts the shanty town of Sainte-Thérèse[46] with Petit-Fond, built and rented out by poor whites to the black servants of the rich whites of the Route Didier. Conversely, and in an almost utopian vein, he celebrates Sainte-Thérèse as a space that is claimed, colonized, and inhabited by blacks newly migrated to the town. This 'New World', free of any oppressive project, calls forth creativity

---

[46] See Zobel, *La Rue Cases-Nègres*, 252–4.

and a sense of community. Moreover, although José is initially inclined to disparage Petit-Fond, the purpose-built servant quarter, as passively reproducing the paternalistic plantation ethos of the Rue Cases-Nègres and as contrasting, therefore, with Sainte-Thérèse, he concludes that the servants of Petit-Fond idealized their employers in a way that the field-workers of the Rue Cases-Nègres never did. In other words, to the ills of exploitation and segregation, these urban blacks add alienation from black cultural values or a sort of servile admiration of their landlord bosses. This damning judgement of urban alienation completes José's evolution from an initially naive perception of plantation space and rural workers to his ultimate ability to discern both the limits and the repetition of plantation structures of alienation. Whereas Sainte-Thérèse bears witness to a spirit of initiative and self-determination, plantation workers passively accept plantation structures; yet the latter manage at least to retain a sense of cultural apartness lost by the urban servants and labourers of Petit-Fond, whose immersion in the living space of their bosses has alienated them from themselves.

In so far as *La Rue Cases-Nègres* is structured around José's 'progress' through proto-urban, then urban space, this novel might appear to break away from the plantation paradigm. Yet the narrator tirelessly revisits in memory his grandmother's cabin on the Rue Cases-Nègres, and all his subsequent places of dwelling—from the room that he inhabits with his grandmother in the village to the urban dwellings of Petit-Fond and Sainte-Thérèse—are ineluctably compared to that original spatial paradigm. Furthermore, urban structures of division and segregation clearly repeat the plantation paradigm, just as the distinction between the Petit-Fond servants and the plantation labourers reproduces the intra-plantation distinction vividly observed in Chamoiseau's *Texaco* between so-called domestic and field slaves (*nègres de case* and *nègres des champs*). Moreover, when José castigates the stereotypical (or what he himself calls the 'Rue Cases-Nègres') cinematic and literary treatment of blacks, he is commenting on the tentacular spread of the structures of slavery deep into modern culture. As in Maximilien Laroche's opposition between the plantation and the 'habitation' referred to in the previous chapter, in his mobilization of 'Rue Cases-Nègres' as an epithet, José uses a 'habitational' and plantation analogy to suggest that racist stereotyping reproduces the restricted, segregated dimensions of Caribbean social and geographical space under slavery. The overwhelming implication of this reproduction is the perennial nature or persistence of the colonial past.

Many *créoliste* novels continue the discourse of segregation that is so predominant in *La Rue Cases-Nègres,* in that they represent urban space as bifurcating into the prosperous 'En-ville' or the modern, planned centre, on the one hand, and the less salubrious quarters, the shanty satellites, on the other. The centre, or down-town, is the site of privilege and officialdom, while the non-white-identified majority congregate on the town margins, alienated not just spatially, but from historical time too (Confiant's Rigobert, for example, knows neither his own age nor the current date or year).[47]

A distinction is made, however, in *Texaco,* between the urban anatomy of Saint-Pierre as the quintessential nineteenth-century plantation town, and the shape of the late-twentieth-century town of Fort-de-France. The impenetrable, exclusionary space of Saint-Pierre is compared to the Big House of the plantation. The order, history, rituals, and monumentality of the town thus confirm the homology of plantation and urban space.

Ville massive. Ville porteuse d'une mémoire dont ils étaient exclus. Pour eux l'En-ville demeurait impénétrable. Lisse. Ciré. Que lire dans ces fers forgés? Ces volets de bois peint? Ces grosses pierres taillées? Ces parcs, ces jardins, tous ces gens qui semblaient en manier les secrets? Bonbon lui dit un jour, et il avait raison, que l'En-ville c'était une Grande-case. La Grande-case des Grandes-cases. Même mystère. Même puissance.[48]

Fort-de-France also recalls the plantation, but not in the same way as Saint-Pierre. Whereas Saint-Pierre was closed in on itself, Fort-de-France integrates oppositional forces within its perimeter. It brings the space of *marronnage* inside, in other words. Moreover, in their portrayal of Fort-de-France, it is as though Chamoiseau and Confiant dismiss the universal, if diversely inflected, structures that typify most late-twentieth-century towns and cities in an effort

---

[47] Confiant, *Le Meurtre du Samedi-Gloria,* 88.
[48] Chamoiseau, *Texaco,* 94; 'Massive City. City from whose memory they were excluded. For them City remained impenetrable. Smooth. Waxed. What to read in this wrought iron, these painted wood shutters, these enormous cut stones? These parks, these gardens, of which all these city people seemed to master the secrets? Bonbon once said to him, and he was right, that city was a Big Hutch. The Big Hutch of all Big Hutches. Same mystery. Same power': tr. 80.

to highlight what is different or unique about the Caribbean urban experience. One could see this as an effort to underline—for outside consumption in the first instance, perhaps, and in memorialist or mythologizing vein for home consumption—all that is or was unique and/or threatened in the Caribbean town. Consumerism, importation, and imitation of Western models are all negatively connoted. And, in *Texaco*, the historical heart of the town is represented as destroying memory wantonly, whereas the most recent urban accretions on the margins are seen as preserving it. Yet, as the following extract confirms, there is a certain amount of circulation between the two poles, even if it is, principally, conflictual:

Elle m'apprit à relire les deux espaces de notre ville créole: le centre historique vivant des *exigences neuves de la consommation*; les couronnes d'occupation populaire, *riches du fond de nos histoires*. Entre ces lieux, la palpitation humaine qui circule. *Au centre, on détruit le souvenir* pour s'inspirer des villes occidentales et *rénover*. Ici, *dans la couronne, on survit de mémoire*. Au centre, on se perd dans le moderne du monde; ici, on ramène de très vieilles racines, non profondes et rigides, mais diffuses, profuses, épandues sur le temps avec cette légèreté que confère la parole. Ces pôles, reliés au gré des forces sociales, structurent de leurs conflits les visages de la ville.[49]

Zobel's positive view of Morne Pichevin and Sainte-Thérèse as representing a creative and collective appropriation of space thus prefigures the 'shantytown' orientation of the *créolité* movement of the 1980s and 1990s. Indeed, a self-reflexive passage in Raphaël Confiant's novel *Le Nègre et l'amiral* outlines the terms of Amédée Mauville's writing project which corresponds to the thrust of *Texaco* as well as of many other works of the *créolité* movement, namely, the privileged portrayal of the urban margins.

---

[49] Chamoiseau, *Texaco*, 188–9; tr. 170. Emphasis mine. 'She taught me to reread our Creole city's two spaces: the historical center living on the new demands of consumption; the suburban crowns of grassroots occupations, rich with the depth of our stories. Humanity throbs between these two places. In the center, memory subsides in the face of renovation, before the cities which the Occident inspires. Here, on the outskirts, one survives on memory. In the center all dissolves in the modern world; but here people bring very old roots, not deep and rigid, but diffuse, profuse, spread over time with the lightness of speech. These two poles, linked by social forces, mold the faces of the city with their push-and-pull.'

Le spectacle hallucinant de cette cour en terre battue entourée de cases peinturées criardement et éclairée par les ampoules blafardes des poteaux électriques fascinait l'imagination du professeur, qui méditait depuis longtemps la rédaction d'un roman. Il voulait brosser une vaste fresque populaire . . .[50]

Unlike Zobel, however, both Chamoiseau and Confiant highlight the urban margins as a site of resistance. Indeed, they represent the conflictual relation between the two polarized urban spaces, 'en-ville' and 'cités', or downtown and liminal ghettoes, as reproducing the oppositional relation between the plantation and the rebel *marrons* who prey on its edges from their retreats in the hills or *mornes* (and the word 'morne' in the name of Fort-de-France's foremost urban margin is significant): 'Arrivé à Morne Pichevin où la Loi n'osait guère s'aventurer, Rigobert fut livré à la drivaille quotidienne et fit très vite l'apprentissage du maniement du couteau à cran d'arrêt, instrument indispensable de la rapine et terreur des bourgeois mulâtres du centre-ville.' ('Once in Morne Pichevin where the Law barely dared to venture, Rigobert joined the general daily drift and was quickly initiated into the use of a switchblade, the essential tool of terror and plunder for preying on the mixed-race bourgeoisie downtown').[51] Yet in *Texaco*, conflict and opposition leave room for circulation and creolization, just as many literary representations of *marronnage* underline the dialectical dependence of the *marrons* on the plantation. As Marie-Sophie puts it, the first inhabitants of Texaco wanted to play 'marron' to the town-centre's 'Habitation': 'Nous voulûmes, face à l'En-Ville, vivre dans l'esprit des Mornes' ('And we wished, confronted with City, to live in the spirit of the Hills').[52]

As a corrective to the *créoliste* celebration of polarization between the centre, on the one hand, and the marginalized urban culture of resistance, community, solidarity, creativity, and autonomy on the other, it is interesting to consider the much more political and materialist critique of urban polarization in Caryl Phillips's *A State of Independence*, where the Caribbean town is viewed through the eyes of an exile returned from England:

---

[50] Confiant, *Le Nègre et l'amiral*, 49; 'The hallucinatory sight of this backyard surrounded by garishly painted cabins and lit by the weak bulbs of street lights captured the imagination of the teacher who had been thinking for a long time of writing a novel. He had in mind a vast popular fresco . . .'.

[51] Ibid. 12.   [52] Chamoiseau, *Texaco*, 348; tr. 317.

like most Caribbean towns, it was originally part slave-market and part harbour . . . Firstly, there were the well-patrolled middle-class estates of the possessors; neat, planned, perfumed, and often affording spectacular views of both the mountains and the sea. And then down by the harbour, and for a few streets in each direction, the low commercial buildings of trade and government. Finally, there existed a hellish and labyrinth-like entanglement of slums in which lived the dispossessed in their broken-down wooden buildings and under their rusty iron roofs . . .[53]

This novel's avowed political agenda (evident in the title that refers, albeit equivocally, to 'independence') dictates the terms of this description. The inheritance of the imperial order is stigmatized as widespread poverty and naked inequality, and explicit references to 'tropical squalor'[54] underline this impression. Far from idealizing the slum, there is not even the slightest sense here of there being 'nothing lovelier than the allotments of the poor'.[55] Geographers such as Marc Pain point out that 'the opposition between what is perceived as 'la Ville' (belonging to the rich and to the world of work) and the 'Cité' (the poor man's city) remains the basic urban structure in the post-colonial world.[56] Janice Spleth considers that this 'socio-economic duality' is a vestige of a colonial past,[57] and quotes the Zairean novelist Mpoyi-Buatu, author of the aptly titled *La Re-production*, for whom renaming does not guarantee change: 'La ville se nomme aujourd'hui Kinshasa . . . Encore que cela ne suffise pas à parier pour une société nouvelle.'[58] Although the writing of the *créolité* movement insists that this duality is highly productive on a socio-cultural level, their cult of urban polarization is not shared by all contemporary authors. French Caribbean writing is not devoid, in other words, of indictments of ghettoization or destitution, and Guadeloupean (women) writers are particularly alive to this question: Gerty Dambury's story 'Le Lit' discreetly evokes the shame and concealment that often accompanies poverty

[53] Phillips, *A State of Independence*, 57.
[54] Ibid. 19.
[55] Walcott, *What the Twilight Says*, 4.
[56] 'L'opposition demeure fondamentale entre ce qui est perçu comme "la Ville": la ville des riches, la ville du travail et "la Cité": la ville des pauvres': Marc Pain, *Kinshasa. La Ville et la cité* (Paris: ORSTOM, 1984).
[57] Janice Spleth, 'Kinshasa: The Drama of the Post-Colonial City', in Buford Norman (ed.), *The City in/and French Literature* (Amsterdam: Rodopi, 1997), 215–28: 217.
[58] Thomas Mpoyi-Buatu, *La Re-production* (Paris: L'Harmattan, 1986), 7.

and social exclusion,[59] while much of Gisèle Pineau's work delineates the cycle of abuse and neglect that spins off the systemic material and social deprivation and the misogynistic oppression inherited from the institution of slavery. Concentrating more specifically on the urban context, Lucie Julia's *Mélody des faubourgs* is a condemnation of the tardy modernization of the disenfranchised quarters of Pointe-à-Pitre.

CREOLIZATION: A TIME AND A PLACE?

Why do the *créolistes* dwell loudly on the internal polarization of urban space and time? Chris Bongie, in his work on exoticism, a phenomenon that he has defined as 'a discursive practice intent on recovering 'elsewhere' values 'lost' with the modernization of European society',[60] has much to say about the desire for a lost elsewhere or a lost 'other time'. It is important to note, however, that what the *créolistes* are fixated on is not just rural space and time, but rather a social and economic system that generated a unique social dynamic, and a particular culture (Creole culture) around that dynamic. It is this oppositional moment, this process of emergence or creolization that they seek to recreate, over and over. They view the town as reproducing the selfsame creative process that gave rise on the plantations to Creole culture. Just as the plantation system, with transportation and slavery at its heart, gave rise to a culture of ruse and of resistance (direct and indirect), so too the centre of Fort-de-France, unproductive and consumerist in a way that the plantation never was, a place of alienation where the Creole culture born of the plantation is devalued, produces in turn a culture of resistance. In a vision underwritten by Édouard Glissant in his preface to Chamoiseau's first novel, the *créolistes* represent the marginalized urban population—not just the 'démunis', but the 'djobeurs' (essentially the jobless)—as surviving by

---

[59] Gerty Dambury, *Mélancolie. Nouvelles* (Paris: La Flèche du temps, 1999).

[60] Chris Bongie, *Exotic Memories: Literature, Colonialism, and the Fin de Siécle* (Stanford: Stanford University Press, 1991), 5. He has also defined it as a 'ninteenth-century literary and existential practice that posited another space, the space of an Other, outside or beyond the confines of a "civilization" . . . that, by virtue of its modernity, was perceived by many writers as being incompatible with certain essential values—or, indeed, the realm of value itself' (ibid. 4–5).

their wits (or wit) on the fringes of bourgeois society, where they reinvent Creole culture. Beyond the pale of the *en-ville*, the quarters of Texaco or Morne Pichevin thus secrete the 'culture de ruse et de paradoxe qu'est la créolité' ('Creole culture of cunning and paradox'),[61] a culture of 'débrouillardise et entraide' ('resourcefulness and helping out').[62] In a particularly rich image of creolization, Texaco's town-planner calls these quarters 'une mangrove urbaine' ('an urban swamp'),[63] neither land nor sea, urban nor rural.

If—in the name of Creole creativity—Caribbean urban space is held to reproduce plantation structures, more specifically to re-enact the kind of cultural resistance for which the plantation is celebrated, how, then, does that space relate to time? More specifically, to what extent does this 'reproduction' or this nostalgia leave room for modernity? Does Chamoiseau's radiant writing of the Creole town in *Texaco* and in *Antan d'enfance*, or Confiant's portrait of the raucous, demotic street life of Fort-de-France give a sense of a town with municipal structures and a modern working centre? In reading these works, we can, in fact, get a certain feel for the atmosphere of French Caribbean hospitals and offices, supermarkets and garages, schools and public transport, art galleries and shopping malls. But always in a context of polarization. The view of Fort-de-France and of Caribbean society that emerges from Roger Parsemain's writing, on the other hand, is not at all constrained by that agenda of dichotomy. Thus the vivid and detailed social and cultural backdrop to his story 'Je ne suis pas la diablesse' is a country 'congestionné jusqu'à l'étranglement' ('congested to suffocation point') with cars and other consumer durables, a country highly aware of a very different past—'le jadis du pays touffu d'arbres, de jardins, de champs de cannes, de cases minuscules' ('the land of the past, dense with trees, gardens, canefields, and tiny huts')—but not paralysed or polarized by memory. The chasm between this perspective on Caribbean space and time and the received Creole view is clearly pointed up in the identity of the first-person narrator of the story: a lesbian, divorced civil servant and mother of three.[64]

---

[61] See Burton, *Le Roman marron*, 184.   [62] Ibid. 188.
[63] Chamoiseau, *Texaco*, 289.
[64] Parsemain, *Il chantait des boléros*, 38, 43.

When *créoliste* descriptions of Caribbean urban space do not represent it as reproducing plantation polarization, this is usually because the town is being opposed *as a whole* to the plantation and urban space to rural space. Thus, in Confiant's *Commandeur du sucre*, Firmin Léandor's wife wistfully speaks of the 'douceur de la vie' in the capital. 'Les gens y étaient propres, bien habillés. Ils ne parlaient pas créole ou peu et donc n'injuriaient pas à tout propos. Chacun était à ses affaires et personne ne s'intéressait de se mêler de votre vie ni de vous critiquer' ('The people there were clean and well-dressed. They didn't speak Creole, or very little, and didn't insult you all the time. Everybody was minding their own business and people weren't all the time sticking their nose into your business or criticizing you').[65] The end of this novel, however, sees even Firmin's wife resisting the attractions of the town, loyally remaining with her husband who cannot bring himself to abandon, not even for his own highland plot, the lure of the sugarcane plantation. Set in the 1930s like *La Rue Cases-Nègres*, this novel suggests that the social advancement, comfort, and refinement apparently promised by urban life are not necessarily irresistible. Far, then, from collapsing the distinction between town and plantation space, *Commandeur du sucre* allows the 'en-ville' of Fort-de-France to figure metonymically the entire undifferentiated urban experience.

A rather different polarization underlies the plot of Roland Brival's *Biguine Blues*, although the town itself is represented as a more or less undifferentiated space. In this novel, set in the present, the pole opposed to the urban hell of petrol fumes and social problems is not the time of the plantation but rather the countryside, specifically the hills. Théodore had lived in the town and had seen people 'sans racines, sans ailes, qui tournaient en rond entre les murs de Fort-de-France' ('without roots and without wings, wandering round in circles within the walls of Fort-de-France').[66] He knew that the luxurious urban villas, no less than the corrugated steel shacks, were home to 'parents blessés . . . familles torturées . . . enfants déchus de l'enfance' ('stricken parents, tormented families, children robbed of their childhood').[67] He had dreamed of healing the urban wounded, rich and poor alike, and of gathering them all in the countryside to teach them how to live

---

[65] Confiant, *Commandeur du sucre*, 301–2.
[66] Brival, *Biguine Blues*, 84.   [67] Ibid.

again, but he decided that he was too old to become the leader of an alternative village set in the island's highlands 'comme à l'époque de l'ancien temps' ('like in the old times').[68] In Brival's novel too, there is a sense of the past. Specifically, Théodore remembers that the hills were the site of alternative *marron* communities. The novel also highlights the urban–rural schism and to this end minimizes the meaning of intra-urban distinctions. Despite its superficial social polarization into villas with swimming pools and security fences and squalid squats, there is no suggestion that the town can incorporate a space of resistance. Rather, the only alternative to pan-urban alienation lies in rural space.

An even less (internally) polarized account of urban space is given in Maryse Condé's autobiographical *récit d'enfance, Le Coeur à rire et à pleurer*, and in the fiction of Daniel Maximin, both of whom write sympathetically of the lives and aspirations of inhabitants of the 'en-ville', mostly teachers (purveyors of cosmopolitan, if not assimilated, culture) and intellectuals. It is no accident that both Maryse Condé and Daniel Maximin have kept their distance from the aspirations of the *créolité* movement and that their commitment to Creole orality is qualified. Maximin's narrators and characters speak, indeed, rather unmarked French, and are given to poetic intellectual analysis. Furthermore, in Maximin's work, the banal workings of urban bureaucracy are acknowledged in a non-conflictual, matter-of-fact manner.

Arrivée au bourg, au lieu de rentrer directement par le chemin du cinéma, Angela passe du côté du marché pour acheter de la main de Mme Dora deux ou trois bouts de boudin, puis elle remonte à sa case tout en haut du bourg, passé [*sic*] l'hôpital général et la résidence du préfet, presque là où la route commence à chercher le volcan.[69]

The above evocation of Basse-Terre is a good example of the kind of spatial *récitative* that is the backdrop to the narrative of ceaseless circulation across Guadeloupe, through urban and rural space and from one to the other, that predominates in *Soufrières*. In

---

[68] Brival, *Biguine Blues*, 84
[69] Daniel Maximin, *Soufrières* (Paris: Seuil, 1987), 26 ('When she gets to the village, instead of going straight home by the cinema, Angela goes by the market to buy from Mme Dora's stall two or three slices of sausage, before going up to her house right at the top of the village, way past the hospital and the Prefect's residence, almost as far as the point where the road starts to seek out the volcano').

Condé's autobiographical narrative too, although the rural–urban divide is highlighted in the portrayal of the family's circulation between country and town, both spaces are represented without reference to the plantation past. It is no doubt significant that both Maximin and Condé are Guadeloupean, and that Guadeloupe is less urbanized than Martinique. While rural settlement certainly features prominently in the fiction of Guadeloupean writers like Condé, Schwarz-Bart, Pineau, or Pépin, what is much more remarkable is the fact that these writers do not idealize the plantation, nor do they create a sort of surrogate, oppositional rural or plantation space within the town, as the *créoliste* writers tend to do. Like Roland Brival, both Daniel Maximin and Maryse Condé claim the 'whole town' as a legitimate setting for their fiction or autobiography, respectively.

In the previous chapter, I noted Maximilien Laroche's use of the plantation as a metaphor of literary and cultural ghettoization, and I have located a similar connection in Zobel's novel. To what extent, however, does the urban French Caribbean novel imagine a 'New World', different from the 'Old World' of the plantation, to what extent does the urban habitat that it represents escape the structures of the *Habitation*? It is important here not to confuse the two levels of spatial creolization that I have already noted, that is, the interpenetration of two coeval or synchronous spaces, urban and rural, on the one hand, and the persistence or reproduction of plantation structures in the shanty towns, on the other, a temporal resonance that Édouard Glissant evokes in *Poétique de la Relation*:

le bourgeonnement des bidonvilles a aimanté les masses des démunis et changé le rythme de leurs voix. . . . Une littérature urbaine est apparue ainsi, à Bahia, à New York, à Jacmel ou à Fort-de-France. L'aire de la Plantation, ayant conjoint aux surfaces infinies de l'hacienda ou du latifidium, s'est éparpillée pour finir dans ces dédales de tôles et de béton où se risque notre commun devenir.'[70]

---

[70] Glissant, *Poétique de la Relation*, 87. 'In the Caribbean and in Latin America, the burgeoning shantytowns drew masses of the destitute and transformed the rhythm of their voices. Thus, urban literature made its appearance in Bahia, New York, Jacmel or Fort-de-France. The Plantation region, having joined with the endless terrain of haciendas or latifundio, spread thin to end up in mazes of sheet metal and concrete in which our common future takes its chances' (*Poetics of Relation*, 72–3).

Although Glissant uses here the spatial term 'aire' or 'sphere' to refer to the plantation, the temporal reference of the ghostly homonym 'ère' or 'era' is reinforced by the unequivocal temporal reference of the expressions 'pour finir dans', and 'notre commun devenir'. Glissant thus recognizes that plantation space mutates into urban space and that there is a continuity between the plantation culture of the past and the urban future. Moreover, this mutation (discontinuity within continuity) is expressed in terms of a relocation or dissemination, as though, in other words, the lingering vestiges of the plantation somehow creolize urban space, setting up a dynamic of repetition versus creation.

How, then, does Édouard Glissant regard Caribbean urban space? Although his novels, particularly *Le Quatrième Siècle* and *La Case du commandeur*, do not go so far as to represent the town as a degraded cultural space, or to idealize the plantation, they do nonetheless associate urban space with a sense of loss, drift, and vacuum. Chris Bongie observes that in Glissant's work 'the hills serve as the site par excellence of authentic resistance and *grand marronnage*',[71] whereas the 'lowlands symbolize submission'. However, Bongie also claims that the lowlands symbolize the

compromised (or from another perspective creolized) identity that was to emerge on the plantations and then later be refined in the degraded urban setting that the narrator of *Le Quatrième Siècle*—in a typically modernist attack on cities—revealingly identifies as 'the unspeakable thing that raises its voice in order to muffle the call of the heights . . . the vacuum into which the history of the land and the knowledge of the past is sucked, and in which it gets lost'.[72]

This comment suggests that Glissant associates the compromise of creolization with the lowlands only (and this is not so, as we saw in the previous chapter). It also implies that Glissant is somehow hostile to the space of creolization and that he dismisses or condemns both plantation space and urban space as a vacuum. Again, this is a misrepresentation. Certainly, both Chamoiseau and Confiant go much further than Glissant in their endorsement of the cultural value both of the plantation and of the town as sites of creolization *qua* resistance and subversion. Since they see rampant Frenchification as being linked with the 'en-ville' ('town centre' or

---

[71] Bongie makes this point in his *Islands and Exiles*, 152–3.
[72] Ibid.

'official town') only, the mass movement of the ex-slaves towards urban centres is, for them, a shift, not a hiatus in Creole culture. They view the plantation as a culturally creative space, and the town as being made in the same mould, the polarization (between the centre and the fringes) encouraging the marginalized to re-mobilize the resistant, creative strategies of displaced plantation culture (oral culture and 'petit marronnage'). Édouard Glissant, on the other hand, refrains from positing such highly polarized spaces, whose price is both temporal and spatial closure; closure both to 'becoming' and to what he terms extension or 'l'étendue'. This is why Glissant's *marrons* do not forget the sea any more than they turn their backs on that open, unrestricted space that becomes connoted as the space of Africa, or suppress the Middle Passage. And this is why Glissant, far from decrying it, tirelessly promotes creolization. His writing does link the urban environment with inauthenticity and with the hollowness of consumerism, and the plantation with colonial compliance, but to suggest that his high-lands are hostile or even impervious to creolization is a distortion of his whole project. As we saw, the two 'seminal' *marrons*, Louise, a plantation slave, and Longoué, the 'aboriginal' *marron*, gradually come to communicate in Creole. Moreover, the consummation of their relation is itself a highly symbolic act of mutual creolization that will render it henceforth impossible to claim that space is polarized into high and low ground. As we have seen, even if the lowlands (not just the towns, but also the plantations) are constructed as the space of capitulation, compromise, and amnesia, Glissant's principal concern is to show that no space, culture, language, or time is purely this or that. 'Nothing is but what is not', and creolization is not a chemical reaction that makes of several pure elements an indivisible compound. Rather, in the (unrecover-able) beginning was the uncertain, the unstable, the compounded. And, rather than suggesting that they dwell in a nostalgically inflected memory (ultimately, plantation memory), or that they hold out as the guardians of the precarious past of Creole culture, he sees the urban 'labyrinths of corrugated iron and concrete' as holding the key not just to the Caribbean present and future, but to humanity's shared being in time, to our common habitat in a 'becoming'.

CHAPTER SEVEN

French Connection, Metropolitan Mirror

Martinique is France[1]

'CHAMP D'ILES': A MAGNETIC FIELD

The Caribbean is a field—a 'champ d'îles'[2]—upon which many other spaces exert powerful forces of attraction or appropriation. How do these tiny spaces accommodate such pulls? How, for example, do French Caribbean writers balance the call of Africa, Europe, or other parts of the so-called 'New World' against the need to dwell in and on the Caribbean itself? Is it not so that the Caribbean is axiomatically relational, and that it inevitably seeps out, leaking into other spaces, its own reach being too restricted and its past too impacted for autonomy to be a plausible option?

In a process crucial to its every attempt to envision itself, the (French) Caribbean continues to position itself in relation to other poles. On the one hand, it gravitates towards the origins elsewhere of the vast majority of its population, and although these are frequently identified as continental Africa and Metropolitan France, this foundational model is notoriously restrictive in its binarity, most notably excluding Asia; on the other hand, it inclines towards contiguous spaces or kindred cultures with which it might more readily identify in the present. This latter attraction is confirmed by the interest shown by French Caribbean writers in the culture and history of other islands of the Caribbean, particularly Haiti, as well as various parts of continental America (Quebec

---

[1] Naipaul, *The Middle Passage*, 212.

[2] Glissant's poem sequence entitled 'Un champ d'îles', dated 1952, first appeared along with 'La Terre inquiète' and 'Les Indes' in *Poèmes* (Paris: Seuil, 1965).

and the Deep South, for example) and in some Indian Ocean islands, for several reasons, not least a shared history of extensive *métissage*, plantation culture and intensive Eurocentric acculturation.

The old triangular model in which the Caribbean was seen as stretched between the competing calls of two separate source spaces (Africa and Europe) is glaringly reductive. However, the alternative triangular model involving gravitation towards foundational space on the one hand, and local or kindred space on the other, could also be criticized on that count. If one thinks of Édouard Glissant's insistence on global awareness, especially in his *Poétique de la Relation* and in his writing on 'Tout-Monde' and 'Chaos-Monde', or if we take Patrick Chamoiseau's avowed and textually substantiated leaning towards Celtic and Nordic cultures, in particular Ireland and Iceland,[3] it is clear that Caribbean writers are not simply impelled towards originary and/or comparable spaces, but that they may wish to connect with places much further afield. The tripartite structure of this section might then be criticized on precisely the grounds that it does not leave space for the attractions and affinities that might overspill the three fundamentally foundational or mirroring attractions taken account of here.

The anomalous, anachronistic political status of the French Caribbean undoubtedly impinges on the relative strengths of its various cultural inclinations and tangencies. That the colonies' 'naturalization' in 1946 has not been revoked arouses both inside and outside the French Caribbean a combination of censure and envy, admiration and incredulity. It has also, of course, provoked sporadic outbreaks of violent resistance to the political status quo, particularly in Guadeloupe. However, that largely contained dissent has done little to lessen the economic and political dependency which is the legacy of almost three and a half centuries of French tutelage. Necessarily, the arterial attachment of the French Caribbean as peripheral region to France as distant European centre overshadows and restricts all economic, political, and cultural exchange with the rest of the Caribbean basin. And this remains true despite protestations that increasingly multilateral cultural exchange has eroded the centrality of the distinction

---

[3] In the conclusion to Gallagher (ed.), *Ici-Là*, I consider a number of Chamoiseau's allusions to Ireland.

between centre and periphery. Hence the French Caribbean has been clearly set apart in the region, and this despite its numerous geo-historical and cultural affiliations with its neighbours. To begin with, the standard of living in the *départements d'outre-mer* is vastly higher than in the rest of the Caribbean. Based almost wholly, however, on Metropolitan transfusions, this conspicuous and covetable buoyancy is belied by the much-lamented underproductivity of the local economy and by the disproportionate presence and power of Metropolitan interests. Moreover, on the literary front, France is still institutionally and intellectually the *locus princeps*. Not only are literary texts, essays, and histories usually published in Paris, but it is first and foremost there that they are commissioned, reviewed, and commended. The majority of established French Caribbean authors became famous initially in France, and the United States has only really courted French Caribbean writers to the extent that Paris had already made their reputations; in other words, their route onto the American lecture circuit and publication track had to traverse France first.

The particular strength of the Metropolitan–Antilles connection has a long history. In the 1850s Anthony Trollope was infinitely more impressed by the French West Indies than by any of the English Caribbean colonies, even those that had been French at one time, such as Dominica and St Lucia. He locates the superiority of the French Caribbean not just 'in the outward appearance of things' but also in the islands' administration and productivity, and he explains it in terms of the Frenchman's object being 'to make a Paris for himself, whether it be in a sugar island in the Antilles, or in a trading town upon the Levant'.[4] For Trollope, the 'French colonists . . . cast no wistful looks towards France', whereas the English colonies are 'considered more as temporary lodging-places, to be deserted as soon as the occupiers have made money enough by molasses and sugar to return *home*'.[5]

But how has French Caribbean writing since 1950 constructed the French connection? What are the opportunities and compromises, tensions and ambivalences generated by that attachment? To what extent do French Caribbean authors continue to look

---

[4] Anthony Trollope, *The West Indies and the Spanish Main* (1859; New York: Hippocrene, 1985), 75.
[5] Ibid. 120–1.

towards France, to what extent has France been perfectly internalized in the French Caribbean?

In the 1950s, the literary hold of the *négritude* movement, conceived within expatriate black intellectual circles in 1930s Paris, was beginning to fray. At the same time, a robust second vein of expatriate French Caribbean writing was emerging, as newly emigrated authors began to explore in prose (rather than through poetry, which had been the dominant genre of *négritude*) their usually rather unrevolutionary, first-hand experience of living in France. Whereas Césaire's *Cahier* had articulated a dramatic return to the 'pays natal' from Metropolitan distance, writing from the 1950s onwards often focuses instead on the relation to Metropolitan France. This trend reflects the political realities of *départementalisation* and of French Caribbean economic emigration to France in the 1950s and 1960s, a movement amplified and harnessed by Metropolitan France through the official immigration agency, the BUMIDOM.[6] Françoise Éga's *Lettres à une noire*[7] is one of the more traditional texts of this transcription of immigration. Éga's autobiographical, epistolary text, written throughout the early 1960s, records an experience of menial labour, exploitation, and racism in Metropolitan France, while celebrating the lifeline provided by expatriate society and solidarity. The author does not hesitate to refer to the status of the immigrant Caribbean population in terms of slavery and the slave trade, even if her discourse is much less polemical than the text of Daniel Boukman's play *Les Négriers* (1978). Another important work in this tradition is Joseph Zobel's novel *Quand la neige aura fondu*, which is the sequel to the story of José Hassam. Whereas France per se had barely featured in *La Rue Cases-Nègres*, that novel was significantly signed in Fontainebleau. Its sequel, originally entitled *La Fête à Paris*, takes up José's story after he emigrates to Paris to continue his studies there, and shows him oscillating between

---

[6] Bureau des migrations des DOM/TOM. This agency was set up in 1963 to encourage and regulate migration from the Caribbean to Metropolitan France.

[7] Françoise Éga, *Lettres à une noire* (Paris: L'Harmattan, 1978).

enthusiastic discovery of the cosmopolitanism of the promised land and a combination of climate-shock and culture-shock as he is exposed to the misery of a cold, damp, interminable winter and the contagious depersonalization of Parisian life.

Whereas these two works by Éga and Zobel approximate to a naive form of ethnographic discourse in their concern to give an account of the encounter with the host culture,[8] Édouard Glissant's essay *Soleil de la conscience*, dating from 1956, is a more sophisticated text in rhetorical and intellectual terms, largely because it injects a certain epistemological reflection and a poetic vibration into the ethnography in reverse. On the very first page of his text, Glissant declares his Francotropism. France, he claims, is a reality from which he 'cannot abstain', Europe a 'vaccine' he can no longer do without.[9] The negative formulation of both characterizations suggests the ambivalence of the Metropolitan compulsion: for Glissant, Europe (or France) is not just an addiction, but a virus. If this essay is particularly illuminating, it is firstly because it performs a subtle dance of cultural identification and separation and secondly because it is truly seminal. Indeed, the development of Glissant's thinking over the forty-five years to come is strikingly prefigured in the opening pages of *Soleil de la conscience*. For example, his prophetic view that it will no longer be possible for any one culture to be positioned as the metropolis (mother country or capital) of another. Or his intuition that no poet will henceforth be ignorant of the 'movement of History', and, perhaps most significantly of all, that 'no culture will be possible in the absence of all cultures'.[10] There is no sense whatsoever in this work of the searing inferiority complex attributed to the painter Camille Pissarro by Derek Walcott: 'the pain of being provincial was a scab'.[11] Yet Glissant's text opens with the declaration that for eight years (the year of writing is 1954–5), the author has been involved in what he terms a 'solution française' ('French solution').[12] The ambiguity of the image translates a certain hesitation between resolution and

---

[8] Émile Monnerot in his preface to Éga, *Lettres à une noire*, 6, uses the term ethnography to describe the author's perspective.

[9] Glissant, *Soleil de la conscience*, 11.

[10] 'Je devine peut-être qu'il n'y aura plus de culture sans toutes les cultures, plus de civilisation qui puisse être métropole des autres, plus de poète pour ignorer le mouvement de l'Histoire': ibid.

[11] Walcott, *Tiepolo's Hound*, 105.　　　　　　[12] Glissant, *Soleil*, 11.

dissolution. Glissant suggests that this process of [dis]solving (integration, assimilation, disappearance . . .) refers back to the *terminus a quo* that was the act of *départementalisation* of 1946, and that it corresponds to the gradual dawn and development of a (double) consciousness combining 'le regard du fils et la vision de l'Étranger' ('the gaze of a son and the vision of a foreigner').[13] Glissant's double vision has taken hold and matured over the eight years that he has devoted to studying 'ces paysages de la connaissance française' ('the landscape of French knowledge'), not as an intellectual tourist viewing the surface of landscape, but as a (re)searcher registering the epistemological resonance of landscape and climate, relating it back to himself, and becoming 'l'ethnologue de moi-même' ('the ethnologist of myself').[14]

Soleil de la conscience celebrates the deep intellectual excitement generated by Glissant's encounter with otherness: 'Dehors, c'est la vérité française s'opposant à la mienne; par cette alliance révélée d'un contraire à son autre' ('Outside, French truth opposes mine through that alliance that emerges between an opposing value and its other').[15] Like Éga and Zobel, he singles out climate, and snow in particular, as emblematic of that extraordinarily tangled relation to France. Snow is a potent counter-cliché of tropical discourse on Europe,[16] as are Europe's four seasons: thus, in Patrick Chamoiseau's first novel, *Chronique des sept misères*, France is dubbed the 'pays aux quatre saisons'.[17] Snow offers tangible proof of the distance between Europe and the Caribbean, and writers as diverse as V. S. Naipaul, Alejo Carpentier, and Ernest Pépin have written of the discovery of ice as a fundamental rite of passage. However, Glissant, unlike any of the aforementioned authors, irrigates this inverted exoticism with reflection on the epistemological punch of the encounter: 'Avec elle je sors de l'indécis pour être porté jusqu'à l'extrême contraire de mon ordre' ('Through snow I leave behind me all that is indistinct and am carried to the opposite extreme of my own order').[18] The hard, compact extremeness of snow, its whiteness, brightness, and clarity, are aligned with a

---

[13] Ibid.   [14] Ibid. 15.   [15] Ibid. 16.

[16] 'I have seen much snow. It never fails to enchant me, but I no longer think of it as my element. I no longer dream of ideal landscapes or seek to attach myself to them': V. S. Naipaul, *The Mimic Men* (London: André Deutsch, 1967), 10.

[17] Chamoiseau, *Chronique des sept misères*, 54.

[18] Glissant, *Soleil*, 18.

particular 'distinctness'. Again, admiring the intricate and orderly patience of patchwork field patterns in the French landscape, Glissant distances himself from that order based on sharp divisions, explaining that a long Caribbean history of dispossession has ruled out any atavistic interest on his part in territorial tidiness. Modulating, however, this double declaration of ethnographic distance, Glissant maintains that Paris highlights what he regards as both the most barren and the richest part of himself. The richest because this city, in its concentration of diversity, both mirrors and extends his consciousness of cultural variation; the most barren, because its individualism inhibits the expansive Caribbean sense of community, the gregariousness of Caribbean culture.

The paradoxical construction of Metropolitan France as totalizing, if not totalitarian, because all-encapsulating (revealing both the privilege and the impoverishment of the Caribbean subject transplanted there) continues as Glissant claims that it embraces the extremes of both order and disorder and, even more significantly, that Paris is both Glissant's opposite (other, outside and different)—'Dehors, c'est la vérité française s'opposant à la mienne' ('outside, French truth opposes mine')—and his mirror-image: 'Je sais soudain son secret: et c'est que Paris est une île, qui capte de partout et diffracte aussitôt' ('Suddenly I discover its secret: that is, that Paris is an island, immediately diffracting what it takes in from all sides').[19] In a further 'totalitarian' twist, the rhetoric of opposition combines with the rhetoric of reflection as the cold of the northern winter becomes a paradoxical image of mirroring. Because the word 'glace' in French has two meanings, Europe is both mirror and ice. So, the Martinican looking upon Paris sees both the other extreme of his own reality, solid cold (*glace*), and also the reflection of his own insularity in the mirror (*glace*) held up to him by the city. Hence France, and Paris in particular, doubly helps Glissant to deepen his consciousness of his own doubleness. On the one hand, it reflects him because it is similar; on the other hand, it shows him what he is not because it is radically different. Developing these paradoxical associations, Glissant thus acknowledges himself both as son and as foreigner in relation to France. Hence the French connection is seen to be partly generative. It has in some sense produced Glissant and is thus familiar and even

---

[19]　Glissant, *Soleil*, 68.

familial; yet he also feels his displacement or strangeness relative to this dominant, Oedipal 'other'. Glissant's use of the imagery of mirroring is thus much more positive and constructive than Fanon's recourse to it in *Peau noire, masques blancs*. Fanon's approach is more Lacanian in that the mirroring that he associates with ego-formation (or identity formation) is undercut by the self-destructive alienation associated by Lacan with narcissism.[20] Although for Glissant, as for Fanon, the Other acts as the mirror— 'toute action de l'Antillais passe par l'Autre ... parce que c'est l'Autre qui l'affirme dans son besoin de valorisation' ('Everything that an Antillean does is done for The Other ... because it is The Other who corroborates him in his search for self-validation')—[21] Glissant's motive in approaching the mirror is less a need for affirmation than a more detached epistemological interest in consciousness.

FROM MIRRORING TO ALIENATION

Continental France continues to figure in French Caribbean writing of the 1960s and 1970s. However, the encounter between the French Caribbean subject and the *métropole* is represented in the majority of texts dating from this period as being much more alienating than in Glissant's demanding prose or in Zobel's and Éga's narratives. Clearly, for some time after 1946, France could still occupy a largely idealized position in French Caribbean discourse. Hence, Zobel's *Quand la neige aura fondu* emphasizes the eagerness and enthusiasm of exile in a highly cosmopolitan setting, and represents Metropolitan France as less racist and more open to difference than the French Caribbean. However, with the winds of decolonization gathering velocity, both Zobel's cultural appreciation and Glissant's epistemological fascination are swept away in the 1960s by a groundswell of resentment, incommunicability, and ambivalence. Moreover, some writing of this second post-war period—that is, from the 1960s through to the mid-1980s—illustrates the pull of

---

[20] 'Je suis Narcisse et je veux lire dans les yeux de l'autre une image de moi qui me satisfasse': Fanon, *Peau noire, masques blancs*, 172; 'I am Narcissus, and what I want to see in the eyes of others is a reflection that pleases me': *Black Skin, White Masks*, 212.

[21] *Peau noire, masques blancs*, 172; *Black Skin, White Masks*, 212–13.

a counter-pole, namely Africa. This can be seen, for example, in Myriam Warner-Vieyra's *Juletane* (1982) and in the earlier novels of Maryse Condé.

It is perhaps no accident that both Condé and Warner-Vieyra are Guadeloupeans rather than Martinicans—the latter having a reputation for being more unequivocally drawn towards France—nor that they both have extensive experience of living in Africa and that their Francotropism is consequently balanced and, in the case of the earlier Condé, cancelled, initially at least, by the pull towards Africa. In the work of other Guadeloupean writers of the 1960s, however, Jacqueline Manicom and Michèle Lacrosil, for example, the Metropolitan connection is examined frontally and there is much less emphasis on any alternative pole of attraction or identification. Lacrosil's work dwells both on the paternalism of Metropolitan attitudes towards the French Caribbean and on the pathology of internalized racism. Manicom's *Mon examen de blanc* (1964) and Lacrosil's *Demain Jab-Herma* (1967) are set in the Caribbean, where the Metropolitan is represented as a powerful player who intrudes into and even takes over the Caribbean plot. Cyril in *Mon examen de blanc* is the white French doctor who comes to work in Guadeloupe, and who says of the Caribbean population that they 'réclament de se faire en quelque sorte "materner" par la France' ('demand to be "mothered" by France').[22] It is partly as a reaction to being patronized by Cyril for whom she feels acute distaste that Madévie becomes politically mobilized on the side of Guadeloupean independence. His 'regard glacé' ('frozen gaze'),[23] far from mirroring Madévie, profoundly misjudges her loyalties. In Lacrosil's *Demain Jab-Herma*, Philippe is the Metropolitan who eclipses the White Creole or 'Grand Blanc', Sougès, in a Metropolitan takeover of the plantation, allying himself instead with the eponymous black *quimboiseur*. However, unlike Cyril's advances, which propel Madévie towards political self-affirmation, the actions of Philippe push the already deeply envious, neurotic, and doomed *métis* Cragget towards suicide. A dysfunctional Caribbean–Metropolitan relation is also represented in Vincent Placoly's *La Vie et la mort de Marcel Gonstran*, a novel set mostly in France and partly in the Caribbean. Gonstran's unions with Frenchwomen are both failures: his first marriage is to a

---

[22] Manicom, *Mon examen de blanc*, 13.   [23] Ibid.

Bretonne who turns out to be a prostitute; the child born of this doomed union has Down's syndrome (described in the text as a 'monstrous' anomaly of nature) and is committed at the age of 7 to an institution where he dies following months of suffering. Of his subsequent relationship with (He)Léna, Gonstran writes self-pity-ingly (in the section 'Autobiographie de Marcel Gonstran') 'Pourquoi ne t'ai-je pas connue dans notre pays où les femmes . . . sont pures comme du cristal?' ('Why did I not meet you in our country where women . . . are pure as crystal?'),[24] and the implied negative construction of Europe as tainted or debased is reinforced by the image of darkness that marks the end of the novel's epilogue: 'Tel nègre qui meurt en France a besoin d'un peu de soleil' ('The black who dies in France needs a little sun').[25] Many texts of this period, especially those set in Metropolitan France, represent the Metropolitan–Caribbean relation as vitiated and unviable, and the outcomes of madness, incarceration, death, or suicide are common. Cajou, a Guadeloupean living in France, in Michèle Lacrosil's novel of the same name,[26] suffers from a particularly extreme, indeed fatal, form of racist self-hatred. The catalogue of casualties continues in the work of Miriam Warner-Vieyra, whose two novels, both published in the early 1980s, feature young women who are not simply marginalized, but ultimately incarcerated in and by an alien society. In *Le Quimboiseur l'avait dit*, Zétou finds herself committed to a French mental hospital, having been brought to France and exploited there by her (lighter-skinned) mother and her mother's lover. Zétou's breakdown in exile in France is represented not just through the oppressive imagery of landscape and climate, but also in terms of linguistic alienation. If France as M/Other seems hostile, non-mirroring, and non-nurturing, it is betrayal by her literal, Caribbean mother that in fact destroys Zétou. This Caribbean mother, having rejected the Caribbean for Europe, and what she regards as the stigma of blackness for whiteness, effec-tively sells her own daughter body and soul.

What is unusual about *L'Autre qui danse*, a novel by Martinican author Suzanne Dracius-Pinalie, is not so much the level of abjec-tion and self-destruction that it recounts, nor the fact that they are

---

[24] Placoly, *La Vie et la mort de Marcel Gonstran*, 109.
[25] Ibid. 172.
[26] Michèle Lacrosil, *Cajou* (Paris: Gallimard, 1961).

triggered primarily by those who claim the superiority, rather than the inferiority, of African-identified values or characteristics, but rather that the novel shows that abjection is not a necessary outcome. One Martinican sister—the dancer—is thus utterly at home both in her *métisse* body and in the cosmopolitan context of Paris. The other, Rehvana, is tormented in both, to the point of immolating herself on the altar of what she sees as the ideal of black or African purity from which she herself as a *métisse* has fallen, or indeed that more obvious oxymoron, Caribbean purity, from which she again, as a second generation immigrant in France has been cut off. It is symbolically significant that it is in the Paris area that she starves to death with her baby, having failed both in a symbolic 'return to Africa' in Paris and in an actual, but unsuccessful, return to the Caribbean. In this novel too, then, Metropolitan France is the catalyst of Caribbean self-confrontation, forcing the issues of identity, identification, and difference.

As might be expected, in addition to making it the trigger of the internal haemorrhage of Caribbean identity, some narratives circumscribe the Metropolitan relation, disinfecting themselves of its hegemony by containing it as a brief episode or interlude that fails to contaminate the narrative as a whole. That this is a strategic containment, designed to circumvent the dispossession or alienation diagnosed by Édouard Glissant in *Le Discours antillais*, is indirectly confirmed perhaps by the plethora of self-reflexive references to France in Schwarz-Bart's *Pluie et vent sur Télumée Miracle*. Of Amboise, a character who spends seven years in France, it is said that he avoided speaking to his compatriots of France, fearing that the description would poison the soul of his listeners. Again, Schwarz-Bart is a Guadeloupean writer and her two novels to date present only the most brief and schematic evocations of France. Amboise's reluctance seems, then, to explain self-reflexively his author's preference for scrutiny of local Caribbean space and relations. However, even the brief glimpse given of his experience of France, this experience of which he is so significantly loath to speak, is telling. Although he frequents the small ghettoes of black musicians, waiters, and dancers scattered over Paris, the main emphasis is on his initial admiration of the inner strength of the French, who appear to him to be godlike in their self-sufficiency. His admiration of their autonomy wilts, however, in the wake of his own feelings of exclusion and invisibility. His idols do not appear to see him, and this lack of mirroring is reinforced when even his attempts to imitate them go unnoticed. Here the image of mirroring, so positively connoted by Édouard Glissant, has taken on the most negative of meanings. France and the French are represented as denying the French Caribbean subject both in his/her difference and in his/her similarity to themselves. Following this experience of invisibility, Amboise revels, upon his return to Guadeloupe, in the solidarity of language, community, and affirmation, thus justifying at a metafictional level the fact that the author concentrates in her book on Guadeloupe itself. This outcome also legitimates the heroine's words at the outset of the narrative to the effect that her native island had never seemed to her to be too small to contain her life. Ti Jean, the principal character of Schwarz-Bart's next novel, *Ti Jean L'horizon* also sojourns in what are termed the 'terres arides et glacées de la métropole' ('arid, frozen acres of the *métropole*').[27] However, this interlude is, again, skimpily presented, thus minimizing rather than simply relativizing the importance of Metropolitan France in Ti Jean's quest.

AUTOPSIES OF EMIGRANT SPACE AND TIME

From the Caribbean 'home' perspective, the Metropolitan connection is often viewed as a problematic of emigration rather than immigration. For example, in Glissant's novel *La Case du commandeur*, it is learned that Thaël, a character who has already appeared in *La Lézarde*, has settled in France. Mention of his departure destabilizes the already fragile Mycéa, who feels his emigration as a defection, less perhaps a sign of the 'cursed colonial hunger for the metropolis',[28] than a vote of no confidence in the French Caribbean: 'Je ne veux pas partir, le pays n'est pas perdu, ce n'est pas vrai de vérité' ('I don't want to leave, the country is not finished, that just isn't true at all').[29] Mycéa's turmoil is not abated by the notion that pursuit of knowledge can be the trigger to emigration: in her evocation of the demeaning clichés of exile (the slow erosion of identity; the ritual parcels of tropical fruits, rum,

---

27 Simone Schwarz-Bart, *Ti Jean L'horizon* (Paris: Seuil, 1979), 221.
28 Walcott, *What the Twilight Says*, 32.
29 Glissant, *La Case du commandeur*, 190.

and hot peppers; the nostalgic idealization of the lost landscape) she suggests that migration to the Metropolis has no heuristic value; rather, the emigrant stagnates in exoticism.

In Daniel Boukman's play *Les Négriers*, the BUMIDOM is represented as promoting a latter-day slave trade, alternately accelerating and slowing down the importation of 'bras et cerveaux d'outre-mer selon les exigences du Plan' ('bodies and brains from overseas to respond to the needs of its Economic Plan').[30] The cynical manipulation and exploitation of the Caribbean labour force is condemned in this play, as is the self-interested remote control exerted by the *métropole* over the Martinican and Guadeloupean economy: for example, the fact that the importation of Metropolitan retail chains forces small Caribbean shops to close down. Conversely, in Maryse Condé's novel of 1989, *Traversée de la mangrove*, it is the Caribbean itself, in this instance Guadeloupe, that is indicted in rather summary fashion for exporting its natives to France where they freeze in the unwelcoming unskilled or semi-skilled working environments where they end up:

la Guadeloupe marâtre ne nourrit plus ses enfants . . . tant d'entre eux se gèlent les pieds en région parisienne. Pourtant là où ils sont, les fils de Rivière au Sel gardent la religion du travail. Dans les tristes officines ou les chaînes de montage automobile où ils peinent, ils se rappellent qui ils sont.[31]

Here, the symbolic cold of France is again emphasized, as is the largely menial and unrewarding 'immigrant', like the Renault production line on which the eponymous Marcel Gonstran labours. The emigrant father of the first-person narrator of Daniel Radford's novel *Le Maître-Pièce* works in a bank rather than on a production line, but his sad memories of his father's submission to the joylessness of his daily grind emphasize the narrator's inability to comprehend his family's exile. Why, he asks himself, when they had been relatively prosperous in the Caribbean, had they emigrated to France, a place 'qui nous n'allait pas et semblait ne

---

[30] Daniel Boukman, *Les Négriers* (Paris: L'Harmattan, 1978), 11.

[31] Maryse Condé, *Traversée de la mangrove* (Paris: Mercure de France, 1989), 38; 'Guadeloupe is no longer nourishing her stepchildren . . . how many of them are in Paris with frozen feet. Yet wherever they find themselves, the sons of Rivière au Sel are faithful to the religion of work. Toiling in dismal dispensaries or on car-manufacturing production lines, they recall who they are'.

vouloir de nous' ('which didn't suit us and which didn't seem to want anything to do with us').[32] This mystery motivates the entire effort of recollection and interpretation on which the novel is based. Other novels of immigration, most notably perhaps Gisèle Pineau's *L'Exil selon Julia* (1996), explore the notion of the immigrant as cultural misfit. The eponymous Julia, the narrator's grandmother, is like a fish out of water in France but, as in *Le Maître-Pièce* and other novels of the mobile 1990s, the increased accessibility of travel and the corresponding intensity of circulation between Europe and the Caribbean considerably reduce the residual, subliminal echo of the Middle Passage and of the *métropole* as a Babylonian place.

The tragicomic hero of the depiction of French Caribbean emigration must surely be Jojo of Ernest Pépin's *Tambour-Babel*, an anachronistic, anti-colonial freedom-dreamer: 'Jojo tournait et virait, se démenait dans son appartement de Sarcelles où, depuis des siècles, il rêvait de révolution pour libérer la Guadeloupe' ('Jojo twisted and turned, thrashing about in his Sarcelles apartment where, for centuries, he had been dreaming of the revolution that would liberate Guadeloupe').[33] Having simply hopped on a plane to Paris on an off-day, he has stayed on in Paris 'au cœur de la Bête' ('in the belly of the Beast') more from inertia than conviction or necessity, yet he deeply resents the cultural riches of Paris, so many windmills at which he tilts furiously:

Son Paris à lui était un Paris d'immigré en révolte contre le colonialisme. Il haïssait l'Arc de Triomphe, dont l'arrogance était à la mesure de l'abaissement des peuples dominés et écrasés. Il aurait voulu arracher l'Obélisque pour le restituer aux Égyptiens. Il vomissait de dégoût dans le musée de l'Homme, baptisé par lui Temple du racisme![34]

Not only does Jojo dream of putting together a mercenary army to decolonize France's 'last colonies', but he feeds his discontent with all the clichés of Metropolitan evil: the cold, police harassment, ghettoization, discrimination, racist taunts, and so forth. His

---

[32] Daniel Radford, *Le Maître-Pièce* (Paris: Éditions du Rocher, 1993), 161.

[33] Ernest Pépin, *Tambour-Babel* (Paris: Gallimard, 1996), 193.

[34] Ibid. 194; 'His Paris was the Paris of an immigrant rebelling against colonialism. He hated the Arc de Triomphe, whose arrogance was proportional to the humiliation of dominated and crushed peoples. He would have liked to tear up the Obélisque to return it to the Egyptians. He threw up in disgust in the Anthropology Museum, the Musée de l'Homme, which he called the Temple to Racism'.

battle-cry 'Fwansé déwo!' ('French Out!')[35] makes little sense, however, when appropriated by a Guadeloupean 'Frenchman' who himself no longer lives in the Caribbean. Moreover, in the context of this novel's undiluted celebration of anchorage in the labile space and time of *créolité*, Jojo appears as a comical misfit, a foil for the sense of well-being of those characters at home in the mobility conferred by their passion for traditional drumming.

NÉGROPOLITAINS OR COSMOPOLITANS?

Not only is Jojo anomalous in the context of the plot of Pépin's novel itself, but he clashes with the widespread perception that Paris is a sort of 'troisième île' due to the extent of its Caribbean immigrant population. It is, indeed, in relation to the intense Metropolitan–Caribbean dynamic that the term 'négropolitain' was coined, to refer to an Antillean born and resident in the *métropole*. But it is a specifically circulatory economy of exchange that gives Daniel Maximin's *œuvre* its particular timbre. In *Soufrières*, for example, Maximin's France is a hub of cosmopolitan cultural activity, and a particularly vibrant home to music and drama from several continents. French Caribbean artists and intellectuals like Adrien dip into this artistic ferment at will, moving freely to and from the *métropole* and contributing there to a generalized cosmopolitan effervescence. Echoing the creative ferment of the 1930s that gave rise to the *négritude* movement, Metropolitan France is represented as providing an opportunity for French Caribbean dramatists and musicians to meet their African counterparts:

... Wole Soyinka avec qui Adrien et moi avons travaillé au cours d'un stage à Paris sur le théâtre rituel africain.
Quand est-ce qu'il rentre ici-dans, Adrien?
Il doit venir en août, justement, car il est pris en France tout juillet. Il participe à une pièce antillaise qui sera au programme du festival d'Avignon, la *Mulâtresse Solitude*.[36]

[35] Pépin, *Tambour-Babel*, 196.
[36] Maximin, *Soufrières*, 18; '... Wole Soyinka with whom Adrien and I did a workshop on African ritual drama. || —When does Adrien come back home, then? || —He's to come in August because he's busy in France all July. He's taking part in a Caribbean play scheduled for the Avignon festival—*La Mulâtresse Solitude*.'

As the above conversation between Antoine and his father Rémy indicates, the *métropole* is figured first and foremost as an 'exchange', connecting blacks of the diaspora with each other and with Africans, just as it did in the 1930s. It is perhaps ironic that it is in *Soufrières* too, however, that the option of Metropolitan emigration is vehemently rejected when Toussaint expresses deep exile-fatigue: he argues that one is better off being a prisoner of all the restrictions implied by living on a small island, than living in exile with no deep attachment to place:

je ne reviendrai plus jamais en France; en Guadeloupe, je veux vivre, à Port-Louis je veux mourir. Et toi-même, Adrien, qu'espères-tu encore là-bas? Sache qu'il vaut mieux pour nous tous être un captif des îles qu'un libre exilé. La plus belle liberté, c'est de s'enraciner quelque part par amour, une fois revenu de tout. . . .[37]

Ironically, these sentiments are inscribed in the novel of a Guadeloupean author who would seem to be a confirmed immigrant in Metropolitan France. Although his characters are cosmopolitan in spirit, Maximin himself could be deemed to be a *négropolitain*, that is, a Caribbean emigrant resident in Metropolitan France: one of these 'négropolitains qui depuis des années jaunissent leur cuir par les hivers sans soleil de la banlieue parisienne' ('Negropolitans who have been letting their tans fade over years of sunless winters in the Paris suburbs').[38] The neologism 'négropolitain' is usually defined, however, not just as an 'Antillais' resident in France but as someone who has been born there and thus as a Creole in reverse. The unadulterated singularity of the racial reference suggests, however, a rejection of creolization as mixture. The term of reference in the neologism being racial identity, the person thus identified is confined inside the limits of a race label and, in an echo of *négritude* thinking, is classified as a citizen of his/her race. Usage confirms that the term is intended to create a resonance with 'métropolitain', since it is applied to those born in the Metropolis and is used as a synonym of the more transparent

---

[37] Ibid. 133; 'I will never go back to France; it is in Guadeloupe that I want to live, in Port-Louis that I want to die. And yourself, Adrien, what is keeping you over there? You know, it is better for all of us to be prisoners in the islands than free and in exile. The best freedom is to take root somewhere out of love, having tried everywhere else . . .'.

[38] Condé, *Traversée de la mangrove*, 31.

'negzagonal', a neologism that refers to the term 'Hexagone', used as a synonym for Metropolitan France.[39] However, the alternative echo of 'cosmopolitain' emphasizes the radically restrictive vision that produced the expression 'négropolitain', a reductive orientation diametrically opposed to Daniel Maximin's portrayal of free-spirited circulation of people and ideas between and across continents, islands, and seas.

TOWARDS A DECENTRED APPROACH: IRONIC RELATIVIZATION

Although the writing of circulation and emigration shows that Metropolitan France continues to impinge on the imagination of French Caribbean writers, the primary effort of most writers in the wake of post-*négritude* consciousness-raising was focused on recovery of the local. In much of the writing of the *créolité* movement, validation of the local is reinforced by the representation of Metropolitan France in an overwhelmingly ironic and critical vein. For example, Europe's shameless exploitation of its Caribbean subjects as cannon fodder in the two world wars is recalled in *Texaco*, and the credulous reverence in which those subjects hold *la mère patrie* is derided:

La guerre avait surgi sans raison, en dehors de nous et de nos élans pour pénétrer l'En-ville. Nous ne sûmes qu'une chose: la doulce France, berceau de notre liberté, l'universelle si généreuse, était en grand danger. Il fallait tout lui rendre.[40]

Chamoiseau emphasizes also the delusions of the powerful urban 'mulâtre' population, who cling to an idealized image of Metropolitan France viewed as utterly benign in contrast to the *béké* plantocracy: 'Contre la férocité békée, ils dressaient l'éternité généreuse de la France, O mère bonne perdue dans l'horizon et gonflant tous les cœurs' ('Against the *béké* ferocity, they erected

---

[39] Glissant, *Tout-monde*, 578. In a note, Glissant gives the two terms as synonyms.

[40] Chamoiseau, *Texaco*, 210; 'The war had broken out for no reason, that is for nothing to do with us and our attempts to penetrate City. We only knew one thing: Sweet France, crib of our liberty, that so-generous land of the universal, was in great danger. Everything had to be paid her back': tr. 190).

France's generous eternity, Oh goodly mother lost in the horizon and filling our hearts').[41]

The to and fro of economic and professional emigration between the *métropole* and the islands is not hidden, certainly, in the literary work of the *créolité* movement. But derision is the predominant mode of evocation of the competitive plot of demotion and promotion, and competition for local jobs, a theme treated both in *Solibo Magnifique* and in *Bassin des ouragans* (1994). In both works it is well salted with biting irony, for example in the allusion to the practice of making police officials pay for promotion by sentencing them to the *métropole*: 'sans voir accompagner ces promotions de l'exil habituel dans le givre des commissariats parisiens' ('without their promotion being accompanied by the usual exile in the frost of Parisian police stations'),[42] or in the allusion to the fact that all senior officials tend to be Metropolitan tourists: 'Inspecteurs et commissaires, pour la plupart métropolitains . . . en chemise à fleurs et bermuda, ils traquaient nos mœurs carnavalesques pour leur album de souvenirs' ('Inspectors and Superintendents, metropolitans for the most part . . . [in] flower print shirts and Bermuda shorts, left to hunt down our carnivalesque mores for their scrapbooks').[43] In Confiant's *Bassin des ouragans*, the irony is double-edged in the depiction of the Martinican, newly awarded with a French state doctorate in anthropology, who returns from France and hails a taxi at the airport directing the driver 'au poste'. The latter takes this to mean the police station ('poste de police') whereas his passenger, whose sole luggage is all ten tomes of his doctoral thesis, means to his post, that is, to the post that he intends to snatch from beneath the nose of its current Metropolitan incumbent, the museum administrator lulled into a false sense of security by the thought that no Martinican would dream of spending a decade on studies not guaranteeing instant affluence.[44]

Along with such ironic reversals, the European claim to constitute the central pole of all reference is further punctured by the regular reversal of the more flagrant Eurocentric references, in

[41] Ibid. 83; tr. 70.
[42] Chamoiseau, *Solibo Magnifique*, 55; *Solibo Magnificent*, 30.
[43] *Solibo Magnifique*, 165; *Solibo Magnificent*, 112.
[44] Raphaël Confiant, *Bassin des ouragans* (Paris: Mille et une nuits, 1994), 31–3.

other words, by the implicit adoption of the Caribbean as standard and the characterization of France as the other, as the place that lies 'overseas'. In an eminently economical and witty manner, Chamoiseau thus undoes the assumption that the 'over' of 'overseas' is monodirectional. 'C'est quoi, han? dit-il (Ce qui, traduit en français d'outre-mer, donnerait: Pouvez-vous m'expliquer ce qui est à l'origine de cette situation déplorable?)' ('What is it, huh? he said. (Which, when translated into colonial French, would be something like: Might you explain to me what is the origin of this deplorable state of affairs?)').[45] In this way, the Metropolitan connection is frequently highlighted in an ironic vein based on 'galloping relativization' or *relativisation à outrance*.

CONTAINED RELATION?

From the 1970s onwards, French Caribbean authors concentrated increasingly on declining a specificity that most have been at pains to locate in the complex relationality of Caribbean identity and/or in the specificity of Caribbean space and time, including the substratum of Creole orality and myth. But, although the language and style of their work are often inflected by orality or by Creole morphology and vocabulary, Creole is itself, as we have seen, a language of relation. Hence, although the creative and distinctive modulation of French and its exploration of a specific history and spatial order might set French Caribbean writing apart from continental writing in French, this discourse of separation is, to a large extent, a contained discourse. That is, it is, if not embedded in, then inextricably linked to the French language and it is, furthermore, circulated in the first instance to France (and its DOM) and the French (its implicit readership is French- rather than Creole-speaking). Both diachronically and synchronically, then, it is overdetermined by relation to France. Already in 1980, the critic Jacques André was insisting that it is impossible for the French Caribbean to recover for itself an origin untainted by history and its compromises, or an identity outside or beyond relation.[46] As we have seen,

---

[45] *Solibo Magnifique*, 58; *Solibo Magnificent*, 32.
[46] See André, *Caraïbales*, and 'L'identité ou le retour du même', *Les Temps Modernes*, 441–2, 'Antilles' (Apr.–May 1983), 2026–37: 2035. 'La relation à l'Autre est constitutive de l'identité.'

the major speculative visions to emerge of and from the French Caribbean at the end of the twentieth century rest precisely upon the singularly intense and ongoing relationality of Caribbean identity and culture. To what extent, however, is that relationality explored as something ongoing and dynamic, and to what extent is it seen as purely foundational, or past-centred? And can it relativize the Metropolitan connection?

From the 1960s to the early 1980s, Édouard Glissant actively promoted the political imperative of economic and political independence in the French Caribbean. The Martinican radical who co-founded the *Front antillano-guyanais* envisioned the formation of Martinique, Guadeloupe, and Guyana into a federation that would eventually integrate the entire Caribbean basin. In his more recent work, however, Glissant seems to have all but renounced this political agenda, which has been transcended by the more soft-focus idea of a poetics of relation, *créolisation*, and *tout-monde*. What is significant in the limited convergence at the end of the twentieth century between Glissant's perspective and that of the *créolité* movement is their common belief that the future of Caribbean culture inheres in its hyper-relationality. In this poetics of relation, the Caribbean is held out as a model for the transcendence of all nostalgia for pure origins or roots. Glissant, for example, writes at length on the need to substitute for the single underground root the multiple and often aerial root system of the rhizome.[47] However, to be faithful to this alternative emphasis, the Caribbean must somehow break free of the fascination exerted by the subterranean system of historical relations upholding and sustaining its sense of identity and branch out into unprescribed, unpredictable relations in the present and future.

Given the implied relativization of the French connection in Glissant's vision of 'chaos-monde', we would expect that Metropolitan France would not be particularly favoured as a pole of relation in writing attuned to Glissant's ideas, but that an ongoing 'relativizing' relation with the Metropolitan *imaginaire*, and with Metropolitan thinking and writing, would subsist. And indeed that expectation is largely confirmed. Moreover, few contemporary Guadeloupean or Martinican writers focus on Metropolitan France and, when they do, it is rarely for long. This waning of engagement

---

[47] Glissant, *Poétique de la Relation*, 187.

with the *métropole* must be seen in terms of the pledge made by the movements of *antillanité* and *créolité* to privilege the local Caribbean context and the inscapes of Creole culture respectively. And yet the highly paradoxical, if unspoken, ghost of a relation with Europe hangs over the writing of these movements in that the majority of their readers and publishers are Metropolitan French. In practical, institutional terms, the most prominent French Caribbean writing is overdetermined by the French connection. In the work of Confiant and Chamoiseau, this vital attachment is heavily implied by intensive cultural self-representation, by allusions within the texts to spatial distance and to linguistic and cultural difference, and by copious use of meta-discourse proffered in the textual polyps that their texts have tended to sprout: periphrastic footnotes, terminal glossaries, in-text translations, and so forth. Indeed, the texts teem with indications, ironic or not, that the expected or implicit readership is in part if not largely non-Caribbean. Moreover, texts like Chamoiseau's *Écrire en pays dominé* (1997) place the neo-colonial relationship at the heart of the author's entire writing project. In this context, can the poetics of place and ironic de-hierarchization short-circuit the neo-colonialism that structures the political and socio-economic modalities of the Metropolitan relationship? Can it in fact break with the containment and with the mirroring accepted in previous decades? Or does it simply displace those phenomena into the reception process? In publishing and reading, in rewarding and analysing new so-called Creole texts in French, do not France and the French continue, in fact, to mirror the Caribbean subject, and this just as French Caribbean writers seem to declare the notion of political independence to be an irrelevance?

CHAPTER EIGHT

Africa, a Critical Displacement: Between Authenticity and Ambivalence

Traces-mémoires d'Afrique ... ne reconstruisirent nulle Afrique au pays, mais tissèrent le pays d'un scintillement d'afriques mouvantes, en dérive dans leurs diversités propres, et en dérive dans toutes les autres.[1]

Is Africa still accorded a place of honour in French Caribbean writing after 1950? Is it still claimed as an extension of Caribbean identity, serving as a distant continental backdrop, a vital, alternative hinterland? Does it afford a sense of continuity or of tension or ambivalence? To what extent is Africa viewed as 'other', to what extent as an inherent part of the Caribbean constitution? Is the continent embraced in its contemporary and multifarious reality, or is it instead romanticized or mythologized, reduced, or even rejected? And how did the relation to Africa evolve over the second half of the twentieth century?

The continent as it is configured in French Caribbean writing could be usefully compared with its representation in those indigenous or external Africanist discourses studied by Christopher Miller in *Theories of Africans*, more especially Michel Leiris's *L'Afrique fantôme*, since the author of this monumental opus on

---

[1] Chamoiseau, *Écrire en pays dominé*, 128; 'Memories-traces of Africa ... reconstructed no Africa in this country, but wove the land here from a shimmering of moving africas, each drifting within its own diversity, and drifting within all the others.'

Africa as construct, projection, or mirror went on to write an ethnological study of the populations of Martinique and Guadeloupe.[2] Because, from the Caribbean perspective, the continent is neither completely distant nor completely familiar, because it is both identified with as foundational and regarded as 'other', Caribbean constructions of Africa are more complex than those of outright 'insiders' like V. Y. Mudimbe or outright 'outsiders' like Leiris. 'The' Caribbean perspective is, of course, highly variable, but its heterogeneity can be fruitfully considered in terms of time and space. Approaching French Caribbean literary discourse on Africa from 1950, we find, as one might expect, that the 'African' preoccupation is strongest in the immediate post-*négritude* era, a period still convulsed by the aftershocks of that movement of radical re-evaluation. The continent continues, then, to loom large in the writing of figures such as Aimé Césaire, Guy Tirolien, Paul Niger, and, incomparably of course, Frantz Fanon.

AFRICA IDEALIZED: A LOST AUTHENTICITY

Since Africa is identified, not as the sole or common origin of the Caribbean people, but at least as the origin of those who suffered the most massive and most unspeakable rupture of the continuity between space and time, it has been the pre-eminent locus of the pre-Creole past for many Caribbean writers. It is in this sense that Maryse Condé's anti-heroine Véronica in *Heremakhonon* hopes that her encounter with Africa will enable her to penetrate beyond the 'family saga': 'c'est d'abord pour cela que je suis ici. . . Pour essayer de voir ce qu'il y avait avant' ('that is the main reason why I'm here . . . To try to see what was there before').[3] For writers in tune with the *négritude* movement, Africa is the symbol not only of a doubly distant past, but also of the lost authenticity that the 'diaspora' aspires to recover. And there is much of this mentality in Condé's Véronica, who anticipates that Africa will not just tell her who she is, but also repair her damaged self-image, arming her against the inferiority complex lurking beneath her family's

---

[2] Michel Leiris, *L'Afrique fantôme* (Paris: Gallimard, 1934) and *Contacts de civilisations en Martinique et en Guadeloupe* (Paris: Gallimard/Unesco, 1955).

[3] Maryse Condé, *Heremakhonon* (Paris: UGE, 1976), repr. as *En attendant le bonheur: Heremakonon* (Paris: Seghers, 1988), 31.

perverse sense of caste as white-identified blacks. Véronica is fascinated by the aura of assurance surrounding continental Africans,
an aura that she imputes to their endowment with a continuous
past and a complete and legitimate family tree. For example, the
corrupt government minister with whom she has an affair in
Africa beguiles her because he is a 'nègre avec aïeux' ('black with
ancestors').[4] However if, in Véronica's eyes, the traceability of
their lineage affords Africans a legitimacy denied to their
Caribbean relatives, African men also attract her because they are
not the descendants of slaves; they are, as she herself puts it,
unbranded. At the outset of her stay in Africa, then, Véronica
wants to reconnect with her own distant past, to cathect a lost
nobility and continuity, and even more significantly, a lost ancestral power, even if that potency is corrupt. No 'ordinary' or familiar African brother is going to be able to requite that desire.
Saliou, her friend and colleague in Africa, is, for example, a mere
'Africain, un homme d'Afrique, qui pour moi ne saurait être
l'Afrique et, partant, cristalliser l'amour qu'à travers elle je
cherche à me porter ('an African, a man from Africa, who cannot
be Africa for me, and so he cannot inspire the love that I want to
lavish on myself in lavishing it on Africa').[5] What is the difference
between a 'man from Africa', like Saliou, and a man who can
embody the time-space that Véronica calls 'Africa' and thereby
cure the sense of inferiority that undermines her, healing her
'blessure narcissique'? It would appear that such an 'Africa-man'
must have power and must be 'vieille Afrique', that is, possess
antique aristocratic connections. Hence, the past and present
crimes of Ibrahima Sory and his family pale into insignificance for
her beside the notion that he is a commanding man descended
from an old and privileged ruling family: 'Parce qu'en fait, c'est
cela que je suis venue voir. D'authentiques aristocrates. Pas des
singes. Des petits-fils d'esclaves dansant le menuet et méprisant les
autres ... Ainsi donc, ce nègre a des aïeux!' ('Because that is in
fact what I have come to see. Real aristocrats. Not apes. Not the
grandsons of slaves who can dance the minuet and look down on
everybody else ... So then, this black has ancestors!').[6] In
Véronica's view, such a caste would have been untouched by slavery, untainted by assimilation.

---

[4] Condé, *En attendant*, 14.   [5] Ibid. 207.   [6] Ibid. 47.

The narratological subtlety of Condé's novel has inspired a number of sophisticated readings that concentrate on the representation of the problematic relation to Africa.[7] Véronica's oscillation between lucidity and gullibility, and between irony and naivety, is rendered by particularly sustained yet highly dialogical and discontinuous use of what Françoise Lionnet terms 'direct free thought'.[8] However, the end of the novel sees Véronica flee in unambiguous disillusion from the (repressive and corrupt) power by which she has allowed herself to be sexually beguiled and politically compromised. This débâcle thoroughly discredits the myth that Africa can provide the Caribbean subject with either a link to the lost past or a true sense of legitimacy. Indeed, it is as though Véronica has a premonition of this fact at the very start of the novel, when her response to the warm welcome that she receives on her arrival in Africa—'Vous êtes ici chez vous' ('Here you can feel at home')[9]— is a sceptical thought to the effect that three and a half centuries cannot be so easily erased. At the end of her quest, then, Véronica is obliged to admit her failure: 'Mes aïeux, je ne les ai pas trouvés. Trois siècles et demi m'en ont séparée. Je n'ai trouvé qu'un homme avec aïeux qui les garde jalousement pour lui seul, qui ne songe pas à les partager avec moi' ('I have not found my ancestors. Three and a half centuries have separated me from them. All I have found is a man with ancestors whom he keeps strictly for himself and who would not dream of sharing them with me').[10] Worse still, she realizes too late that she lacks the ability to read the real Africa correctly—'je me suis trompée d'aïeux. J'ai cherché mon salut là où il ne fallait pas. Parmi les assassins' ('I adopted the wrong ancestors. I looked for my salvation in the wrong place, amongst the assassins').[11]

Like the work of Édouard Glissant, who criticized the nefarious representation of Africa as the pure Origin, or the authentic, continental paradise to which the 'diaspora' must aspire to return, other novels by Condé—such as *Une saison à Rihata* (1981) or *Les Derniers Rois mages* (1992)—and novels by other writers such as Simone Schwarz-Bart's *Ti Jean L'horizon* (1979) and Myriam Warner-Vieyra's *Juletane* (1982) similarly negate the notion that

[7] See especially Françoise Lionnet, *Autobiographical Voices: Race, Gender, Self-Portraiture* (Ithaca and London: Cornell University Press, 1989), 173–90.
[8] Ibid. 184. [9] Condé, *En attendant*, 21.
[10] Ibid. 207. [11] Ibid. 244.

Africa is 'Home' or that it can provide a rehabilitating route to the ancestral past. This realization can be represented as positive in so far as initial disillusionment gives way to a liberated and creative identity quest closer to home. Indeed the trajectory of Condé's work—from writing centred on Africa to work set more in the context of the 'New World'—endorses Édouard Glissant's view that the history of local, Caribbean place provides the Caribbean subject with a much more authentic foundation than Africa. This is also the favoured version of Caribbean identity in Simone Schwarz-Bart's writing, especially in *Ti Jean L'horizon*, where Africa is tested and found wanting.

Seeing in the Caribbean primarily—as Condé's Véronica does— a scene of dislocation or disjunction from the 'real' or 'authentic' past suggests that it is merely a debased Africa. This notion that the Caribbean is a fallen Africa emerges not just within Caribbean writing, but also in the work of non-Caribbean authors. In his *Hiver caraïbe*, for example, the French writer and diplomat Paul Morand wrote: 'J'aurais vu les Antilles après l'Afrique, *la copie après l'original*, que ma déception eût été profonde' ('Had I seen the Caribbean after Africa, the copy after the original, how deeply disappointed I would have been').[12] In Morand's portrayal, Africa represents an authenticity that makes the French Caribbean appear as a deficient ersatz. In his novel *Tambour-Babel*, Ernest Pépin approaches this question from a humorous perspective, through an encounter between an African and a Guadeloupean drummer: 'Tu ne peux pas jouer du tambour comme ça et t'appeler Jean-Claude Antoinette!—C'est la faute à Napoléon! Je veux dire la faute à l'esclavage! Eh oui, frère africain! Je comprends ton désarroi . . .' ('You can't possibly play the drums like that and have a name like Jean-Claude Antoinette!—Well it's all Napoleon's fault. I mean the fault of slavery! Ah yes, my African brother, I understand your

---

[12] Morand, *Hiver caraïbe*, 37. Morand continues: 'mais les visitant après les États noirs de l'Amérique du Nord, je suis charmé au contraire de leur couleur et de leur poésie . . . Le "tignon" de Madras déjà oublié à La Nouvelle-Orléans et qui coiffe si bien les négresses est encore porté partout. Il y a plus de caractère original dans ce petit monde de Pointe-à-Pitre que dans toute l'Amérique du Nord' ('but since I am visiting [the Caribbean] after the black states of North America, I am on the contrary charmed by their colour and poetry . . . The Madras headdress abandoned in New Orleans and which so becomes black women is still widely worn here. There is more originality and character in the little world of Pointe-à-Pitre than in all of North America'). Emphasis mine.

incomprehension ... For you my name and my drum don't go together').[13] Here, the Guadeloupean drummer clearly regards the African as his brother and Africa as their common mother, but the African is disconcerted by the Guadeloupean's name. Familial imagery recurs further on in the novel when the African past is likened to rediscovered snapshots in a family album that are found eminently worthy of being reclaimed: 'Comme des enfants émerveillés devant un album de famille, nous découvrîmes notre antan et nous sûmes qu'il valait son pesant d'humanité' ('Like children looking in wonder at a family photograph album, we came across our past and we realized that it was worth its weight in humanity').[14] For the characters of Pépin's novel, the relation to Africa is dictated by fidelity to the phantom murmur of the distant African past in the Guadeloupean mind. If the drum gives meaning to the lives of Vélo, of Eloi, and his son Napo, it is because drumming reinforces the sense of temporal continuity between Africa and the Caribbean, a continuity expressed in spatial terms, however: 'Chaque chose à sa place! Le tambour est bon pour maintenir le lien (une chaîne de morts sous les eaux salées) entre la terre de Guinée et Grosse-Montagne' ('Everything in its place! The drum is there to maintain the link (a chain of deadmen beneath the saltwater), between Guinée and Grosse-Montagne').[15] This connection between Guinée and Guadeloupe is deemed sacred, and is to be respected at all costs because of its mystical, spiritual charge. The drum not only connects two geographical spaces and two historical times, past and present, but also life with the afterlife.

Certains ont tourné fou pour avoir enjambé les usages transmis depuis le ventre de la bête flottante à l'époque où dans certaines contrées de l'ancestrale Guinée des tam-tams ensorcelaient les esprits et rappleaient les défunts sur terre. On ne manie pas à la légère un instrument aussi chargé de puissance et de souffrance.[16]

---

[13] Pépin, *Tambour-Babel*, 233. The text continues by stressing the double consciousness that makes of Jean-Claude and his kind 'les hommes à deux visages' or 'men with two faces': 'celui que nous montrons et celui qui nous regarde' ('the one we show and the one that looks at us').

[14] Ibid. 230.   [15] Ibid. 24.

[16] Ibid. 27; 'There are those who have lost their reason because they trampled the customs handed down from the time we were in the belly of the floating beast. That was in the time when, in certain parts of ancestral Guinée, tam-tams cast spells on the spirits and called the dead back to earth. Nobody handles lightly an instrument so loaded with power and suffering.'

Pépin's portrayal of a broadly harmonious, benign, and fluid relation between Guadeloupean culture and its African ancestry and between past and present, life and death, is, however, rather unusual in French Caribbean writing.

'OLD WORLD', 'NEW WORLD', AND 'OTHER WORLD'

In many texts of the French Caribbean tradition, as in Pépin's novel, the principal conduit of ancestral memory leading back towards Africa is folk culture (music, drumming, or the *conteur*'s tales, for example).[17] However, as Colette Maximin observes in relation to Zobel's Médouze, folk culture serves to consummate a purely mystical relationship with an 'ancestral land' or 'pays d'avant' that is, in reality, an inaccessible dream, a land of the mind. According to Colette Maximin, this abstract archetype is destined to be replaced by an equally mythical but more readily accessible dream, namely France.[18] When ancestral memory weakens, what happens to the notion of Africa? Does it not become respatialized, reconfigured, that is, not as the land of the past (or the 'pays d'avant') but as 'elsewhere'? And in those circumstances is it not finally recognized as 'other', rather than as the place of the Caribbean's *own* past? In *Texaco*, as Ninon ponders her mother's tomb, she sees there the vanishing point of the African connection: 'La mort de l'Africaine ouvrit un nouveau temps' ('The death of the African woman marked a new era').[19] Just as the death of Médouze preceded and even signalled José's death to the folk culture of the plantation and thereby to the myth of Africa, so too

---

[17] Régis Antoine comments on the substratum of African imagery in Césaire's writing, arguing that it illustrates 'non plus donc une africanisation de la pensée mais l'effet d'un dépôt, au fond de soi' ('not so much "Africanized" thought processes as a sort of deposit in the depths of one's self'). He goes on to note a convergence in thought patterns between continental and diasporic blacks: 'même confiance dans la force de la parole ou nommo, même érotisation de la nature, qu'elle soit africaine ou antillaise' ('the same trust in the power of the word (or *nommo*), the same eroticization of nature, whether African or Caribbean'): Régis Antoine, 'La littérature antillaise francophone, voie de connaissance vers l'Afrique', in Annie Wynchank and Philippe-Joseph Salazar (eds.), *Afriques imaginaires: Regards réciproques et discours littéraires 17e–20e siècles* (Paris: L'Harmattan, 1995), 103–12: 110.

[18] Colette Maximin, *Littératures caribéennes comparées*, 41.

[19] Chamoiseau, *Texaco*, 134; tr. 118.

the death of Ninon's mother occasions (and symbolizes) the definitive demise of an ancestral, Africa-centred memory, and if not the
dawn of an autonomous time, then at least a reinforced consciousness of local space:

Ninon resta devant la tombe. Seul, désormais, ce retourné de terre décoré
de calebasses attestait que sa mère lui provenait d'Afrique ... Ninon ne
savait pas encore que tout en cultivant le souvenir de sa mère, elle
oublierait l'Afrique: resteraient la femme, sa chair, sa tendresse, le bruit
particulier des sucées de ses pipes, ses immobilités malsaines, mais rien de
l'Autre Pays. Pas même le mot d'un nom.[20]

Here, Africa is named 'l'Autre Pays'. It has become 'Other' and is
about to become this 'vaste pays dont on ne savait hak' ('that enormous country about which none knew squat').[21] As long as
Ninon's mother was alive, her presence preserved the illusion of a
living link with Africa. Her death dealt to Ninon, however, what
Chris Bongie would term an 'amnesiac blow'[22] transforming Africa
from the 'pays d'avant'—the land of before (or of the past)—into
'l'Autre Pays', an indeterminate and unfamiliar space. Africa thus
recovers its synchrony, but loses its intimate connection with the
Caribbean (as the site of the Caribbean past). Yet, as if to suggest
the radical otherness of Africa—even when it is still functioning as
the 'pays d'avant'—Caribbean culture identifies it as the location of
the afterlife. The expression 'emporté à la terre de Guinée' is widely
used as a euphemism for death, which it configures as a return
voyage, a reversal of the Middle Passage, a repatriation. Clearly,
the representation of Guinea as the 'Other World' suggests above
all its remoteness, since it is constructed as the space of a spiritual
'hereafter', beyond 'this world' and outside lived time. A further
implication of this representation concerns the Caribbean itself,
which becomes a sort of parenthesis, a holding place and time, or
limbo, meaningless in itself, less a chiastic space than a hiatus
between Africa as origin and Africa as return destination.

[20] *Texaco*, 134; 'Ninon remained by the grave. The only thing that now attested
that her mother was from Africa was this fresh mound of earth decorated with
calabashes. ... Ninon didn't know that though she honored her mother's memory
she would forget Africa. All that would remain would be the woman, her flesh, her
tenderness, the sucking noises she made with her pipe, her insane immobility, but
nothing of the Other Country. Not even the word of a name' (tr. 118).
[21] *Texaco*, 134; tr. 118.
[22] Bongie, *Islands and Exiles*, 378–89.

'PAYS RÊVÉ' AND 'PAYS RÉEL'

Like the term 'Congo', the name 'Guinée' bespeaks the mythifica-
tion of Africa, a continent not just displaced into the realm of the
Past or the Afterlife, but also shrunk by the Caribbean imagination
into the Horn of Africa that was the principal site of embarkation
for the Middle Passage. Although many commentators have noted
the persistently reductive metonymization of the continent in the
Caribbean imagination, all of Africa being retracted into the tiny
space of one region linked to the Middle Passage, alongside this
reduction Africa often remained, paradoxically, an image of
immensity or Ninon's 'vaste pays' in the Caribbean imagination.
Clearly, the Western reduction of Africa is very pervasive and is
evident, for example, in the minimalization of its cultural stature,
the dismissal of its institutional structures, or the infantilization of
its people. In the Caribbean such diminishment can be glossed in
terms of the insecurity, or neurosis even, of an offshoot culture,
branded as enslaved, assimilated, and secondary, orphaned from
vastness and cast adrift from continuity of space and time.

Il cherchait dans le livre aux feuilles jaunes épaissies par l'usage la trace de
ce pays jadis marqué d'immensité. L'immensité nous a quittés. Nous
taraudons le même carré de terre qui s'offre aux eaux de deux mers. Ce
pays-d'avant nous démarra de nos corps, que nous n'avons pas ensouchés
dans le pays-ci. . . .[23]

Representations of Africa as the 'pays d'avant' and as 'l'Autre
Pays' are both entirely relational, in that they construct Africa not
as a place in itself, but strictly in terms of its contextualization of
the Caribbean: it is either reduced to its status as the land of the
pre-Creole past, or else it is positioned within a dialectic of iden-
tity/difference, or sameness/otherness. In *La Case du commandeur*,
a distinction is made between the 'temps d'avant'[24] which is not the
African, but rather the Caribbean past, that is, the past anchored
in the Caribbean itself, on the one hand, and on the other the 'pays

---

[23] Glissant, *La Case du commandeur*, 32; 'He searched through the yellowed
pages thickened by age for the trace of this land that had formerly been the site of
vastness. The vastness has abandoned us. We are now worrying away at the same
patch of land laid out between the waters of two seas. This land-of-the-past severed
us from our bodies and we have not transplanted them in this country . . .'.
[24] Ibid. 227, 235.

d'avant'. Use of the latter collocation thus underlines the failure to conceive of Africa as a *separate place*, with its own present, past, and future, rather than simply as the location of the ('New World') past.

In Glissant's poem cycle *Pays rêvé, pays réel*,[25] the very landscape of the Caribbean is said both to hold and to withhold the lost landscapes of Africa. Hence although Glissant can write that 'l'anse du morne ici recomposée nous donne | L'émail et l'ocre des savanes d'avant temps' ('the loop of the hill reconfigured here gives us | the enamel and ochre of the savanna of prior time'), he can also affirm, conversely, that 'la rivière la mer | Nous donnent vie nous ôtent mémoire' ('the river the sea | give us life take away our memory').[26] Here, the hills recall or retain the African past, while the flow and currents of the river and the sea cancel memory and awaken the Caribbean mind to the shifting nature of life rather than recalling its retentiveness.

Africa as motherland has been identified as a dominant theme of Glissant's poetry and poetics.[27] However, while it is true that his poems present many clear evocations of African landscape and culture (images of the African bush and desert, of totems and baobabs), it is important to recognize the full force of the relationality at the heart of this poetics. Yves-Alain Favre agrees that Glissant is constantly thinking of Africa, but notes that Africa appears in and through the Caribbean.[28] Favre stresses that the 'pays rêvé' is imagined in terms of the 'pays réel', and that the word 'rêvé' does not mean unreal, fictitious, or utopian. Rather it means that Africa per

---

[25] Glissant, *Pays rêvé, pays réel* (Paris: Seuil, 1985).

[26] Ibid. 98, 70.

[27] Michel Bernier, 'L'Afrique dans la poésie d'Édouard Glissant', in Yves-Alain Favre (ed.), *Horizons d'Édouard Glissant* (Biarritz: J&D Éditions, 1992), 255–68; 'l'Afrique en tant que terre-mère s'impose comme le trait déterminant, le thème fondateur de la poésie et de la poétique d'Édouard Glissant' ('Africa as motherland is the principal characteristic and paramount theme of Édouard Glissant's poetry and poetics').

[28] Yves-Alain Favre, 'Le songe, le réel et le chant dans la poésie d'Édouard Glissant', in id. (ed.), *Horizons d'Édouard Glissant*, 171–82: 'Le pays rêvé existe bel et bien, mais il demeure hors des prises du poète, éloigné dans l'espace et dans le temps. Si l'on peut encore abolir l'espace en franchissant l'océan, il reste impossible de supprimer l'histoire passée: l'Afrique reste un rêve pour le poète' ('The dreamed-of land exists in reality but remains beyond the poet's reach, distant in space and in time. If space can be abolished by crossing the ocean, it is impossible to cancel time. Africa remains a dream for the poet').

se is distant in space and out of reach altogether in time. Most of
the citations adduced by Favre—'Ce pays | s'élonge d'un tel songe'
('This land | is extended by such a dream'),²⁹ 'Nous fêlons le pays
d'avant dans l'entrave du pays-ci' ('We are cracking the mould of
the land of before in the grip of this land here')³⁰—confirm that
Glissant is fascinated less by Africa than by the texture of the
Caribbean–African connection. In other words, what he highlights
is the manner in which Africa is refracted by and within the
Caribbean.

In Glissant's first novel, Mathieu enjoins his people to face the
sea and to remember their origins elsewhere: 'Ne craignons pas de
nous tenir sur le rivage, face au large, et de peser notre histoire.
Nous venons de l'autre côté de la mer, rappelle-toi' ('Let us dare to
stand on the shore, looking out to sea, and to measure our history.
We come from the other side, remember').³¹ This plea to weigh up
Caribbean history highlights the space between the Caribbean
shore and the 'other side': that is, the space of the sea and the
Middle Passage or historical dislocation itself. Again and again,
then, Glissant emphasizes the relation between Africa and the
Caribbean, rather than one place or the other. And the fundamental characteristic of this relation is that it superimposes time on
space and vice versa. And yet, on another level, Glissant is
concerned to acknowledge the separateness and independence of
Africa and the Caribbean, as well as the fundamental assymmetry
of the relation. In *Le Discours antillais*, he notes that Africa was for
a long time a projection of Western desire. However, he considers
that in facing the reality of Africa's current, dynamic state, 'we',
that is, the rest of the world, including the Caribbean population,
can no longer project our own identity onto it. Instead, we now
know that we have to 'try to be ourselves', and, by extension, allow
Africa to be itself.

Il est vrai que, tout comme l'"Orient', l'Afrique a été objet de fascination,
du moins tant qu'elle a paru dans la Relation mondiale comme fantasme
(fantôme, ambiguë) de l'autre. Les mouvements révolutionnaires en
Afrique, l'énorme effort entrepris par les peuples, les ravages qui visent à
les anéantir, ont imposé une image moins 'malléable' du fait africain.

²⁹ Glissant, *Pays rêvé*, 14.
³⁰ Ibid. 17.
³¹ Glissant, *La Lézarde* (Paris: Seuil, 1958), 29.

L'Afrique qui se fait nous oblige à quitter les fantasmes de projection et à tâcher d'être nous-mêmes.[32]

In these comments, Glissant indicates his awareness that the dynamic reality of the African continent greatly exceeds its Caribbean mythification as origin/past/history/dream. He also sketches out the plot of what we could term the French Caribbean's 'Africa complex', that is, its difficulty in separating from a source that is reduced to the manageable, but grossly distorted proportions of a monolithic 'country'. A powerful 'effet d'identification' had driven Césaire to write in the 1930s: 'A force de penser au Congo, je suis devenu un Congo bruissant de fleuves et de forêts' ('I have thought of the Congo and so I have become a | Congo rustling with rivers and forests').[33] This bald identification is textured, of course, by the fact that the term 'Congo' in Caribbean parlance means an African freshly arrived in the 'New World'. Nonetheless, the extraordinarily powerful presence of African imagery in Césaire's poetry appears to be criticized and the relation to Africa relativized in Glissant's novel *La Case du commandeur*. Through the character Pythagore, Glissant represents the disorienting and destructive effect of the inability to distinguish between Africa and the Caribbean. If Pythagore is adrift, if he does not know his (own) place, it is because he has lost the capacity to distinguish the Caribbean from Africa, and insists on projecting the latter onto the former. Not only does he identify Africa with the Caribbean, but he shrinks it down to the dimensions of the familiar, believing it to be constructed in the image and likeness of the 'pays-ci': 'persuadé que le pays d'avant, ce qu'il n'appelait pas l'Afrique mais la Guinée ou le Congo, était à l'image de ce pays-ci (car il ne pouvait concevoir que ce pays-ci fût peut-être l'image remodelée du pays d'avant)' ('certain that the land of the past, that he didn't call Africa, but rather Guinea or Congo, was modelled on this land (for he could not imagine that this land might perhaps be

---

[32] 'It is true that, as was the case for the "Orient", Africa was an object of fascination, at least as long as it seemed to offer itself as a worldwide fantasy of the other (a phantom figure or a figure of ambiguity). African revolutions, the immense effort of the peoples of Africa, and the repression that attempted to destroy them, have all imposed a less malleable image of Africa. Africa as it is being constructed today forces us to abandon these projections and to try to be ourselves': *Le Discours antillais*, 392. This has not been included in *Caribbean Discourse*. Emphasis mine.

[33] Césaire, *Cahier d'un retour au pays natal*.

the remodelled image of the land of the past)').[34] To explain and to situate Pythagore's confusion, this novel weaves Africa into a complex poetics of place. More precisely, Pythagore's confusion would seem to be inevitable given the fact that the *Habitation* that he remembers comprises spaces called Guinée and Congo. The geometry of projection is thus collective, and is inscribed in particular in this naming of the 'New World' in terms of the 'Old': 'La case du commandeur était le centre de l'Habitation, au quartier Grand Congo. C'est au soleil tombant que se situait la Petite Guinée' ('The driver's cabin was at the heart of the plantation in the quarter called Great Congo. Little Guinea was located in the direction of the setting sun').[35]

Pythagore était passé du côté des songes errants, qui ne repèrent pas leur paysage et ne s'ancrent dans aucune argile. C'est-à-dire qu'il perdit à jamais la possibilité (qui en vérité ne l'avait qu'effleuré) de distinguer entre le paysage du pays d'avant . . .: ce recommencement sans fin de terres labourées d'eaux, de bois ravinés, de villes taillées dans l'argile et le sable— l'Afrique—, cet infini qui vous portait à la limite de vos pas, ménageant partout des îlots tranquilles où les hommes et les bêtes voisinaient et s'aidaient comme le font à coup sûr les amas d'étoiles dans le firmament, et le paysage du pays-ci, où tout se répétait à toute allure dans un concentré tourbillonnant de tous les paysages possibles . . . qu'il perdit donc la voyance de ces deux paysages, la connaissance de leur écart.[36]

What Pythagore lacks, then, is the ability to locate and to measure the gap between the two landscapes and, with that, the ability to distinguish them and *de facto* to relate them the one to the other. And yet, he does envision the two spaces in radically different terms. Africa is represented as a timeless, infinite utopia. The fact that this Africa is purely imaginary, a figment of Pythagore's

---

[34] Glissant, *La Case du commandeur*, 33.   [35] Ibid. 88.

[36] Ibid. 41–2; 'Pythagore had become one of those roving dreams, who no longer recognize their own landscape and who are anchored in no clay. He lost for ever the ability (that he had only ever vaguely glimpsed anyway) of distinguishing between the landscape of the land of the past, on the one hand . . . that never ending stretch of watered earth, of valleyed woods, of towns sculpted in sand and clay—Africa— that infinity that brings you to the limit of your footsteps, creating everywhere peaceful islands where man and beast side by side assisted each other just like the stars in the firmament no doubt, and the landscape of this land, on the other, where everything was repeated at full speed in a compressed whirlwind of all possible landscapes—to such an extent that he lost the vision of both landscapes, and all knowledge of the gap between them.'

fantasy, is underlined by the ironic, anthropomorphic likening of the utopian African oases of peace where man and beast work in perfect harmony together, to the firmament where the stars are supposed to coexist in a state of cosmic collaboration. The landscape of the Antilles on the other hand is compressed into a frenzied, compacted mass of words meaning little, a vortex of repetition and speed.

COLONIAL ENCOUNTERS WITH THE 'PAYS RÉEL'

The Caribbean colonial administrators posted to Africa had a golden opportunity to measure the gap between Africa as 'pays rêvé' and as 'pays réel'. At least four major writers were in this privileged, if ambivalent, position: René Maran, Albert Béville,[37] Guy Tirolien, and Joseph Zobel. Régis Antoine considers that the relation between French Caribbean writers and Africa was always been one of solidarity, although it did not usually go as far as the engagement of Frantz Fanon, who joined the FLN during the Algerian war as well as following the Mau Mau revolt in Kenya, the Angolan guerrilla war, and the situation in the Congo, advocating indeed a pan-African revolution. Antoine has in mind in particular congruences like the one between Césaire and Sékou Touré, the former having prefaced the latter's work, *Expérience guinéenne et unité africaine*.[38] Whereas Césaire's polemical *Discours sur le colonialisme* and Fanon's *Les Damnés de la terre* (1961) are unambiguous in their support for decolonization, revolutionary anti-colonial discourse would ill befit the likes of Niger, Maran, or Tirolien, who were writing of Africa with one hand tied behind their backs in their capacity as foot soldiers of empire in Africa.

If the deep ambivalence of the Caribbean–African relation is particularly well illustrated in writing that confronts the imagined or mythical Africa with contemporary African realities, it is compounded by the compromised position of those Caribbean writers who found themselves enforcing European hegemony in Africa, if only as educators or cultural policy-makers. The nuances

---

[37] Béville, born in Marie-Galante, wrote under the pseudonym, Paul Niger; Édouard Glissant dedicated his novel *Le Quatrième Siècle* to him.

[38] See Antoine, 'La littérature antillaise', 103. Sékou Touré's text was published in Paris in 1961 by Présence africaine.

of their situation are particularly well captured in the outlook of René Maran, Martinican-born author (of Guyanese origin) of the self-styled 'véritable roman nègre' *Batouala*, which was awarded the Prix Goncourt in 1921. Maran was sent by the French colonial administration to Africa, to Bangui, 'pour accomplir un métier de garde-chiourme que j'abomine' ('to be a prison-warder, a position that I abominate'), as he wrote in 1901 in a letter to a friend (a letter quoted by Régis Antoine). 'Je sens', he continues, 'que je suis sur le sol de mes ancêtres, ancêtres que je réprouve parce que je n'ai pas leur mentalité primitive ni leurs goûts. Mais ce n'en sont pas moins mes ancêtres' ('I feel that I am on my ancestors' ground, but I reprove them because I share neither their primitive mentality nor their tastes. But they are, nonetheless, my ancestors').[39] That judgement, which makes Maran appear as a perfectly alienated and assimilated colonial, the model *évolué*, belies the writer's commitment to many of the values that the *négritude* movement would, a few decades later, enthusiastically espouse. Yet what is particularly significant is that, despite the fact that Maran is experiencing the 'real' Africa, he does not seem to recognize its coevalness. Instead, his use of the present tense is suggestive of what Johannes Fabian would term 'allochronic discourse'; in other words, Maran seems to situate Africans in a different time-frame to his own. He sees the Africans that he encounters in Africa, his contemporaries in fact, as his 'ancestors'. Moreover, if he ascribes to them a primitive mentality from which he feels obliged to distance himself, it is precisely because he has collapsed the temporal distance between the Africans from whom he is descended and those amongst whom he works in Bangui.

As many of its critics have pointed out, the greatest failing of *négritude* was that it relegated to a second level of importance the indelible cultural effects—positive as well as negative—of time, displacement, contact, and complexity. However, French Caribbean writers associated with the movement did not necessarily peddle a mythical, static, or idealized Africa. Those who devoted much of their lives to Africa, like Guy Tirolien and Paul Niger, who were both posted to Africa in the same year (Tirolien to Guinea, Niger to Mali), were capable of political engagement with the 'present' of Africa, and even showed, in the case of Niger, a

[39] Quoted in Antoine, '*La littérature antillaise*', 104.

certain ambivalence regarding African political reality. The follow-ing lines from his poem 'Je n'aime pas l'Afrique' are quite telling in this respect:

> L'Afrique des yesmen et des beni-oui-oui.
> L'Afrique des hommes couchés attendant comme une grâce le réveil
>   de la botte
> L'Afrique des boubous flottant comme des drapeaux de capitulation[40]

For his part, the Guadeloupean writer Guy Tirolien joined the Rassemblement démocratique africain and was politically active in Guinea alongside Sékou Touré. Because of his political activity he had to leave Guinea for Niger, and, after decolonization, repre-sented the United Nations in Mali and Gabon.

The increasingly discerning, questioning, and sometimes highly critical light in which Africa was represented in writing of the 1970s and 1980s (a trend most apparent, perhaps, in Simone Schwarz-Bart's *Ti Jean L'horizon*, Myriam Warner-Vieyra's *Juletane*, and many of Maryse Condé's novels, most notably *Heremakhonon*, *Une saison à Rihata*, and *Les Derniers Rois mages*) bespeaks a complexity and an ambivalence already latent and sometimes explicit, then, in these earlier approaches to the continent, and even in the writing of certain apologists of *négri-tude*.[41] I could instance, for example, Césaire's play *Une saison au Congo*, with its equivocal resonances of Rimbaud's title *Une saison en enfer* that are again picked up by Maryse Condé in *Une saison à Riyhata*. These writers all bear witness to the complexity of the relation between Africa and the Caribbean and they illustrate how recognition of the realities of that continent can puncture inflated expectations of Africa and lead to a certain cultural disappoint-ment, or even alienation. This might not necessarily, of course, lead to the rehabilitation of the Caribbean sense of self-worth and could, indeed, have the opposite effect, depending on the degree of (foundational) identification with Africa. Both Guy Tirolien and Paul Niger, unlike Frantz Fanon, eventually returned from Africa to the Caribbean, and turned their attention to Caribbean politics. But whereas Niger returned in the early 1960s and acted upon his

---

[40] Paul Niger, *Inquisitions* (Paris: Seuil, 1954), 31; 'Africa of the yesmen and the yes-sir-no-sirs | Africa of the supine awaiting the indulgence of a rousing kick | Africa of the bubus flapping like flags of capitulation.'
[41] See ibid. 110.

hostility to colonization by co-founding, along with Édouard Glissant, the *Front antillais-guyanais* (Caribbean and Guyanese Independence Front), Tirolien did not return until the mid-1970s, when he stood for election to the French parliament, admittedly as a candidate in favour of Caribbean 'self-determination'. Simone Schwarz-Bart and Maryse Condé, who also spent spells in Africa, subsequently returned to the 'pays natal' literally (and for Maryse Condé, in terms of the focus of her writing as well). It is worth repeating, however, that Maryse Condé would come back to the question of Africa again and again after *Heremakhonon*, notably in *Une saison à Rihata* and in *Les Derniers Rois mages*, translated, significantly, as *The Last of the African Kings*.[42]

CRITICAL PERSPECTIVES ON AFRICA (AS 'PAYS RÉEL'?)

In the light of the frequently highlighted dissonance between an imagined Africa and a real Africa, it is important to distinguish between writing that approaches Africa as a coeval space (and the authors of such writing have often spent—sometimes quite protracted—periods of time on the continent), and writing in which Africa retains that rather abstract quality of distant origin, homeland of the mind. We have seen how, often, as though to underline the abstraction and reduction inherent in this latter approach to an entire continent, Africa becomes quite simply 'Guinée', or 'Congo', more vaguely the 'land of before' ('pays d'avant'), or in any case a more or less monolithic block which is allowed to stand for 'the past' claimed by (some) Caribbean subjects. And we have seen also that three Guadeloupean women writers, Maryse Condé and Myriam Warner-Vieyra in particular, and, to a lesser extent, Simone Schwarz-Bart, in engaging with Africa as a contemporary, but significant 'other', attempted in the 1970s and 1980s a literary 'return to Africa', following to a certain extent in the realist footsteps of the earlier generation of pre-*négritude*, *négritude*, and post-*négritude* writers like Maran, Niger, Tirolien, and also, of course, Fanon.

---

[42] Condé, *Les Derniers Rois mages* (Paris: Mercure de France, 1992); tr. Richard Philcox as *The Last of the African Kings* (Lincoln: University of Nebraska Press, 1998).

However, it would be quite wrong to claim that any of these writers portrays an 'Afrique réelle' which contrasts with the 'Afrique imaginaire' of other writers such as Édouard Glissant. It is not because Maryse Condé herself, like her two compatriots Schwarz-Bart and Warner-Vieyra, chose to write about the encounter in Africa between an Antillean subjectivity and contemporary Africa(ns), that what is represented in their writing is a real as opposed to an imagined Africa. On the contrary, in each case we read of the very specific and often complex and even contradictory encounter of a particular imagination with a vast and highly differentiated continental space and history. In one case, however, Africa is represented more insistently as lying outside the Caribbean subjectivity—thus as an 'other', separate space-time which can only be encountered by a major displacement of the imagination. This is as true of the surreal Africa encountered by Ti Jean, the mythical hero of Schwarz-Bart's magic realist novel, as it is of the thinly disguised Guinea of Sekou Touré to which Véronica turns in *Heremakhonon*. In the other case, for example in the writing of Édouard Glissant, Patrick Chamoiseau, or Raphaël Confiant, this 'external' Africa is only confronted 'in theory' and what the writing focuses on is an 'Africa within'.

REJECTION OF AFRICA (AS 'PAYS RÊVÉ'?)

The sense of the disproportion between Africa and the Caribbean is a function in the first place of the vastness of the continent. However, the assumed assurance of Africans, related as it is to the aura of continuity and legitimacy surrounding African cultural tradition, combined with present-day African independence and sovereignty, feed into the Caribbean inferiority complex that is sometimes represented as a defensiveness and even as an aggressive rejection. In *La Case du commandeur*, Pythagore's veneration of the figure of King Béhanzin serves in this sense as a foil for the pettiness and insecurity of the clerks whom he encounters in his search through the archives for information about the exiled Dahomean king.

À propos d'un Africain prisonnier qui avait passé dans le pays quelque trente ans auparavant et avait laissé le souvenir (non, le vague relent si vite évanoui) d'un pantin en robe, encanaillé de combien de femmes qu'il avait

eu l'audace d'appeler ses épouses. . . . Les petits employés, qui s'estimaient
à combien de hauteur au-dessus d'un Africain (et qui peut-être connaî-
traient la bonne fortune—parce qu'ils avaient rencontré à un repas de
Pentecôte le cousin du commis d'un chef de service du secrétaire général
du gouverneur, qu'ils avaient eu la grâce de lui plaire et de le faire rire
avec des plaisanteries du cru—d'être bientôt nommés à Dakar ou à
Cotonou) . . .[43]

This passage exposes the prejudices of assimilated Caribbeans
against what they suppose to be African culture—for example,
non-European dress and the practice of polygamy. The description
is heavy with implied criticism of the closed minds and complacent
alienation of these bureaucrats who ironically combine colonial
discourse and values with a particularly servile mentality, as they
compete for the dubious and, of course, paradoxical privilege of
being appointed as officials to the African colonies. The pettiness
of these critics of Africa, the smallness of their ambitions, and their
utter dependence on the colonial hierarchy contrast with the
grandeur and immensity of Africa as Pythagore perceives it.

Raphaël Confiant also uses irony to underline what Glissant
identifies as the increasingly remote and indeed demoted status of
Africa in the French Caribbean imagination. For Glissant, the
dethronement of Africa signals not only the failure or rejection
both of imagination and of memory, but also the repudiation of
relation and relativization, and with it, of full self-situation. In his
depiction of contemporary urban values in Martinique, Raphaël
Confiant exposes on several occasions the rejection of memories of
'l'horrible Afrique-Guinée'.

Pour nous autres, natifs-natals, le bourg de Grand-Anse était le mitan du
monde. Certes, nous rêvions d'ailleurs, d'En Ville, d'en France, de la Syrie
ou de l'Inde et certains qui avaient voyagé, de Panama ou de l'Amérique,
mais la plupart d'entre nous doutaient que ces contrées merveilleuses

---

[43] Glissant, *La Case du commandeur*, 41; 'All about an African prisoner who had
passed through thirty years previously and had left the memory (no, the vague whiff
quickly faded) of a berobed figure, weighed down with all those women that he had
the effrontery to call his wives . . . The petty officials, who considered themselves
infinitely above any African, and who would one day perhaps have the good fortune
to be posted to Dakar or to Cotonou—having met at a Whitsun feast the cousin of
the assistant of one of the governor's secretary generals, and having been lucky
enough to have struck him favourably and to have made him laugh with some local
jokes.'

(hormis l'horrible Afrique-Guinée que nous avions enfouie au plus obscur de notre moi) fussent vraiment réelles.[44]

It is ironic that it is the reality of Africa, its all too real reality (a memory rather than a dream, an inheritance rather than a project) that makes the Caribbean subject repress all thought of it. However, Julien Thémistocle, described as having 'the bad manners of a maroon' ('des mauvaises manières de nègre marron'), berates this betrayal of Africa by his fellow-citizens:

Vous êtes en admiration devant la France et la Syrie, bandes de couillons, mais vous tournez le dos à la Guinée! pas un qui veuille y retourner, compères! Moi, je n'attends que la mort, tuez-moi et vous verrez que mon cadavre ne sera plus dans ma tombe le lendemain matin. J'ai ma place en Guinée![45]

This outburst meets only with mockery, however, with the single exception of the comical intellectual, Émilien Bérard:

Le monde se gaussait de lui ... Nous n'avions que faire de cette Guinée dont il nous bassinait les oreilles, de ce pays de nègres sauvages et de canni-bales, et il n'y avait que ce liseur de livres d'Émilien Bérard pour être d'ac-cord avec lui. [46]

The salty humour of Confiant's rumbustious style does not take away from the bite of the notion that only diehard anti-Creoles or fey intellectuals would be caught beating the African drum at the end of the twentieth century. Given, then, the irony that increas-ingly relativizes and subverts not only the Metropolitan connec-tion, but also the African heritage, and given the apparent lack of interest in contemporary Africa, it would surely seem that Caribbean subjectivity as constructed in literature gradually turned

---

[44] Confiant, *Le Nègre et l'amiral*, 179; 'For us natives the village of Grand-Anse was the centre of the world. Sure, we dreamed of other places, of the town, of France, of Syria, and of India, and those of us who had travelled dreamed of Panama and America. But most of us doubted that these magic countries really existed (all of them, that is, except for that horrible Africa-Guinea that we had buried in the darkest regions of our selves).'

[45] Ibid. 88; 'You are lost in admiration for France and Syria, you idiots, but you are turning your back on Guinea! Not one of you wants to return there, my friends! As for me, I am just waiting for death; kill me and you'll see that my corpse won't be in my tomb the next day. I have my seat booked in Guinea!'

[46] Ibid. 'Everybody was laughing at him ... we wanted nothing to do with this Guinea that he was forever on about, this land of savage blacks and cannibals, and the only person who agreed with him was that bookworm Émilien Bérard.'

away in the course of the twentieth century from these two poles of attraction. However, in his second novel, *Soufrières*, Daniel Maximin modulates this impression in his poetic reading of the sliding of the continental shelf:

Aujourd'hui, même les savants affirment que les continents dansent, les pieds cachés sous l'eau pour garder en surface leur sérieux. L'Amérique s'éloigne en douce de l'Afrique qui concède trente centimètres par décennie. Et la plaque caraïbe, qui supporte tout notre archipel, fait résistance à cet éloignement au prix des éruptions et des séismes dans nos îles arc-boutées, fidèles et fragiles au souvenir du continent noir.[47]

According to this lyrical logic, America is slowly but surely distancing itself from Africa, while the Caribbean shelf is being pulled between the two, resisting this distancing, and paying for its fidelity to the 'continent noir' by being rocked by eruptions and quakes, tremors, and aftershocks. Whatever the accuracy in geological terms of this poignant perspective on the Caribbean, it is a poetic and suggestive one. However, although the literary equivalent of the Richter scale might give confirmatory readings for 'fidelity' to the 'memory of the dark/black continent' in the work of Édouard Glissant and Daniel Maximin themselves, as well as in works such as Maryse Condé's *Le Dernier des rois mages* or Ernest Pépin's *Tambour-Babel*, even then, it is important to understand that what is being registered for the Caribbean–African relation is, simply, a variable combination of memorial fragility and fidelity, a fundamentally precarious resistance to an inexorable displacement, that is, to irreversible tectonic movement, which symbolizes here the movement of time. If the resistance is fragile, it is not simply because the faultline of the African connection is so deeply submerged (in time). It is also because of the existence of a third plate, not mentioned by Maximin. The European continental shelf exerts, after all, a certain torsion on the African–American drift. This is particularly obvious, indeed, in the case of Maximin's own *imaginaire*. For example, in *Soufrières*, Africa is brought to mind in France: Soyinka is encountered in Avignon, and Adrien is reminded

---

[47] Maximin, *Soufrières*, 29; 'Today, even scientists agree that the continents are dancing, their feet hidden in the water so as to look serious on the surface. America is slowly drifting away from Africa which is conceding thirty centimetres each decade. And the Caribbean shelf that bears the weight of our entire archipelago is resisting this drift and is paying for its resistance with the eruptions and quakes that shake our braced islands, frail in their fidelity to the memory of the dark continent.'

of the anti-apartheid struggle in the Latin quarter. In *Heremakhonon* too, Véronica leaves for Africa from France; in *L'Autre qui danse*, Africa is envisioned within France; and the eponymous Juletane meets her African husband Mamadou in Paris. Certainly, the 'pays rêvé' is not just envisioned in French Caribbean writing as the 'pays d'avant'; yet, when Africa is seen to be a coeval 'pays réel' in its own right, the vision is often routed via Metropolitan France, suggesting, perhaps, that for the Caribbean subject an unmediated and synchronous relation to, or vision of, Africa is an impossibility.

CHAPTER NINE

'New World' Synchrony: Imagining the Local

Je ne suis pas attaché à une île. Mes racines couvrent les côtes américaines et maillent l'archipel de la mer des Antilles.[1]

In his noted study *The Black Atlantic*, Paul Gilroy concentrates on transatlantic movement between the 'New World' and the 'Old World', thus limiting the scope of his resonant title. This neglect of Atlantic crossings within the 'New World' is faithful, however, to the binary thrust of Gilroy's subtitle, which refers to 'double consciousness'. The decision to focus on the 'image of ships in motion across the spaces between Europe, America, Africa, and the Caribbean'[2] perhaps prevents Gilroy's study from validating the specificity, the potential, and meaning of 'New World' relationality as revealed in intra-American circulation. For such gravitation towards other parts of the 'New World' could, perhaps, counterbalance the obsessive triangulation that Édouard Glissant once stigmatized as imprisoning the Caribbean mind within the dead-end orientations of the 'Détour' towards France | Europe and the 'Retour' towards Africa. Surely 'New World' vistas could offer the possibility of a relationality enriched by both solidarity and reflection? As we have seen, preponderantly foundational relations, like the Caribbean relation to Africa, Europe, or the Indian sub-continent, do tend to be passive and

---

[1] 'I am not attached to an island. My roots are spread across the American coastlines and they are like netting cast over the archipelago of the Caribbean sea': Chamoiseau, *Écrire en pays dominé*, 110.

[2] It is significant that Paul Gilroy's index does not feature the names of Césaire or of Fanon, and that, under *négritude*, there is just one reference. Glissant fares better: his thinking on modernity features in an epigraph to the first chapter, and he is also quoted on black kinetic consciousness and musical awareness. Paul Gilroy, *The Black Atlantic: Modernity and Double Consciousness* (London: Verso, 1993).

ultimately self-reflexive or centripetal. Unlike such constitutive relations, which are 'givens' or products of the past, and thus inherent in Caribbean memory, language, culture, and identity, the relation to the rest of the Caribbean and the 'New World' more generally could be expected to entail a more outward-looking and less historically preoccupied disposition. In other words, connection with other 'New World' space can more readily take place in a preponderantly synchronic framework. In contrast, the French Caribbean relation to France and to Africa is always (already) diachronic even if a synchronic relation can be superimposed by an effort to engage with the present of those spaces. Moreover, whereas relation to France and Africa typically involves a quest for a version or a fraction of the self, relation to the 'New World' might permit connection on a less solipsistic, less self-referential and less predetermined plane.

LATE *NÉGRITUDE* AND THE NEW WORLD: FROM RETURN TO CIRCULATION

The writing of late French Caribbean *négritude* might be expected to demonstrate not just an awareness of developments in black cultural consciousness within North America (and New York in particular, specifically the Harlem Renaissance), but also some recognition of those elements of black culture prominent in parts of South America and much of the American South, as well as movements of cultural consciousness in the Anglophone and Hispanophone Caribbean. And indeed, José in *La Rue Cases-Nègres* does claim a certain familiarity with nascent Caribbean and African-American literature. In fact, this wider literary context is represented as being instrumental in developing his awareness of his own *négritude*. Claude McKay's *Banjo* and René Maran's *Batouala* are mentioned specifically in Zobel's novel, and more generally, José's disillusionment with the programme of studies at the *lycée* in Fort-de-France is contrasted with his new-found interest in 'New World' writing by blacks. His enthusiastic exploration of this corpus does not appear, however, to develop José's geographical or spatial awareness. Nor does it deepen in any explicit way his ability to situate his subjectivity as specifically Caribbean. Indeed, it is precisely this approach to the 'New World' that identifies José's outlook as more akin to the values of *négritude* than to those of Caribbeanness. It is as though these texts are despatialized, dislocated from the specific cultures in which they were produced, since no note is taken of the particularity of Maran's Africa or of McKay's Harlem. The value attributed to these works in the novel is that they foreground and rehabilitate blackness or black culture, regardless of cultural context. Not only is there no sense of relating to a different, neighbouring space in the 'New World', but there is no sense either of relating to a different (Anglophone) language or culture. Rather, the distressed and alienated subject is relieved to find himself mirrored in the discourse of a similarly alienated black subjectivity under comparable cultural strain.

In contrast to Zobel's novel, many Francophone Caribbean texts—Roumain's *Gouverneurs de la rosée* (1946) and Césaire's *Cahier d'un retour au pays natal* (1939), for example—show that the dynamic of foreign sojourn followed by return to the native island is a significant source of messianic inspiration in Caribbean writing. In Césaire's case, however, the native land is envisaged and returned to from Metropolitan France and Africa rather than from another 'New World' space, whereas in the case of Roumain's novel, Manuel returns from Cuba, bringing with him the Good News of a local Caribbean tale of solidarity and collective enterprise. Maryse Condé's *Traversée de la mangrove* rewrites the *Cahier* and repeats the plot of *Gouverneurs de la rosée* in so far as her anti-hero, Francis Sancher, also returns to Guadeloupe from Cuba. However, in general, in French Caribbean writing of the second part of the twentieth century, the notion of return is less important than the idea of circulation. And much of that circulation is local rather than transatlantic.

ANTILLANITÉ, OR THE (UNKEPT?) PROMISE OF CARIBBEAN COMMUNITY

Some writers show greater commitment than others to the parameters of 'New World' space. Some communicate a strong sense of the local geographical configuration (both of other islands in the Caribbean archipelago and of contiguous continental space), as well as a strong sense of community with other places sharing a similar history of colonization and diaspora, slavery and plantation culture. Predictably, this is the case of Édouard Glissant, as the prophet of *antillanité*, but it is also true of the writings of Simone Schwarz-Bart, Maryse Condé, and Daniel Maximin. However, following the publication of *Le Discours antillais* in 1981, Édouard Glissant's thinking developed in two quite different, if related, directions: firstly, towards that opening evident in his subsequent essay collections—*Introduction à une poétique du divers* (1997), *Poétique de la Relation* (1990), and *Traité du Tout-Monde* (1998)—where, as the titles indicate, the author's principal concern is with global diversity and mobility, rather than with problematics specific to the Caribbean. Indeed, the later essays look back in this sense to the less strictly Caribbean-centred perspective of *Soleil de la connaissance* (1956) and *L'Intention poétique* (1969) and, secondly, towards further elaboration of his long-standing interest in general 'New World' cultural dynamics, a new direction evident in his work on William Faulkner and the American South, *Faulkner Mississippi* (1996). However merely apparent this dilution of the perspective on the Caribbean, we must wonder about the degree of commitment within the French Caribbean to location within the 'New World', when Édouard Glissant, undoubtedly the writer most closely associated with relocating Caribbean identity in relation to the specifics of 'New World' space, has been so insistently drawn towards the exploration and articulation of a far broader canvas, that is, towards a concern with worldwide cultural circulation. One could argue, of course, that the logic of these later essays is based on observation of the Caribbean laboratory. Yet it is true that Glissant's primary concern since the early 1990s (that is, in *Poétique de la Relation* and *Traité du Tout-Monde*, as indeed in his novel *Tout-monde*) has been with reverberations of the global, while the specificity of the 'New World' and in particular of the Caribbean has receded into a kind of empirical source for this much more broadly focused vision of creolization and relationality.

ANTILLANITÉ AS AMÉRICANITÉ

In *Le Discours antillais*, Glissant makes no distinction between the Caribbean novelist's preoccupations and those of American writers in general, noting that in 'the Americas' the novelist is defined by a crucial obsession, namely the strain of time.[3] The expression 'in the Americas' recurs in a further generalization, according to which a concern with the past is one of the essential hallmarks of American literature.[4] Even more significantly, Glissant does not distinguish, within that shared 'New World' poetics, between the European and the African diasporas. For him, 'ce temps éclaté, souffert est lié à des espaces "transportés". Je pense aussi bien aux espaces africains qu'à un espace breton, dont les "souvenirs" viennent se plaquer sur la réalité spatiale que nous vivons les uns et les autres' ('exploded, suffered time is linked to "transferred" space, I have in mind African space as much as Breton space, the "memory" of which has become stamped on the spatial reality that we all live').[5] It is as though Glissant views the shock of space and time consequent on displacement from the 'Old World' to the 'New World' as super-seding any distinctions that might be made between European migration and African transportation, between voluntary and forced displacement, and, more fundamentally, between free and enslaved Americans. More specifically, in an attempt to explain the parameters of the shock common to both elements of the displaced population, Glissant claims that the discontinuous frame of refer-ence in which they operate can be read as the superimposition not just of time on space but also of two spaces and two desires: one space merely remembered (or reimagined?) and the other present and real, one lost and distant, the other local, and neither experi-enced entirely in itself but perceived rather as intersecting.

However, within American writing, Glissant identifies a subset that operates as a sort of internal 'other', comprising South America and the Caribbean. And this America he terms the 'Other America', suggesting that it is moving towards the vision of a 'new man' alive in a new way to relation and relativity. In defiance of the

---

[3] He outlines 'autour de quelles données il me semble que l'ouvrage du romancier s'articule volontiers dans les Amériques: une obsession essentielle, oui, que je résume ainsi: la crispation du temps' ('the assumptions around which I feel the work of writers in the Americas instinctively revolves. Certainly, one essential obsession that I characterize in these terms: a tortured sense of time') *Le Discours antillais*, 254; *Caribbean Discourse*, 144.

[4] 'la hantise du passé . . . est un des référents essentiels de la production littéraire dans les Amériques' ('the haunting nature of the past . . . is one of the essential points of reference in the works produced in the Americas') *Le Discours antillais*, 254; *Caribbean Discourse*, 144.

[5] *Le Discours antillais*, 254; *Caribbean Discourse*, 144.

fact that Faulkner's ideas are very far removed from that 'Other America', Glissant believes that the author of *Sartoris* shares with writers from the 'Other America' a certain temporal consciousness, that is, a yearning for history and a tragic sense of return.

Édouard Glissant's interest in pan-Caribbean literary and intellectual activity is obvious in all his writing. In his preface to Chamoiseau's *Chronique des sept misères*, for example, he mentions Jamaican Dub poetry, the work of the Cuban Alejo Carpentier, and the writing of the Haitian Franketienne, and also refers in this context to an inclusive entity that he terms 'nos Amériques' ('our Americas').[6] This vision of Caribbean cultural rootedness in local American space pervades Glissant's novels too. J. Michael Dash notes of *Malemort* (1975), for example, that the novel indicts the isolation(ism) of a Martinique

> oblivious to the nature of the region that surrounds it. There is no longer salvation in the *morne* but it might just lie in the interrelationships with the world on the outside. The idea of Caribbean identity for Martinique is sketched out as Dlan, Medellus and Silacier gaze out to sea. St Lucian workers who were brought in to break a strike and sided with the Martiniquan workers; the self-sustaining productivity of Dominica; Haiti with its legendary past and frightening present; the exploits of the Cuban general Maceo—all these are juxtaposed with a Martinique more and more alienated from itself and prone to self-destruction.[7]

In this novel, other Caribbean islands are thus represented as models of creative identity, local sovereighty, neighbourly solidarity, and/or rootedness in an indigenous identity project, all in stark contrast to the isolation of the French Caribbean which is still in thrall to a doubly distant past and ever more controlled by forces far beyond and foreign to it. Glissant's emphasis is not primarily, or not directly, on the possibility of active, bilateral relation to a real place or a real population, however. It is more a question of specular or intellectual engagement with the very notion of diversity or of a multiplicity of 'others'. Similarly, in the novel that appeared in the same year as the *Discours antillais*, namely *La Case du commandeur*, local Caribbean relationality is explicitly represented in terms of a lost opportunity for speculative, heuristic

---

[6] Glissant, 'Un marqueur de paroles', preface to Chamoiseau, *Chronique des sept misères*, 6.
[7] Dash, *Édouard Glissant* (Cambridge: Cambridge University Press, 1995), 124.

connection with the rest of the Caribbean. More specifically, Martinicans are said to have failed to use the stock-taking time of the post-war period to climb the hills and to reflect from that high ground (not just a topographical, but also a highly symbolic vantage-point) on the immediate environment of the island, that is, on the neighbouring islands, said to be unknown quantities in Martinique:

Le pays était comme éclairé de ces ardeurs de l'après-guerre. C'était là une occasion de monter vraiment sur les mornes, de sonder le temps qui s'y était amassé, de regarder sur la mer vers ces autres îles dont nous ne supposions même pas comment leurs habitants les peuplaient.[8]

The relation envisaged in this novel is again rather limited in that it is restricted to a mere looking out towards, or at the very most, as we shall see, a hailing of the other. If even that level of connection is avoided by Martinicans, it is allegedly because they are 'surexcités d'espace', opting to 'courir en imagination, et par consentement de tous, au loin de cette mer et de ses couis de terre' ('run in their imagination and by common consent far away from this sea and its islands like hollowed out half-calabashes').[9] Not all the foregrounded characters of the novel turn or run away, however: Marie Celat, for example,

apostrophait les îles. Répondez, la Dominque. Je vous appelle à conférence. . . . ho répondez Jamaïque. Venez à la naissance et appelez dans la danse, Haïti ho Haïti. Et toutes sortes de tirades qu'elle improvisait en actrice inspirée, riant d'elle-même et de ces simagrées. Comprenant toutefois que si elle parlait à ces pays comme à des personnes vivantes, ombrageuses ou bonnes, c'est parce qu'elle était restée si longtemps à venir là se baigner au soleil sans jamais lever les yeux sur l'horizon où les mêmes mornes là-bas se profilaient.[10]

---

[8] Glissant, *La Case du commandeur*, 173; 'The country was lit up, as it were, by this post-war passion. This was the moment to climb the hills, to sound out the time that had accumulated there, and to look out towards those other islands whose settlements we could not even imagine'.

[9] Ibid. 174.

[10] Ibid. 215; '[Mycéa] hailed the islands. Reply, Dominica. I am calling you to talk . . . ho, reply Jamaica. Come to the birthing and call out in the dance, Haiti, ho Haiti. And so went the declamations that she improvised like an inspired actress, laughing at herself and at her own posturing. But she understood too that if she was speaking to these places as though they were living people, tetchy or good-natured, it was because she had been coming there for so long to sun-bathe without ever looking up towards the horizon where the same hills stood out over there.'

This passage evokes an evolution in Marie Celat's awareness as she, all of a sudden and for the very first time, is led to look towards the immediate horizon. What she sees there is a distant place, a 'là-bas' or an 'over there' which is yet the same as her own island. Rather than occupying an irremediably different time-space, it is in the same time-frame as Martinique and presents the same topography. This passage, in which Mycéa hails Dominica, Jamaica, and Haiti, rewrites the poem in which Césaire too calls out, not to the other Caribbean islands, however, but to Africa. In his mind's eye, Césaire sees, not the *mornes* that remind him of his own island, but rather the proud banners of new African nations whose birth the poet salutes from his distant Caribbean island:

je vois pousser des nations.

Vertes et rouges, je vous salue,
bannières, gorges du vent ancien,
Mali, Guinée, Ghana

et je vous vois, hommes,
point maladroits sous ce soleil nouveau! Écoutez!
de mon île lointaine
de mon île veilleuse
je vous dis Hoo!
Et vos voix me répondent

et ce qu'elles disent signifie:
'Il y fait clair'. Et c'est vrai:
même a travers orage et nuit
pour nous il y fait clair.
D'ici je vois Kiwu vers Tanganika descendre . . .[11]

In Césaire's poem, Africa responds to the poet's greetings, whereas Mycéa's speeches, although projected much less far, are left without response. Moreover, it is implied that she finds her own histrionics comical, and that they are an overreaction to her

---

[11] 'I see nations grow | Banners, green and red, | I salute you, throats of the ancient wind, | Mali, Guinea, Ghana || and I see you, men | not awkward under this new sun | Listen! | from my remote island | from my watchful island | I cry Hoo to you. | And your voices answer me. || and what they are saying means: "There is plenty of light here!" and that is true! | Even during the storm and the night | for us there is plenty of light here | From here I see the Kiwu descend Ruziz's | silver stairway toward Tanganyika'; from 'Pour saluer le Tiers Monde' (A Salute to the Third World) dedicated to Senghor in Aimé Césaire, *Ferrements* (Ferraments), in *Collected Poetry*, 351–3.

previous obliviousness to the other islands' distant presence on the horizon.

EMBRACING THE AMERICAS: THE GUADELOUPEAN REACH

A specific kind of openness to the other islands of the Caribbean, and indeed to continental American space too, prevails in the writing of a number of Guadeloupean authors. Simone Schwarz-Bart's play *Ton beau capitaine* is centred, for example, on the Guadeloupean exile of a Haitian worker. Similarly, Schwarz-Bart's novels feature some characters (usually men) who circulate between one island and another. For example, in *Pluie et vent sur Télumée Miracle*, Toussine's father came to Guadeloupe from Dominica and departed again in a hurry before his daughter's birth.[12] Ernest Pépin's *Tambour-Babel*, Dany Bébel-Gisler's *Léonora*, and Daniel Maximin's trilogy also confirm the view that Guadeloupean writers are perhaps less constrained than many Martinican writers by a need to connect with Europe, or by a self-analytical compulsion that turns them in on their own identity; hence they seem freer to concentrate on other spaces of circulation, and on less restrictive trajectories.

L'accès de démence du vent vous éclaire le cœur, qui se met à penser aux autres îles Caraïbes, balayées par la queue du cyclone sur le dernier cercle des Antilles. L'Atlantique mis au courant reflue à grandes vagues vers l'Europe entre les mers de nuages.[13]

At the end of the previous chapter I noted that Daniel Maximin in *Soufrières* profiles the American continent as sliding away from Africa, with the Caribbean islands resisting this distancing. In Maximin's writing, Africa is indeed represented as an important pole of Caribbean affiliation. Yet his subscription to a vision of what we could term 'antillanité' works against this atavistic pull, and so the presence and the draw of the local prevails over the

---

[12] Schwarz-Bart, *Pluie et vent sur Télumée Miracle*, 12.
[13] Daniel Maximin, *L'Ile et une nuit* (Paris: Seuil, 1995), 37; 'The wind's burst of dementia lightens our heart, and we begin to think of the other Caribbean islands on the outer circle, being swept by the tail end of the cyclone. The Atlantic, now brought into the picture, surges backwards towards Europe between seas of clouds.'

attraction of Africa. A similar forcefield can be sensed at work in Ernest Pépin's *Tambour-Babel*, a novel in which music, and the circulation of musicians, is also the primary factor of mobility towards Africa and Europe, certainly, but also within the 'New World' itself. Moreover, in *Soufrières*, Maximin highlights the strategic importance of the French Caribbean as a Central and South American base for Metropolitan economic and political interests.

Les îles Caraïbes ont ouvert l'appétit des requins. Et le gouvernement français a décidé de jouer à fond la carte de l'agro-business et des multi-nationales du transport. L'avenir, c'est Pointe-à-Pitre et Fort-de-France, grands ports d'éclatement entre l'Europe, la Caraïbe et l'Amérique latine, sous l'aile protectrice de la France qui envoie déjà ses ministres de la Coopération cajoler tous vos voisins de droite à gauche, à Haïti comme à Cuba.[14]

Its critical position within the highly polarized Caribbean, and its strategic position in relation to Europe and Latin America, also, however, makes the French Caribbean vulnerable to exploitation as a pawn, a victim of dubious political courtesies designed to promote European business interests. Not only does France extend its right hand to Duvalier and its left to Castro ('la main droite à Duvalier et la main gauche à Castro'), but it also extends dubious civilities to undesirable neighbours like Pinochet; thus its inhabitants note that: 'un navire de guerre chilien avait droit depuis deux jours à un amical accueil dans nos belles eaux territoriales' ('a Chilean warship benefited from a friendly welcome in our beautiful territorial waters').[15] Metropolitan tutelage is a political liability, since it means that France, like a parent of questionable judgement, chooses the French Caribbean's friends for it, thereby queering the local political pitch for the DOM. Further emphasizing that Martinique and Guadeloupe are located in the Americas and that they belong geopolitically to the Caribbean and not to

---

[14] Maximin, *Soufrières*, 88; 'The Caribbean islands have aroused the appetite of the sharks. And the French government has decided to go for bust with agro-business and multinational hauliers. It sees the future as lying in Pointe-à-Pitre and Fort-de-France, these big ports split between Europe, the Caribbean, and Latin America, and nestling beneath the protective wing of France who is already sending her development ministers to woo all our neighbours, both right- and left-wing, Haiti no less than Cuba.'

[15] Ibid. 89.

France, Rosan (in *Soufrières*), having acknowledged that French Caribbeans are ignorant of the geographical details of the Caribbean archipelago, notes that the French would be unable to list all the departments of France or the Americans all the states in the USA. Rosan thus implies that the French Caribbeans are no more French than they are American.

Tu sais, je ne connais pas un seul Antillais capable de donner dans l'ordre la liste des îles qui composent toute la Caraïbe. Mais ne t'en inquiète pas trop. Aucun Français d'aujourd'hui ne connaît la liste de ses départements—et aucun Américain la liste de ses États dit unis.[16]

It would seem, then, that in comparison with *La Case du commandeur*, for example, regional circulation, interests, and solidarities impinge in many specific ways on the characters of Maximin's work. In another striking example of this regional inflection, Rosan rescues a young girl who is being coercively spirited in a reversal of the slave trade from Dominica through Guadeloupe en route to the brothels of Europe.[17] However, like Édouard Glissant's writing, Maximin's work still implies a degree of remoteness from the rest of the 'New World'. Indeed, in Caribbean writing in general, consideration of the local environment does not usually transcend a certain level of general awareness; it eschews in particular the physical displacement that might involve moving beyond the limits of the immediate island environment. The 'other' space close by is thus observed from the vantage-point of the home island, either visually or through contact with emigrant workers or islanders in transit from other islands. It is less often sought out and explored in itself as a separate place.

The same could certainly not be said, however, of the work of Maryse Condé. Indeed, the most concerted representation of mobility across the Americas is to be found in the writing of this prolific author. In *La Colonie du nouveau monde* set in Colombia, not to mention *Desirada*, *Les Derniers Rois mages*, and *Moi, Tituba sorcière . . . Noire de Salem*, Condé has her characters and narrators circulate and settle in various parts of the 'New World',

---

[16] Ibid. 238–9; 'You know, I don't know a single West Indian capable of listing all the islands of the Caribbean. But don't worry. No Frenchman today knows the whole list of French *départements*, and no American could list all the so-called United States.'

[17] Ibid. 246.

and she also has them actively analyse and interpret the distance and the proximity between the French Caribbean on the one hand, and, on the other, the often very different cultures and also very different constructions of post-diasporic black culture. In *La Vie scélérate*, for example, the construction of the Panama canal looms large as a symbolic pan-American venture on which black Americans and Caribbeans worked together along with labourers from the entire world.

Les Américains n'avaient peur de rien. Voilà qu'ils touchaient à la structure du monde et coupaient des continents en deux. A Panama, ils creusaient un canal qui allait permettre à leurs bateaux de naviguer plus rapidement de New York à San Francisco sur la côte Pacifique et pour ce dessein surhumain, ils faisaient appel à des travailleurs du monde entier.[18]

The novel mentions in particular the casualties of the enterprise from Barbados, Montserrat, and Haiti and charts the friendship that develops between the Guadeloupean Albert and Jacob, an American from Louisiana, a bond that becomes central to the entire plot of the novel. Ironically, it is Jacob, the continental American, who introduces Albert to the thinking of the Jamaican Marcus Garvey.[19]

In telling the story of Marie-Noëlle in *Desirada* (1997) Condé explores the sensibilities of the black American diaspora, staging not only a whole cast of black American characters and a very wide range of settings—clubs, universities, urban decay, fast-food rot, and racial discrimination—but also imagining the intricate networks of intercultural relation across the various sites of this secondary black diaspora: for example, between the English-born and educated Stanley, on the one hand, and, on the other, the Guadeloupean born and raised, but Paris-educated, Marie-Noëlle. She further writes of the searing confrontation between Stanley and the Caribbean that he had never seen but around which he had built ambitious plans, and Marie-Noëlle's equally fraught return to the place and the past that haunt her every breath.

---

[18] Condé, *La Vie scélérate*, 17; 'The Americans were afraid of nothing. Here they were, changing the structure of the world, cutting continents in two. In Panama they were building a channel that would allow their ships to sail faster from New York to San Francisco on the Pacific Coast, and for this superhuman project they were calling on labourers from all over the world.'

[19] Ibid. 43.

In *Les Derniers Rois mages*, set in the United States, Debbie Middleton is a black American historian who is obsessed with racial politics. She marries the Guadeloupean Spéro largely because he is of royal African lineage. Unfortunately for Debbie, Spéro is politically unaware and, even worse, pushes racial incorrectness to the point of having an affair with a white woman. In her portrayal of extreme black or African-Americanism, Condé satirizes myths of racial purity or integrity (it emerges that Debbie's own ancestor was a valuer of 'slave stock' in South Carolina). However, in this novel, as in *La Colonie du nouveau monde* (1993), she is also concerned to exercise imaginative freedom and thus explores a wide range of relations and connections within the Caribbean and between the Caribbean and the rest of the Americas, just as she had previously exercised her right to write both an African epic (*Ségou*) and also a number of novels centred more on the Caribbean relation to contemporary Africa.

HAITI, A SPECIAL RELATION

Haiti holds up a very specific sort of mirror to French Caribbean consciousness. It is interesting to observe how the latter, with its history of assimilation, has faced the radically different revolutionary history of Haiti, the first independent black republic. Not only does Haiti's history and political status diverge dramatically from those of the French Caribbean, but traditionally it is held to be more African, or more African-identified, than the French Caribbean. For Chris Bongie, 'it is generally agreed that Haiti, Cuba, and Jamaica are, in this order, the islands whose cultures show a greater degree of Africanization. Moreover, among the Antillean islands with the least African culture, Barbados is usually presented as the first example.'[20]

Césaire's play *La Tragédie du roi Christophe* and Glissant's drama *Monsieur Toussaint* (1961, definitive version 1978) tackle head-on the question of Haitian history in subtle representations of the two figures that are arguably the most symbolic figures of that half-an-island's eventful past. However, at a much more pervasive level Haiti haunts much contemporary French Caribbean writing,

---

[20] Bongie, *Islands and Exiles*, 355–6.

if only as an immense *refoulé*. Daniel-Henri Pageaux, in his *Images et mythes d'Haïti*, notes that Alejo Carpentier, who set his two most famous novels in Haiti, realized that Haiti was a particularly propitious space for the creative imagination.[21] Colette Maximin observes for her part that, within the Caribbean in general, Haiti enjoys the status of a symbolic land and is, moreover, regarded by ethnologists as the Caribbean Africa.[22]

Without denying the admiration and fascination aroused by Haitian history, Édouard Glissant also notes that the troubled state of Haiti was one of the arguments used in the French Caribbean to justify the political status quo: ' "Voilà où mène l'indépendance!" ' is a slogan guaranteed to stifle velleities of sovereignty or independence. Yet for Adrien, in Maximin's *L'Isolé Soleil*, Guadeloupe is a place in which 'liberation' in the true sense of the word has not taken place: reflecting upon the Haitian revolution, he muses that 'nous aurions été un peuple libre à la même date que Haïti si la Soufrière avait explosé sur Basse-Terre en 1802, applaudie par la joie du peuple insurgé' ('we would have been a free people at the same time as Haiti if the Soufrière had erupted onto Basse-Terre in 1802, to the joyful applause of an insurgent people').[23] Yet the ambiguity of the status of Haiti is confirmed in Maximin's next novel in the image of 'Inès, partie enseigner aux Abricots, un loin-tain petit village haïtien, pour se perdre ou pour se retrouver' ('Inès, gone to be a teacher in Les Abricots, a small and distant Haitian village, where she was going to either find or lose herself').[24] Here Haiti appears both as a place of pilgrimage and of self-discovery and as a country in need of volunteered aid. And it is Haiti's failure that is foregrounded in its literary depiction as the homeland of the immigrant workers who are the target of anti-migrant intoler-ance in the *départements d'outre-mer*. In *Traversée de la mangrove*, for example, Francis Sancher is said to have been unable to find anybody, 'pas même un clandestin haïtien, pour l'aider à remettre son bien en état' ('not even a Haitian illegal to help him restore his property').[25] Several other remarks about Haitians in *Traversée de*

[21] Daniel-Henri Pageaux, *Images et mythes d'Haïti* (Paris: L'Harmattan, 1984), 12.
[22] Colette Maximin, *Littératures caribéennes comparées*, 13.
[23] Maximin, *L'Isolé soleil*, 88.
[24] Maximin, *L'Ile et une nuit*, 118.
[25] Condé, *Traversée de la mangrove*, 36.

la mangrove further testify to Condé's concern to highlight, as Simone Schwarz-Bart had done in her play *Ton beau capitaine*, the desperate plight of Haitian economic and political refugees and the discrimination directed against them in the comparatively prosperous DOM islands.[26]

In addition to condemning French Caribbean hostility and prejudice against Haitians, writers also underline instances of solidarity. When Glissant writes in *Le Discours antillais* of a 'Haitian evening' that brought together French Caribbean and Haitian writers, he recalls that the talk was of exile: 'Peut-être qu'on parlait aussi des rigueurs de l'exil. Il y a un exil intérieur, moins pressant, mais tout aussi lancinant. Nous n'avons pas cessé de le combattre' ('Perhaps there was talk too of the rigours of exile. There is an internal exile, less urgent but just as painful. We are still fighting it').[27] Here the first subject, the 'on', seems to refer to the Haitians who suffer literal exile and the second subject, the 'nous', to the French Caribbean subject whose exile is internal and no less urgent or searing. Yet the sense of (Francophone) Caribbean solidarity is reinforced by the fact that the distinction is not made explicit.

THE *CRÉOLITÉ* MOVEMENT AND 'NEW WORLD' SPACE AND TIME

How do the cultural and geographical proximity of other Caribbean islands and of South, Central, and North America impinge on the vision communicated by the novels and essays of Patrick Chamoiseau and Raphaël Confiant? At first sight, this relation might appear rather slight, and, as we have already seen, some critics of the *créolité* movement have indeed discerned in it a lack of interest in Anglophone and Hispanophone Caribbean thought, an indifference consistent with its stated concern to concentrate on exploration of the complexity within. And yet, Patrick Chamoiseau's *Écrire en pays dominé* communicates a nostalgic sense of the pre-Columbian unity of 'New World' space, a unity

---

[26] 'Mon père me dit que je finirai par charroyer du fumier comme les Haïtiens' ('My father says that I will end up shovelling manure like the Haitians'), ibid. 102–3.
[27] Glissant, *Le Discours antillais*, 266. This is not one of the essays translated in *Caribbean Discourse*.

now impossible to imagine: 'Aujourd'hui, derrière les murs imposés par les colonialistes, il nous est impossible de concevoir ces circuits frémissants dont Caraïbes et Taïnos nourrissaient l'archipel, et avec lui le continent américain' ('Today, behind the partitions imposed by colonization, we can no longer imagine the vibrating circuits bestowed upon the archipelago and even upon the American continent by the Caribs and the Tainos').[28] In its openness to the sea, an orientation that I have already noted as being somewhat exceptional in the writing of the *créolité* movement, Confiant's *Eau de café* does, however, register some interest in the general, coeval Atlantic environment of the Caribbean. On the first page of the novel, for example, the narrator acknowledges that the village of Grand-Anse turns its back towards the Atlantic, and to the ocean surf that rolls all the way from Miquelon right down to Martinique.[29] Much further on in the novel, the parochialism of Grand-Anse is mocked, as we have already seen, in the following terms:

Pour nous autres, natifs-natals, le bourg de Grand-Anse était le mitan du monde. Certes, nous rêvions d'ailleurs, d'En Ville, d'en France, de la Syrie ou de l'Inde et certains qui avaient voyagé, de Panama ou de l'Amérique, mais la plupart d'entre nous doutaient que ces contrées merveilleuses . . . fussent vraiment réelles.[30]

Here, 'elsewhere' is thus first and foremost urban and original space, whether dreamed of or repressed, and only secondarily adjacent or American space. Moreover, the American continent seems just as unreal as France. Indeed Bérard, one of the villagers who has 'done' France, tries to convince fellow cinema-goers back in Martinique that Monument Valley is in Central France and the Amazon in Alsace. This spatial confusion—however comical and satirical the effect of the collision in scale and atmosphere between the vast and empty Arizona desert and the busy and tidy central plain of France, and the tropical jungle and the Franco-Germanic order of Alsace—suggests a disorientation not dissimilar to

[28] Chamoiseau, *Écrire en pays dominé*, 113.
[29] Confiant, *Eau de café*, 11.
[30] Ibid. 179; 'For us natives, the village of Grand-Anse was the centre of the world. Certainly, we dreamed of elsewhere, of the town centre, of France, of Syria or of India, and some who had travelled dreamed of Panama or America, but most of us doubted that these wonderful lands really existed.'

Pythagore's confusion in *La Case du commandeur* (see p. 236). Underlying both episodes is the notion that there can be no relation without a certain ability to differentiate. To relate France to America, or Africa to the Caribbean, one must first be able to perceive the two spaces as distinct.

Although Confiant's novel gently mocks the insularity of the villagers of Grand-Anse, the *créolité* movement is not in fact distinguished by its interest in 'other places'. Its other concern is with Creole space defined as post-plantation space, or space where Creole is spoken: that is, Haiti, Dominica, St Lucia, and the American South, in particular Louisiana. Moreover, unlike Glissant, the authors of *Éloge de la créolité* are at pains to emphasize the difference between Americanization and creolization. For them, not all Americans are Creoles, and not all Creoles are American. And yet, they would probably not accept Antonio Benítez-Rojo's statement that a 'Haitian or a Martinican feels closer to France than to Jamaica, and a Puerto Rican identifies better with the United States than with Surinam'.[31] Not only would Haitians respond that they feel closer to Quebec and Florida than to France, but *créolistes* insist that, although their primary cultural allegiance is to fellow Creoles, their second loyalty is to the Caribbean basin rather than to France.

Les Créoles que nous sommes sont aussi proches, sinon plus proches, anthropologiquement parlant, des Seychellois, des Mauriciens ou des Réunionnais que des Portoricains ou des Cubains. Nous, Antillais créoles, sommes donc porteurs . . . d'une double solidarité:

—d'une solidarité antillaise (géo-politique) avec tous les peuples de notre Archipel, quelles que soient nos différences culturelles : notre Antillanité;

— d'une solidarité créole avec tous les peuples africains, mascarins, asiatiques et polynésiens qui relèvent des mêmes affinités anthropologiques que nous: notre créolité.[32]

---

[31] Benítez-Rojo, *The Repeating Island*, 37.

[32] *Éloge de la créolité*, 32–3; 'As Creoles, we are as close, if not closer, anthropologically speaking, to the people of the Seychelles, of Mauritius, or Reunion, than we are to the Puerto Ricans or the Cubans . . . We, the Caribbean Creoles, enjoy, therefore, a double solidarity:—a Caribbean solidarity (geopolitical) with all the peoples of our Archipelago regardless of our cultural differences—our Caribbeanness; and—a Creole solidarity with all African, Mascarin, Asian, and Polynesian peoples who share the same anthropological affinities as we do—our Creoleness': *In Praise of Creoleness*, 94.

Implausibly, in this Caribbean/Creole configuration, Europe and France do not figure at all among the cultural affinities claimed for Martinicans.

PAN-CARIBBEAN TIME

At the outset of this chapter, I noted Paul Gilroy's failure to engage with circulation within the American Atlantic. Indeed a certain indifference to the French Caribbean black Atlantic connection is symptomatic of this failure. And at the end of the first chapter of this study, we saw that the *créolité* movement has been much criticized as isolationist. Both instances of disconnection should be situated in the context of a tradition of French Caribbean apartness. Régis Antoine observes that the three centuries leading up to the Second World War were a period of absolute isolation for the French-speaking Caribbean, not just economically and politically, but also culturally and intellectually. As Antoine puts it, 'On ignorait les voisinages caraïbes, ceux des littératures anglophones et hispanophones, et les déplacements d'intellectuels d'île en île étaient des plus rares' ('Writing from the neighbouring Caribbean islands was unknown and intellectuals hardly ever circulated between the islands').[33] Antoine goes on to point out that Paris served as a meeting-place in between the two world wars, and he further identifies the wartime blockade of Martinique as a decisive influence on Caribbean intellectual gravitations, strengthening resistance to Metropolitan French influence and encouraging the French Caribbean to turn towards its immediate environment. A number of cultural links were thus created during that period with Venezuela, Cuba, and Haiti. Even though Régis Antoine admits that, in the final analysis, Paris remained the principal pole of cultural reference, he argues that, from 1960 onwards, the waves of African and Caribbean decolonization made themselves felt in Martinique, as teachers of English introduced their students to George Lamming and teachers of Spanish spoke of the Cuban writer Ortíz or the Puerto Rican Pedroso. He also notes the immense interest generated by the writings of the Trinidadian Eric Williams, the Cuban Alejo Carpentier, and by the Casa de las

[33] Antoine, *Rayonnants écrivains de la Caraïbe*, 249.

Americas in Cuba. In more recent times, there have been what Antoine terms a further loosening of the ties of Frenchness and clear progress in the development of an archipelagic consciousness.[34] For Régis Antoine, the ascendant of the idea of creolization signifies above all the retreat of the French tropism as a result of the cultural cross-fertilization attendant on globalization. Both Antoine and Gilroy emphasize the crucial connection between music and the decolonization of the black Caribbean mind. Indeed, several French Caribbean authors, notably Ernest Pépin, Roland Brival, and Daniel Maximin, confirm the role of drumming, *bel air* song, and jazz respectively in the efflorescence of Caribbean cultural consciousness, circulation, and mobility. Paradoxically, North American continental space can be seen to be as much a limiting as an enabling influence on the scope of this mobility.

THE NORTH ATLANTIC CIRCUIT

If the French Caribbean relation to Haiti is a special case, so too is the North American connection. Although Canada, and Quebec in particular, would afford the French Caribbean writer the possibility of continuing to write in a French-speaking environment, it is the United States that has attracted French Caribbean authors. Haitian writers do, however, tend to live and work in Canada, their history of occupation by US forces having no doubt made them more inclined to look towards (Francophone) Canada than the United States as a place of refuge. The American academy has, since the late 1970s at least, been noticeably in thrall to French literary and cultural theory, and in the late 1980s and 1990s, post-colonial theory notably. That French Caribbean writers who have associated themselves or who have been associated with 'theory' should be courted by the US academy cannot, therefore, be regarded as unexpected. Furthermore, these writers, unlike their Haitian counterparts, would not associate the USA, but rather Metropolitan France, with cultural assimilation and imperialism. The French academy is not, however, particularly fascinated by 'post-colonial' writing and does not, furthermore, tend to fund writers by visiting professorships as is common practice in the

---

[34] Ibid. 252.

United States. Like Maryse Condé and like Derek Walcott too, indeed, Édouard Glissant has held various posts in American universities. Working as he did for some years in Baton Rouge, Glissant was able to explore in Louisiana another pole of creolization, a former outpost of plantation culture. Moreover, the USA is an important centre for research into French Caribbean writing, and the bibliographical investment of the university presses in this area is remarkable. The University of Virginia Press is a notable powerhouse which commissions and supports both critical studies and translations of the writing emanating from Guadeloupe and Martinique. Other university presses such as Florida, Nebraska, and Michigan have, however, also commissioned studies or translations.

North American sponsorship has thus contributed significantly not just to the dissemination but also to the professionalization of Caribbean writing with all that this implies.[35] Without denying other aspects of the indisputably positive impact of this development, such as 'New World' localization and cross-fertilization, not to mention the enabling and empowering effects of the cultural recognition and material security of authors and artists, its principal impact is probably to balance the cultural force of Europe, extending and reinforcing the field of resonance of Caribbean writing within the 'New World' itself. The drawbacks are less obvious and more uncertain; there may be, for example, a certain danger of the Narcissus factor coming into play. After all, if gravitation towards France, Africa, and also the 'New World' is motivated in each case by a (different) self-reflective impulse, when is the French Caribbean writer to look beyond the mirror?

I have suggested that Patrick Chamoiseau's writing occasionally breaks out of the three spheres of gravity that appear to limit and to vectorize the vast part of French Caribbean imagination of space. Yet, let us take as an example of this 'breaking out' the handful of references to Ireland that we can read in *Texaco*. Unlike Daniel Maximin, who integrates a knowing reference to Northern Ireland into *Soufrières*, the Celtic twilight clichés of *Texaco*[36] cancel all possibility of envisaging the space-time connection

---

[35] Bruce King's biography, *Derek Walcott: A Caribbean Life* (Oxford: Oxford University Press, 2000), draws out these implications fully.
[36] Maximin, *Soufrières*, 58.

and/or specificity of the place in question. That seeming lack of concern in *Texaco* with the 'pays réel' as opposed to the 'pays rêvé' is not, perhaps, unrelated to the historical tradition of French Caribbean isolation. Yet it is disconcerting to find it surfacing in the context of such thoroughgoing and passionate commitment to the idea of cultural diversity and to the ideal of authentic connection with the other.[37] Moreover, this question raises the broader issue of the (frangible) relation between poetics and ethics. In the imaginative or represented mobility studied over the last three chapters, a recurrent concern has been indeed what Christopher Miller terms the 'ethic of flow'. Criticizing much postmodern theorization of movement as 'utopian . . . arrogant . . . messianic', Miller wonders about the possibility of a mobility 'that remains meticulously aware of localities and differences', in other words a 'more convincing ethic of flow'.[38]

[37] Ibid. 574. Bruce King notes Derek Walcott's appearance at the Cúirt cultural festival in Ireland despite the fact that the festival could not afford his full appearance fee. It is not always easy, then, to meet the expectations of writers accustomed to the well-endowed American literary circuit.

[38] Christopher L. Miller, 'The Postidentitarian Predicament: On the Footnotes of *A Thousand Plateaus*', *Diacritics*, 23/3 (1993), 6–35: 33.

Conclusions

The narrative of Caribbean consciousness articulated in the late 1980s and in the 1990s by the *créolité* movement suggests that the Caribbean reached the historical terminus or plateau called 'globalization' sooner than the rest of the world. Hence the 'mangrove swamp' of Caribbean relationality is proposed as the mirror in which the entire world can contemplate its hyperrelational future. In overwriting the teleology of narrative with textual and intertextual circulation, many French Caribbean writers seem to suggest that history, understood as endless linearity or, at least, as the endless forward-driving spiral of dialectic, has collapsed into endlessly proliferating loops. Indeed, their work foregrounds writing itself as the space where the open, potentially boundless intertext that is the 'tout-monde' is woven and rewoven. The creolizing 'chaos-monde' envisioned in Glissant's *Traité du Tout-Mmonde* does not so much undo the teleology of narrative as overlay it with the more retentive space of writing. Indeed, the polysemy of 'traité' (treatise and treaty) suggests the denial not only of dialectic and of conflict in their drive towards substitution, but also of a mathematical model of time, in favour of the *détente* and *étendue* of duration.

Is *durée*, however, just another word for space? At the outset of her persuasive study of Édouard Glissant's novels, Celia Britton suggests that one of the messages of Glissant's *Poétique de la Relation* is that 'particularly in the Caribbean, the "space" of relation has supplanted the linear time-span of filiation'.[1] She also notes that the authors of *The Empire Writes Back* present hybridity in terms of 'the privileging of "space" over "history, ancestry and the past" '.[2] In her reading of *La Case du commandeur*, Celia Britton returns to this point, noting that Mycéa's recovery from delirium is triggered not by the thought of the ancestors, but by the

---

[1] Britton, *Édouard Glissant and Postcolonial Theory*, 15.
[2] Ibid. 16.

thought of the archipelago: 'this would suggest that it is less "filiation" than the "space" of Relation with the world in the present that cures her. Relation, in fact, is the project of a cure for unhomeliness.'[3] The tentativeness of the claims made here for the importance of space in Caribbean writing is evident in the ubiquitous hedging quotation marks. That affiliation replaces filiation in Glissant's writing is incontestably true. But the unease surrounding the notion that the dimension of affiliation is space rather than time is well founded too. It derives from the sense that there is another sort of time, that is not linear, successive time (a blind alley in the Caribbean mind), but rather retained time.

'Et Mathieu voyait le Temps désormais noué à la terre ... Qu'est le passé sinon la connaissance qui te roidit dans la terre et te pousse en foule dans demain?' ('And Mathieu saw Time henceforth bound up with the earth. ... What is the past if not the knowledge that braces you in the earth and thrusts you in huge numbers into tomorrow?').[4] In this way, Édouard Glissant underlines the intricate, knotted link between place on the one hand, and on the other duress, endurance, duration, and crucially, projection (into 'tomorrow'). Apart, however, from the question of the relation between space and time, one of the most persistent preoccupations in French Caribbean writing concerns the tension between reaching out and looking within. While Édouard Glissant and Daniel Maximin both focus on the tension between space and time, the concern with each dimension can be directed inwards or outwards. Its reach can be local or wide; it can involve an awareness of the 'semi-totality of human cultures'[5], or it can favour a more or less localized focus. Chamoiseau for his part predicts that the *créolité* movement's outward-looking concern with diversity will never be superseded:

Moi je crois que ce qui reste dépassable dans l'histoire de la créolité, ce sont ... la revalorisation de la langue créole, la préservation interne des choses, l'inventaire des traditions pour densifier le lieu ... Par contre, ce qui est indépassable, c'est le positionnement de la diversité, l'identité relationnelle.[6]

[3] Ibid. 129.
[4] Glissant, *Le Quatrième Siècle*, 279; *The Fourth Century*, 285.
[5] Glissant, *Traité du tout-monde*, 23.
[6] 'De la problématique du territoire à la problématique du lieu' (interview with M. McCusker), 731–2; 'I believe for my part that what can be superseded in the

It is the central insight of Glissant's entire writing project that is thus identified by Chamoiseau as lying at the indestructible heart of the *créolité* project also, namely consciousness of 'la totalité du monde dans la relativisation de l'humanité' ('the unsurpassable totality of the world and the concomitant relativization of all humanity').[7]

It is undeniably difficult to balance belief in circulation, relativity, and relationality with a sense of the present and the past of place, that is, to exorcize the ghosts of essentialism and particularism, without sacrificing the specificity of Caribbean place and time.[8] It is in this context that Édouard Glissant reconciles, or recomposes the specifically Caribbean sense of time and space, on the one hand, and on the other, the wide sea and the vast and diverse world onto which it opens. For Glissant, there is no contradiction between the concern with Caribbean time and the concern with global space; indeed, he links both time and space, and the Caribbean and the world, when he expresses Caribbean endurance in terms of a sense of the vastness of the world. 'Ce que nous ne manquions jamais de faire, c'était de considérer les pays au loin. Comme si l'image des étendues nous répondait pour l'insouci de la durée' ('What we never forgot to do was to look towards distant lands. It was as though the thought of these expanses underwrote our carefree outlook on duration').[9] To date, however, the *créoliste* focus on a specific past and place more or less to the exclusion of the chaos of the world has prevented this movement from joining Glissant's novel *Tout-monde* and his poem 'Les Grands Chaos' on the other side of that threshold of the globalized future.

When Daniel Maximin writes 'nous manquons d'espace',[10] or when he writes 'mais que de temps et d'espace il faut pour venir à

history of creoleness are the things that needed to be addressed urgently: the positive re-evaluation of Creole; the inner preservation of things, the inventory of endangered traditions and thereby the according of a certain density to place; all that can be transcended. Once we have affirmed the positive value of place, for example, then we can move on. However, what we cannot move beyond is the positioning necessitated by diversity, or the relationality of identity.'

  [7] Ibid.
  [8] '*Éloge de la créolité* risks undoing the epistemological break with essentialist thinking that he [Glissant] has always striven to conceptualize': Dash, *Édouard Glissant*, 23.
  [9] Glissant, *Traité du tout-monde*, 44.   [10] Maximin, *L'Isolé Soleil*, 263.

l'existence',[11] he is articulating that insatiable longing for a sense of spatial and temporal thereness that we have noted throughout this study. It would seem, indeed, that French Caribbean writing is required to requite that desire by either concentrating on Caribbean space and time (and this would explain, for example, the totemic status of deictics in French Caribbean writing) or by reaching out towards distance and straining towards temporal depth. This is so not just of writing that some regard as the only one worthy of the name, that is, writing that privileges the text, the intertext, and the metatext, but in fact *all writing* that, by its very existence, expands and 'thickens' the space and the time required if the Caribbean is to be and to have a real place in the local and also in the global mind. In other words, the work of Joseph Zobel, Roland Brival, Roger Parsemain, Xavier Orville, or Vincent Placoly, for example, along with the writing of Guadeloupean women authors, contributes to that sense of cultural incipience and existence referred to by Maximin, and gestures, in addition to the endurance, texturing, and diversity of Caribbean culture.

The surfeit of intertextuality pervading late-twentieth-century French Caribbean writing creates a sense of extension, density, and relation-ality that at once compensates for the limits and marginality of island space and reflects the hyperrelational culture of the Caribbean. However, it also produces an impression of temporal depth; not a sense of succession, that mathematical march of moments, each of which replaces or abolishes the previous one, and not just a sense of synchronous relation in the present either, but the reverberation of textual memory, the vibration of the past propagated in the present, creating there a sense of duration and endurance. Intertextuality implies both repetition and accumulation, and is thus potentially suggestive of tradition as an enduring and continuous effort. Furthermore, the textual and intertextual processes of writing trigger a dynamic entirely consonant with the transformations and processes of lived time, just as their infinite paradigmatic potential underlines the unpredictability associated with time.

Internal intertextuality has been identified as one of the signal tendencies of the writing of the Guyanese author Wilson Harris. In

---

[11] Ibid. 255.

his review of a collection of Harris's selected essays, Bruce King notes that 'to come across without preparation some of the later essays, or to see Harris radically rewriting in later novels, placing material from the earlier novels at different places and times, can be a shock'.[12] That shock is one with which the reader of much French Caribbean writing will be more than familiar. In the essay 'Apprenticeship to the Furies', the text of a talk given by Harris in 1996 on his novel *Jonestown*, Harris rewrites his early notion of the Caribbean as emerging from the 'shock' of place and time—a notion on which the subtitle of my study is based. A quarter of a century later, the shock has become a 'womb' and a 'cradle of dream'. More precisely, Wilson sees his novel as gathering motifs 'from the past and present and future in the womb of space and time into a revisionary gestation or arousal of the light of consciousness'.[13] And he envisions freedom as 'the action of the past to acquaint us deeply, profoundly, with the perilous voyage of humanity out of its cradle of dream in space and time'.[14] Here the 'revisionary gestation' and the perilous journey of creation from 'big bang' to matrix to cradle is, of course, being actualized at the level of the writing itself.

Supériorité? Infériorité?

Pourquoi tout simplement ne pas essayer de toucher l'autre, de sentir l'autre, de me révéler l'taure?

Ma liberté ne m'est-elle donc pas donnée pour édifier le monde du *Toi*?
A la fin de cet ouvrage, nous aimerions que l'on sente comment nous la dimension ouverte de toute conscience.[15]

It is worth setting briefly against the (inter)textual aspiration and the narrative, memorial, and/or identitarian motive marking so much French Caribbean writing the apparent modesty of Frantz Fanon's final position in *Peau noire, masques blancs*. Rather than

---

[12] Bruce King, in *World Literature Today* (Summer 2000), section on Africa and the West Indies.
[13] Wilson Harris, 'Apprenticeship to the Furies', in *Selected Essays*, 233.
[14] Ibid.
[15] Frantz Fanon, *Peau noire, masques blancs*, 188; 'Superiority? Inferiority? | Why not the simple attempt to touch the other, to feel the other, to explain the other to myself? | Was my freedom not given to me then in order to build the world of the You! At the conclusion of this study, I want the world to recognize, with me, the open door of every consciousness' (*Black Skin, White Masks*, 230–1).

leading him to 'writing' in the restrictive sense of textuality,[16] towards the dance of diversity, or to an exploration of place or a search for depth, duration, or distance, Fanon's effort to counter the reductions of polarization brought him, at the end of this work, to an appeal for an ethics of relation. Not, therefore, to a totalizing ontological or poetic exploration of the Caribbean and the World, or to a sounding of the accumulated depth of memory, but instead to a reaching out towards the pre-ontological I/Thou of ethics.

As this study was nearing completion, a third Caribbean-born writer was honoured by the Nobel Prize for Literature. And, a short time afterwards, Patrick Chamoiseau delivered his fifth novel. Although Chamoiseau's title—*Biblique des derniers gestes*—communicates the 'sense of an ending', we can perhaps assume its antiphrastic tenor, given the endurance implied by this very big book.[17] French Caribbean writing is not just voluminous, however; indeed, it is remarkable less for its volume, than for its tuning, and less for its stamina than for its resonance, as Édouard Glissant recognized when he marvelled that such a tiny part of the world 'soit à ce point remplie du bruit de l'univers'—'should hold so much of the sound of the universe'.[18]

---

[16] See, for example, Dominique Chancé's comments on Dany Bébel-Gisler (Ch. 1, n. 23).

[17] Patrick Chamoiseau, *Biblique des derniers gestes* (Paris: Gallimard, 2002).

[18] Glissant, *L'Intention poétique*, 62.

Bibliography

AFFERGAN, FRANCIS, *Anthropologie à la Martinique* (Paris: Presses de la fondation nationale des sciences politiques, 1983).

ANDRÉ, JACQUES, 'L'identité ou le retour du même', *Les Temps Modernes*, 441–2, 'Antilles' (Apr.–May 1983), 2026–37.

—— *Caraïbales. Études sur la littérature antillaise* (Paris: Éditions caribéennes, 1981).

ANTOINE, RÉGIS, *Les Écrivains français et les Antilles: Des premiers Pères blancs aux surréalistes noirs* (Paris: Maisonneuve et Larose, 1978).

—— 'La Littérature antillaise francophone, voie de connaissance vers l'Afrique', in Annie Wynchank and Philippe-Joseph Salazar (eds.), *Afriques imaginaires. Regards réciproques et discours littéraires 17e–20e siècles* (Paris: L'Harmattan, 1995), 103–111.

—— *La Littérature franco-antillaise. Haïti, Guadeloupe, et Martinique* (Paris: Karthala, 1992).

—— *Rayonnants écrivains de la Caraïbe* (Paris: Maisonneuve et Larose, 1998).

ARNOLD, A. JAMES, 'The Gendering of *Créolité*: The Erotics of Colonialism', in Maryse Condé and Madeleine Cottenet-Hage (eds.), *Penser la créolité* (Paris: Karthala, 1995), 21–40.

ASHCROFT, BILL, GARETH GRIFFITHS, and HELEN TIFFIN, *The Empire Writes Back: Theory and Practice in Post-Colonial Literatures* (New York: Routledge, 1989).

AUGÉ, MARC, *Non-Lieux. Introduction à une anthropologie de la surmodernité (Paris: Seuil, 1992)*; tr. as *Non-Places: Introduction to an Anthropology of Supermodernity* (London: Verso, 1995).

BACHELARD, GASTON, *La Poétique de l'espace (*Paris: Presses universitaires de France, 1970; 1st edn. 1957).

BÉBEL-GISLER, DANY, *Le Défi culturel guadeloupéen. Devenir ce que nous sommes* (Paris: Éditions caribéennes, 1989).

—— *La Langue créole, force jugulée. Étude des rapports de force entre le créole et le français aux Antilles* (Paris: L'Harmattan, 1976).

—— *Léonora. L'histoire enfouie de la Guadeloupe* (Paris: Seghers, 1985); tr. Andrea Leskes as *Leonora: The Buried Story of Guadeloupe* (Charlottesville and London: University Press of Virginia, 1994).

BENÍTEZ-ROJO, ANTONIO, *The Repeating Island: The Caribbean and the Postmodern Perspective*, tr. James Maraniss (Durham: Duke University Press, 1992).

BENOÎT, CLAUDE, 'La symbolique de l'espace dans *La Lézarde*', in Yves-Alain Favre (ed.), *Horizons d'Édouard Glissant* (Biarritz: J&D Éditions, 1992), 367–79.

BERNABÉ, JEAN, PATRICK CHAMOISEAU, and RAPHAËL CONFIANT, *Éloge de la créolité | In Praise of Creoleness*, bilingual edn., tr. M. B. Taleb-Khyar (Paris: Gallimard, 1993; 1st edn. (French only) 1989).

BERNIER, MICHEL, 'L'Afrique dans la poésie d'Édouard Glissant', in Yves-Alain Favre (ed.), *Horizons d'Édouard Glissant* (Biarritz: J&D Éditions, 1992), 255–68.

BHABHA, HOMI K. (ed.), *Nation and Narration* (London: Routledge, 1990).

BLANCHOT, MAURICE, *L'Entretien infini* (Paris: Gallimard, 1969).

BONGIE, CHRIS, *Exotic Memories: Literature, Colonialism, and the Fin de Siècle* (Stanford: Stanford University Press, 1991).

—— *Islands and Exiles: The Creole Identities of Post/Colonial Literatures* (Stanford: Stanford University Press, 1998).

—— 'Resisting Memories: The Creole Identities of Lafcadio Hearn and Édouard Glissant', *Sub-Stance*, 84 (1997), 153–78.

BOUKMAN, DANIEL, *Les Négriers* (Paris: L'Harmattan, 1978).

BOWIE, MALCOLM, *Lacan* (London: Fontana, 1991).

BRATHWAITE, EDWARD KAMAU, *The Development of Creole Society in Jamaica, 1770-1820* (Oxford: Oxford University Press, 1971).

—— *History of the Voice: The Development of Nation Language in Anglophone Caribbean Poetry* (London: New Beacon, 1984).

BRAUDEL, FERNAND, *Écrits sur l'histoire* (Paris: Flammarion,1969); tr. Sarah Matthews as *On History* (Chicago: University of Chicago Press, 1980).

BRENNAN, TIMOTHY, 'The National Longing for Form', in Homi Bhabha (ed.), *Nation and Narration* (London: Routledge, 1990), 44–70.

BRITTON, CELIA, 'Collective Narrative Voice in Three Novels by Édouard Glissant', in Sam Haigh (ed.), *An Introduction to Francophone Caribbean Writing: Guadeloupe and Martinique*(Oxford: Berg, 1999).

—— *Édouard Glissant and Postcolonial Theory: Strategies of Language and Resistance* (Charlottesville: University Press of Virginia, 1999).

BRIVAL, ROLAND, *Biguine Blues* (Paris: Phébus, 1999).

BRUNER, JEROME, 'Life as Narrative', *Social Research*, 54 (1987), 11–32.

BURTON, RICHARD D. E., *Le Roman marron. Études sur la littérature martiniquaise contemporaine* (Paris: L'Harmattan, 1997).

CAILLER, BERNADETTE, *Conquérants de la nuit nue: Edouard Glissant et l'H(h)istoire antillaise* (Tübingen: Gunter Narr, 1988).

—— 'From "Gabelles" to "Grands Chaos": A Study of the Disode of the Homeless', in Mary Gallagher (ed.), *Ici-Là: Place and Displacement in Caribbean Writing in French* (Amsterdam and Atlanta: Rodopi, forthcoming).

CALDWELL, ROY CHANDLER JR., 'Créolité and Postcoloniality in Raphaël Confiant's *L'Allée des soupirs*', *The French Review*, 73/2 (2000), 301–11.

CANNY, NICHOLAS, 'Early Modern Ireland *c*.1500–1700', in R. Foster (ed.), *The Oxford Illustrated History of Ireland* (Oxford: Oxford University Press, 1989), 104–60.

CARR, DAVID, *Time, Narrative, and History* (Bloomington and Indianapolis: Indiana University Press, 1986).

CÉSAIRE, AIMÉ, *Cahier d'un retour au pays natal/Notebook of a Return to the Native Land*, tr. Mireille Rosello and Annie Pritchard (London: Bloodaxe, 1995).

—— *The Collected Poetry*, tr., introd., and notes by Clayton Eshleman and Annette Smith (Berkeley and London: University of California Press, 1983).

—— *Discours sur le colonialisme* (Paris: Présence africaine, 1950).

CHAMOISEAU, PATRICK, *Antan d'enfance* (Paris: Hatier, 1990); tr. Carol Volk as, *Childhood* (London: Granta, 1999).

—— *Biblique des derniers gestes*. (Paris: Gallimard, 2002).

—— *Chemin d'école* (Paris: Gallimard, 1994); tr. Linda Coverdale as *School Days* (London: Granta, 1998).

—— *Chronique des sept misères* (Paris: Gallimard, 1986).

—— *Écrire en pays dominé* (Paris: Gallimard, 1997).

—— *Elmire des sept bonheurs*, photographs by Jean-Luc de Laguarigue (Fort-de-France; Paris: Fort de France: Habitation Saint Etienne; Paris: Gallimard, 1998).

—— *L'Esclave Vieil Homme et le molosse* (Paris: Gallimard, 1997).

—— *Guyane: Traces-mémoires du bagne* (Caisse nationale des monuments historiques et des sites, 1994).

—— *Solibo Magnifique* (Paris: Gallimard, 1988); tr. Rose-Myriam Réjouis and Val Vinokurov as *Solibo Magnificent* (London: Granta, 1999).

—— *Texaco* (Paris: Gallimard, 1992); tr. Rose-Myriam Réjouis and Val Vinokurov as *Texaco* (London: Granta, 1997).

—— and RAPHAËL CONFIANT, *Lettres créoles: Tracées antillaises et continentales de la littérature 1635–1975* (Paris: Hatier, 1991).

CHANCÉ, DOMINIQUE, *L'Auteur en souffrance. Essai sur la position et la représentation de l'auteur dans le roman antillais contemporain (1981–1992)* (Paris: Presses universitaires de France, 2000).

CHAUDENSON, ROBERT, *Des îles, des hommes, des langues. Langues créoles—cultures créoles* (Paris: L'Harmattan, 1992).

CHAULET-ACHOUR, CHRISTIANE, and DANIEL MAXIMIN, ' "Sous le signe du colibri": traces et transferts autobiographiques dans la trilogie de Daniel Maximin', in Alfred Hornung and Ernstpeter Ruhe (eds.),

Postcolonialisme & Autobiographie (Amsterdam and Atlanta, Ga.: Rodopi, 1998), 203–18.

CHERUBINI, BERNARD, 'La créolisation socioculturelle à l'heure de la mondialisation: interculturalité, créolités, système monde', *Études Créoles*, 22/1 (1999), 119–36.

CHEVRIER, JACQUES, *Poétiques d'Édouard Glissant* (Paris: Presses universitaires de Paris-Sorbonne, 2001).

CLARK, GREGORY, *Dialogue, Dialectic, and Conversation: A Social Perspective on the Function of Writing* (Carbondale: Southern Illinois University Press, 1990).

COATES, NICK, ' "Gardens in the Sands": The Notion of Space in Recent Critical Theory and Contemporary Writing from the French Antilles' (Ph.D. dissertation, University College London, 2001).

—— ' "The Sigh of History": Space and the Caribbean', in Ann Amherst and Katherine Astbury (eds.), *Dialogues 2: Endings* (Exeter: Elm Bank, 1999), 39–49.

COMPAGNON, ANTOINE, *La Seconde Main, ou le travail de la citation* (Paris: Seuil, 1979).

CONDÉ, MARYSE, *Le Cœur à rire et à pleurer* (Paris: Robert Laffont, 1999).

—— *La Colonie du nouveau monde* (Paris: Robert Laffont, 1993).

—— *Les Derniers Rois mages* (Paris: Mercure de France, 1992); tr. Richard Philcox as *The Last of the African Kings* (Lincoln: University of Nebraska Press, 1998).

—— *Heremakhonon* (Paris: UGE, 1976); repr. as *En attendant le bonheur: Heremakonon* (Paris: Seghers, 1988).

—— *Moi, Tituba sorcière . . . Noire de Salem* (Paris: Mercure de France, 1986).

—— 'Order, Disorder, Freedom, and the West Indian Writer', *Yale French Studies*, 83/2: *Post/Colonial Conditions: Exiles, Migrations, and Nomadisms*, ed. F. Lionnet and R. Scharfman (1993), 121–35.

—— *La Parole des femmes. Essai sur des romancières des Antilles de langue française* (Paris: L'Harmattan, 1979).

—— *Traversée de la mangrove* (Paris: Mercure de France 1989).

—— *La Vie scélerate* (Paris: Seghers, 1987).

—— and MADELEINE COTTENET-HAGE (eds.), *Penser la créolité* (Paris: Karthala, 1995).

CONFIANT, RAPHAËL, *Aimé Césaire. Une traversée paradoxale du siècle* (Paris: Stock, 1993).

—— *Bassin des ouragans* (Paris: Mille et une nuits, 1994).

—— *Commandeur du sucre* (Paris: Écriture, 1994).

—— *Eau de café* (Paris: Grasset & Fasquelle, 1991).

—— *Le Meurtre du Samedi-Gloria* (Paris: Mercure de France, 1997).

—— *Le Nègre et l'amiral* (Paris: Grasset, 1988).

CONFIANT, RAPHAËL, 'Quelques questions d'écriture créole', in Ralph Ludwig (ed.), *Écrire la 'parole de nuit'. la nouvelle litterature antillaise* (Paris: Gallimard, 1994), 171–80.

—— *Ravines du devant-jour* (Paris: Gallimard, 1993).

—— *Régisseur du rhum* (Paris: Écriture, 1999).

CORZANI, JACK, *La Littérature des Antilles-Guyane Françaises* (Fort-de-France: Désormeaux, 1978).

——with LÉON-FRANÇOIS HOFMANN and MARIE-LYNE PICCIONE, *Littératures francophones*, vol. ii: *Les Amériques* (Paris: Belin, 1998).

CROSTA, SUZANNE, *Le Marronnage créateur. Dynamique textuelle chez Édouard Glissant* (Laval: GRELCA, 1991).

DAMBURY, GERTY, *Mélancolie. Nouvelles* (Paris: La Flèche du temps, 1999).

DASH, J. MICHAEL, *Édouard Glissant* (Cambridge: Cambridge University Press, 1995).

—— *The Other America: Caribbean Literature in a New World Context* (Charlottesville: University of Virginia Press, 1998).

DE LAGUARIGUE, JEAN-LUC, and PATRICK CHAMOISEAU, *Cases en Pays-Mêlés* (Habitation Saint-Étienne: Traces, 2000).

DE SOUZA, PASCALE, '*Traversée de la mangrove*: éloge de la créolité, écriture de l'opacité', *The French Review*, 73 (2000), 822-33.

DEBIEN, GABRIEL, 'Les Grand'cases des plantations à Saint-Domingue aux XVIIe et XVIIIe siècles', *Notes d'histoire coloniale*, 138 (1970).

DEGRAS, PRISKA, 'Édouard Glissant, préfacier d'une littérature future', Glissant in conversation with Priska Degras and Bernard Magnier, *Notre Librairie*, 74 (1986), 14–20.

DERRIDA, JACQUES, *De la grammatologie* (Paris: Minuit, 1967).

—— *L'Écriture et la différence* (Paris: Seuil, 1967).

DIMOCK, WAE CHEE, 'A Theory of Resonance: Literature and Temporal Extension ', *PMLA* 112/5 (1997), 1046–59.

EAKIN, PAUL JOHN, *Touching the World: Reference in Autobiography* (Princeton: Princeton University Press, 1992).

ECO, UMBERTO, 'Postmodernism, Irony, the Enjoyable', in Peter Brooker (ed.), *Modernism/Postmodernism* (London: Longman, 1999), 225–8.

ÉGA, FRANÇOISE, *Lettres à une noire* (Paris: L'Harmattan, 1978).

FABIAN, JOHANNES, *Time and the Other* (New York: Columbia University Press, 1983).

FANON, FRANTZ, *Les Damnés de la terre* (Paris: Maspéro, 1961).

—— *Peau noire, masques blancs* (Paris: Seuil, 1952); tr. Charles Lam Markmann as *Black Skin, White Masks* (London: Pluto, 1986; 1st edn. New York: Grove, 1967).

FAVRE, YVES-ALAIN, 'Le songe, le réel et le chant dans la poésie d'Édouard Glissant', in id. (ed.), *Horizons d'Édouard Glissant* (Biarritz: J&D Éditions, 1992), 171–82.

FOUCAULT, MICHEL, *L'Archéologie du savoir* (Paris: Gallimard, 1969).

—— *Dits et écrits, 1954–1988, iv: 1980-88*, ed. Daniel Defont and François Ewald (Paris: Gallimard, 1994).

GALLAGHER, MARY, 'La poétique de la diversité dans les essais d'Édouard Glissant', in Yves-Alain Favre (ed.), *Horizons d'Édouard Glissant* (Biarritz: J&D Éditions, 1992), 27–36.

—— 'Seminal Praise: The Poetry of Saint-John Perse', in Sam Haigh (ed.), *Introduction to Francophone Caribbean Writing: Guadeloupe and Martinique* (Oxford: Berg, 1999), 17–33.

GILROY, PAUL, *The Black Atlantic: Modernity and Double Consciousness* (London: Verso, 1993).

GIRAUD, MICHEL, 'La créolité: une rupture en trompe-l'oeil', *Cahiers d'études africaines*, 148 (1997), 795–811.

GLISSANT, ÉDOUARD, *La Case du commandeur* (Paris: Seuil, 1981).

—— 'Le Chaos-Monde: l'oral et l'écrit', in Ralph Ludwig (ed.), *Écrire la 'parole de nuit'. La Nouvelle Littérature antillaise* (Paris: Gallimard, 1994), 111–29.

—— *Le Discours antillais* (Paris: Seuil, 1981); tr. J. Michael Dash as *Caribbean Discourse: Selected Essays* (Charlottesville: University Press of Virginia, 1989).

—— *Faulkner Mississippi* (Paris: Stock, 1996).

—— *L'Intention poétique* (Paris: Seuil, 1969).

—— *La Lézarde* (Paris: Seuil, 1958).

—— *Mahagony* (Paris: Seuil, 1987).

—— *Pays rêvé, pays réel* (Paris: Seuil, 1985).

—— *Poèmes* (Paris: Seuil, 1965).

—— *Poèmes complets* (Paris: Gallimard, 1994).

—— *Poétique de la Relation* (Paris: Gallimard, 1990); tr. Betsy Wing as *Poetics of Relation* (Ann Arbor: University of Michigan Press, 1997).

—— *Le Quatrième Siècle* (Paris: Seuil, 1964); tr. Betsy Wing as *The Fourth Century* (Lincoln and London: University of Nebraska Press, 2001).

—— *Sartorius. Le Roman de Batoutos* (Paris: Gallimard, 1999).

—— *Soleil de la conscience* (Paris: Seuil, 1956).

—— *Tout-monde* (Paris: Gallimard, 1997).

—— *Traité du Tout-Monde* (Paris: Gallimard, 1997).

GRESSET, MICHEL, 'Going la maison', *Corps écrit*, 9, *La Demeure* (1984), 119–26.

HAIGH, SAM (ed.), *An Introduction to Francophone Caribbean Writing: Guadeloupe and Martinique* (Oxford: Berg, 1999).

—— *Mapping a Tradition: Francophone Women's Writing from Guadeloupe*, MHRA Texts and Dissertations 48 (London: Maney, 2000).

HARRIS, WILSON, 'History, Fable, and Myth in the Caribbean and Guianas', *Caribbean Quarterly*, 16 (June 1970), 1–32.

HARRIS, WILSON, *Selected Essays of Wilson Harris: The Unfinished Genesis of the Imagination*, ed. Andrew Bundy (London: Routledge, 1999).

—— *The Womb of Space: The Cross-Cultural Imagination* (Westport, Conn.: Greenwood, 1983).

HEARN, LAFCADIO, *Youma: The Story of a West Indian Slave* (New York: Harper and Bros., 1890).

HILLIS MILLER, J., *Topographies* (Stanford: Stanford University Press, 1995).

HOBSBAWM, ERIC, *On History* (London: Weidenfeld & Nicolson, 1997).

HORNUNG, ALFRED, and ERNSTPETER RUHE, *Postcolonialisme & Autobiographie* (Amsterdam and Atlanta, Ga.: Rodopi, 1998).

HULME, PETER, 'The Locked Heart: The Creole Family Romance of Wide Sargasso Sea', in Francis Barker, Peter Hulme, and Margaret Iversen (eds.), *Colonial Discourse/Postcolonial Theory*, Essex Symposia on Literature Politics Theory (Manchester and New York: Manchester University Press, 1994), 74–5.

HUTCHEON, LINDA, 'Telling Stories: Fiction and History', in Peter Brooker (ed.), *Modernism/Postmodernism* (London and New York: Longman, 1992), 229–42.

JACK, BELINDA, *Francophone Literatures: An Introductory Survey* (Oxford: Oxford University Press, 1996).

—— *Negritude and Literary Criticism: The History and Theory of 'Negro-African' Literature in French* (Westport, Conn.: Greenwood, 1996).

JAMESON, FREDRIC, *Postmodernism, or, the Cultural Logic of Late Capitalism* (London: Verso, 1991).

JONES, BRIDGET, and SITA E. DICKSON LITTLEWOOD, *Paradoxes of French Caribbean Theatre: An Annotated Checklist of Dramatic Works, Guadeloupe, Guyane, Martinique, from 1900* (London: Roehampton Institute, n.d.).

JULIA, LUCIE, *Les Gens de Bonne-Espérance* (Paris: Temps actuels, 1982).

—— *Mélody des faubourgs* (Paris: L'Harmattan, 1989).

JUMINER, BERTÈNE, *Au seuil d'un nouveau cri* (Paris: Présence africaine, 1963).

—— 'La parole de nuit', in Ralph Ludwig (ed.), *Ecrire la 'parole de nuit'. La Nouvelle Littérature antillaise* (Paris: Gallimard, 1994), 131–49.

KHALFA, JEAN, with JÉRÔME GAME, 'Pustules, Spirals, Volcanos: Images and Moods in Césaire's *Cahier d'un retour au pays natal*', *Wasafiri*, 31 (Spring 2000), 43–51.

KING, BRUCE, *Derek Walcott: A Caribbean Life* (Oxford: Oxford University Press, 2000).

LABAT, LE R. P. JEAN-BAPTISTE, *Nouveau voyage aux isles d'Amérique*, iii (1742); repr. Fort-de-France: Éditions des Horizons Caraïbes, 1972).

LACLAU, ERNESTO, *New Reflections on the Revolution of our Time* (London: Verso, 1990).

LACROSIL, MICHÈLE, *Cajou* (Paris: Gallimard, 1961).

—— *Demain Jab-Herma* (Paris: Gallimard, 1967).

LAMMING, GEORGE, *The Pleasures of Exile* (1960; Ann Arbor: University of Michigan Press, 1992).

LAROCHE, MAXIMILIEN, *La Double Scène de la représentation*, GRELCA Essais 8 (Quebec: Université de Laval, 1991).

—— *Sémiologie des apparences*, GRELCA Essais 11 (Quebec: Université de Laval, 1984).

LE GOFF, JACQUES, *History and Memory*, tr. Steven Rendall and Elizabeth Claman (New York: Columbia University Press, 1992); *Histoire et Mémoire* (Paris: Gallimard, 1986).

LEERSEN, JOEP, *Remembrance and Imagination: Patterns in the Historical and Literary Representation of Ireland in the Nineteenth Century* (Cork: Cork University Press, 1996).

LEFEBVRE, HENRI, *La Production de l'espace* (1974; Paris: Anthropos, 2000).

LEIRIS, MICHEL, *L'Afrique Fantôme* (Paris: Gallimard, 1934).

—— *Contacts de civilisations en Martinique et en Guadeloupe* (Paris: Gallimard/Unesco, 1955).

LEJEUNE, PHILIPPE, *Le Pacte autobiographique* (Paris: Seuil, 1975).

LEROI-GOURHAN, ANDRÉ, 'Demeure: "Espace construit dans lequel on vit" ', *Corps écrit, La Demeure*, 9 (1984), 9–13.

LÉVI-STRAUSS, CLAUDE, *Tristes tropiques* (1955; Paris: Plon, 1993).

LIONNET, FRANÇOISE, *Autobiographical Voices: Race, Gender, Self-Portraiture* (Ithaca and London: Cornell University Press, 1989).

LOWE, LISA, 'Literary Nomadics in Francophone Allegories of Postcolonialism: Pham Vanky and Tahar Ben Jelloun', *Yale French Studies*, Post/Colonial Conditions, 1 (1993), 43–61.

LUDWIG, RALPH (ed.), *Écrire la 'parole de nuit'. La Nouvelle Littérature antillaise* (Paris: Gallimard, 1994).

MADOU, JEAN-POL, *Édouard Glissant, de mémoire d'arbres* (Amsterdam and Atlanta, Ga.: Rodopi, 1996).

MANICOM, JACQUELINE, *Mon examen de blanc* (Paris: Presses de la cité, 1972).

MARAN, RENÉ, *Batouala. Véritable roman nègre* (Paris: Albin Michel, 1938).

MARIMOUTOU, JEAN-CLAUDE CARPANIN, 'Créolie et créolité', *Notre Librairie, Dix ans de littératures 1980–1990*, II. *Caraïbes—Océan Indien*, 104 (Jan.–Mar. 1991), 95–8.

MARSHALL, PAULE, *The Chosen Place, the Timeless People* (New York: Harcourt, Brace, & World, 1969).

MASSEY, DOREEN, 'Politics and Space/Time', in Michael Keith and Steve Pile (eds.), *Place and the Politics of Identity* (London and New York: Routledge, 1993).

MAXIMIN, COLETTE, *Littératures caribéennes comparées* (Pointe-à-Pitre and Paris: Jasor and Karthala, 1996).

MAXIMIN, DANIEL, 'Entretien', *France-Antilles*, 315, 7–13 Oct. 1995.

—— *L'Ile et une nuit* (Paris: Seuil, 1995).

—— *L'Isolé Soleil* (Paris: Seuil, 1981).

—— *Soufrières* (Paris: Seuil, 1987).

MCCUSKER, MAEVE, 'De la problématique du territoire à la problématique du lieu: un entretien avec Patrick Chamoiseau', *The French Review*, 73/4 (Mar. 2000), 724–33.

—— 'No Place Like Home? Constructing an Identity in Patrick Chamoiseau's *Texaco*', in Mary Gallagher (ed.), *Ici-Là: Place and Displacement in Caribbean Writing in French* (Amsterdam and Atlanta, Ga.: Rodopi, forthcoming).

—— ' "Une rencontre multiple": A Study of the Work of Patrick Chamoiseau' (Ph.D. dissertation, Queen's University Belfast, 2001).

MCKAY, CLAUDE, *Banjo* (New York: Harper and Bros., 1929).

MILLER, CHRISTOPHER L., 'The Postidentitarian Predicament: On the Footnotes of *A Thousand Plateaus*', *Diacritics*, 23/3 (1993), 6–35.

—— *Theories of Africans: Francophone Literature and Anthropology in Africa* (Chicago: University of Chicago Press, 1990).

MILNE, LORNA, 'From *Créolité* to *Diversalité*: The Postcolonial Subject in Patrick Chamoiseau's *Texaco*', in Paul Gifford and Johnnie Gratton (eds.), *Subject Matters: Subject and Self from Descartes to the Present* (Amsterdam: Rodopi, 2000), 162–80.

MINH-HA, TRINH T., 'An Acoustic Journey', in John C. Welchman (ed.), *Rethinking Borders* (Minneapolis: University of Minnesota Press, 1996), 1–17.

MORAND, PAUL, *Hiver caraïbe* (1928; Paris: Flammarion, 1991).

MOREAU DE SAINT-MÉRY, *Description topographique, physique, civile, politique et historique de la partie française de l'isle Saint-Domingue* (1779; Paris: Société française d'outre mer, 1984).

MOUDILENO, LYDIE, *L'Écrivain antillais au miroir de sa littérature* (Paris: Karthala, 1997).

MPOYI-BUATU, THOMAS, *La Re-production* (Paris: L'Harmattan, 1986).

MURDOCH, H. ADLAI, *Creole Identity in the French Caribbean Novel* (Gainesville: University of Florida Press, 2001).

NAIPAUL, V. S., *The Middle Passage: Impressions of Five Societies, British, French, and Dutch in the West Indies and South America* (London: André Deutsch, 1962).

—— *The Mimic Men* (London: André Deutsch, 1967).

NEPVEU, PIERRE, *Intérieurs du nouveau monde. Essai sur les littératures du Québec et des Amériques* (Quebec: Boréal, 1998).

NIGER, PAUL, *Inquisitions* (Paris: Seuil, 1954).

NORA, PIERRE, 'Between Memory and History: *Les Lieux de Mémoire*', *Representations*, 26 (Spring 1989), 7–25; repr. in Geneviève Favre and Robert O'Meally (eds.), *History and Memory in African-American Culture* (New York and Oxford: Oxford University Press: 1994), 284–300.

OLLIVIER, ÉMILE, *Passages* (1991; Paris: Le Serpent à Plumes, 1994).

ONG, WALTER, *Orality and Literacy: The Technologizing of the Word* (London and New York: Methuen, 1982).

ORMEROD, BEVERLEY, *An Introduction to the French Caribbean Novel* (London: Heinemann, 1985).

ORVILLE, XAVIER, *Moi, Trésilien-Théodore Augustin* (Paris: Stock, 1996).

PAGEAUX, DANIEL-HENRI, *Images et mythes d'Haïti* (Paris: L'Harmattan, 1984).

PAIN, MARC, *Kinshasa. La Ville et la cité* (Paris: ORSTOM, 1984).

PARSEMAIN, ROGER, *L'Absence du destin* (Paris: L'Harmattan, 1992).

—— *Il chantait des boléros* (Pointe-à-Pitre: Ibis Rouge, 1999).

PATTERSON, ORLANDO, 'Recent Studies on Caribbean Slavery and the Atlantic Slave Trade', *Latin American Research Review*, 17 (1982), 251–75.

PÉPIN, ERNEST, *Coulée d'or* (Paris: Gallimard, 1995).

—— *Tambour-Babel* (Paris: Gallimard, 1996).

PERRET, DELPHINE, 'L'écriture mosaïque de *Traversée de la mangrove*', in Maryse Condé (ed.), *L'Héritage de Caliban* (Pointe-à-Pitre: Éditions Jasor, 1992), 187–200.

PFAFF, FRANÇOISE, *Entretiens avec Maryse Condé* (Paris: Karthala, 1993).

PHILLIPS, CARYL, *A State of Independence* (London, Faber & Faber, 1986).

PINEAU, GISÈLE, *L'Exil selon Julia* (Paris: Stock, 1996).

—— *La Grande Drive des esprits* (Paris: Le Serpent à Plumes, 1993).

PLACOLY, VINCENT, *La Vie et la mort de Marcel Gonstran* (Paris: Éditions Denoël, 1971).

PLUCHON, PIERRE, *Histoire des Antilles et de la Guyane* (Toulouse: Privat, 1982).

PONNAMAH, MICHEL, *Dérive de Josaphat* (Paris: L'Harmattan, 1991).

PRICE, RICHARD and SALLY PRICE, 'Shadowboxing in the Mangrove: The Politics of Identity in Post-Colonial Martinique', in Belinda Edmondson (ed.), *Caribbean Romances: The Politics of Regional Representation* (Charlottesville: University Press of Virginia, 1999), 123–62.

RADFORD, DANIEL, *Le Maître-Pièce* (Paris: Éditions du Rocher, 1993).

RICŒUR, PAUL, *La Mémoire, l'Histoire, l'Oubli* (Paris: Seuil, 2000).

—— 'Narrative Time', *Critical Inquiry* (Autumn 1980), 169–90.

ROSELLO, MIREILLE, *Littérature et identité créole aux Antilles* (Paris: Karthala, 1992).

ROUMAIN, JACQUES, *Gouverneurs de la rosée* (Paris: Éditeurs français réunis, 1944); tr. Langston Hughes and Mercer Cook as *Masters of the Dew* (Reynal & Hichcock, 1947); repr. with introd. by J. Michael Dash (London: Heinemannn Educational, 1978).

SACKS, OLIVER, *The Man who Mistook his Wife for a Hat and Other Clinical Tales* (New York: Harper, 1987).

SAINT-JOHN PERSE, *Éloges and Other Poems*, tr. Louise Varèse (New York: Pantheon Books, 1956).

—— *Œuvres complètes*, Bibliothèque de la Pléiade (Paris: Gallimard, 1972).

SAINVILLE, LÉONARD, *Au fond du bourg* (Paris: Messidor, n.d.).

SCHWARZ-BART, SIMONE, *Pluie et vent sur Télumée Miracle* (Paris: Seuil, 1972); tr. Barbara Bray as *The Bridge of Beyond*, introd. Bridget Jones (London: Heineman, 1982).

—— *Ti Jean L'horizon* (Paris: Seuil, 1979).

SEGAL, RONALD, *The Black Diaspora* (London: Faber & Faber, 1995).

SÉKOU TOURÉ, AHMED, *Expérience guinéenne et unité africaine* (Paris: Présence africaine, 1961).

SMYTH, GERRY, *Space and the Irish Cultural Imagination* (Basingstoke and New York: Palgrave, 2001).

Société et littérature antillaises aujourd'hui, Cahiers de l'Université de Perpignan, 25 (1997).

SOJA, EDWARD, *Postmodern Geographies: The Reassertion of Space in Critical Social Theory* (London: Verso, 1989).

SPEAR, THOMAS C., 'L'enfance créole: la nouvelle autobiographie antillaise', in S. Crosta (ed.), *Récits de vie de l'Afrique et des Antilles* GRELCA Essais 16 (Quebec: Presses universitaires de Laval, 1998).

SPLETH, JANICE, 'Kinshasa: The Drama of the Post-Colonial City', in Buford Norman (ed.), *The City in/and French Literature* (Amsterdam: Rodopi, 1997), 215–28.

SPROUSE, KEITH ALAN, 'Lieu de mémoire, lieu de créolité: The Plantation as Site of Memory', *Cincinnati Romance Review*, 18 (1999), 153–61.

THEUNISSEN, MICHAEL, *The Other: Studies in the Social Ontology of Husserl, Heidegger, Sartre, and Buber*, tr. Christopher Macann (Cambridge, Mass.: MIT, 1984).

THRIFT, NIGEL, *Spatial Formations* (London: Sage, 1996).

TIROLIEN, GUY, *Balles d'or* (Paris: Présence africaine, 1961).

TORRES-SAILLANT, SILVIO, *Caribbean Poetics: Towards an Aesthetic of West Indian Literature* (Cambridge: Cambridge University Press, 1997).

TOUMSON, ROGER, 'Les Écrivains afro-antillais et la réécriture', *Europe*, 612 (Apr. 1980), 115–227.

—— *La Transgression des couleurs: Littérature et langage des Antilles, 18e, 19e et 20e siècles* (Paris: Éditions caribéennes, 1989).

TROLLOPE, ANTHONY, *The West Indies and the Spanish Main* (1859; New York: Hippocrene, 1985).

TUAN, YI-FU, *Space and Place: The Perspective of Experience* (Minneapolis: University of Minnesota Press, 1977).

WALCOTT, DEREK, *The Antilles: Fragments of Epic Memory* (London: Faber & Faber, 1993).

—— *Omeros* (London: Faber & Faber, 1990).

—— *Tiepolo's Hound* (New York: Farrar, Straus, & Giroux, 2000).

—— *What the Twilight Says* (London: Faber & Faber, 1998o).

WEBB, BARBARA, *Myth and History in Caribbean Fiction* (Amherst: University of Massachusetts Press, 1992).

WHITE, HAYDEN, 'The Value of Narrativity in the Representation of Reality', *Critical Inquiry* (Autumn 1980), 5–28.

WILLIAMS, RAYMOND, *The City and the Country* (1973; London: Hogarth Press, 1985).

ZIMRA, CLARISSE, 'Daughters of Mayotte, Sons of Frantz: The Unrequited Self in Caribbean Literature', in Sam Haigh (ed.), *An Introduction to Francophone Caribbean Writing: Guadeloupe and Martinique* (Oxford: Berg, 1999), 177–94.

ZOBEL, JOSEPH, *Diab'là* (Paris: Présence africaine, 1946).

—— *Quand la neige aura fondu* (Paris: Éditions caribéennes, 1979); 1st pub. as *La Fête à Paris* (Paris, 1953).

—— *La Rue Cases-Nègres* (Paris: Présence africaine, 1950); tr. Keith Warner as *Black Shack Alley* (London: Heinemann, 1980).

Index

292 *Index*

relationality, 6, 22, 27, 38, 203, 223, 247, 270
relativization, 41, 222–3, 270
Ricœur, Paul, 61–2, 82–3, 88, 117–18
Rosello, Mireille, 10, 181 n. 20
Roumain, Jacques, 151 n. 22, 249
rural–urban transition, 183, 187–8

Sacks, Oliver, 88
Saint-John Perse, 14, 54, 91, 130, 131, 135–44, 156, 170, 177–80
Saint-Pierre, 177, 182
Sainville, Léonard, 163
Schoelcher, Victor, 161 n. 48
Schwarz-Bart, Simone, 15, 111, 240, 241, 242; *Pluie et Vent*, 69–70, 97–8, 116, 155,157, 159, 163, 165, 188–9, 214, 255; *Ti Jean*, 111, 215, 228–9, 240; *Ton beau capitaine*, 255
sea, 262, 270; *see also* Atlantic; Caribbean, sea
Segal, Ronald, 8
Sékou Touré, 238, 240, 242
Senghor, Léopold Sédar, 23
shock of space and time, 2, 251, 272
slavery, 29, 58, 78, 146, 157, 159, 161, 163, 168, 197; and Abolition, 76, 161; as a space, 49, 69; narratives of, 48–9
Soja, Edward, 4 n. 10, 129
space 4–6, 12–13, 24, 30, 37; and disorientation, 236–7; and duration, 104, 155; appropriated and dominated, 185; domestic and extra-domestic, 103, 140; enclosed, 146, 149, 185; Euclidean, 147; local vs distant 26, 60, 253, 257, 264, 269; rural, 165; spatial récitative, 73, 200; spatial rhetoric, 53–4; textual, 25, 123; versus filiation, 269; *see also* coevalness; dwelling; plantation; rural–urban; urban space
Spear, Thomas, 189
Sprouse, Keith Alan, 145 n. 2
St Lucia, 14, 35, 206
synchrony, 46, 68, 128, 232, 248; *see also* coevalness

teleology, 11, 22, 35–8, 46, 69, 96, 268

temporal depth, 3, 177; *see also* duration
text, *see* writing
theory, 8–9, 265; and teleology, 35–8; criticized, 38–43; disavowed, 43–6
Thrift, Nigel, 6
time, 1, 3, 4–6, 11, 25–6, 27, 32, 65, 66, 83, 88, 115, 120, 122, 174, 198, 239, 245; and displacement, 67, 78–80, 139; and narrative, 61, 98, 106; and space 5–6, 59, 61,62, 67, 68, 75–5, 112, 116, 129–30, 189, 197, 242, 251, 254, 268–71; and the present, 75, 98; arrested, 78; calendar 76; cyclical 68, 70; detemporalization, 71; disjunctive, 66, 76, 81; lived, 81, 85 (*see also* duration); negated in folktale, 76–7; neutralized, 75–80; Newtonian 147; repossessed, 57; spatialized, 70–3, 74–5; successive, 25–6, 47, 55, 62, 65, 66, 69, 71, 84–5, 86, 107, 153, 155, 183, 268
time–space continuum, 5–6, 57, 74–5
Tirolien, Guy, 24, 187, 226, 238, 239, 240, 241
topography, 253, 254
toponyms, 73, 86, 133
Toumson, Roger, 23, 135
tout-monde, 23, 223
transmission: and dislocation, 101; and writing, 98, 103
Trollope, Anthony, 150, 206
Tuan, Yi-Fu, 60

urban space: and growth, 181; and memory, 194; and mobility, 183, 184; and modernity, 194, 200; and time, 193, 202; intra-urban polarization, 193–6, 200; market towns, 179; pathology, 175, 177–8, 180; reproducing plantation, 143, 185, 191–2, 197–9, 201, 203; segregation, 192; shanty towns, 183, 191–2; slums, 196; stagnation, 178, 180 (*see also* Césaire; Saint-John Perse); undifferentiated, 199, 201
urban–rural schism, 187–8, 200

vernacular, 39, 111, 118, 119
voice, 24, 115, 116, 122–3, 168, 269

Walcott, Derek, 2, 19, 20, 39, 47, 50,

AEH-8292

WITHDRAWN